Where to

THE *WHERE TO WATCH BIRDS* SERIES FOR THE BRITISH ISLES

Where to Watch Birds in Britain
Simon Harrap and Nigel Redman

Where to Watch Birds in Devon and Cornwall
David Norman and Vic Tucker

Where to Watch Birds in Dorset, Hampshire and the Isle of Wight
George Green and Martin Cade

Where to Watch Birds in East Anglia
Peter and Margaret Clarke

Where to Watch Birds in the East Midlands
Rob Fray

Where to Watch Birds in Ireland
Clive Hutchinson

Where to Watch Birds in Kent, Surrey and Sussex
Don Taylor, Jeffery Wheatley and Paul James

Where to Watch Birds in the London Area
Dominic Mitchell

Where to Watch birds in Scotland
Mike Madders

Where to Watch Birds in Somerset, Gloucestershire and Wiltshire
Ken Hall and John Govett

Where to Watch Birds in Thames Valley and The Chilterns
Brian Clews and Paul Trodd

Where to Watch Birds in Northeast England
Dave Britton and John Day

Where to Watch Birds in North West England
Pete Marsh, Alan Conlin, Chris Sharpe, Judith Smith, Stephen Williams

Where to Watch Birds in Wales
David Saunders

Where to Watch Birds in the West Midlands
Frank Gribble, Graham Harrison, Helen Griffiths, Jim Winsper and Steve Coney

Where to Watch Birds in Yorkshire and North Humberside
John Mather

Where to Watch Birds in the
East Midlands

Derbyshire, Leicestershire, Lincolnshire, Northamptonshire and Nottinghamshire

Rob Fray

Second edition

CHRISTOPHER HELM
LONDON

Dedication

Dedicated to Samantha Lee – thanks for everything

Published 2006 by Christopher Helm, an imprint of
A & C Black Publishers Ltd., 38 Soho Square, London W1D 3HB
www.acblack.com

Copyright © 2006 Rob Fray
Line drawings by John Wright

ISBN-10: 0-7136-7530-6
ISBN-13: 978-07136-7530-6

A CIP catalogue record for this book is available from the British Library

All rights reserved. No part of this publication may be reproduced in any
form or by any means — graphic, electronic or mechanical, including
photocopying, recording, taping or information storage and retrieval systems
– without the prior permission of the publishers.

This book is produced using paper that is made from wood grown in
managed, sustainable forests. It is natural, renewable and recyclable.
The logging and manufacturing processes conform to the environmental
regulations of the country of origin.

Printed in Great Britain by Caligraving Ltd, Thetford, Norfolk

10 9 8 7 6 5 4 3 2 1

CONTENTS

ACKNOWLEDGEMENTS

The production of this second edition would not have been possible without help and guidance from many people. In particular I would like to thank Bob Bullock, who single-handedly updated the information on all the sites in Northamptonshire, Roy Frost, who not only provided various contacts but also gave advice on a number of sites in Derbyshire and Nottinghamshire, and Steve Botham, who did likewise in Lincolnshire. In Derbyshire, Rod Key and Mark Reeder were invaluable in providing various contacts, as were Bernie Ellis and Andy Hall in Nottinghamshire. The following local birders have all provided information regarding the sites mentioned, and without them this book would not have come to fruition: in Derbyshire, Mark Beevers (Carr Vale Nature Reserve and Pools Brook Country Park); Loz Brooks (Pleasley Pit Country Park); Roy Frost (Cromford Canal, Derbyshire Dales, East Moors, Longshaw Estate and Ogston Reservoir); Richard James (Willington Gravel Pits); Rod Key (Long Eaton Gravel Pits, Trent Meadows and Wyver Lane Nature Reserve); Richard Spowage (Willington Gravel Pits); Keith Turton (Ogston Reservoir); Mick Taylor (Upper Derwent), in Lincolnshire, Steve Botham (Boultham Mere, Covenham Reservoir, Laughton Forest, Messingham Sand Quarry and North Witham Fens); Dave Bradbeer (Cleethorpes to Humberstone Fitties and Tetney to Northcoates Point); Stuart Britton (Linwood Warren and Willingham and Walesby Woods); Paul French (The Wash); Grahame Hopwood (Whisby Nature Reserve, North Hykeham Pits, Hartsholme Country Park and Swanholme Park); Alex Lees (Marston Sewage Treatment Works); Kevin Marshall (Kirkby on Bain area); Andrew Powers (Laughton Forest); John Walker (Donna Nook to Mablethorpe and Sutton on Sea to Chapel St Leonards) and Kev Wilson (Gibraltar Point), and in Nottinghamshire, Carl Cornish (Girton, Besthorpe and Collingham Pits); Tony Critchley (Holme Pierrepoint); Steve Dunn (King's Mill Reservoir); Bernie Ellis (Hoveringham Gravel Pits); Roy Frost (Idle Valley and Sherwood Forest); Andy Hall (King's Mill Reservoir and Sherwood Forest); John Hopper (Colwick Country Park); Pete Smith (Netherfield Lagoons); Mark Speck (Attenborough Nature Reserve).

Further information has been extracted from the annual bird reports published by the Derbyshire Ornithological Society, Leicestershire and Rutland Ornithological Society, Northamptonshire Bird Club and Nottinghamshire Birdwatchers. These reports would not have been published without the diligence of local recorders and editors, along with thousands of hours of fieldwork by many hundreds of observers; their contributions in helping to produce this book and to local ornithology in general are gratefully acknowledged. Unfortunately, no bird reports have been published in Lincolnshire for a number of years. In addition, the websites of the the various local Wildlife Trusts and bird clubs, particularly that of the Lincolnshire Bird Club, have been mines of information.

The excellent illustrations which enrich this book were provided by Leicestershire artist John Wright, who is not only a long-standing friend but is also remarkably good at finding rare birds in Leicestershire and Lincolnshire.

Finally, the staff at Christopher Helm provided support throughout the preparation of this guide. In particular, I would like to thank Susan McIntyre (designer), Brian Southern (cartographer), Marianne Taylor (copy editor) and Sophie Page (editor) for their help.

INTRODUCTION

For the purposes of this book, the five counties which make up the East Midlands region are Derbyshire, Leicestershire, Lincolnshire, Northamptonshire and Nottinghamshire. The small county of Rutland is included within Leicestershire, as this is how local recording arrangements have been carried out for the last 65 years.

The five counties provide some excellent and varied habitats, which in turn attract a wide range of bird species. The region encompasses areas such as the internationally important estuaries of the Humber and Wash, the rivers Trent, Nene, Welland and Witham with their extensive sand and gravel workings and flooded pits, historic ancient woodland and its modern coniferous counterpart in Sherwood Forest, old parkland such as that at Bradgate and Fawsley, and the limestone dales and wild gritstone moorlands of Derbyshire. Inland reservoirs within the region include Britain's largest man-made lake at Rutland Water, and it and other such waterbodies are magnets for birds and birdwatchers alike. Small remnants of lowland heath still survive, most of them protected as nature reserves. For the most part, however, the area is dominated by arable farmland, with more pastoral areas to the west. Most of the land lies at low altitudes, only rising to any notable height in north Derbyshire and to a lesser extent in Charnwood Forest. Derby, Nottingham, Leicester and Northampton are all sizeable conurbations, while Lincolnshire is more sparsely populated.

As of April 2006, the combined species total of the five counties was 414. While the 40 miles (64 km) of Lincolnshire coastline is well known as a prime area for watching migrant birds, and includes such famous sites as Gibraltar Point and Donna Nook, the four inland counties may apparently lack similar pleasures. One of the aims of this book is to show otherwise. A glance through the respective county lists will reveal exceptional records from each of the five areas: Black-browed Albatross and Pallid Swift in Derbyshire, Crag Martin and Red-flanked Bluetail in Leicestershire, Green Heron and American Redstart in Lincolnshire, Sooty Tern and Pacific Swift in Northamptonshire, and Blyth's Pipit and Cedar Waxwing in Nottinghamshire, to name but a few. These kinds of sightings are obviously likely to be one-offs, but it does show the potential of even inland areas to produce something out of the ordinary.

Details of 16 sites that were not included in the first edition can be found in this guide. A number of these were not even in existence ten years ago, being the results of factors such as aggregate extraction and the closure of opencast mines. Several other similar sites, most notably Aston-upon-Trent Gravel Pits in Derbyshire and Langford Lowfields in Nottinghamshire, would undoubtedly have qualified for inclusion had their access arrangements been straightforward; indeed, all sites without legitimate public access have been excluded. It is worth bearing in mind that, while all access details regarding sites mentioned in this book were correct at April 2006, local circumstances may change at any time. If your personal favourite is not mentioned in this book then I can only apologise; space simply does not permit the inclusion of every site with birding potential. Pioneering readers could take note of some of the areas not included and attempt to make their own discoveries, which will perhaps in turn appear in future editions of this book.

HOW TO USE THIS BOOK

The 79 major sites in this guide are arranged into county groups and, as the counties in the region are not arranged in an obvious geographical line they are presented alphabetically. Within each county section the sites are, in the main, again listed alphabetically. Some large areas, such as the Peak District in Derbyshire and the Charnwood Forest area of Leicestershire, are given a brief overview then broken down into two or more specific 'attached sites'. In the majority of such cases, the attached sites are listed in a logical geographical order if possible; the overview makes it clear how the attached sites have been arranged. The sites in Lincolnshire have been treated slightly differently; as this is the only coastal county its sites are divided into 'coastal' and 'inland' sections, with the coastal section arranged geographically north to south and the inland sites presented alphabetically.

Each locality within the guide has a major heading with a reference number which relates to the species index at the back of the book. The relevant Ordnance Survey Landranger (1:50,000) and Explorer maps (1:25,000) are noted alongside each site name. Appendices to this book comprise a recommended reading list, a selection of useful addresses and websites, and indexes for place names and species mentioned.

Within each site account there are sections covering Habitat, Species, Timing, Access and Calendar; the content of each is described below.

Habitat

This section defines the area covered and describes its main features; which may include geology, geography, vegetation, size in acres and hectares (ha), altitude in metres and feet (ft), status, and ownership.

It is important to bear in mind that some localities, particularly working gravel pit complexes, are continually changing, and this may influence which birds use the site. The details given are correct as at April 2006.

Species

The more interesting birds likely to be encountered at specific times of year are detailed here, but the reader should not expect to find, either in this section or in the subsequent 'Calendar' section, a definitive species list. To this end, certain widespread and common species such as Pheasant, Woodpigeon, Collared Dove, Wren, Dunnock, Robin, Blackbird, Song Thrush, Blue Tit, Great Tit, Magpie, Rook, Carrion Crow, Starling, House Sparrow, Chaffinch and Greenfinch are not usually mentioned, unless it is in relation to specific movements or large flocks.

The presence of some birds is very dependent on weather conditions; this particularly applies to passage migrants on the coast and waders and terns at inland reservoirs and gravel pits. Of course, the fact that a species is listed as occurring at a certain season does not mean it will be seen; there are always days when even the most obvious species will, for some reason, remain uncooperative.

Some sites are well-known for attracting rarities and other scarce migrants, and past occurrences of these are listed for information. Such birds should not be expected on a routine visit, but they do demonstrate the potential of the locality for attracting rarer species.

The species names used in this guide are in accordance with those in the most recently published checklist of the birds of Britain – Birds of Britain: the Complete Checklist, compiled by Dominic Mitchell and Keith Vinicombe. This list, while up-to-the minute with its recognition of recent and proposed splits such as Caspian Gull and Siberian Stonechat, takes a more conservative approach with nomenclature. It is hoped that the use of familiar English names instead of their 'global' alternatives, for example Dunnock rather than Hedge Accentor and Nuthatch rather than Wood Nuthatch, will make the use of this book more straightforward for readers. Copies of Birds of Britain: the Complete Checklist can be ordered from Solo Publishing – call 0208 8810550.

Timing

Some sites are at their best at certain times of year, or at certain times of day, and this section gives information to assist you in timing your visit so as to get the most out of the site. In general, early mornings are best at all times of year, when bird activity is at its greatest and human disturbance is usually low. There are occasions, however, when evening visits will be more productive; for instance, when viewing winter gull roosts or if searching for crepuscular species such as European Nightjar, Nightingale and Grasshopper Warbler. Weather patterns often play an important part in determining which species are likely to be seen. During spring and autumn migration periods, winds with an easterly element to them – especially when accompanied by rain – are ideal for bringing migrant passerines to the Lincolnshire coast. At the same time, these conditions usually see movements of waders and terns inland. Seawatching, however, is most productive during periods of strong winds with a northerly component, and on rare occasions severe gales can provide the land-locked counties of the region with unexpected seabird records. Other important considerations include the times of high tides on the coast, which influence the roosting and feeding patterns of many birds, and additional human pressures on the site, which might vary from excess disturbance from anglers to the use of the area as a bombing range! In all cases, such information is detailed in this section.

Access

As mentioned previously, the relevant Ordnance Survey map references are given alongside each site heading. These maps provide full details of public rights of way and it is recommended that they are used in conjunction with the details given in this part of the guide. The information in this important section is as detailed as possible and gives full directions, often from several different major roads or towns. Longer distances are given in miles and kilometres (km) and shorter ones in metres (m) only (1 metre = 1.0936 yards). Information on access to the site itself is also given, especially where this is restricted, and includes details of permits (if required) and opening times among other things. On-site details of hides, footpaths and other facilities such as toilets are given where appropriate. Access details are subject to change and, although all information was correct as at 2006, visitors are advised to always check local information sources.

Calendar

This section lists by season the species which one may reasonably hope to encounter during a visit to the site concerned in the right conditions. The status of some species, particularly those which are weather-dependent or passage migrants, is qualified by the use of phrases such as 'scarce' or 'rare'.

As mentioned in the Introduction, certain very common species have been excluded to avoid repetition. The first list includes species which may be seen at any time of year, but it should be noted that even such resident species may be present in larger numbers at certain times of year. Other lists broadly cover winter (October to March), spring passage (April to June), spring and summer (April to July) and autumn passage (July to October). However, each site is different with regards to the birds that visit, and a combination of these periods may be used where necessary. Each list of species is presented in the order recommended by the British Ornithologists' Union.

KEY TO THE MAPS

℗	Car park		Marsh
Ⓗ	Hide		Scrub
★	Viewpoint		Reedbeds
Ⓥ	Visitor centre		Lakes
ⓅⒽ	Public house		Sea
🗼	Lighthouse		Railways
ⓌⒸ	Public toilet		Main roads
ⒸⒼ	Coastguard		Minor roads
►ⒼⒸ	Golf course		Tracks
✝	Church		Footpaths
	Towns		Embankment
	Conifers		
	Deciduous		

THE AREA COVERED BY
THIS GUIDE

DERBYSHIRE

1. Carr Vale Nature Reserve
2. Carsington Water
3. Cromford Canal and Shiningcliff Wood
4. Foremark Reservoir
5. Ogston Reservoir
6. The Peak District
6A. The Upper Derwent Valley
6B. Longshaw Estate and Padley Gorge
6C. The Derbyshire Dales
6D. The East Moors
7. Pleasley Pit Country Park
8. Pools Brook Country Park
9. Staunton Harold Reservoir
10. Trent Valley Gravel Pits
10A. Long Eaton Gravel Pits and Trent Meadows
10B. Willington Gravel Pits
11. Wyver Lane Nature Reserve

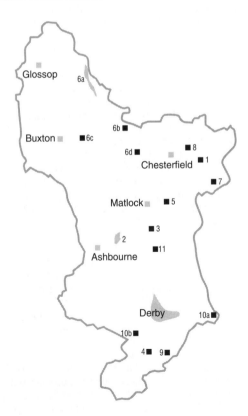

1. CARR VALE NATURE RESERVE

Habitat

Carr Vale Nature Reserve was created in two stages, with the first 8 acres (3.25 ha) of pool and marsh being declared a nature reserve by the Derbyshire Wildlife Trust (DWT) in 1992. What is now known as the Reserve Pond was formerly a fishing pond used by members of Bolsover Miners' Welfare Angling Club. This pond formed in the 1950s as a result of mining subsidence and the area consists of a shallow pool flanked on the west and southern edges by reedmace, with dense hawthorn scrub to the west. Along the northern edge there is a footpath that leads to the Peter Fidler Reserve, a small reserve maintained by Derbyshire County Council following reclamation of the Bolsover Colliery south spoil tips. Running south on the eastern side of the pool, adjacent to the River Doe Lea, there is another footpath leading to the more recently developed area of the reserve. Following successful applications for various grants, this second area was acquired by the Derbyshire Wildlife Trust in 1996 and developed in 1998. The area was formerly a 22 acre (9 ha) field but over a three-month period it was transformed into the most important part of the reserve. Just beyond the Reserve Pond there is a smaller pond, surrounded by *Phragmites*, which is known locally as the Southern Marsh, adjacent to which there is a small shallow scrape. The main areas of water are viewable from an observation mound. The nearest stretch of water to the mound is known as Meadow Flash. The northern section of this flash is man-made but the southern part is a naturally formed subsidence flash. The southern section of the flash is outside the official reserve area and therefore not under the control of the DWT, but it is owned by a sympathetic farmer who is happy for it to be treated as a conservation area. In the centre of the reserve lies the unoriginally named Middle Flash, which is roughly circular in shape, has shallow muddy edges and a controllable water level. Further west of here is another small pool surrounded by *Juncus*. The grassland surrounding these pools is managed using sheep to produce short grass sward that is beneficial to breeding Northern Lapwings and wintering Eurasian Wigeons.

The remaining recording area lies outside the boundaries of the DWT reserve and consists of rough grassland, arable crops, hawthorn scrub and more mature trees. This ensures that there are a wide variety of habitats within in a reasonably compact area.

Species

The most obvious birds during the winter period are ducks; up to eight species are regularly present with up to 230 Eurasian Wigeons, 100 Gadwall, 180 Common Teal and 200 Mallards being the most prevalent. These are joined by small numbers of Shovelers, Pochards, Tufted Ducks and Goosanders, while a few Ruddy Ducks from the breeding population may linger into the winter. Shelduck and Goldeneye are rare visitors in winter and there are single records during this period of Common Eider and Red-breasted Merganser. Cold, clear frosty mornings during November and December sometimes encourage Pink-footed Geese to move from north-west England to Norfolk and occasionally good numbers can be seen flying over, the best time being between 9-11 am. However, the largest counts have been of birds making the return journey in January, when up to 2,750 have

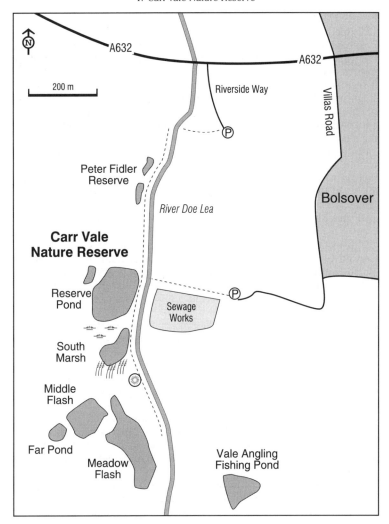

been logged flying north-west. Whooper Swans are occasionally noted flying through the valley, but Bewick's Swan remains a very rare visitor with just four records.

Water Rails are often heard calling around the reserve, with up to five regularly scattered around the Reserve Pond. They often provide very good views, the best places to view them being the west bank of the Reserve Pond or the stream adjacent to the Vale Angling Fishing Pond. Very few waders are present in winter but both Northern Lapwing and European Golden Plover are regular with Common Snipe a little less so. Jack Snipe used to be frequent but are now barely annual and Woodcocks are occasionally flushed by dog-walkers. The only other waders likely to be encountered are very occasional Dunlins and Redshanks, although out-of-season Grey Plover, Black-tailed Godwit, Knot and Curlew have all been recorded during the winter period. Occasionally large numbers of gulls are present on and around the pools and careful scrutiny may pay dividends as there have been ten Mediterranean, two Little, three Caspian, 14 Iceland and 12 Glaucous Gulls recorded since 1996.

Kestrel and Sparrowhawk are the raptors most likely to be seen during the winter but careful scanning of the electricity pylons to the west of the reserve often produces a Peregrine Falcon or two. Common Buzzard is fairly regular, Merlin and Barn Owl are occasional winter visitors and there is a single record of Hen Harrier. Two winter feeding stations provide close views of Willow Tit along with good numbers of Reed Buntings, with the one adjacent to the observation mound being the most productive. Chiffchaffs are regular during the winter and there have been at least seven records of eastern-type birds (Siberian Chiffchaff). In addition, single Firecrests have wintered four times since 1996. The place to look for these wintering warblers is the hawthorn embankment next to the sewage works, although the air is not too pleasant at times! Finally, in good winters there are mobile flocks of Siskins and Lesser Redpolls to chase.

By late March duck numbers have declined, but in spring there is more chance of Shelduck being present and there have been a dozen records of Garganey. Great Crested and Little Grebes arrive back by early spring and Greylag Geese are almost daily visitors in small numbers. Ospreys and Marsh Harriers are almost annual at this time of year and other raptors noted during spring have included Honey Buzzard, Red Kite and Derbyshire's second Black Kite in April 1997 – it pays to watch the skies at Carr Vale.

Little Ringed Plovers are usually present from late March and Ringed Plover starts to be seen regularly from the beginning of March, as do Oystercatcher, Dunlin, Curlew and Redshank. Other species of wader recorded occasionally during spring are Grey Plover, Knot, Sanderling, Ruff, Bar-tailed Godwit, Whimbrel, Greenshank and Wood Sandpiper and, while none are guaranteed, at least one or two of these species makes an appearance each year.

Spring is the most likely time to see Kittiwake, which often appears in either March or April. There have also been spring records of Mediterranean and Yellow-legged Gulls. Common Terns are fairly regular and there have been about a dozen records of Arctic Tern, but Black Terns are very rare with just two spring records.

April sees the arrival of most of the expected summer visitors. Yellow Wagtails are sometimes joined by migrant White Wagtails, Northern Wheatears and Whinchats, while the occasional Scandinavian Rock Pipit and Blue-headed Wagtail have also been seen.

The pools at Carr Vale have a good population of breeding birds, particularly wildfowl, with Mallard, Gadwall (up to eight pairs), Tufted Duck and Ruddy Duck (up to six broods) all nesting annually. Additionally, Garganey have bred successfully once and up to four pairs of Shovelers have attempted to nest with some success. Unfortunately, the single breeding attempt by Common Teal was ended by predation. Two pairs each of Great Crested and Little Grebe, a pair of Mute Swans and several pairs of Canada Geese add to the array of waterbirds during the breeding season. But it is not all about ducks, as up to nine pairs of Northern Lapwings and up to four pairs of Little Ringed Plovers usually breed as well. Redshanks, which used to breed annually, are now more sporadic but courting adults are usually present during the summer, and in 2005 Oystercatchers bred for the first time. Water Rails are occasionally noted as a breeding species but whether chicks are observed depends very much on the water level in the Reserve Pond. Common Tern, although not breeding yet, is fairly regular throughout June and July. The variety of habitat ensures that nine species of warbler are present during the breeding season, including up to four reeling Grasshopper Warblers, 20 pairs of Reed Warblers and ten of Sedge Warblers. As many as three pairs of Willow Tit breed but Turtle Dove, Little Owl, Tree Sparrow and Corn Bunting have all been lost.

By late June or early July the first returning waders start to appear; Common Snipe, Curlew, Black-tailed Godwit and Green and Common Sandpiper are usually logged during this period. As summer progresses into early autumn, species such as Dunlin, Ruff and Greenshank can also be expected at some stage. In total, 28 species of wader have been recorded at Carr Vale, including Avocet, Little Stint, Spotted Redshank, Turnstone, Pectoral Sandpiper (two records) and Derbyshire's only Lesser Yellowlegs (in August 1998).

Late summer sees an increase in wildfowl numbers, notably Canada Goose (maximum 600), Gadwall (maximum 144) and Mallard (maximum 300). The first Eurasian Wigeon appear in early September along with the occasional Pintail and more rarely Garganey. August is proving to be the best month for seeing the increasing Little Egret, and August and September are good months for migrant Marsh Harriers and Ospreys. Also at this time Hobbies often put on a good display as they hunt dragonflies over the pools.

By the end of September the birding emphasis changes and most visitors come to observe visible migration. Some notable counts have been made of birds moving through the valley, such as 1,600 Meadow Pipits and 2,000 Redwings. Other species such as Rock Pipit, Brambling, Lesser Redpoll and Siskin are regularly recorded and occasional rarities such as Woodlark and Snow Bunting have been picked up on the migration watches. Pink-footed Geese can be expected from mid-September and there is usually a large-scale movement on at least one date before the end of October, provided the conditions are right.

Carr Vale is a very well-watched site; so much so that the regular watchers clocked up their 2,000th consecutive daily visit in September 2005. It has produced some excellent inland birds, including Corncrake, two Wrynecks, Yellow-browed Warbler and Lapland Bunting; even more notable have been a flock of nine Little Auks, a Red-rumped Swallow, a group of three Shore Larks and Derbyshire's first Common Rosefinch.

An annual report is produced and is available from the Derbyshire Wildlife Trust, Bolsover and Chesterfield Libraries, the Local Studies Department at Derbyshire County Council Offices in Matlock and The Blue Bell public house on High Street, Bolsover.

Timing

The site is worth visiting at any time of the year, although in March to May and July to early November you'll have a better chance of finding something unusual. The winter months are good for wildfowl and the chance of a rare gull, while June and July provide an opportunity to look for evidence of breeding. Whatever the month it should be borne in mind that for most of the time birdwatchers will be looking south or west; therefore to avoid glare from the sun and poor light a morning visit is recommended.

Access

Carr Vale Nature Reserve is 6 miles (9.6 km) east of Chesterfield on the south-west edge of Bolsover. From Chesterfield travel east along the A632 towards Bolsover and after 6 miles (9.6 km) at the bottom of Bolsover Hill turn right (third exit) at the roundabout onto Riverside Way. Continue to the industrial units and use the car park at SK463207. Go through the A-frames, bear right and follow the path to the River Doe Lea and onto the Peter Fidler Reserve. From here, follow one of two paths south to the DWT reserve.

Alternatively, at the roundabout on the A632 mentioned above, go straight ahead towards Bolsover and at the next crossroads (with the Castle Arms public house on the left) turn right onto Villas Road. Follow this road for 600 m and at the end of the Model Village on a 90-degree left-hand bend there is an unmade track going straight ahead with some garages on the left-hand side. Go down this track and after 100 m, ignoring the gate in front of you, turn right and follow the track to the sewage works entrance (SK461702). Go through the left-hand A-frame and follow the path between the hawthorn covered embankment and the sewage works to the River Doe Lea (about 150m). From here, walk south (upstream) along the riverside path to reach the observation mound at SK458698.

Calendar

Resident: Mute Swan, Canada Goose, Gadwall, Shoveler, Tufted Duck, Grey Heron, Water Rail, Northern Lapwing, Kingfisher, Willow Tit, Yellowhammer, Reed Bunting.

October–March: Whooper Swan (scarce), Pink-footed Goose, Eurasian Wigeon, Common Teal, Pochard, Goldeneye (scarce), Goosander, Cormorant, Common Buzzard, Peregrine Falcon, European Golden Plover, Jack Snipe (rare), Common Snipe, Woodcock, Mediterranean Gull (scarce), Caspian Gull (rare), Iceland Gull (scarce), Glaucous Gull (scarce), Kittiwake (scarce, March), Green and Great Spotted Woodpeckers, Water Pipit (scarce), Rock Pipit (October and November), Grey Wagtail, European Stonechat (scarce), Fieldfare, Redwing, Chiffchaff, Firecrest (rare), Brambling, Siskin, Lesser Redpoll.

April–September: Greylag Goose, Shelduck, Pintail (August onwards), Garganey (scarce), Ruddy Duck, Little Grebe, Great Crested Grebe, Little Egret (scarce), Marsh Harrier (scarce), Osprey (scarce), Hobby, Oystercatcher, Little Ringed and Ringed Plovers, Dunlin, Ruff, Black-tailed Godwit, Whimbrel (scarce), Curlew, Redshank, Greenshank (scarce), Green Sandpiper (July onwards), Wood Sandpiper (rare), Common Sandpiper, Yellow-legged Gull (August onwards), Kittiwake (scarce, April), Common Tern, Arctic Tern (scarce, April and May), Yellow Wagtail, White Wagtail (April), Whinchat (scarce), Northern Wheatear, Grasshopper, Sedge, Reed and Garden Warblers, Lesser Whitethroat, Common Whitethroat.

2. CARSINGTON WATER
OS Landranger 119
OS Explorer 24

Habitat

Set in beautiful countryside on the south-eastern edge of the Peak District National Park, and with a maximum surface area of 740 acres (300 ha), Carsington Water is England's ninth largest reservoir. It is also one of the country's newest; planning began in the 1960s and construction started in the early 1980s but, following the collapse of part of the original dam in

1984, the reservoir was not completed until 1991, being officially opened in May the following year. Water is pumped into the reservoir from the River Derwent via a 6.5 mile (10.4 km) aqueduct, and is returned to the river during times of low water flow. The retaining dam, which forms the south-western side of the reservoir, rises to a height of 128 feet (38.5 m) but the banks are gently sloping and grassed. Much of the land surrounding the reservoir consists of grazed fields divided by hawthorn hedgerows. The principal areas of mature woodland are found in Hall and Middle Woods, both on the eastern side of the reservoir. Hall Wood has extensive areas of pine and larch, but the central section contains oak, beech and ash trees, with a springtime carpet of bluebells, wood anemones and wood sorrel. Over 500,000 trees and shrubs have been planted to create new woodland areas since the construction of the reservoir, and these consist mainly of a mixture of willow, alder, ash, guelder rose, rowan and hawthorn. At the south-eastern end of the reservoir, rough grassland with patches of gorse dominates the hillside. There are several small islands around the reservoir, most of which are covered in rough grassland.

A large visitor centre on the west bank forms the focus of recreational facilities and provides exhibitions, shops, toilets and refreshment facilities. A specific Wildlife Centre, situated in a double-glazed and centrally-heated hide, is located to the north-east of the visitor centre and is used for educational purposes. Three other hides are also situated on the west bank of the reservoir. The visitor centre, Wildlife Centre and hides all have good wheelchair access.

The northern part of the reservoir has been set aside as a wildlife study zone and as such remains generally free from major disturbance, unlike the southern section which is used for a variety of recreational pursuits including fishing and sailing.

Carsington Bird Club, established in 1992, collates records from the reservoir and produces regular newsletters and an annual report.

Species

Carsington Water has rapidly become the most important site in Derbyshire for wintering waterbirds, with peak counts in recent years of the dominant species being 2,048 Coots, 1,248 Tufted Ducks, 1,141 Eurasian Wigeons, 1,001 Canada Geese, 779 Common Teal, 593 Pochards, 400 Mallards, 199 Ruddy Ducks, 105 Little Grebes, 55 Gadwall, 39 Goldeneyes and 24 Goosanders. In addition, smaller numbers of Pintails and Shovelers winter, and a few Shelducks can be found from February onwards. Several Red-crested Pochards are usually present throughout much of the winter, and one or two Smew are recorded most years. Cormorants can be found all year round, although do not breed, with numbers regularly exceeding 50. Large skeins of Pink-footed Geese are seen flying to and from their wintering grounds in East Anglia, especially during October and January. Small parties of Whooper Swans are becoming a regular feature in November and December, although Bewick's Swans remain much scarcer. In view of Carsington's size, it is no surprise that vagrant seaducks, divers and grebes are found with some regularity. Scaup are annual in small numbers between October and March, while Red-breasted Mergansers also appear relatively frequently. Common Eider, Long-tailed Duck and Velvet Scoter have all been recorded, as have the three scarcer grebes, with Black-necked the most regular. Of the divers, Great Northern is the most likely, although both Red-throated and Black-throated have been seen on several occasions and, exceptionally, one of the latter summered at the reservoir in 2003.

Another winter attraction is the large gull roost, which is best watched from either the Sheepwash or Lane End hides. Black-headed Gull is the most numerous species, with as many as 10,000 present in December 2003, and these are joined by three-figure totals of Herring Gulls and smaller numbers of Common and Great Black-backed Gulls. Lesser Black-backed Gull numbers usually peak during the late autumn, with up to 6,000 birds being a regular number. Yellow-legged Gulls frequently accompany the Lesser Black-backs and tend to be seen most reliably from August to November, with one or two remaining throughout the winter. Mediterranean Gulls usually occur between October and March, with as many as six different birds during the winter not unusual. One or two Iceland and Glaucous Gulls are picked out annually, usually in January and February, and several Ring-billed Gulls have been found in recent years. Kittiwakes sometimes put in an appearance in the winter roost, but are more regularly seen during the early spring when small flocks may pause briefly; an exceptional group of 74 was seen in March 2003.

Flocks of European Golden Plovers and Northern Lapwings make up the majority of the wader interest during the winter months, although depending on water levels there may be reasonable numbers of Common Snipe along with a few Dunlin. Oystercatchers, Ringed Plovers and Redshanks begin to appear from February, as do Curlews which build up during the early spring to reach their peak numbers of up to 50 birds in March.

Feeding stations at the Wildlife Centre and in Sheepwash and Millfields car parks attract groups of tits, finches and Tree Sparrows, along with small numbers of Yellowhammers and Reed Buntings. Bramblings may occasionally visit these feeding stations, although their appearances are erratic. European Stonechats sometimes winter in the areas of rough grass around the reservoir and flocks of Siskins and Lesser Redpolls are a regular feature at this time of year. Raptors are represented by the resident Sparrowhawks, Common Buzzards and Kestrels, which are joined in the winter by one or two Peregrine Falcon Falcons and occasional Merlins.

Spring migration can be an exciting time as it offers the chance to find scarce migrants. Easterly winds usually result in the appearance of parties of Little Gulls and Common, Arctic and Black Terns during April and May, and Little and Sandwich Terns have been encountered during such conditions. Common Scoters are most regular in April and May, although they can appear at virtually any time of year. Spring is also the best season for seeing Black-necked Grebes and the odd Garganey. Ospreys are now a feature of spring, and Carsington is the most reliable site in Derbyshire to catch up with this impressive raptor; in recent years, birds have been seen regularly from April through to August. The short-grazed grass on the dam wall is attractive to insect-eating passerines during spring migration, with Yellow and White Wagtails and Northern Wheatears occurring regularly during April and early May.

Spring wader passage is variable and is dependent on weather conditions and water levels; even so, the regular inland species such as Ringed Plover, Dunlin, Ruff and Common Sandpiper can be relied upon at some stage. Black-tailed Godwits are becoming ever more frequent and recent records have included a flock of 138 in April 2004. Of the scarcer species, Sanderling, Bar-tailed Godwit, Whimbrel and Turnstone are the most likely at this time of year.

Breeding wildfowl include the expected Mute Swan, Canada Goose, Mallard, Coot and Moorhen, as well as up to 15 pairs of Tufted Ducks, one or two Ruddy Ducks and a few Little and Great Crested Grebes. A feral

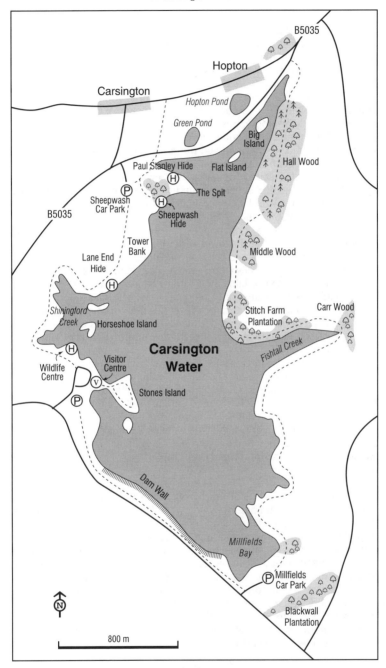

population of Barnacle Geese has become established, and five pairs bred in 2003. Several pairs of Northern Lapwings and Redshanks nest each year, while Little Ringed Plovers do so occasionally and a pair of Common Sandpipers bred in 1992.

The woodland residents such as Sparrowhawk, Kestrel, Tawny Owl, Great Spotted Woodpecker and Treecreeper are joined by a good selection of warblers, with Blackcap, Garden Warbler, Common Chiffchaff and Willow Warbler arriving in good numbers. Three or four pairs of Common Redstarts nest annually in the woodlands around the reservoir, where they are joined by declining numbers of Spotted Flycatchers. In recent years, one or two male Pied Flycatchers have arrived during the spring and set up territory, and have even been seen inspecting nest-boxes; it remains to be seen whether this is the start of a permanent colonisation by this attractive species. Other breeding species around the reservoir include Little Owl, Grey Wagtail, Sedge Warbler, Lesser Whitethroat, Common Whitethroat, Tree Sparrow and Reed Bunting.

Return wader passage commences in July, and as the water level falls muddy margins along the shallower eastern banks are exposed. The variety and number of birds involved is usually greater in the autumn than earlier in the year, and in addition to those species seen during the spring, waders such as Grey Plover, Knot, Little Stint, Curlew Sandpiper, Spotted Redshank, Greenshank and Wood Sandpiper become more likely. Black-necked Grebes often arrive during August, and records at this time of year usually involve juveniles. Later in the autumn, the stonework of the dam is a good place to search for Rock Pipits, which are not infrequent between late September and November.

Due perhaps to Carsington's location away from any major river valley, national rarities are extremely unusual at the site, with the only ones to date being Baird's Sandpiper and Bonaparte's Gull which both occurred in 1996. Nevertheless, the reservoir has hosted a number of local rarities, including a remarkable total of ten different Great Skuas, as well as Ring-necked Duck, Fulmar, Manx Shearwater, Leach's Storm-petrel, Gannet, Avocet, Temminck's Stint, Purple Sandpiper, Red-necked and Grey Phalarope, Pomarine and Arctic Skua, Shore Lark and Great Grey Shrike.

Timing

There is something to see at all times of year at this impressive reservoir, with winter bringing large numbers of wildfowl and gulls and spring and autumn passage periods offering the chance of scarce migrants. The reservoir is very popular, particularly at weekends and bank holidays, and is used for a wide range of recreational pursuits; therefore a visit in the early morning or evening sees the least disturbance. The northern section is, however, a wildlife study zone and is thus not disturbed, so visits at any time should still be productive. Owing to the location of the sun, evening provides better light conditions for watching from the west bank, which is the best area for wildfowl and waders. Visitors wanting to watch the gull roost, which can be observed from either the Sheepwash or Lane End hides, should aim to arrive at least two hours prior to dusk.

Access

Carsington Water is 12 miles (19.2 km) north-west of Derby and 4 miles (6.4 km) north-east of Ashbourne. There are three car parks which give access to the reservoir, with the main one being at the visitor centre (SK241516); this is reached from the minor road which leaves the B5035 south-eastwards 1.5

miles (2.4 km) south-west of Carsington village. This is a pay-and-display car park (£1.50 for up to two hours, £3.50 all day). The visitor centre, which incorporates exhibitions, shops, restaurant, refreshments, toilets, a children's play area and first aid, is open all year except Christmas Day from 10 am. The reservoir site, however, is open every day of the year from 7 am until sunset. From the visitor centre it is only a short walk to the Wildlife Centre.

The Sheepwash car park (SK248528) is on the north-west side of the reservoir and is signed off the B5035 just south-west of Carsington village. This car park is free and is locked at dusk; exact closing times are shown on signs in the car park. From here it is possible to access the Sheepwash, Lane End and Paul Stanley hides.

The Millfields car park (SK248499) is approached via the minor road which runs along the dam wall south-east from the visitor centre. This is a pay-and-display car park (£2), although anybody who has already paid at the main car park can obtain a token from the visitor centre allowing free access.

There is a circular walk around the reservoir covering a distance of approximately 8 miles (12.8 km), which for 2 miles (3.2 km) follows minor public roads and is shared with a horse riding and cycling route.

Calendar

Resident: Mute Swan, Canada Goose, Tufted Duck, Ruddy Duck, Little and Great Crested Grebes, Cormorant, Sparrowhawk, Common Buzzard, Kestrel, Northern Lapwing, Redshank, Little and Tawny Owls, Kingfisher, Great Spotted Woodpecker, Grey Wagtail, Raven, Tree Sparrow, Yellowhammer, Reed Bunting.

October–March: Bewick's Swan (scarce), Whooper Swan (scarce), Pink-footed Goose, Eurasian Wigeon, Gadwall, Common Teal, Pintail, Shoveler, Red-crested Pochard, Pochard, Scaup, Common Scoter (scarce, mainly October and November), Goldeneye, Smew (scarce), Red-breasted Merganser (scarce), Goosander, Black-necked Grebe (scarce), Merlin (scarce), Peregrine Falcon, European Golden Plover, Dunlin (scarce), Common Snipe, Curlew (February onwards), Mediterranean Gull, Yellow-legged Gull (scarce), Iceland Gull (scarce), Glaucous Gull (scarce), Kittiwake (scarce), Rock Pipit (scarce, mainly October and March), European Stonechat, Fieldfare, Redwing, Brambling, Siskin, Lesser Redpoll.

April–September: Shelduck, Garganey (scarce), Common Scoter (scarce, mainly April), Black-necked Grebe, Osprey, Oystercatcher, Ringed and Little Ringed Plovers, Knot, Sanderling, Little Stint (scarce August and September), Curlew Sandpiper (scarce, August and September), Dunlin, Ruff, Black-tailed Godwit, Bar-tailed Godwit (scarce), Whimbrel, Curlew, Greenshank, Common Sandpiper, Turnstone, Little Gull, Yellow-legged Gull (August onwards), Kittiwake (scarce, April), Common, Arctic and Black Terns, Cuckoo, Yellow Wagtail, White Wagtail (April), Common Redstart, Whinchat, Northern Wheatear, Sedge Warbler, Blackcap, Garden Warbler, Lesser and Common Whitethroats, Spotted Flycatcher, Pied Flycatcher (scarce).

3. CROMFORD CANAL AND SHININGCLIFF WOOD

Habitat

The Cromford Canal, which runs from Cromford Wharf to Ambergate, lies adjacent to the River Derwent and is designated as a Site of Special Scientific Interest. The stretch from Whatstandwell to Ambergate is a Derbyshire Wildlife Trust nature reserve. The canal is bordered by deciduous woodland, gardens and riverside meadows and there is a small sewage works at High Peak Junction, which is where the canal and the High Peak Trail join. On the eastern side of Cromford lies the Derbyshire Wildlife Trust reserve of Rose End Meadows, an area of 11 fields which have never been treated with artificial fertilisers or herbicides and therefore represent how Derbyshire's limestone farmland would have looked 100 years ago.

Shiningcliff Wood, a mixed deciduous and coniferous wood on the west bank of the River Derwent, is also a Site of Special Scientific Interest and stretches from just south of Whatstandwell almost to Ambergate.

Species

This site is well known for its wintering Hawfinches. Small numbers are regularly seen between October and March, with recent counts including up to 11 in the winter of 2005-06 and 19 in January 2002. The best areas to look are around the churchyard at Cromford Wharf, the nearby entrance to Willersley Castle, and the Rose End Meadows reserve, although patience may be necessary as Hawfinches can be very elusive and wary birds.

Roving flocks of tits, Treecreepers and other woodland birds are a feature of the winter months in Shiningcliff Wood, with smaller numbers present along the canal. Flocks such as these should be carefully scrutinised, as there have been several recent records of Firecrest, particularly at High Peak Junction. Chaffinches and variable numbers of Bramblings should be in evidence and there may be a sizeable roost of finches in Shiningcliff Wood. Riverside alder trees produce suitable food for wintering groups of Lesser Redpolls and Siskins, with flocks of the latter numbering in excess of 100 in

Hawfinch

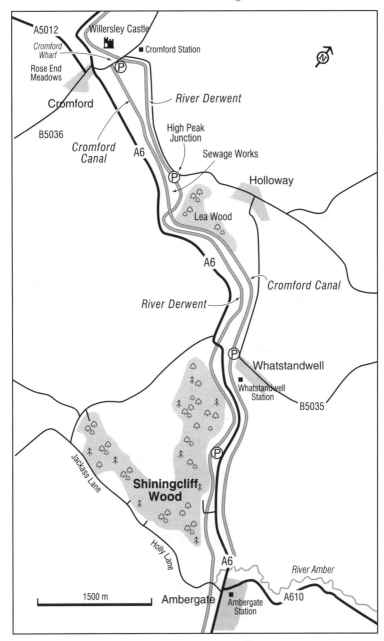

good years. Fieldfares and Redwings appear in large numbers, often feeding in the riverside meadows and roosting in the woodlands. The River Derwent may produce sightings of Goosander and, more rarely, Red-breasted Merganser at this time of the year.

Early spring is a good period to look for some of the resident birds of the area. All three species of woodpecker will be proclaiming their territories, although as everywhere Lesser Spotted is the most difficult to find. Up to five pairs of Little Grebes breed on the canal, where Grey Wagtails, Dippers and Kingfishers can be found displaying in March and April. Woodcocks begin their peculiar roding antics early in the spring over Shiningcliff Wood.

The woodlands come to life with the arrival of the first singing Common Chiffchaffs in late March, followed in April by Blackcaps, Garden Warblers, Common Whitethroats and Willow Warblers. The delightful shivering song of the Wood Warbler can be heard from suitable spots in the woodlands, while Common Redstarts breed in the open woodland edges. Spotted Flycatchers still maintain a reasonable presence and Pied Flycatcher has recently colonised the area, with up to four singing males being recorded in recent years. The River Derwent, particularly at High Peak Junction, has also played host to breeding Goosanders on a few occasions.

Timing

An early morning visit on a bright day with little wind between October and March provides the best chance of seeing Hawfinches. The summer visitors are usually at their most obvious just after they have arrived in April and May, when they are singing and displaying. The resident woodpeckers, Kingfishers, Grey Wagtails and Dippers should be displaying in March and a fine sunny day at this time would offer a good opportunity for searching for these species. This is a popular tourist and walking area, so sunny summer weekends are best avoided unless an early start is made.

Access

The majority of car parks in the area are accessed off the A6 Derby to Matlock road which runs through the Derwent Valley. For Cromford Wharf there is a pay-and-display car park opposite the church just east of the A6 in Cromford village (SK300570). From here a footpath follows the canal tow-path south all the way to Ambergate. The High Peak Junction car park, along with visitor centre, toilets, shop and picnic area, is off the A6 1.2 miles (2 km) south-east of Cromford (SK315561). A further car park is located at Whatstandwell, another 1.25 miles (2 km) south from High Peak Junction. Alternatively, a very pleasant way to birdwatch here is to take the train from Cromford to Whatstandwell or Ambergate stations, or vice-versa, and walk back along the canal towpath.

Rose End Meadows reserve, which is open at all times, is situated between the A5012 and the B5036 just east of Cromford. Two public foot-paths leave the B5036 (Cromford Hill) at SK293566 and SK292564, and these cross the site to reach Albaster Lane at the north end of the reserve. Access to Shiningcliff Wood is via various footpaths from the minor roads between Ambergate and Alderwasley.

Calendar

Resident: Little Grebe, Sparrowhawk, Woodcock, Kingfisher, all three wood-peckers, Grey Wagtail, Dipper, Nuthatch, Treecreeper, Jay, Bullfinch.

October–March: Red-breasted Merganser (scarce), Goosander, Fieldfare, Redwing, Brambling, Siskin, Lesser Redpoll, Hawfinch.

April–September: Goosander (scarce), Common Redstart, Blackcap, Garden Warbler, Common Whitethroat, Wood Warbler, Common Chiffchaff, Willow Warbler, Spotted and Pied Flycatchers.

4. FOREMARK RESERVOIR

Habitat

Completed in 1977, this 230 acre (93 ha) reservoir is owned and managed by the Severn Trent Water and is used extensively for sailing and trout fishing; however, the southern end of the south arm is kept free from disturbance. The reservoir is situated to the east of the Trent Valley floodplain, at an altitude of 365 feet (110 m). The surrounding banks are sandy and steeply sloping, with shallow banks only exposed during dry periods when the water levels are low. The dam, which is covered with rock, has an attractive steep grassy bank. The surrounding land is mainly hilly farmland but the large coniferous plantation of Repton Shrubs lies to the south-west of the reservoir.

At the southern end of the reservoir is the Derbyshire Wildlife Trust's reserve of Carver's Rocks, which comprises mainly of deciduous woodland and wetland with small areas of bracken and heather.

Species

Winter is the best time to visit, with the principal attraction being wildfowl. Diving ducks usually dominate, particularly Tufted Ducks, which reached 320 in November 2003. Smaller groups of Pochard and Goldeneye are present, but it is the wintering flock of Goosanders that the reservoir is best known for; totals sometimes reach three-figures and have topped 200 on occasions. Dabbling ducks are less numerous, although Eurasian Wigeon may be seen in reasonable numbers, and Gadwall, Common Teal and Shoveler are usually to be found, along with the occasional Pintail. Other regular waterbirds at this time of year include Great Crested Grebe, which may number well over 100, Little Grebe and Cormorant. In periods of severe weather, the reservoir becomes an important site for wildfowl that have been frozen out of nearby water areas, and in these conditions some of the scarcer species may appear. Scaup and Smew are not infrequent, and there have been records of Common Eider, Long-tailed Duck, Velvet Scoter and Red-breasted Merganser. Red-throated, Black-throated and Great Northern Divers have all occurred, with some individuals remaining for lengthy periods, while both Red-necked and Slavonian Grebes have appeared on several occasions.

Mediterranean and Black-headed Gulls

Another winter attraction at the reservoir is the large gull roost. Recent estimates of the commoner species have included 10,000 Black-headed Gulls (December 2000), 2,300 Lesser Black-backed Gulls (November 2004), 1,200 Herring Gulls (January 2003) and 650 Great Black-backed Gulls (December 2000). Inevitably, a roost of this size attracts some of the scarcer species: Mediterranean Gulls are annual in small numbers, as are Yellow-legged and the increasingly regular Caspian Gull, while Iceland and Glaucous are found most years. Kittiwakes sometimes occur in the late winter period, and there have been a couple of recent mid-winter records of Little Gull in the roost.

Wintering passerines are best looked for at Carver's Rocks, where birch and alder trees attract groups of Siskins and Lesser Redpolls. Small flocks of Tree Sparrows and Bramblings are often present and one or two European Stonechat normally overwinter. Carver's Rocks is also a good place to look for Woodcocks in the winter months, although they are more likely to be accidentally flushed. The same can be said for Jack Snipe, which may frequent boggy areas on the reserve. On calm days in late winter and early spring, a scan of the skies may reveal Common Buzzards and Ravens, both of which are now resident in the area.

As the reservoir occupies an elevated position adjacent to the Trent Valley, it acts as a beacon to overflying migrants. Common and Arctic Terns are regular during April and May, with the latter sometimes occurring in good numbers during periods of north-easterly winds. During such movements, occasional Sandwich Terns appear and often use the numerous buoys as perches. Black Terns, however, are strangely scarce in the spring. Small flocks of Kittiwakes sometimes arrive between mid-March and mid-April, although their appearances are unpredictable. Parties of Common Scoters pause briefly on their cross-country migrations in spring, especially during April, and Black-necked Grebes in their fine breeding dress sometimes arrive at this time of year.

The water level is generally too high in the spring to produce much in the way of waders, although the dam wall attracts Common Sandpipers and occasionally other species. However, a few migrants may betray their presence by calling as they fly over, with Whimbrel being the most likely in the spring.

Northern Wheatears and Yellow Wagtails are attracted to the concrete walls and grassy banks of the dam, and a few Whinchats are located most springs. Foremark is a regular site for Ospreys in the spring and particularly the late summer and autumn, and some birds may linger for extended periods. Also seen on passage are occasional Marsh Harriers, while sightings of Hobby are fairly frequent.

Summer tends to be a rather quiet time, with a high level of disturbance from water sports, and the only birds of note tend to be the breeding species. Numerous Willow Warblers sing around the reservoir, with smaller numbers of Lesser Whitethroats and Common Whitethroats. A few pairs of Grasshopper Warblers can be found, especially around the Carver's Rocks reserve, and the same area is good for Woodcocks, which can be seen roding on spring evenings. The nature reserve itself has Blackcaps and Garden Warblers, and a few Turtle Doves hang on in this area. Other breeding species around the reservoir include Tufted Duck, Great Crested Grebe, Sparrowhawk, Kestrel, Kingfisher, Green Woodpecker and Marsh Tit. The elusive and declining Lesser Spotted Woodpecker probably still breeds in the area, and there is a small heronry at Repton Shrubs.

Autumn migration brings movements of Common Terns with occasional Sandwich, Arctic and Black Terns, while Little Gulls are not uncommon. In

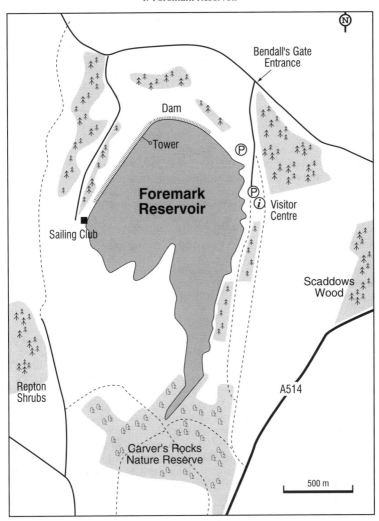

dry summers, low water levels may expose some sandy and muddy shore-lines, and small numbers of waders may be found. Following the hot summer of 2003, for example, there were autumn records of Knot, Sanderling, Ruff and Turnstone, along with the more regular Ringed Plover, Dunlin, Greenshank, Green Sandpiper and Common Sandpiper. Other species such as Grey Plover, Little Stint, Curlew Sandpiper and Black-tailed Godwit have all been noted in the past.

Small numbers of Yellow Wagtails, Whinchats and Northern Wheatears are noted on autumn passage, and there are occasionally sightings of slightly less usual species such as Common Redstart and Pied Flycatcher. During August and September a few Tree Pipits usually pass overhead, while October regu-larly produces records of Rock Pipits, which often frequent the stonework of the dam. Observers prepared to watch the gull roost from late summer may be rewarded with an early Mediterranean Gull, while a few Yellow-legged Gulls should be present from August onwards. Wildfowl numbers begin to build up during the autumn, and this period offers a good chance of finding a Black-necked Grebe; most records are of juveniles in September or October. Late autumn often sees the arrival of Common Scoters and there have been several sightings of Red-throated Diver at this time of year.

The reservoir is rather underwatched, but has produced a number of local rarities, including three Fulmars, four Honey Buzzards, Grey Phalarope, Great Skua and Little Auk. The biggest surprises, however, have been three Arctic Redpolls in the winter of 1995-96 and Derbyshire's first Surf Scoter in November 2005.

Timing

The best period is during the winter between November and March, when wildfowl numbers are at their greatest. As the reservoir is very deep it seldom freezes, and it is therefore well worth a visit during spells of severe weather when birds from surrounding frozen waters will seek refuge at the site. There is also the added attraction of the gull roost during the winter, which is best watched from the main car park near the dam. Visitors should arrive a couple of hours prior to dusk to view the roost; overcast evenings are best, as the sun can be a problem during the afternoons. The spring and autumn migration periods can offer some rewards, particularly if the water levels are low. Passage waders and terns usually appear following spells of easterly winds.

Access

Foremark Reservoir is 5 miles (8 km) south of Derby and lies to the west of the A514 Ticknall to Hartshorne road. From the A514 at the west end of Ticknall, take the minor road west towards Milton and after 1 mile (1.6 km) turn left at the Bendall's Gate entrance (£1.50 entry fee for vehicles). This road leads to two public car parks; there is a visitor centre and toilets in the southern car park (SK336242). Public access is only allowed on this side of the reservoir. The entrance gates are locked around dusk; precise closing times are shown on signs in the car parks.

Carver's Rocks Nature Reserve, which is open at all times, is reached by using the footpath that leaves the A514 1 mile (1.6 km) north-east of Hartshorne at SK334227, although parking facilities here are rather limited. Alternatively, the reserve can be accessed by walking south for 0.75 miles (1.2 km) from the visitor centre in the southern public car park.

Calendar

Resident: Tufted Duck, Little and Great Crested Grebes, Grey Heron, Sparrowhawk, Common Buzzard, Kestrel, Woodcock, Barn, Little and Tawny Owls, Kingfisher, Green and Lesser Spotted Woodpeckers, Marsh Tit, Raven, Yellowhammer, Reed Bunting.

October–March: Eurasian Wigeon, Gadwall, Common Teal, Pintail (scarce), Shoveler, Pochard, Scaup (scarce), Goldeneye, Smew (scarce), Goosander, Ruddy Duck, divers (rare), Red-necked Grebe (scarce), Slavonian Grebe (rare), Cormorant, Jack Snipe, Common Snipe, Mediterranean Gull, Yellow-legged Gull, Caspian Gull, Iceland and Glaucous Gulls (scarce), Kittiwake (scarce), Rock Pipit (scarce, October), Grey Wagtail, European Stonechat, Fieldfare, Redwing, Tree Sparrow, Brambling, Siskin, Lesser Redpoll.

April–September: Common Scoter (scarce), Black-necked Grebe (scarce), Marsh Harrier (scarce, mainly May and August), Osprey (scarce), Hobby,

Kittiwake (scarce, April), Ringed Plover, Dunlin, Whimbrel, Greenshank, Common Sandpiper, Mediterranean Gull (scarce, August onwards), Little Gull (scarce), Yellow-legged Gull (August onwards), Sandwich Tern (scarce), Common Tern, Arctic Tern (passage), Black Tern, Turtle Dove, Cuckoo, Tree Pipit, Yellow Wagtail, Whinchat (passage), Northern Wheatear (passage), Grasshopper Warbler, Blackcap, Garden Warbler, Lesser and Common Whitethroats, Willow Warbler.

5. OGSTON RESERVOIR

OS Landranger 119
OS Explorer 269

Habitat

Ogston Reservoir was created in the late 1950s when the River Amber was dammed near Ogston Hall, flooding a total of 206 acres (83 ha). The reservoir banks are all natural; those on the northern and western sides shelve gently, while those on the east are much steeper. The water level usually falls in the summer and autumn periods, exposing muddy margins. A few small woodlands lie close to the water's edge, including the Derbyshire Wildlife Trust's Ogston Woodlands reserve, for which an entry permit is required. Otherwise, the surrounding area is largely pastoral farmland. Recreational sailing, which was introduced soon after the reservoir was flooded, occurs over much of the water area and causes some disturbance to wildlife, as does trout fishing, which takes place during the period mid-March to October.

Species

The main interests for birdwatchers at Ogston are the gull roost, wintering wildfowl and, especially when water levels are low, migrant waders.

The most numerous wildfowl in winter are Eurasian Wigeon, Common Teal and Mallard, all of which may be present in three-figure flocks. By contrast, diving ducks occur generally in small numbers, though Tufted Duck numbers have reached over 100 and Pochard nearly 400. Goldeneyes have been rather erratic in their appearance of late but Goosanders have increased in the last decade, with small numbers often present. Also showing signs of a rapid recent increase are Cormorants, which used to commute from Attenborough Nature Reserve in Nottinghamshire but now roost at Ogston, with up to 70 recorded. A flock of Canada Geese is usually present, with their numbers peaking during the autumn when up to 492 have been counted. Small numbers of both Little and Great Crested Grebes overwinter, with the latter often increasing considerably when severe weather freezes small surrounding waters. A few Gadwall and Shovelers may be present at any time of year, and more occasional visitors among the wildfowl include Shelduck, Mandarin Duck, Garganey, Pintail, Long-tailed Duck, Velvet Scoter, Smew, Red-breasted Merganser and Scaup, a flock of 17 of which wintered on one occasion. Bewick's and Whooper Swans occasionally call in on migration but rarely stay for long. Bitterns have been seen on a very few occasions, usually in the willows at the north-west and south-west ends of the reservoir.

All three divers have been recorded, with Great Northern and Black-throated having on occasions stayed for long periods, while the less regular Red-throated Diver tends to be more transitory. Red-necked, Slavonian and

Black-necked Grebes are all very infrequent visitors, with the latter most often seen in spring, although the highest count of four birds occurred in December. Grey Herons are present in all but the most severe weather. Common Snipe have peaked at 167 in the winter but they are often difficult to locate when the water level is high. Up to four Jack Snipe are very occasionally seen, usually from the hides.

The winter gull roost is of considerable interest as it regularly attracts some of the rarer species and is easily viewed from the roads and car parks. Typically the roost forms in late October, reaches its largest numbers at the turn of the year and is abandoned in late March or early April. In recent years the largest counts of the regular species have been: Black-headed Gull (8,300), Common Gull (90), Lesser Black-backed Gull (1,700), Herring Gull (3,000) and Great Black-backed Gull (800). Mediterranean, Yellow-legged, Caspian, Iceland and Glaucous Gulls are frequently present and the chance of seeing some of these species at relatively close range is one of the prime reasons why many birdwatchers visit Ogston. In the early days of the roost, Glaucous Gulls were much more regular than Iceland Gulls. The latter then became dominant but in recent years the two species have occurred with roughly equal frequency: there may be ten or more individuals of both species identified during the course of a winter. Mediterranean Gulls are fairly regular and a few have been seen as migrants at other times of year. Gales in winter, and occasionally at other times of year, may bring in small numbers of Kittiwakes. Intense scrutiny of the gull roost has also resulted in sightings of five Ring-billed Gulls, at least three Kumlien's Gulls and more notably a Laughing Gull (in 1980) and a remarkable four Bonaparte's Gulls. Gull-watchers may notice other birds flying over just before dark; small flocks of finches, often including Bramblings, roost in rhododendron cover in Carr Wood, an area which also often holds large numbers of roosting corvids, Woodpigeons and Stock Doves. Woodcocks lurk here in bracken cover during the day and can often be seen at dusk as they fly out to feed in fields and boggy spots beyond the reservoir.

Spring is usually a rather quiet time at Ogston as trout fishing commences and some of the banks may be lined with anglers; in addition, water levels are usually high. As a consequence, migrant waders at this time are often seen only flying over, though it is hoped that the Ogston Bird Club's recent creation of pools, spits and an island on the western bank will tempt more waders to rest and feed at the site. The island has already supported Derbyshire's largest recorded flock of Black-tailed Godwits, when 170 stayed briefly in April 2004. Easterly winds (as in autumn) may produce such scarce migrants as Common Scoter, Little Gull and Black Tern, while Arctic Terns are regular and flocks have sometimes peaked at over 100 birds. Ospreys have been seen on many occasions and some have stayed for long periods.

Several pairs of Mallard and Coot and smaller numbers of Canada Geese, Tufted Ducks and Little and Great Crested Grebes all breed, and Ruddy Duck and Goosander have each bred once. The presence of nesting Little Ringed Plovers and Northern Lapwings used to be dependent on the water level but the recent habitat changes mentioned above will hopefully result in regular breeding. A pair of Oystercatchers nested unsuccessfully on the island in 2003. The installation in 1990 of two rafts for Common Terns was immediately successful, but they have now been deserted – hopefully just temporarily. There is a well-established heronry in adjacent Carr Wood; 15-20 pairs of Grey Heron nest in the larch trees, which can be viewed from the road. Kingfishers and Grey Wagtails breed on some of the surrounding streams, Little Owls on the farmland and Sparrowhawks and all three

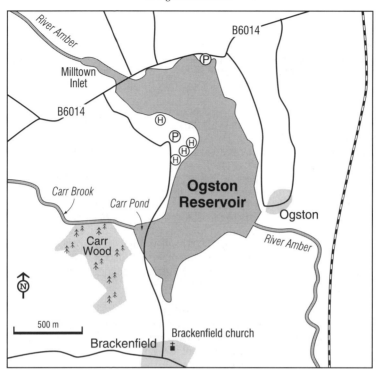

woodpeckers in nearby woodlands. Two very welcome recent additions to the area's breeding birds are Common Buzzard and Hobby, while Peregrine Falcons and Ravens are seen more regularly now, commensurate with their spread into nearby parts of the Peak District. The scrubbier parts of the reservoir margins and adjacent hedgerows support Grasshopper and Sedge Warblers, Common Whitethroats and Lesser Whitethroats, while nearby Brackenfield churchyard is a good place to find Spotted Flycatchers.

Following a dry summer the water level will begin to fall in the early autumn, producing areas of exposed mud and shallow water attractive to waders. Regular species include Little Ringed and Ringed Plovers, Dunlin, Greenshank and Common Sandpiper, while Black-tailed Godwits are becoming more frequent. Less usual are Knot, Sanderling, Ruff, Whimbrel, Spotted Redshank and Wood Sandpiper. Thirty-four species of waders have been recorded at Ogston, including Avocet, Kentish Plover, Temminck's Stint, Pectoral and Purple Sandpipers and Grey Phalarope. Rarer still were Derbyshire's third Spotted Sandpiper (in 2003) and one and only Wilson's Phalarope (in 1965).

Later in the autumn, usually in October, the presence of one or two Rock Pipits (and, more rarely, Water Pipits) is betrayed by their sibilant calls.

Ogston Reservoir is one of the most regularly watched sites in Derbyshire, and consequently has the longest bird list of any place in the county. Unusual species, in addition to those already mentioned, have included Green-winged Teal, Ferruginous Duck, Common Eider, Fulmar, European and Leach's Storm-petrels, Gannet, Honey Buzzard, Rough-legged Buzzard, Corncrake, Common Crane, all four skuas, Sabine's Gull, Caspian, Roseate and White-winged Black Terns, Alpine Swift, Red-rumped Swallow, Woodlark, Great Grey Shrike and Snow Bunting.

Timing

The best time to visit is from October to March when disturbance is low and waterbird numbers are at their highest. The gull roost is generally best viewed from the road and car park at the western side of the reservoir, and visitors should aim to arrive at least two hours prior to dusk to watch the roost. In spring and early summer there may be relatively few birds present.

Access

Ogston Reservoir lies 1.5 miles (2.4 km) south-west of Clay Cross and immediately north of the village of Brackenfield. It is most easily reached from the B6014 Stretton to Matlock road which runs along the northern edge of the reservoir, cutting off a small water area known as Milltown Inlet. Immediately west of here a minor road runs south to Woolley and Brackenfield and gives good views of the southern two-thirds of the reservoir, though periodically these are somewhat restricted by a dense growth of scrub. There is no access to the water's edge, but public car parks can be found at the north-eastern end of the reservoir (SK375610) and on the central west bank at Woolley (SK373604), where there is also a large public hide. Ogston Bird Club, which has a membership of over 1,000, owns three hides on the west and north-west banks, giving excellent close-range views of the birds. The club publishes regular bulletins and an annual report.

Calendar

Resident: Canada Goose, Mallard, Tufted Duck, Little and Great Crested Grebes, Cormorant, Grey Heron, Sparrowhawk, Common Buzzard, Peregrine Falcon, Coot, Little and Tawny Owls, all three woodpeckers, Kingfisher, Grey Wagtail, Nuthatch, Treecreeper, Raven.

October–March: Eurasian Wigeon, Gadwall, Common Teal, Shoveler, Pochard, Goldeneye, Goosander, Jack Snipe (scarce), Common Snipe, Woodcock, Mediterranean, Yellow-legged, Caspian, Iceland and Glaucous Gulls, Rock Pipit (scarce October), Brambling.

April–September: Osprey (scarce), Hobby, Little Ringed and Ringed Plovers, Dunlin, Black-tailed Godwit, Greenshank, Common Sandpiper, Kittiwake (scarce April), Common Tern, Arctic Tern (mainly April and May), Cuckoo, Swift, hirundines, Grasshopper, Sedge and Garden Warblers, Lesser and Common Whitethroats, Spotted Flycatcher.

6. THE PEAK DISTRICT
OS Landrangers 110 and 119
OS Explorers 1 and 24

The Peak District was Britain's first national park, established in 1951, and covers 555 square miles (1,438 square km). It can be divided in to two distinctly different regions: the Dark Peak in the north and north-west, which is typified by gritstone moors such as those found in the Upper Derwent region, and the White Peak to the south and south-west, where the underlying carboniferous limestone forms a gentle landscape of rolling hills with occasional deep valleys.

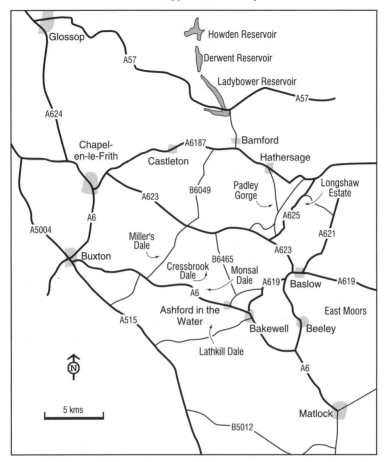

6A. THE UPPER DERWENT VALLEY

OS Landranger 110
OS Explorer 1

Habitat

This very impressive area, located in the Dark Peak region of the Peak District, is one of great scenic beauty. Being within easy reach of the large centres of population of Sheffield, Chesterfield and Manchester, it attracts huge numbers of visitors. The major feature of the valley is the string of reservoirs – Howden, Derwent and Ladybower – which were formed when the valley was flooded at the turn of the 20th century to provide water for the urban areas nearby. The reservoirs are deep with steep sides and lack any extensive areas of emergent vegetation around their edges. When the water level falls in Ladybower Reservoir in dry summers, the remnants of the flooded village of Derwent may be visible. As most of the water in the reservoirs drains off the surrounding peat moorlands it is rather acidic, and as such the reservoirs themselves generally provide little of interest in the way of birds, in direct contrast to the surrounding forests and moorland.

The valley sides have been extensively planted with conifers, mainly larch and pine with some spruce. There are areas of deciduous trees, and

37

also the remnants of old oak woodlands on some of the hillsides. In several places, the woodlands run right down to the edge of the reservoirs. The forestry companies are now beginning to fell some areas of conifers and replant with a more varied mix of tree species.

Above the plantations the valley slopes are covered with large expanses of rough sheep-grazed grassland and mixed heather and grass moorland. This habitat dominates the tops of the surrounding hills, which rise to over 1,700 feet (520 m).

Species

Winter birding is highly dependent upon the weather, as rain, wind and low cloud/fog and mist will hamper the chances of seeing the speciality species of the area. Although the reservoirs may have a few Goosanders, Tufted Ducks, Pochards and sometimes Goldeneyes, there is usually little to see on the open water. Nevertheless, it is always worth a scan as Bewick's and Whooper Swans, Common Scoter, Long-tailed Duck, all three divers, Grey Phalarope and Kittiwake have been recorded in the recent past. Watch out for the resident Grey Wagtails around the water's edge and near the dams and inlet streams, where Dippers can also occasionally be found.

A walk through the lower woodlands will reveal the typical flocks of tits and other small passerines, which are usually dominated by Coal Tits along with a few Treecreepers and Goldcrests. Flocks of Siskins can be found in the larches and areas of alders, and may be accompanied by Lesser Redpolls and Goldfinches. Any group of Lesser Redpolls encountered is worth scrutinising further, as Mealy Redpolls have been seen on several occasions and during early 1996 up to seven Arctic Redpolls were found. Bramblings are regular, and in good winters flocks of over 200 may be found. One of the key species of the area is Common Crossbill, which is best looked for in the plantations of larch; numbers of this species vary, but in good years there may be over 200 birds in the valley. In the winter of 1982–83, large flocks of Common Crossbills were accompanied by up to 25 Parrot Crossbills and a male Two-barred Crossbill, and another of the latter species was found in November 1990. Flocks of Redwing and Fieldfare are often seen throughout the winter in the dale, in addition to which good numbers pass through on migration.

Resident raptors such as Sparrowhawk can be seen hunting the woodlands, and on fine sunny days from the turn of the year they will be indulging in display flights over the plantations and lower moorland. This is one of the best areas in the country to observe Goshawks, which can be seen from the public roads and footpaths without causing disturbance. At any time from January to April local pairs may be seen displaying around the valley, with one of the best spots being the larch plantation north of Windy Corner, to the west of Howden Reservoir. As with all raptors, patience, perseverance and luck are the key elements to successful sightings but, given a fine day with some blue sky and light to moderate winds, then a watch of an hour or two should produce sightings of these magnificent raptors over the plantations and intervening ridges. They are often seen in the air with Sparrowhawks, allowing the obvious differences in size and proportions to be compared. As they are resident in the area Goshawks can be seen in midwinter, when they also hunt over the adjacent moorland, but when not in display a larger degree of luck is required to locate them.

The moorland has a reputation for producing other raptors during the winter months. The resident Peregrine Falcons make regular appearances, a few Hen Harriers are seen most winters (mainly 'ringtails'), as are Merlins and

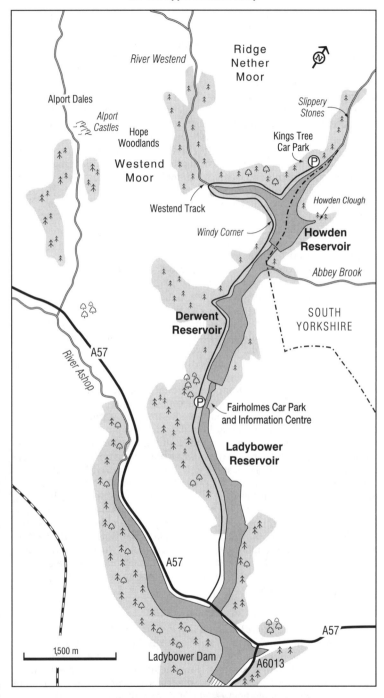

Ridge Nether Moor

River Westend

Alport Dales

Alport Castles

Hope Woodlands

Westend Moor

Slippery Stones

Kings Tree Car Park

Westend Track

Howden Clough

Windy Corner

Howden Reservoir

Abbey Brook

Derwent Reservoir

SOUTH YORKSHIRE

River Ashop

A57

Fairholmes Car Park and Information Centre

Ladybower Reservoir

A57

1,500 m

A57

Ladybower Dam

A6013

occasional Rough-legged Buzzards. Wandering Red Kites have also been noted on several occasions recently. The path which leads up onto the moorland, following the River Derwent valley from Slippery Stones to the north of Howden Reservoir, offers good views over the surrounding crags for raptors. On clear winter days with blue skies, skeins of Pink-footed Geese are often seen high over the moorland on one of their midwinter migrations between feeding sites in Lancashire, Scotland and East Anglia. A pair of European Stonechats sometimes winter up the valley beyond Howden Reservoir and the resident Red Grouse will be present on the heather tops, where you may also see Mountain Hares in their white winter dress. The area has produced several records of wintering Great Grey Shrikes in the past, and there is always the possibility of one of these fine northern winter visitors being located around the plantations and clear-fells. There is also a chance of seeing some of the reintroduced Black Grouse in these areas.

A visit in mid to late March may produce sightings of displaying Peregrines and a pair or two of Ravens, the latter having returned to the area in recent years. Any breeding Common Crossbills will have young by March and April, and roving family parties may be obvious in the plantations. During April and May, Red-breasted Mergansers and Common Sandpipers return to breed around the reservoirs and the resident woodland bird population is swelled by the arrival of Common Chiffchaffs and Willow Warblers. Tree Pipits sing from the woodland slopes and a few pairs of Common Redstarts, Wood Warblers and, in some years, Pied Flycatchers can be found in the older deciduous blocks. Firecrests bred in 1995 and singing males have been heard in a couple of subsequent summers, while Dippers frequent the Derwent downstream of the Ladybower Dam.

Raptors are less obvious when nesting but hunting male Sparrowhawks are a regular sight around the plantations and Goshawks are also seen. Peregrines can be watched from the National Trust hide at Alport Castles if they are breeding at this site. One or two pairs of Merlin sometimes breed on the moors but they are seldom noted during the summer months, and non-breeding Hobbies are found irregularly in July and August, when they can be watched hawking Emperor and Northern Eggar moths. Other raptors are sometimes encountered in the area; Ospreys have been seen on spring passage on several occasions and a Red-footed Falcon was located in 1977.

On the moors Red Grouse become more visible as the males display and their calls echo around the valley. On the moorland tops breeding Curlews, European Golden Plovers and, in some years, the occasional pair of Dunlins take up summer territories. Passage Dotterel have been located occasionally on the moors during late April and May. Ring Ouzels breed on the valley slopes, although they can be particularly elusive when nesting and are best seen early in the spring. Black Grouse can also be seen on some of the high tops, with the area between Abbey Brook and Upper Hey being especially favoured.

Timing

This is a very popular tourist site and attracts large numbers of people at all times of year, even in midwinter and bad weather. The worst times are midsummer and on bank holidays and weekends, when congestion can be a real problem for access to the best areas. However, the area as a whole is extensive and, away from obvious attractions like the dams and car parks, the number of visitors is not usually a problem, especially as regards raptor-watching.

The most important factor to bear in mind is the weather. This is an upland region and as such has its own microclimate; the weather can turn

Red Grouse

suddenly from glorious sunshine to torrential rain with strong winds, and the temperature can change dramatically. The chances of bad weather are obviously higher in the winter but always be prepared for the worst and never set off onto the moorland, in particular, without due preparation and sufficient warm and waterproof clothing. The upland areas are also prone to low cloud and mist, which can ruin any attempt to watch raptors, and it is important to obtain a good weather forecast before contemplating a visit for these birds. In general, winter is good for raptors but the best time to see Goshawks is from February to early April; they are least obvious in summer and early autumn. Good raptor weather does not necessarily mean sunshine; high cloud and some blue sky with light or moderate winds is often best, although at peak display periods the birds will be aloft at some time during the day in all but the worst weather.

Access

The Upper Derwent Valley lies about 10 miles (16 km) west of Sheffield and 16 miles (25 km) north-west of Chesterfield. The main A57 Sheffield to Glossop road (Snake Pass) crosses the southern end of Ladybower Reservoir. A minor road signposted to Derwentdale runs north along the western edge of the three reservoirs to Kings Tree, at the northern end of Howden Reservoir where there is a small car park (SK180950). There are a few other car parks along the road and a number of public footpaths lead up onto the moorland. On Sundays and bank holidays throughout the year, and at weekends from April to the end of October, the road is closed at the southern end of Derwent Reservoir at Fairholmes, where there is a car park and information centre (SK171893). This car park soon becomes congested and an early arrival is an advantage at weekends. Cycles can be hired and there is a shuttle service on a minibus around the northern end of the two northernmost reservoirs, which saves a walk of 2.5 miles (4 km) along the road to Windy Corner, the best spot for Goshawks.

One of the best sites for looking for wintering raptors is located by following the path which leads up onto the open moorland from Kings Tree car park at the northern end of Howden Reservoir. Easier access to the higher areas of open moorland is gained by driving west along the A57 to the summit of Snake Pass where the Pennine Way crosses the road. The moorland has open access but is very popular with hill walkers.

Access to the National Trust hide at Alport Castles is via the Westend track at the end of the western arm of Howden Reservoir (SK154927), or along the track that leaves the A57 at Alport Dale (SK133895) up to the Castles. Current information can be obtained from the Ranger's Office and Fairholmes Visitor Centre.

Calendar
Resident: Red Grouse, Black Grouse (reintroduced), Goshawk, Sparrowhawk, Common Buzzard, Peregrine Falcon, Great Spotted Woodpecker, Grey Wagtail, Dipper, Goldcrest, Coal Tit, Nuthatch, Treecreeper, Raven, Siskin, Common Crossbill.

September–March: Pink-footed Goose, Hen Harrier, Rough-legged Buzzard (rare), Merlin (scarce), Fieldfare, Redwing, Brambling, Lesser Redpoll.

April–August: Red-breasted Merganser, Merlin, Hobby (occasional), European Golden Plover, Dunlin, Curlew, Common Sandpiper, Short-eared Owl, Tree Pipit, Common Redstart, Whinchat, European Stonechat, Northern Wheatear, Ring Ouzel, Wood Warbler, Common Chiffchaff, Willow Warbler, Firecrest (occasional), Pied Flycatcher.

6B. LONGSHAW ESTATE AND PADLEY GORGE

OS Landranger 119
OS Explorer 24

Habitat
Overlooking the Derwent Valley at an altitude of around 300 m (1,000 ft) lies the Longshaw Estate. Criss-crossed by old tracks and packhorse trails, the estate is a mix of wet pasture and meadow, heather moorland and semi-natural ancient woodland.

On the east side of the estate is White Edge Moor, which forms part of the long gritstone edge stretching from Stanage towards Birchens Edge south of Chatsworth House. The moor is predominantly comprised of mat grass with patches of heather on the rocky scarp edges. On the eastern side of the moor is the former Barbrook Reservoir, which was drained in 2002; its 30 acres (12 ha) of water is now restricted to a 3 acre (1.2 ha) area of pools.

Padley Gorge lies more or less centrally within the Longshaw Estate, with the gritstone moor of Lawrence Field to the north and the Sheffield plantation, an open coniferous woodland, to the east. The gorge is one of the finest remaining examples of the oak/birch woodland once characteristic of the edges and valley sides of the Dark Peak. The woodland consists mainly of sessile oak and birch, with alder along the stream side and holly and rowan scattered throughout the remainder of the wood. The oaks are only 5 to 12 m in height, a result of being rooted in thin soils. Running through the gorge is Burbage Brook, which originates 427 m (1,400 ft) up on the Hathersage and Burbage Moors and runs into the River Derwent north of Grindleford.

Species
Winter can be a rather quiet time on the Longshaw Estate, with most interest centred on the moorland areas. A few Red Grouse should be found, perhaps with the occasional Hen Harrier, Merlin or Short-eared Owl, while one or two European Stonechats may be evidence. One bird well worth searching for at this time of the year is Great Grey Shrike; though well by any means guaranteed, this splendid species has been noted on a number of occasions in the area during recent winters. Away from the moors, Common Crossbills may be present in the plantations, along with variable numbers of Bramblings, Siskins and Lesser Redpolls; any finch flocks encountered should be carefully scrutinised, as three Parrot Crossbills were found in 1985 and up to three Arctic Redpolls were located in the winter of 1995-96.

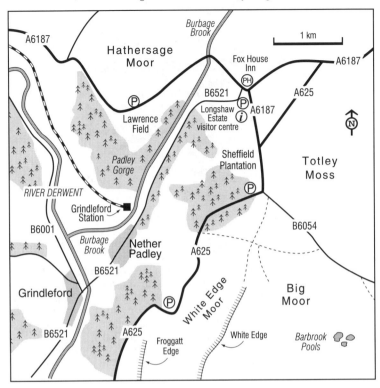

Dippers are resident on the brook through Padley Gorge, where you may flush the odd Woodcock.

Birdlife begins to come into its own in March when Northern Lapwings and Curlews arrive back from wintering areas to display over their moorland breeding territories. A little later in the spring, Common Snipe can be found drumming over boggy stretches of moorland. However, it is the birds of Padley Gorge that attract most interest from birdwatchers. From mid-April onwards, the delightful song of the Wood Warbler fills the air, while up to ten pairs of Pied Flycatchers make use of purpose-built nest-boxes. You may also see a few Common Redstarts here, with more to be found in other areas of the estate. Several pairs of Spotted Flycatchers arrive in May, where they join other typical birds of the sessile oak woods such as Green and Great Spotted Woodpeckers, Nuthatch and Treecreeper. Tawny Owls nest in the woodlands, being most easily located at dusk when calling or feeding young. The elusive Lesser Spotted Woodpecker also breeds here. A late evening walk should produce a few roding Woodcocks, while both Dipper and Grey Wagtail are likely to be seen on the fast-flowing brook.

At the head of the gorge, as the woodlands thin to open moorland, Tree Pipits occur among the birch trees while European Stonechats and Whinchats are found on the more open moorland. At higher elevations Northern Wheatears are fairly common but numbers of Ring Ouzels have declined considerably and pairs are now rather thin on the ground. The breeding populations of Meadow Pipit no doubt account for the high concentrations of Cuckoos, which are more common here than in lowland Derbyshire. Raptors in the area which may be seen overhead include

Pied Flycatcher

Sparrowhawk, Kestrel, Peregrine Falcon and, more occasionally, Goshawk, while Ravens have spread into the area in recent years.

The River Derwent between Hathersage in the north and Froggatt in the south harbours Goosanders throughout the year, and small numbers breed. Red-breasted Mergansers are not infrequent, particularly at Froggatt, with most records between February and June. The Derwent at Froggatt also has a resident population of Mandarin Ducks, numbers of which have increased rapidly in recent times to a peak of 91 in December 2002.

In general, autumn offers fewer rewards, although September to November is the best time for Twite; this species bred in the area until the 1980s but is now a scarce and irregular migrant, with perhaps two or three records a year. Visible migration watches in autumn can produce some impressive numbers of birds over the moors, particularly around Barbrook. Prior to being drained, the reservoir itself had its moments, with records of Baird's and Purple Sandpipers, White-winged Black Tern, Shore Lark and Lapland Bunting being particularly noteworthy.

Timing

April and May are without doubt the best months to visit for a range of woodland and moorland species combined with the special birds of the brook. However, Longshaw is within easy reach of Sheffield and thus attracts large numbers of visitors; it is best to avoid Sundays as the whole area can become very overcrowded. Early morning visits are recommended, allowing most of the singing birds to be located before disturbance and excess noise causes the birds to become quieter and less visible.

Access

The Longshaw Estate is on the county boundary with Yorkshire, 6 miles (9.6 km) south-west of the southern outskirts of Sheffield and immediately north-east of the village of Grindleford. The main car park for the Longshaw Estate Visitor Centre, which has a tearoom, shop and toilets, is by the A6187, 300 m north of the junction with the A625 and 200 m south of the Fox House Inn at SK267801 (pay and display £1). The visitor centre is open from 10.30 am to 5 pm at weekends, and at the same time during most weekdays between late March and late October. There are other parking areas as follows: (1) Lawrence Field by the north side of the A6187 1.5 miles (2.4 km) west of Hathersage village (SK251801); (2) 200 m west of the junction of the A625 and the B6054 (SK267790); (3) Grindleford Railway Station, just off the north side of the B6521 at Nether Padley, 1 mile (1.6 km) north-east of Grindleford village (SK251789). The latter is the best place to park for access to Padley Gorge; there is also limited parking along the B6521 north-east of Grindleford Station. The whole area has open public access at all times.

There is no access inside the perimeter fence at Barbrook Pools, but this area can be viewed from a track which runs alongside the eastern boundary.

Calendar

Resident: Mandarin Duck, Goosander, Red Grouse, Goshawk (scarce), Sparrowhawk, Kestrel, Peregrine Falcon, Woodcock, Tawny Owl, all three woodpeckers, Dipper, European Stonechat, Nuthatch, Treecreeper, Raven.

October–March: Red-breasted Merganser (February and March), Hen Harrier (scarce), Merlin, Great Grey Shrike (rare), Brambling, Siskin, Twite (rare), Lesser Redpoll.

April–September: Red-breasted Merganser (April to June), Northern Lapwing, Common Snipe, Curlew, Cuckoo, Tree and Meadow Pipits, Grey Wagtail, Common Redstart, Whinchat, Northern Wheatear, Ring Ouzel, Wood Warbler, Spotted and Pied Flycatchers.

6C. THE DERBYSHIRE DALES

OS Landranger 119
OS Explorer 24

Habitat

The area to the east of Buxton, within the White Peak, is one of beautiful wooded limestone valleys and craggy gorges, with more open meadows in the lower reaches where the streams meander down to join the River Wye. The valleys are typified by fast-flowing clear trout streams which bubble over stretches of rapids; these alternate with quieter, wider sections, often where the flow of the river has been dammed by old mills such as that at Cressbrook. The woodlands are mainly of ash, with some alders in the lower river sections, but climbing up from the valley floor the trees thin and are replaced with patches of hawthorn scrub, gorse and broom. The valley sides in the upper reaches climb steeply to areas of lush pasture, drystone walls and isolated farms. These higher pastures have few trees, although some small copses exist around farms.

Species

The winter months usually have little to offer apart from typical birds of the streams and some of the resident woodland species. Grey Wagtails are always present on the fast-running streams while the other special bird of the rapids, the inimitable Dipper, is present in good numbers throughout the year. The woodlands contain the usual collection of tits and finches, with Marsh Tit being relatively easy to find, particularly at Monsal Dale. Small parties of Siskins may frequent alder trees, although their numbers vary from year to year. The larger woods hold a few pairs of Nuthatch and both Great and Lesser Spotted Woodpeckers, while Green Woodpeckers are more likely to be encountered in the grassland areas where the trees thin out above the valley floor. Wintering Fieldfares and Redwings join the

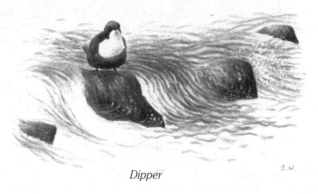

Dipper

resident thrushes in feasting on the berry crop, later feeding out on the pastures in mild weather.

Breeding Northern Lapwings and Curlews arrive from February onwards and indulge in their spectacular display flights before settling to breed on the upland fields. Later in the spring, a wealth of migrants arrives in the area, with Blackcaps, Garden Warblers, Common Chiffchaffs and Willow Warblers frequenting the woodlands, as well as a few pairs of Wood Warblers. Spotted Flycatchers are later arrivals, often being found along the stream sides, and are particularly obvious during the late summer when family groups are in evidence. A few Pied Flycatchers have spread into the area recently, but with the trees in full leaf they can be very elusive. Common Redstarts are a regular sight – 14 males were counted at Lathkill Dale in April 2004. Tree Pipits occupy the interface between wood and pasture, with Meadow Pipits and Skylarks taking over on the higher pastures and rough grassland. Other summer visitors to the open uplands are Northern Wheatears, which arrive from mid-March, and a few pairs of Whinchats, although the latter has declined significantly in recent years. Areas of scrub often harbour Common Whitethroats and Yellowhammers. In addition, good numbers of Common Buzzards breed in the area and, like Peregrine Falcons and Ravens, are regular at all times of the year.

The slower stretches of river have Tufted Duck and Kingfisher as breeding birds, while Little Grebes reach locally important numbers. Mandarin Ducks and Goosanders occur in very small numbers, and both have bred on occasions. The area is not known for attracting rarities, so a drake Blue-winged Teal at Monsal Dale from March–April 1997 was a surprise visitor.

Timing

From an ornithological point of view winter is rather quiet, and the best period to visit is undoubtedly from early April through to June or July when the summer migrants are in residence. However, the area is extremely popular with tourists, rock-climbers, walkers and fishermen and therefore disturbance along the main footpaths is a real problem. On sunny summer days, especially at weekends and bank holidays, the area becomes rapidly overcrowded, making it difficult to find even the resident species. It is therefore best to visit in midweek and also early in the morning before the crowds build up.

Access

Millers Dale, Monsal Dale, Cressbrook Dale and Chee Dale are all just north of the A6 Buxton to Bakewell road. To reach Millers Dale, leave the A6 3 miles (4.8 km) east of Buxton on to the B6049; the road crosses the River

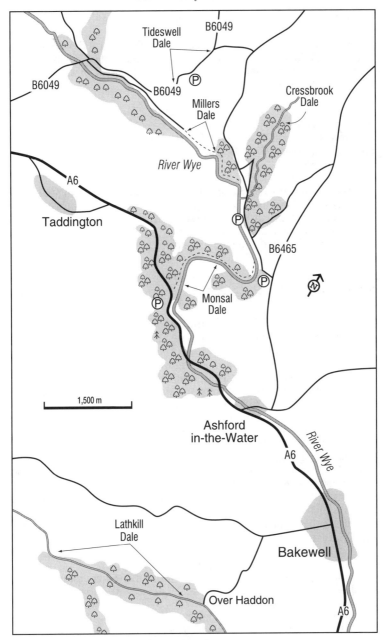

Wye after 1.2 miles (2 km) where there is a car park (SK137733). Another car park, with toilets, is a further 1.3 miles (2.2 km) along this road at Tideswell Dale (SK155743).

For Monsal Dale, Cressbrook Dale and Cressbrook Mill, take the B6465 north-west out of Ashford in the Water for 1.3 miles (2.2 km) to a car park at Monsal Head (SK185715). From here, an unclassified road follows the river north-west to Cressbrook, with a car park 800 m along this minor road at Upperdale (SK177722).

Lathkill Dale is 2 miles (3.2 km) south-west of Bakewell and is approached from the B5055 west of Bakewell and then unclassified roads to Over Haddon. Footpaths are well signposted but all the fields are private and those without public rights of way should not be entered.

Calendar

Resident: Mandarin and Tufted Ducks, Goosander, Little Grebe, Sparrowhawk, Common Buzzard, Kestrel, Peregrine Falcon, Kingfisher, all three woodpeckers, Grey Wagtail, Dipper, Marsh Tit, Nuthatch, Raven, Yellowhammer.

October–March: European Stonechat (scarce), Fieldfare, Redwing, Siskin.
April–September: Northern Lapwing, Curlew, Skylark, Tree and Meadow Pipits, Common Redstart, Whinchat (scarce), Northern Wheatear, Blackcap, Garden Warbler, Common Whitethroat, Wood Warbler, Common Chiffchaff, Willow Warbler, Spotted and Pied Flycatchers.

6D. THE EAST MOORS

OS Landranger 119
OS Explorer 24

Habitat

This is the most south-easterly block of moorland in the Pennines and comprises East Moor, Brampton East Moor, Gibbet Moor, Harewood Moor and Beeley Moor. For simplification, most birdwatchers refer to the area north of Harland Edge as East Moor and the section to the south as Beeley Moor. The moors lie at around 1,000 feet (300 m) above sea level, reaching a maximum of 1,203 feet (360 m) at the eastern end of Harland Edge.

Most of the land is gently undulating and is dominated by heather, which is burned on a rotational basis for grouse management purposes. There are also extensive grassy stretches consisting mainly of purple moor-grass, and some small boggy areas where plants such as round-leaved sundew can be found. Trees are rather scarce, comprising a few scattered small birches and hawthorns. On the fringes of the area, tracts of bilberry support small colonies of the localised Green Hairstreak butterfly. The rocky crags or 'edges', which are such a feature of the Peak District landscape, are represented by the south-facing Harland Edge and the smaller, west-facing Fallinge Edge.

Species

Only a few species are regularly present during the winter months and it is possible to spend some time in the area and see little more than Carrion Crows and Red Grouse. The latter have declined in recent years to the extent that organised shoots take place only occasionally nowadays.

Most birdwatchers visit the moors to look for raptors, particularly Hen Harriers and Merlins. Hen Harriers might be seen at any time between September and April; in some winters there has been a small communal roost on East Moor, but in most recent years birds have not stayed throughout the winter. Sightings of wing-tagged birds indicate that at least some originated in northern Scotland. Hen Harriers are most often seen by scanning the horizons, as they quarter low over the heather in search of small birds and rodents. Sometimes Merlins can be seen flying very close to them,

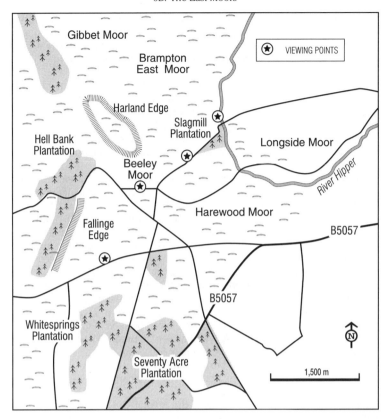

perhaps waiting to attack any small birds put to flight by the hunting harrier. Another good way to find Merlins is to scan large boulders out on the moor, where they spend a lot of time sitting and preening. It is believed that some of the Merlins wintering in the area are of the slightly larger and darker Icelandic subspecies.

Common Buzzard, Peregrine Falcon and Raven are three species which have increased dramatically in the Peak District recently, and all three may now be seen regularly in the area throughout much of the year. During the breeding season, noisy mobbing Curlews and Northern Lapwings might draw attention to the presence of marauding Ravens, while Peregrines can sometimes be seen sitting on the same rocks used by Merlins. Common Buzzards often visit the moors but are more easily found by scanning the skies over woodland in the area, especially around Chatsworth Park to the west. This will often produce sightings of Goshawks too, especially during the chief display period in late winter and spring. Other raptors recorded here have included Marsh Harrier, of which one or two are seen in most years, Red Kite, which is becoming more regular, Honey Buzzard, Montagu's Harrier, Osprey, Rough-legged Buzzard and Red-footed Falcon, while an immature White-tailed Eagle delighted scores of birders in January 2005. Short-eared Owls have nested in the past but are usually encountered as occasional migrants, while Long-eared Owls sometimes breed in small woods and areas of scrub on the fringe of the area – adults are occasionally seen hunting in the evenings when they have young to feed.

In winter passerines are usually few and far between, but small numbers of European Stonechats are present. Since the mid-1990s a few pairs have bred in the area, while up to 17 may be present in late autumn. Great Grey Shrikes and Snow Buntings have wintered in the past but have both become considerable rarities of late.

At any time between September and March transient skeins of Pink-footed Geese may be seen flying over, invariably heading either east-south-east or west-north-west as they commute on an unerringly direct route between their feeding areas in south-west Lancashire and the southern Wash. Mid- to late morning is usually the best time of day to connect with them but they can occur at other times of day and, on rare occasions, have rested and fed on the moors and adjacent fields.

Early spring sees the return of Curlews and Skylarks to the moors, followed in March and April by Meadow Pipits, which may occur in large flocks, Northern Wheatears and Ring Ouzels. The latter species is now very scarce here, with maybe one or two pairs in some years and none at all in others. A few pairs of Whinchats breed, mainly in the large bracken beds along the rocky edges. A more surprising visitor was a Bluethroat, which sang for a day in June 2001. Twite formerly bred, but the population in the eastern Peak District is all but extinct as a result of the loss of the adjacent hay fields, where the birds found the weed seeds on which they depend; it is now only a rare migrant in the area. Curlew numbers are prone to wide annual variations, but these waders are very obvious in spring as they perform their aerial display flight; in midsummer flocks of 30 or so birds can be seen in the newly mown fields adjacent to the moors. A few pairs of Common Snipe frequent the boggy stretches, and very small numbers of European Golden Plovers breed in some years, usually in newly burnt heather. Trips of migrant Dotterels have been seen on several occasions, mainly in late April and May, frequenting the bare areas created by heather burning.

Another attraction of the moors is the regular presence in mid to late summer of Hobbies, especially around Beeley Moor, where up to four birds have been seen together. Though seen annually, these falcons are most obvious in odd-numbered years, which is when Northern Eggar moths (which have a two-year life cycle) fly in large numbers. In even-numbered years, Cuckoos can be seen devouring the larvae of the same moth.

Timing

A visit at any time of year can be rewarding but the winter months are generally the most productive for seeking raptors. Bright and reasonably calm late autumn and winter days are best for seeing movements of Pink-footed Geese. Breeding waders are most conspicuous here during their spring display period, particularly early and late in the day, while late April and May offer the best chance of finding Dotterel. Hobbies may be seen any time during the summer but July seems to be the most likely month.

Access

The East Moors are south-west of Chesterfield and south of the A619 Chesterfield to Baslow road. Very few footpaths cross the moors, which now have open access as a result of the Countryside and Rights of Way Act. However, most local birdwatchers continue to view from the minor roads which cross the area and offer good vantage points. The best spots are west and north of Slagmill Plantation (SK303681 and SK310688), the north side of Beeley Triangle (SK293677) and between the small gas plant and Wragg's Quarry on Beeley Moor (SK285663).

Hen Harrier

Calendar

Resident: Red Grouse, Goshawk, Sparrowhawk, Common Buzzard, Kestrel, Peregrine Falcon, European Stonechat, Raven.

September–March: Marsh Harrier (scarce), Hobby, Dotterel (scarce, April and May), European Golden Plover, Common Snipe, Curlew, Long-eared Owl (scarce), Cuckoo, Skylark, Meadow Pipit, Whinchat, Northern Wheatear, Ring Ouzel.

April–August: Pink-footed Goose, Hen Harrier, Merlin, Short-eared Owl.

7. PLEASLEY PIT COUNTRY PARK

OS Landranger 120
OS Explorers 269 and 270

Habitat

Pleasley Pit Country Park is, as the name suggests, a disused colliery spoil heap and, under Derbyshire County Council's regeneration team and a number of other bodies, the area has been turned into an excellent site for wildlife. The park, which covers some 150 acres (61 ha), is owned by Derbyshire County Council, although 13 acres (5 ha) around the old pit buildings are owned by the East Midlands Development Agency; the pit buildings themselves are now a scheduled Ancient Monument. Pleasley Pit Nature Study Group, which now boasts over 100 members, was formed in January 2000 to monitor and record all aspects of wildlife and carry out management work at the site.

The main feature of the site is a 7.5 acre (3 ha) pool with many shallow areas, spits and islands designed primarily for waders and wildfowl. This pool (the Main Pond) is overlooked by a members-only hide. Water from the Main Pond runs out through a series of run-off pools, adjacent to which is a sizeable reedbed. Three smaller pools, one of which is reed-fringed, have been constructed with dragonflies in mind, and several other water bodies can be found on the site. A large area on the southern slope, close to the Dragonfly Pools, has been set with a wildflower mix, and attracts many butterflies and other insects. A number of pockets of deciduous trees have

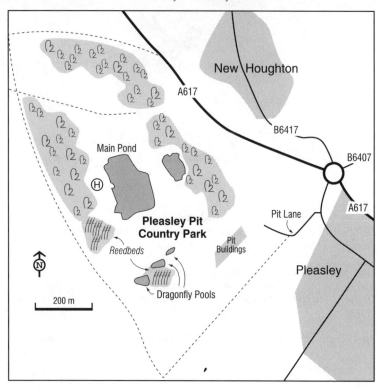

been planted, which are slowly starting to develop, while other areas have been left with pit waste showing, again forming a different type of habitat.

Habitat creation and regeneration work was completed in 2001, so the site is still very much in its infancy; however, as much of the habitat has been created specifically for birds, it will certainly mature and improve in the coming years.

Species

Although there are good resident numbers of some declining species such as Skylark, Meadow Pipit and Reed Bunting, the site is at its best in spring and autumn, when the wetlands attract passage waders. Species such as Dunlin, Ringed Plover, Redshank, Ruff and Common Snipe are the most frequent, while scarcer visitors have included Curlew Sandpiper, Spotted Redshank, both godwits and Wood Sandpiper. The odd migrant tern or gull may appear in suitable conditions. As the pit top offers a commanding view over the surrounding area, it is worth scanning the sky for raptors during passage periods; as well as regular Kestrels and Sparrowhawks, Common Buzzards are not infrequent, and Red Kite, Marsh and Hen Harriers, Goshawk and Osprey have all been recorded.

Summer visitors to the site include Sedge and Reed Warblers, while Grasshopper Warblers appeared for the first time in 2005. The surrounding fields are worth a listen for Quail in the spring, while small parties of Hobbies have been noted later in summer.

Winter can be rather bleak on the pit top. Some good-sized finch flocks may roam the area, and these are worth searching through as both Snow and

Lapland Buntings have been recorded in recent winters. The day may be brightened by the sight of a Merlin or Peregrine Falcon chasing a flock of finches, while the occasional Short-eared or Barn Owl may put in an appearance. Small numbers of wildfowl may be present on the pools and there is always the chance of an oddity such as a Scaup. Large skeins of Pink-footed Geese are regularly noted flying north-west in January, on their way from north Norfolk to Lancashire. Jack Snipe are frequent, if a little difficult to find.

Despite this site only being in existence for a few years, regular watching has produced a number of good local rarities, including Little Egret, Arctic Skua, Wryneck, Woodlark and Shore Lark.

Timing

During passage periods an early morning or evening visit is recommended, as many of the migrant waders drop in at these times. Morning is also a good time to witness passerine movements, particularly during the autumn, when calm days are the best. If searching for raptors, mid-morning on a sunny day is often productive. Pink-footed Geese move over the site in large numbers in January, and crisp sunny days are the favoured conditions to see this spectacle.

Access

Pleasley Pit Country Park is close to the Derbyshire/Nottinghamshire border, 3.5 miles (5.6 km) north-west of Mansfield. From the large roundabout on the A617 at Pleasley, 3 miles (4.8 km) north-west of Mansfield, take the minor road southwards signed to Pleasley and Teversal and then turn right into Pit Lane after about 50 m (SK501644). Park here and head towards the pit buildings; look for a short row of metal posts and walk up the bank parallel with the buildings to access the site. Please keep to the paths and do not enter the fenced conservation area around the main pond. Further parking can be found at the Miner's Welfare at the next turning to Pit Lane.

Calendar

Resident: Kestrel, Little Owl, Skylark, Meadow Pipit, Reed Bunting.

October–March: Pink-footed Goose, Merlin (scarce), Peregrine Falcon, European Golden Plover, Jack Snipe, Short-eared Owl, Fieldfare, Redwing, Siskin.

April–September: Quail (scarce), Hobby, passage waders, Grasshopper, Sedge and Reed Warblers.

8. POOLS BROOK COUNTRY PARK

OS Landranger 120
OS Explorer 269

Habitat

Lying just south-east of Staveley in north-east Derbyshire, Pools Brook Country Park was born out of the reclamation of the Ireland Colliery spoil heaps. The area formerly consisted of a heavily polluted pool, rough grassland and colliery tips, but despite this could be productive; it held a sizeable Swallow roost in autumn and the few who visited regularly found some notable species during the 1970s and 1980s, including Garganey, Hen Harrier, Short-eared Owl and various migrant waders. However, with the closure of the local colliery, regeneration for the community was the order of the day and the county planners designed the current, rather sanitised country park, a haven for dog-walkers, families and fishermen with regular encroachment by youths on motorcycles.

From the derelict pit (coalmine) area a cleaned-up lake was created, complete with encircling footpath, fishing pegs and a pier for the launching of powerboats and canoes, with an adjecent small fishing pool. A maze of footpaths cross the area leading visitors through scrubland and emerging woodland made up of alders, willow and hawthorn. There is a visitor centre on the south-west side of the lake which affords protection from the wind, and occasionally the café is open for light snacks.

Species

On the face of it, this site would appear to have little to offer the visiting birder. However, Pools Brook Country Park lies just 400 m from a working landfill site (accessed by going to the end of North Crescent in the village of Duckmanton and walking around the perimeter fence, or by walking from Pools Brook Country Park) and less than a mile from a second such site at Barrowhill. Consequently, there is a continual movement of gulls over the park as they move between the two sites and they often loaf and bathe on the lake. By late November numbers start to build up and they remain high throughout the winter until reducing in late February.

Among the large gulls Herring dominate, often reaching four figures, and good numbers of Great and Lesser Black-backed Gulls are often present along with a handful of Common Gulls. Black-headed Gulls are frequently present in four figures during this period. Regular birders have grown accustomed to seeing rarer species such as Iceland and Glaucous Gulls frequently and the site saw the third Derbyshire record of Caspian Gull during the late winter of 1999. Nowadays Caspian Gulls are more regular than either Iceland or Glaucous Gull and as many as ten are identified each winter. Mediterranean Gulls occur occasionally but can appear at any time of the year while Kittiwakes, in keeping with most inland sites, are sometimes seen in March and April. The rarest gull recorded so far is a Bonaparte's Gull in December 2000, which was also seen at Ogston Reservoir.

What makes Pools Brook worthy of a visit is that the gulls can be seen in good light and often at extremely close quarters. There is no need to squint into the deepening gloom as can happen at roost sites, including Ogston, and most of the gulls seen at the Ogston Reservoir roost will also visit Pools Brook.

Apart from small numbers of Tufted Ducks and Pochards during the winter, along with the occasional Goosander, very few wildfowl are to be found at the site, although Garganey, Scaup and Red-breasted Merganser have been recorded and given the right conditions Pink-footed Geese can be seen overhead, flying south-east. Whooper Swans have turned up in the past but have never stayed very long.

Spring sees the arrival of Little Ringed Plovers and Redshanks, which breed locally and often fly over the area. Whinchats, Northern Wheatears and Yellow Wagtails like the manicured lawns and sometimes a pair of European Stonechats can be found on fences surrounding the rougher grassland in autumn and winter. Rock Pipits are annual in autumn. Common Terns are regular during the summer, although they have so far failed to breed due to disturbance. By late summer numbers of Lesser

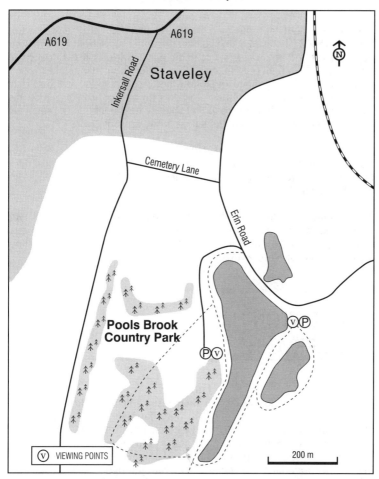

Black-backed Gulls start to increase, bringing with them occasional Yellow-legged Gulls; this species is usually recorded from August through to early January.

Any area of water will eventually attract something of note and, in addition to the species mentioned so far, Red Kite, Marsh Harrier, Osprey, Black Tern and Golden Oriole have all been logged, along with Derbyshire's second Red-throated Pipit (in April 1996).

Timing

While gulls can be present at any time of the day during the winter, the best period for observing them seems to be from mid-morning until about 3.30 pm. There are two viewing points: one below the visitor centre, which affords protection from the wind, and the other from the car park opposite. Various factors have to be considered, such as sunlight and wind direction but as the lake is small you can quickly relocate. At other seasons timing is not too important; it only takes 20 minutes to walk round the lake and no matter what time you arrive it is guaranteed that at least one local dog will have already been walked round the site!

Access

From Chesterfield take the A61 north and then the A619 east towards Staveley. After 3.5 miles (5.6 km) go over the mini roundabout by Morrisons Supermarket and at the next set of traffic lights (with a GK car dealership on the right) turn right onto Inkersall Road. After about 400 m take the second left onto Cemetery Lane and follow this for 150 m to the end. Turn right onto Erin Road and the entrance to Pools Brook Country Park is on the right. Travel further along the road and take the next right into the small car park at SK438736, from where the lake is easily viewable.

Calendar

October–February: Pink-footed Goose, Pochard, Tufted Duck, Goosander, Mediterranean, Yellow-legged, Caspian, Iceland and Glaucous Gulls, Rock Pipit, European Stonechat.

March–September: Ruddy Duck, Great Crested Grebe, Little Ringed Plover, Redshank, occasional passage waders, Yellow-legged Gull (August onwards), Kittiwake (scarce, March and April), Common Tern, Yellow Wagtail, Whinchat, Northern Wheatear.

9. STAUNTON HAROLD RESERVOIR

OS Landranger 128
OS Explorer 245

Habitat

This comparatively new reservoir, which lies in a natural valley surrounded by mainly deciduous woodland and open farmland, was constructed in 1964 to provide drinking water for Leicestershire. Covering 209 acres (85 ha), it is owned by Severn Trent Water and is used for sailing and coarse fishing – only the southern third of the reservoir remains largely undisturbed. The county boundary with Leicestershire runs through the southern part of the reservoir, with the eastern half of this section being in the latter county. Adjacent to the south-eastern corner is the Derbyshire Wildlife Trust reserve of Spring Wood (which is actually in Leicestershire) while at the south end of the reservoir is Dimminsdale, a 16 acre (6.5 ha) area of damp woodland and pools managed as a nature reserve by the Leicestershire and Rutland Wildlife Trust. To the south-west is Calke Park, an area of mature oaks set among open parkland owned by the National Trust.

The geography of the reservoir means that the water is fairly shallow throughout and its gently sloping sandy banks are attractive to wading birds and wildfowl. The water surface is dotted with buoys used for sailing, which in turn form perches for a variety of birds.

Species

The winter wildfowl scene is headed by Eurasian Wigeon, Common Teal, Pochard, Tufted Duck and Goldeneye. The dabbling ducks tend to concentrate at the southern end of the reservoir, where the Eurasian Wigeons graze on a number of grassy fields; numbers of this species usually exceed 200 and peaked at 400 in December 2000. Small groups of Goosanders are often present, while Pintail, Shoveler and Ruddy Duck are scarcer. Occasional

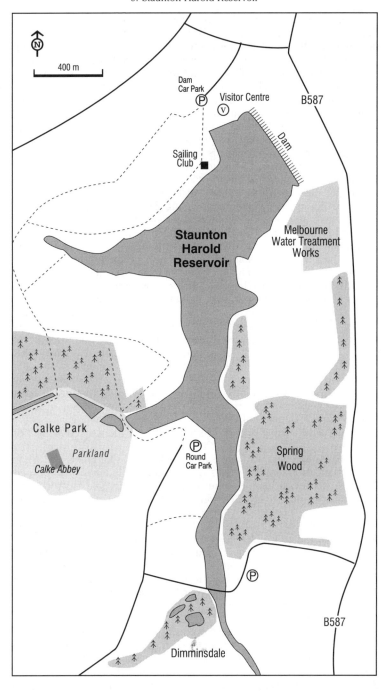

Scaup or Smew are found, and there have also been records of Common Eider and Long-tailed Duck. At this time of year the reservoir is locally important for the concentrations of Great Crested Grebes, with a recent peak of 115 in January 2000. Red-necked Grebes have occurred in a number of winters, and although Slavonian Grebe and all three divers have also appeared, they are much rarer. The buoys scattered over the water surface provide drying-out perches for Cormorants, which also use the trees at the southern end to roost; upwards of 50 birds may be present.

A relatively small gull roost is present during the early winter, although often the site is used merely as a pre-roost gathering before the birds leave for nearby Foremark Reservoir. Several Mediterranean Gulls have been located in recent years, and there have been sightings of Glaucous and Iceland Gulls, but note that this roost is relatively underwatched.

Feeding stations in the Round and Dam Car Parks attract many Tree Sparrows during the winter months, and flocks of Siskins and Lesser Redpolls can be found in the alders at the southern end of the reservoir. The road bridge here is a good place to watch for Water Rails, which occur infrequently in cold weather, while the occasional Green Sandpiper may winter. The surrounding arable fields are also of interest, with Northern Lapwings, Grey Partridges and finch flocks. Little Owls can be heard calling towards dusk and the area has also attracted a wintering Great Grey Shrike.

Spring is one of the best times to visit the reservoir as it offers the potential for locating scarce passage migrants. Summer-plumaged Black-necked Grebes are not infrequent in April, while small flocks of Common Scoters may appear en route to their breeding areas further north. Flocks of Common, Arctic and Black Terns, with occasional Little Gulls, may pass through during late April and May in the right weather conditions, and Little and Sandwich Terns have also been seen at such times. The shallow sandy banks make attractive feeding areas for waders, although in spring the water levels are often rather high. However, there may be a few Ringed and Little Ringed Plovers, Dunlin and Common Sandpipers, and there is always the chance of a something scarcer like a Grey Plover, Black-tailed Godwit or Whimbrel.

The banks and dam wall make good feeding areas for Yellow and White Wagtails and Northern Wheatears during April, while areas of scrub and trees are worth checking for other migrants; Dimminsdale has produced both Firecrest and Pied Flycatcher in spring. Sightings of passage raptors are often a case of pot-luck but Ospreys are probably more frequent than records suggest, while Hobbies may be seen in the evenings, hunting the flocks of hirundines which feed over the reservoir.

During summer the amount of disturbance reaches a peak. The few breeding waterbirds include Greylag Goose and Great Crested Grebe, while a few pairs of Common Terns have recently nested on rafts. Singing Sedge Warblers and Common Whitethroats can be found around the reservoir, perhaps with the occasional Grasshopper Warbler, and Spring Wood has breeding Great Spotted Woodpeckers and Nuthatches.

Autumn migration sees larger numbers of waders than in the spring, particularly if water levels are low. Species such as Ringed Plover, Dunlin, Ruff, Greenshank and Green and Common Sandpipers often stay for longer periods and are occasionally joined by a few Curlew Sandpipers and Little Stints. Tern passage is mainly of Common and Black Terns, with the latter having peaked at 220 birds during favourable conditions. Little Gulls also appear, and Sandwich Terns are slightly more regular in the autumn than in the spring. Black-necked Grebes are again possible at this season. Passerine

Little Ringed Plover

migrants around the hedgerows may include a few Whinchats and the occasional Common Redstart.

Although the reservoir has not been intensively watched over its 40-year history it has still produced a number of scarce birds, including good inland records like Gannet, Purple Sandpiper, Pomarine Skua, Roseate Tern, Razorbill and Little Auk. In addition, two White-winged Black Terns have appeared during the autumn.

Timing
As with most inland reservoirs, winter (November to March) is best for wildfowl, and April-May and August-October are the times for passage migrants. Passing gulls and terns tend to appear following easterly winds and the same conditions are best for passage waders, although water levels will dictate whether they stop off. As access to the main part of the reservoir is only permitted along the western side, the early morning sun can create a problem for viewing. Unfortunately, there is a greater degree of disturbance from water sports during the afternoon and evening periods, so birds are most settled in the early mornings. The gull roost is best viewed from the west bank just south of the sailing club, where the birds can sometimes be reasonably close.

Access
Staunton Harold Reservoir is situated 5 miles (8 km) south of Derby, just to the south of Melbourne and to the east of Foremark Reservoir. The dam car park (£1.50 pay and display) contains a visitor centre, exhibition room and toilets; it is reached from the B587 half a mile (0.8 km) south of Melbourne, and is well signposted (SK376244). The entrance gates are locked at dusk; exact closing times can be found on signs in the car park.

The south arm can be reached by leaving Melbourne south on the B587 and turning right on to a minor road after 2 miles (3.2 km). A car park is on the left after 500 m (SK379220), from where it is possible to walk along the road for 150 m to view the reservoir from the bridge. The entrance to the Dimminsdale reserve is 50 m beyond the road bridge at SK376219. Spring Wood is opposite the car park; entry is by permit only. A further 500 m west of the road bridge a lane heads off northwards and leads to the Round Car Park which overlooks the central part of the reservoir (SK377228).

Calendar

Resident: Greylag and Canada Geese, Grey Partridge, Little and Great Crested Grebes, Sparrowhawk, Common Buzzard, Kestrel, Little Owl, Kingfisher, Green and Great Spotted Woodpeckers, Willow Tit, Nuthatch, Linnet, Reed Bunting.

October–March: Eurasian Wigeon, Common Teal, Pintail (scarce), Shoveler, Pochard, Tufted Duck, Scaup (rare), Goldeneye, Smew (scarce), Goosander, Ruddy Duck, divers (rare), Red-necked Grebe (scarce), Cormorant, Grey Heron, Peregrine Falcon, Water Rail, Northern Lapwing, Common Snipe, Green Sandpiper, Mediterranean Gull (rare), Grey Wagtail, Fieldfare, Redwing, Tree Sparrow, Siskin, Lesser Redpoll.

April–September: Common Scoter (scarce), Black-necked Grebe (scarce), Osprey (scarce), Hobby, Little Ringed Plover, Ringed Plover, Little Stint (scarce August to October), Curlew Sandpiper (scarce (August to October), Dunlin, Ruff, Greenshank, Green Sandpiper, Common Sandpiper, Little Gull, Sandwich Tern (scarce), Common, Arctic and Black Terns, Cuckoo, Yellow Wagtail, White Wagtail (April), Common Redstart (scarce passage), Whinchat (passage), Northern Wheatear (passage), Grasshopper Warbler (scarce), Sedge Warbler, Common Whitethroat, Common Chiffchaff, Willow Warbler.

10. TRENT VALLEY GRAVEL PIT

OS Landrangers 128 and 129
OS Explorers 245 and 260

The River Trent flows roughly south-west to north-east through Derbyshire, forming the county boundary in various places with Staffordshire, Leicestershire and Nottinghamshire. There are many old and current gravel extraction complexes along the Trent's route. Unfortunately, two of the best from an ornithological point of view (Drakelow Wildfowl Reserve and Aston on Trent Gravel Pits) are currently private with no access to the general public. For this reason, these sites are not detailed in this guide.

10A. LONG EATON GRAVEL PITS AND TRENT MEADOWS

OS Landranger 129
OS Explorer 260

Habitat

This area of old flooded gravel pits is an extension of Attenborough Nature Reserve, which is located just over the county boundary in Nottinghamshire. The pits are found either side of Meadow Lane, with three interconnected lakes to the north-east, a large flooded pit to the south-west and a smaller area of water at the southern end of the lane. The pits to the north-east of the lane are used by anglers and the easternmost pit is also used for windsurfing. The paths around the pits and along the river bank are popular with dog walkers. There are wide spits separating the north-east pits from each other but, because of an old channel along the northern edge which was used by flat-bottomed boats to transport gravel, there is no pathway through these pits and much of the viewing has to take place from the

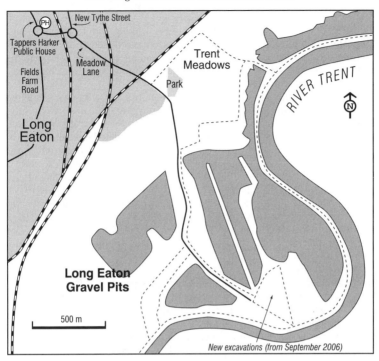

New excavations (from September 2006)

path alongside the river. Between the pits and the River Trent south of the lane is an area of rough grassland that can be good for passerines in winter. However, further excavation commenced in this area in April 2006 and the habitat here is likely to change in the near future.

Trent Meadows, which is a reliable area for Short-eared Owls and European Stonechats in the winter, is very close to this site and can be visited in conjunction with the gravel pits.

Species

The main interest in winter is to be found in the rough pasture at the end of Meadow Lane and in the surrounding hedgerows. In a good year up to ten Corn Buntings and 50 Tree Sparrows may be located among the flocks of finches (consisting mainly of Greenfinches, Linnets and Yellowhammers) which feed on the seed heads in the fields and sit around in the hedgerows. These flocks attract raptors such as Kestrel and Sparrowhawk, with the odd Merlin also being noted. Both Green and Great Spotted Woodpeckers can be found here, while European Stonechat is a regular wintering bird. At dusk look out for Short-eared Owls and the occasional Barn Owl. Nearby Trent Meadows has attracted up to five Short-eared Owls during recent winters; these can be seen quartering rough stubble fields between the River Trent and the main Derby to Nottingham railway line from noon onwards. Other notable birds in the Trent Meadows area at this time of year include Jack Snipe and European Stonechat.

Another attraction in winter is wildfowl, with all the usual species such as Eurasian Wigeon, Gadwall, Common Teal, Mallard, Shoveler, Pochard, Tufted Duck and Goldeneye to be seen. Eurasian Wigeon numbers can build up to nearly 300, with smaller groups of the dabbling ducks and flocks of up to

100 of the two common *Aythya* species. Great Crested Grebes and small numbers of Little Grebes are normally present, along with Cormorants and Grey Herons. A few Greylag Geese stray from Attenborough Nature Reserve, as does the odd pair of Egyptian Geese. Waders are generally scarce at this time of year, but occasionally Jack Snipe, Common Snipe, Redshank and Green Sandpiper are seen.

Waders and terns are the main attractions in spring, with Oystercatcher, Little Ringed Plover, Dunlin and Common Sandpiper to be seen around the shallower edges, especially on the pit to the south-west of Meadow Lane, along with less regular Whimbrel, Curlew and Black-tailed Godwit. Common Terns are normally present from mid-April, although they do not nest here. With south-easterly winds small numbers of Little Gulls and Black Terns can be found and in favourable conditions up to 100 Arctic Terns have been seen hawking over the pits.

Occasional Water Pipits consort with the groups of Meadow Pipits that move through in late March and early April. This is also a good time to look for Northern Wheatears on the short grassy areas. Yellow Wagtails frequent the rough pasture, and Hobbies often appear later in the spring, when they prey on the hirundine flocks.

Because of disturbance in the summer, nesting waterbirds are somewhat restricted, although they do include Greylag Goose, Tufted Duck and Little and Great Crested Grebe. A selection of passerine species breed, among them Sedge and Reed Warblers, which sing from the small areas of reeds along the edges of some of the pits.

It is always worth checking the pits from late July onwards as waders start to move south; similar species are recorded as in spring, although in addition Greenshanks and Green Sandpipers are likely to be found. This is also the time of year when Little Egrets can be seen, especially on the smaller pit near the end of Meadow Lane; up to three birds have been noted in recent years. Again, look among the hirundine flocks for hunting Hobbies, especially from mid-August when the young are on the wing.

Long Eaton Gravel Pits has a good reputation for attracting rare and scarce migrants, most notable of which have been a singing male Bluethroat in April and May 1992 and a Woodchat Shrike in May 2006. Other good birds have included Ring-necked and Long-tailed Ducks, Common Scoter, Black-throated Diver, Black-necked Grebe, Bittern, Osprey, Pectoral and Purple Sandpipers, Great Skua, Sandwich and Little Terns and Great Grey Shrike.

Timing

Winter is the peak time to see the good numbers of wildfowl which can be found here, along with the wintering finches and Short-eared Owls; the latter are best looked for during the late afternoons, but are often seen on the wing from noon onwards. A visit in spring or autumn, particularly during periods of easterly winds, may well turn up a surprise or two.

Access

The area is 1.8 miles (3 km) south-east of Long Eaton and 1 mile (1.6 km) south-west of Attenborough Nature Reserve. From the A6005 Long Eaton to Beeston road, turn south on the eastern outskirts of Long Eaton on to Station Street (SK501339) and continue for 1 mile (1.6 km). Turn left immediately after the petrol station on to New Tythe Street, which after a mini roundabout becomes Meadow Lane. Follow this road over the railway crossing and then turn right onto a single-track metalled road after a further

200 m. Continue to the end of the track, where there is limited parking (SK507318). With the commencement of new excavations in this area in April 2006, parking at the end of the track may become problematic. Alternatively there are conveniently placed gateways along the lane where it is possible to park and view the pits. Please be aware that cars have been broken into here so take valuables with you.

If approaching from the south, leave the A50 near Castle Donington and follow the B6540 north-east towards Long Eaton, passing under the M1 and then crossing the River Trent at Old Sawley. In Sawley, turn right at the small roundabout on to Fields Farm Road (signposted to Acton Road Industrial Estate) and follow the road for 1.5 miles (2.4 km) to another roundabout with the Tappers Harker public house on the opposite side. Turn right here, go across the railway crossing to a mini roundabout, and bear right at this roundabout on to Meadow Lane.

For Trent Meadows, park on Meadow Lane after the railway crossing just before the right turn to the gravel pits (SK502328). Walk north towards the obvious park, crossing a small stile on the left, and follow the path across the park to a raised bank on the left. The path runs alongside the bank before turning left; continue for a further 200 m and the open fields lie in front. Watch for Short-eared Owls from where the path starts to go across the open expanse (SK505328).

Calendar

Resident: Greylag, Canada and Egyptian Geese, Tufted Duck, Little and Great Crested Grebes, Cormorant, Grey Heron, Sparrowhawk, Kestrel, Green and Great Spotted Woodpeckers.

October–March: Eurasian Wigeon, Gadwall, Common Teal, Shoveler, Pochard, Goldeneye, Merlin (scarce), European Golden Plover, Jack Snipe, Common Snipe, Redshank, Green Sandpiper, Barn Owl (scarce), Short-eared Owl, European Stonechat, Fieldfare, Redwing, Tree Sparrow, Siskin, Linnet, Lesser Redpoll, Yellowhammer, Reed and Corn Buntings.

April–September: Shelduck, Black-necked Grebe (rare), Little Egret, Hobby, Oystercatcher, Little Ringed and Ringed Plovers, Dunlin, Black-tailed Godwit, Whimbrel, Curlew, Greenshank, Green and Common Sandpipers, Turnstone (scarce), Little Gull (passage), Sandwich Tern (rare), Common Tern, Arctic Tern (mainly April and May), Black Tern (passage), Cuckoo, Yellow Wagtail, Whinchat, Northern Wheatear, Sedge and Reed Warblers, Lesser and Common Whitethroats.

10B. WILLINGTON GRAVEL PITS

OS Landranger 128
OS Explorer 245

Habitat

Excavated in the late 1970s, this area of approximately 183 acres (74 ha) forms part of an extensive chain of workings along the Trent Valley flood-plain. The site contains a variety of wetland habitats although over the years Willington Gravel Pits, like all similar areas that have not been in-filled, have matured. Gone are the shingle spits, gravel islands and bare earth, and in their place are reedbeds and heavily-vegetated banks. The birdlife during this time of maturation has changed somewhat; although wildfowl still find the habitat suitable, the importance of the site for waders has diminished.

There have, however, been compensations, with reedbed warblers finding the conditions much to their liking and accordingly increasing in numbers. The Derbyshire Wildlife Trust has purchased the land to the north of the lane and is developing it as a nature reserve. This area contains two large pits, along with several smaller reed-fringed pools and areas of rough grassland. To the south of the lane there are another two large expanses of water, both under the control of an angling club.

There is no woodland at the site, but the hedgerows along the lane contain oak, ash and sycamore; there are also thickets of blackthorn, gorse and willow.

Species

Wildfowl are the main attraction during the winter months. Although numbers are often not large when compared to those on some of the neighbouring reservoirs and gravel workings, there is usually a wide range of species to be found. Eurasian Wigeon, Gadwall, Common Teal, Mallard, Shoveler, Pochard, Tufted Duck and Goldeneye are all to be expected, with numbers of the latter often in excess of 30 as they move between the pits and adjacent river. Goosanders also use the river for feeding and may number 20 or more, especially at evening roosts. Pintail are sometimes to be found, particularly in times of winter floods, while Smew are occasionally present. Both Whooper and Bewick's Swans visit infrequently, but their stays are almost invariably short. Canada Geese are ever-present, but other goose species have been recorded and it is always worth scanning the flocks for a few Greylags or a stray Pinkfoot or Brent Goose.

Waders are a little thin on the ground during winter, but large numbers of Common Snipe and a few Redshanks frequent the margins and grassy areas. Jack Snipe are sometimes present but difficult to locate, and Ruff have been found at this time of year. There are usually one or two Green Sandpipers in the area and in recent years a Greenshank has wintered. Large flocks of Northern Lapwings are sometimes joined by European Golden Plovers. Although there is no gull roost at this site all the common species occur, and Mediterranean and Glaucous have been found. Sparrowhawk, Common Buzzard and Kestrel are the most likely raptors to be encountered, but Peregrine Falcons are often present and Merlin very occasionally. In four recent years Long-eared Owls have roosted in hawthorn scrub.

As spring approaches one of the features at this site is the pre-breeding flock of Curlew that can reach three figures in February and March. Other waders begin to arrive and these invariably include Oystercatcher, Little Ringed Plover and Ringed Plover, while Black-tailed Godwits are also often encountered. This is a good time of year to look for Water Pipit although the species has become rare in the last few years. The early part of the period occasionally produces Kittiwake and Garganey. During late April and early May migrating flocks of Common, Arctic and Black Terns appear together with Little Gull and occasionally Sandwich and Little Terns. Although these flocks can pass through quickly, they may linger for a day or two if northerly or north-easterly winds prevail. A typical May might produce records of wader species such as Grey Plover, Sanderling, Dunlin, Ruff, both godwits, Whimbrel, Greenshank, Wood Sandpiper and Turnstone, but all in small numbers.

Raptors, besides the resident species, are often noted during the passage period and include Marsh Harrier and Osprey. The former is attracted to the developing reedbeds and birds occasionally stay to roost, while the latter may commute between the pits and nearby Foremark Reservoir. Hobbies are also found but are more obvious later in the year in August when they

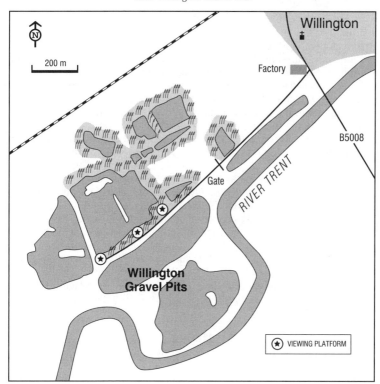

are either feeding large young or when recently fledged juveniles are on the wing. This site is the best in the county to encounter these superb falcons as they hawk dragonflies during the middle of the day or harass evening gatherings of hirundines. Barn Owls are seen irregularly, but Little Owls are resident in the area.

Searching through flocks of Pied and Yellow Wagtails feeding along the muddy margins or in grassy areas will produce some White Wagtails and perhaps a Blue-headed. Northern Wheatears have traditionally appeared, especially when there was less vegetation, and one or two Whinchats may occur. The lane and hedgerows are of interest since all three woodpeckers can be found, although Lesser Spotted has become decidedly rare. Willow Tits are present throughout the year and have not suffered the decline in numbers noted nationally; they can be heard calling from the hedgerows and scrub areas. Warblers are very much in evidence with Blackcap, Garden Warbler and Lesser and Common Whitethroats regular; these are joined in most years by one or two reeling Grasshopper Warblers. Now that the reedbeds have developed large numbers of both Sedge and Reed Warblers are to be found – during 2004 singing birds totalled 45 Sedge Warblers and a county record of 70 Reed Warblers. All this warbler activity attracts the attention of attendant Cuckoos.

Breeding wildfowl include Canada Geese, Mallards and Tufted Ducks, while Gadwall have recently commenced regular breeding and Shelducks sometimes appear with broods. Garganeys have summered at least once and a female Red-breasted Merganser was seen with a brood in 1995. Several pairs of Great Crested Grebes nest and Water Rails do so in some years. Four pairs of Cormorants which bred in 1998 was not only a county first, but also the first time that the species had bred on a pylon in Britain. Oystercatchers, Northern Lapwings and the occasional pair of Redshanks are the only currently breeding waders, although intriguingly a Green Sandpiper displayed and apparently held territory in 1999. Black-headed Gulls have ceased to breed, but Common Terns attempt to do so most years. Kingfishers and Sand Martins nest in banks nearby.

The first returning migrants begin to arrive in July and Greenshank and Green and Common Sandpipers can be expected. Groups of ten or more noisy Oystercatchers often fly in towards dusk. Adult and juvenile Common Terns from other breeding sites gather, sometimes joined by the odd Arctic or Black Tern. There is always the chance of a Little Stint, or Curlew or Wood Sandpiper, and this is probably the best time of year to connect with Little Egret at this site. Loafing gulls are always worth checking in autumn and both Yellow-legged and Caspian Gulls have been discovered. Although difficult to detect, Spotted Crakes have visited in two recent years.

In view of its position in the Trent Valley, it is no surprise that this site has a good list of scarce birds to its name. Spring and early summer has produced Ring-necked Duck, Honey Buzzard, Kentish Plover, Temminck's Stint, Bonaparte's Gull, Caspian Tern, Pallid Swift and Golden Oriole, while excellent birds in the autumn have included Blue-winged Teal, Ferruginous Duck, Spoonbill, Pectoral and Spotted Sandpipers, Red-necked Phalarope, Wryneck and Bearded Tit.

Timing

A visit to Willington Gravel Pits can be worthwhile at any time of the year, but spring and autumn passage periods (April and May and late July to October) are probably the best. As most of the viewing is to be had to the west of Meadow Lane the morning is the best time to watch on sunny days; however, evening visits can be very profitable to watch for Hobbies and birds flying in to roost.

Access

Willington Gravel Pits are situated 6 miles (9.6 km) south-west of Derby. From the A38/A50 junction north of Willington village, take the B5008 south into Willington. Cross the Trent and Mersey Canal and at the two mini roundabouts go straight ahead (signed to Repton) under a railway bridge. The approach road to the gravel pits is on the right by the metal processing factory, 100 m south of the church and 100 m north of the River Trent bridge (SK295280). After 450 m the access track is blocked, at which point there is very limited parking. The land to the south of the lane is owned by Derbyshire County Angling Club, while the area to the north has recently been purchased by the Derbyshire Wildlife Trust; neither side has public access, although both areas can be viewed from the lane. Three viewing platforms have been erected along the lane, overlooking the two large pits north of the track. At present, there is no other access to this site, although this may change as the nature reserve is developed in the future.

Calendar

Resident: Canada Goose, Gadwall, Shoveler, Tufted Duck, Great Crested Grebe, Cormorant, Grey Heron, Sparrowhawk, Common Buzzard, Kestrel, Peregrine Falcon, Northern Lapwing, Redshank, Little Owl, Kingfisher, Green Woodpecker, Great Spotted Woodpecker, Lesser Spotted Woodpecker (scarce), Willow Tit, Bullfinch, Reed Bunting.

October–March: Bewick's Swan (rare), Whooper Swan (rare), Eurasian Wigeon, Common Teal, Pintail (scarce), Pochard, Goldeneye, Smew (scarce), Goosander, Water Rail, European Golden Plover, Jack Snipe (scarce), Common Snipe, Curlew, Green Sandpiper, gulls, Long-eared Owl (rare), Short-eared Owl, Fieldfare, Redwing.

April–September: Shelduck, Garganey (scarce), Little Egret (mainly July to September), Marsh Harrier (passage), Osprey (passage), Hobby, Oystercatcher, Little Ringed and Ringed Plovers, Sanderling (scarce), Little Stint (scarce August and September), Curlew Sandpiper (scarce August and September), Dunlin, Ruff, Black-tailed Godwit, Whimbrel, Greenshank, Green Sandpiper (July onwards), Wood Sandpiper (scarce), Common Sandpiper, Little Gull, Sandwich Tern (rare), Common Tern, Arctic Tern, Little Tern (rare), Black Tern, Cuckoo, Sand Martin, Water Pipit (scarce April), Yellow Wagtail, White Wagtail (April), Whinchat, Northern Wheatear, Grasshopper, Sedge and Reed Warblers, Blackcap, Garden Warbler, Lesser and Common Whitethroats.

11. WYVER LANE NATURE RESERVE

OS Landranger 119
OS Explorer 259

Habitat

Lying next to the River Derwent and within the Derwent Valley World Heritage Site, Wyver Lane Nature Reserve is owned by Amber Valley Borough Council and managed by the Derbyshire Wildlife Trust. It is made up of two pools that vary in size dependent on flooding, surrounded mainly by extensive areas of wet grassland and farmland and set in the wide but steep-sided and well-wooded valley of the Derwent. The largest pool has stands of sedge and reed on its banks and is overlooked by a hide, which has a small feeding station next to it.

Species

Wildfowl are the principal attraction during the winter, with a flock of Eurasian Wigeons using the areas of wet grassland; numbers generally peak at around 200. Common Teal is usually the next most numerous duck, with recent counts in excess of 100, and a few Gadwall, Shovelers and Tufted and Ruddy Ducks are regular; the latter two species often breed in the area. A small wintering flock of Goosanders is usually present in the vicinity, and these birds are best looked for in the late afternoon when they fly in to roost on the pools. There have been occasional visits by scarcer species of wildfowl, including Whooper Swan, Smew and Red-necked and Black-necked Grebes, while a Slavonian Grebe was seen on the River Derwent nearby in Belper one winter.

The pools are used by gulls as a pre-roost gathering site in the late afternoon before leaving for nearby Carsington Water. The majority are Black-headed and Common Gulls, but there have been records of Mediterranean and Ring-billed Gull in recent years.

One or two Water Rails lurk in the sedge around the pools, but as ever are difficult to see well. The same areas harbour groups of Common Snipe, along with the occasional Jack Snipe. The feeding station by the hide attracts a number of Reed Buntings, and flocks of Siskins may be found feeding in nearby alder trees. European Stonechats have wintered on more than one occasion.

Resident breeding birds include Greylag and Canada Goose, Little Grebe, Sparrowhawk, Kestrel, Northern Lapwing, Kingfisher and Jay, and these are joined in the summer by most of the common warblers. All three species of woodpecker occur, although Lesser Spotted is scarce and elusive and is most reliably seen or heard in early spring. Common Buzzard and Raven are now regularly seen throughout the year.

Spring and autumn offer the chance of passage waders, although their appearance is dictated by water levels. The most regular species are Curlew, Redshank (which sometimes breeds in the area) and Green and Common Sandpipers, and there have been recent records of Little Stint, Ruff, Black-tailed Godwit, Spotted Redshank and Greenshank. The wader highlight in the last few years, however, was two Pectoral Sandpipers in September 2003. Hobbies are not infrequent in spring and autumn and, as with any area of water in a river valley, there is always the possibility of a surprise, such as the Great White Egret which appeared in June 2005.

Timing
Passage waders occur during the spring and autumn, which is perhaps the best time to find something out of the ordinary. Wintering wildfowl can be seen between October and March. If viewing from the hide, strong sunlight can be a problem in the mornings.

Access
Wyver Lane Nature Reserve is 1 mile (1.6 km) north of Belper, which in turn is 8 miles (12.8 km) north of Derby. In Belper, turn west by East Mill on to the A517 Ashbourne road, cross the River Derwent and then turn right after 300 m by the Talbot Hotel on to Belper Lane (signed to Belper Lane End). Take an immediate right on to Wyver Lane and the reserve is a further 0.7 miles (1.1 km) along the lane on the right (SK345493). Wyver Lane is very narrow and parking is extremely limited; it is advisable to leave vehicles on Belper Lane and walk. There is no access to the reserve itself, but the area can be easily viewed from the lane or the hide.

Calendar
Resident: Greylag and Canada Geese, Tufted and Ruddy Ducks, Little Grebe, Sparrowhawk, Common Buzzard, Kestrel, Northern Lapwing, Kingfisher, all three woodpeckers, Jay, Raven, Reed Bunting.

October–March: Eurasian Wigeon, Gadwall, Common Teal, Shoveler, Goosander, Water Rail, Jack and Common Snipe, European Stonechat, Fieldfare, Redwing, Siskin.

April–September: Hobby, Curlew, Redshank, Green and Common Sandpipers, passage waders, Cuckoo, Yellow Wagtail, Garden Warbler, Lesser and Common Whitethroat.

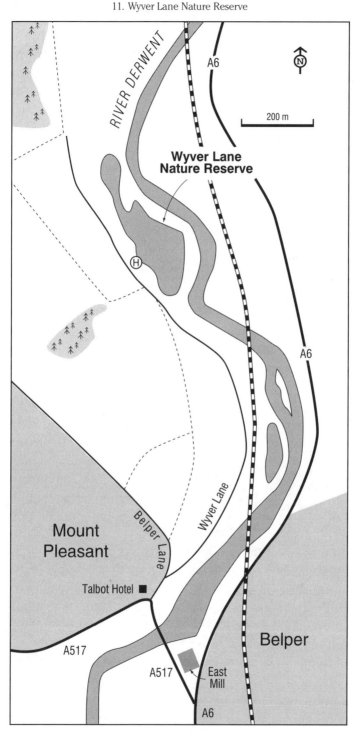

12. Belvoir
13. Charnwood Forest area
13A. Bardon Hill
13B. Beacon Hill Country Park and Deans Lane
13C. Bradgate Park and Cropston Reservoir
13D. Groby Pool
13E. Swithland Reservoir
13F. Swithland Wood
13G. Thornton Reservoir
14. Eyebrook Reservoir
15. Rutland Water
16. Sence Valley Forest Park
17. Soar Valley Gravel Pits
17A. Cossington Meadows
17B. Cossington South Lakes and Wanlip North Lakes
17C. Watermead Country Park North and Wanlip Meadows
17D. Birstall Gravel Pits
17E. Watermead Country Park South, Thurmaston Floodplain
       and Birstall Meadows

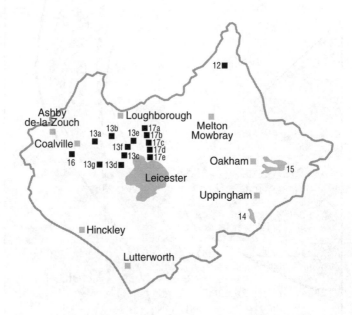

12. BELVOIR

Habitat

The Vale of Belvoir, which is located about 8 miles (12.8 km) north of Melton Mowbray and 5 miles (8 km) south-west of Grantham, is mostly within Leicestershire but lies on the boundaries with Nottinghamshire to the north-west and Lincolnshire to the north-east. The region is dominated by the Belvoir ridge, which rises to a height of 500 feet (150 m), with Belvoir Castle at its eastern end forming a well-known landmark. Along the ridge from Belvoir west to Stathern are extensive stands of mature deciduous woodland with smaller areas of conifers. Barkestone, Plungar and Stathern Woods, which are all part of one large block, are accessible on their southern edge via the Jubilee Way footpath.

To the east and south lie areas of private parkland which contain two small lakes (Belvoir Lakes). Knipton Reservoir, which is also private, can be viewed at its western end from the minor road between Knipton and Branston. To the north runs the disused Grantham Canal which has some large stands of reed and sedge along its banks. Adjacent areas consist of rich arable farmland and grazed grassland. Additionally, there are some lengths of old dismantled railway track, which have become overgrown with hawthorn scrub, birch, bramble and rough grass.

Species

The Vale of Belvoir came to local prominence in the early 1990s, when Leicestershire's first breeding Common Buzzards for over 160 years were found in the area. The region was regularly watched for the next few years and was found to be something of a raptor hot-spot, but with Common Buzzards now being widespread over the county the area has since been rather neglected by birders. The region therefore offers good opportunities for more pioneering visitors to find their own birds.

Winter birdwatching in the Vale of Belvoir concentrates on woodland birds and raptors, although there can be good numbers of Goosanders on Belvoir Lakes and Knipton Reservoir, where they join the resident Greylag Geese, Tufted Ducks and Great Crested Grebes. It is always worth checking the lakes and reservoir, as in the past they have produced Whooper Swan, American Wigeon, Common Scoter, Slavonian Grebe, Gannet and Shag.

Raptor-watching is at its best in winter and early spring, when the resident birds are starting to display. The area holds several pairs of Sparrowhawks and Kestrels, although Common Buzzard is now probably the most numerous raptor in the region and it is not unusual to see as many as 20 birds on a winter visit. The best way of locating raptors is to find a good vantage point and watch for birds soaring over the ridge or hunting over the open fields. Of the rarer species, Merlin and Peregrine Falcon are regular during the winter and there have been several sightings of Hen Harriers; the latter is probably more frequent in the area than records suggest. Red Kites are now more or less resident, and other winter raptors have included several Goshawks and three records of Rough-legged Buzzard, including one which wintered in 1994-95 and attracted large numbers of observers to the area. Barn Owls are present at a number of sites – one of the best areas to see them is over the open fields south of Barkestone-le-Vale. Short-eared Owls are often encountered in the winter, while Long-eared Owls probably still persist in the area and are worth searching for in stands of coniferous

Common Buzzard and Magpies

woodland. On fine sunny days in January, skeins of Pink-footed Geese can sometimes be seen flying north-west, and it is likely that the Vale of Belvoir is on a regular route for these birds as they move between wintering sites in East Anglia and Lancashire.

The woodlands have a typical mix of species. Marsh Tits are common in the area, with good spots to see them being Windsor Hill and Barkestone Wood. Nuthatches are also numerous and all three species of woodpecker are resident. Large groups of Chaffinches frequent suitable fields, particularly areas of set-aside, and in most years these flocks attract Bramblings which can often be found in quite good numbers. Mixed finch and bunting flocks should also be checked for Corn Buntings, which occasionally winter in the area. Siskins are regular, and in irruption years Common Crossbills are usually present, often in sizeable flocks. Locating them can sometimes be difficult, but the best sites are usually Barkestone and Stathern Woods or the stand of larches at Windsor Hill. Woodcocks are often flushed from the woodland floor during the winter months, and by spring several birds may be seen roding over Stathern Wood at dawn or dusk.

In the early spring, some of the nests of the 25–30 pairs of Grey Heron which breed on the Belvoir Estate can be seen in the woodland by looking west from the minor road north of Harston. Curlews breed in the region and usually return to the fields by March, when their distinctive bubbling calls can be heard. From May onwards Hobbies are present and undoubtedly breed in the vicinity; they are, however, more obvious during the late summer, when family parties are attracted to hirundine flocks. It is well worth scanning the broad horizons for other raptors during the spring, as the area has attracted several Marsh Harriers and Ospreys in recent years, as well as a Honey Buzzard in 1998. More regular coverage of the region would undoubtedly produce further similar records. The vale is the most regular site in Leicestershire for Quail, and small numbers are usually present even in years when there are few others elsewhere; the south-facing barley and wheat fields north of Branston village are the favoured area.

The Grantham Canal provides a different range of habitats and, as such, attracts several species not found elsewhere in the area. The reedbeds play host to large numbers of Sedge and Reed Warblers and Reed Buntings, while a few Grasshopper Warblers can usually be heard singing in patches of rough grassland and brambles. The canal banks and adjacent arable land is the summer haunt of several pairs of Yellow Wagtails. Turtle Doves still maintain a presence and can be found during the summer, particularly in

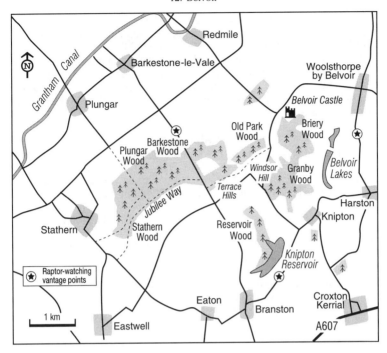

the Barkestone-le-Vale and Plungar areas. Unfortunately, the same cannot be said of Corn Buntings, which were formerly regular around the barley fields north of Branston but now appear to have gone.

Autumn is the least promising time to visit the area, although this may be due to lack of observations by birdwatchers. A few Green Sandpipers visit Knipton Reservoir and there may be diurnal movements of Northern Lapwings, Skylarks, thrushes and finches.

Timing

Winter is probably the best time to visit the area, and raptors are more active on fine days. As a rule, the region is relatively undisturbed, although the Belvoir Estate is heavily keepered and days when shooting is taking place are best avoided.

Access

From the A607 between Melton Mowbray and Grantham take minor roads northwards signposted to Belvoir, Knipton and Branston. The most popular vantage point for watching raptors is by the minor road overlooking Knipton Reservoir half a mile (0.8 km) north-east of Branston at SK818300 although there are several other good spots, including the minor road 1 mile (1.6 km) south-west of Barkestone-le-Vale at SK792333, which gives views over Barkestone and Plungar Woods and the valley to the north-west, and the minor road between Woolsthorpe and Harston at SK837327. Woodland birds may be seen along the Jubilee Way, which passes along the southern edge of Stathern, Plungar and Barkestone Woods and is accessed either just east of Stathern village at SK777309 or from the minor road between Branston and Barkestone-le-Vale at SK797322. Windsor Hill, which is another good spot for woodland birds and offers a good raptor vantage point, is

1 mile (1.6 km) south of Belvoir Castle at SK813322. The Grantham Canal can be accessed from a number of points near Redmile, Barkestone-le-Vale and Plungar; the canal footpath is open to the public all year round.

Belvoir Estate is owned by the Duke of Rutland and much of the area is private. Birdwatchers should keep to public roads and footpaths at all times. Many of the roads in the area have verges wide enough to park a car on; visitors should use discretion, not block gateways and show respect for other road users.

Calendar

Resident: Greylag Goose, Tufted Duck, Red-legged and Grey Partridges, Great Crested Grebe, Grey Heron, Red Kite, Sparrowhawk, Common Buzzard, Kestrel, Woodcock, Barn and Tawny Owls, all three woodpeckers, Skylark, Goldcrest, Marsh Tit, Nuthatch, Treecreeper, Reed Bunting.

October–March: Pink-footed Goose (irregular), Eurasian Wigeon, Goosander, Hen Harrier (scarce), Merlin (scarce), Peregrine Falcon, Long-eared Owl (scarce), Short-eared Owl (irregular), Brambling, Siskin, Common Crossbill (irregular), Corn Bunting (scarce).

April–September: Quail, Hobby, Curlew, Turtle Dove, Yellow Wagtail, Grasshopper, Sedge and Reed Warblers, Blackcap, Garden Warbler, Lesser and Common Whitethroats, Common Chiffchaff, Willow Warbler.

13. CHARNWOOD FOREST AREA

OS Landrangers 129 and 140
OS Explorers 233, 245 and 246

Charnwood Forest is an undulating, rocky upland tract in north-west Leicestershire with an elevation of generally 600 feet (180 m) and upwards. Much of the original forest has long since disappeared, but there are still some extensive areas of woodland to be found and a number of interesting reservoirs. The sites detailed in the following section are arranged in alphabetical order.

13A. BARDON HILL

OS Landranger 129
OS Explorer 245

Habitat

At 912 feet (278 m), Bardon Hill is Leicestershire's highest peak, and from the top commanding views over the surrounding area can be had. A large proportion of the hill has been extensively quarried, and much of the remainder is now given over to pine plantations, parts of which are subject to periodic felling. Bardon Hill is a Site of Special Scientific Interest, as its areas of heath and ancient woodland are some of the last surviving fragments of the original Charnwood Forest. Some heathland restoration is also being carried out by English Nature. 'The Mound' on the northern edge of the quarry provides areas of birch scrub and gorse attractive to migrant passerines.

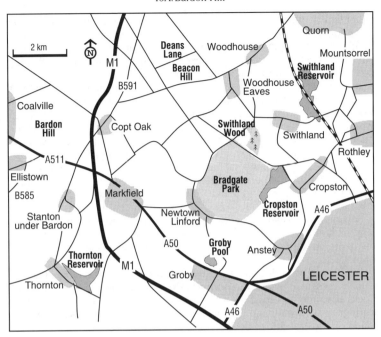

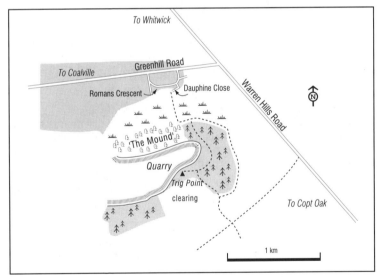

Species

It has recently been discovered that Bardon Hill is an important migration site, especially during the spring, and it is now one of the most reliable places in the region to see passage Ring Ouzels. This distinctive thrush can turn up any time between late March and early May, but the peak period is the third week in April. Up to ten birds have been seen in most recent springs, in groups of as many as six at a time. They are almost always found in the birches and gorse on The Mound – favoured weather conditions are either light south-easterly or cold northerly winds. The Mound is also a good place for Northern Wheatears, and scarcer birds moving through in spring in this area of the hill have included Woodlark and Black Redstart. Several pairs of Tree Pipits breed on the hill; traditional areas include the clearing near the summit and the northern slope of the Mound. The latter area is also a reliable place to hear Grasshopper Warblers singing. Good numbers of Garden and Willow Warblers and Common Chiffchaffs breed in the wooded areas, where they join resident species such as Jay and Green Woodpecker. Little Owls and Red-legged Partridges can often be seen in the quarry itself. Raptors are conspicuous at all times of year, and Sparrowhawk, Common Buzzard, Kestrel and Peregrine Falcon are all likely to be seen.

Autumn coverage of the hill has been patchy, and may well repay further attention. Northern Wheatears are regular during August and September, while Honey Buzzard and Marsh Harrier have been noted flying over at this time of year. There have also been several recent records of Firecrest in September. October sees good numbers of finches moving through, regularly including Brambling, Siskin and Lesser Redpoll. Woodcocks may be encountered during late autumn, most often seen when flushed from areas of bracken.

Winter can be fairly quiet, although one or two European Stonechats are usually present, often on the northern slope of the Mound. Some sizeable flocks of Common Crossbills have been noted on a number of occasions during the late winter and early spring, with a favoured area being the plantation on the east side of the quarry.

Timing

During the spring migration period an early morning visit is recommended, as The Mound is a popular place for dog-walkers. Likewise, a morning visit is essential in autumn for visible migration, which is best observed during calm weather or during light north-westerly winds.

Access

Bardon Hill lies 2 miles (3.2 km) east of Coalville. From junction 22 of the M1, take the A5199 towards Coalville, turning right at the first roundabout on to the B591. At the Copt Oak traffic lights turn left towards Whitwick, and after 1 mile (1.6 km) turn left on to Greenhill Road. Parking is available either in the lay-by on Greenhill Road just past Romans Crescent (SK458142) or nearby at the end of Dauphine Close (SK459141). From here, access is via various well-signed public footpaths; bear in mind that part of the area is a working quarry, so do not stray from the paths.

Calendar

Resident: Red-legged Partridge, Sparrowhawk, Common Buzzard, Kestrel, Peregrine Falcon, Little Owl, Green Woodpecker, Meadow Pipit, Jay, Raven.

September–March: Woodcock, European Stonechat, Brambling, Siskin, Lesser Redpoll, Common Crossbill (irregular).

April–August: Marsh Harrier (rare), Cuckoo, Tree Pipit, Northern Wheatear, Ring Ouzel (mainly April), Grasshopper and Garden Warblers.

13B. BEACON HILL COUNTRY PARK AND DEANS LANE

OS Landranger 129
OS Explorer 246

Habitat

Beacon Hill Country Park, which at 802 ft (245 m) is Leicestershire's second highest point, is owned and managed by the Leicestershire County Council and comprises 335 acres (135 ha) of mixed woodland, heathland, grassland and adjoining farmland on the northern edge of Charnwood Forest. Woodland sections consist mainly of beech, oak and Scots pine, with some stands of birch, and over 100 nest-boxes have been erected in these areas. A long-term programme of heathland restoration is taking place, involving the removal of invasive species to encourage plants such as heather and bilberry.

Due to its great archaeological importance, Beacon Hill is legally protected by English Heritage as a Scheduled Ancient Monument, and the area has also been designated as a Site of Special Scientific Interest.

Species

Wintering birds at Beacon Hill are those typical of woodland habitats. Roving parties of tits, including Marsh Tit, are joined by Goldcrests, Nuthatches, Treecreepers and occasionally Lesser Spotted Woodpeckers, while small flocks of Siskins and Lesser Redpolls may be present in the areas of birch. The upper car park is a regular wintering site for Bramblings and birds can usually be located feeding with Chaffinches on beechmast beneath the trees; in influx years flocks of over 100 may be found, and a remarkable 750 were present in December 1997. One or two European Stonechats usually winter in the country park, with the heathland areas and rocky outcrops being the most likely locations. On clear sunny days in late winter or early spring, a scan from the peak should give views of the resident Common Buzzards, Sparrowhawks and Kestrels, and with a bit of luck they may be joined by a wandering Red Kite. One or two pairs of Ravens are now established in Charnwood, and this is as good a spot as any to look for them.

Spring sees the arrival of a variety of warblers to the area, with Garden Warblers being particularly numerous. Occasional singing Wood Warblers

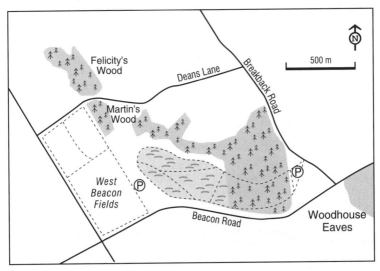

may take up territory, but this species is currently experiencing something of a slump in Leicestershire and its presence is by no means guaranteed. Common Redstarts have also declined markedly in recent years, but every now and again a singing male may appear. Spotted Flycatchers can be found in the wooded areas, particularly near the lower car park, while Leicestershire's first breeding pair of Pied Flycatchers in 1996 caused more interest. Colonisation seemed on the cards when five singing males were located the following spring, but unfortunately, despite one or two males returning each year until 2001 and regularly inspecting nest-boxes, the phenomenon appears to have been rather short-lived. Other breeding species at Beacon Hill include Tawny Owl and all three woodpeckers, while several pairs of Tree Pipits nest on the heathland areas. The rocky outcrops near the peak attract migrant Northern Wheatears in the spring, with irregular sightings of Ring Ouzel and Whinchat. There have also been a couple of records of Black Redstart in this area.

Deans Lane, to the north of the country park, has attracted considerable interest in recent years as a visible migration site. A vantage point next to the road by the new plantation known as Martin's Wood gives commanding views of the valley to the north, and birds pass quite low overhead as they reach the edge of Beacon Hill. From late August to mid-November, large numbers of migrant passerines can be seen, mainly heading south-west. Meadow Pipit is the first species to move in large numbers, followed by hirundines, Siskins and Lesser Redpolls during September. October sees some huge movements of Woodpigeons, along with large flocks of Fieldfares and Redwings, while from mid-October to mid-November good numbers of Chaffinches and Bramblings head south-west. October also offers the chance of seeing transient Pink-footed Geese and even species such as Bewick's Swan have been noted flying over. Several Woodlarks have been seen in recent years in early October, and there have also been records of this species in March on a number of occasions; continued observations may well prove this to be a regular migrant in the area. One or two Merlins are usually seen in the autumn and winter months. Deans Lane is also a good area for Common Crossbills, and small flocks may be encountered during influx years.

Inevitably for a site which is higher than much of the surrounding land, a few scarcities have been found over the years, including Honey Buzzard, Dotterel, Hoopoe, Nutcracker and Snow Bunting.

Timing

This site is worth a visit at any time of year, although from an ornithological point of view summer is probably the quietest. The country park can become busy at weekends, but the size of the area means that direct disturbance to birdlife is minimal. Visible migration watches from Deans Lane are best from late August to mid-November, and to a lesser extent in March; calm weather with a light south-westerly breeze produces the best results.

Access

Beacon Hill Country Park lies 2.5 miles (4 km) south of Loughborough on the northern edge of Charnwood Forest. From junction 23 of the M1, take the A512 east towards Loughborough and turn right after 0.6 miles (1 km) onto a minor road signed to Nanpantan. Go straight ahead at the crossroads, passing the small concrete-sided Nanpantan Reservoir on the left, and the lower car park for Beacon Hill is on the right after a further 1.5 miles (2.4 km) at SK521148. The upper car park is 0.6 miles (1 km) to the west at

SK510145. Both car parks are pay and display, cost £1.50, and are open from 8 am to dusk (exact times of closing are displayed on signs). A network of footpaths extends through the country park from the car parks and, in addition, permissive paths have been developed across adjoining farmland.

Deans Lane runs east to west along the northern boundary of the Country Park, with the best point for observing visible migration being at SK505152.

Calendar

Resident: Red Kite, Sparrowhawk, Common Buzzard, Kestrel, Peregrine Falcon, Woodcock, Tawny Owl, all three woodpeckers, Meadow Pipit, Marsh Tit, Nuthatch, Raven, Yellowhammer, Reed Bunting.

October–March: Pink-footed Goose (scarce), Merlin (scarce), Woodlark (rare October and March), European Stonechat, Fieldfare, Redwing, Brambling, Siskin, Lesser Redpoll, Common Crossbill (irregular).

April–September: Tree Pipit, Common Redstart (scarce), Whinchat (passage), Northern Wheatear (passage), Ring Ouzel (scarce, April), Garden Warbler, Wood Warbler (scarce), Spotted Flycatcher, Pied Flycatcher (scarce).

13C. BRADGATE PARK AND CROPSTON RESERVOIR

OS Landrangers 129 and 140
OS Explorer 246

Habitat

Bradgate Park lies at the south-eastern edge of Charnwood Forest, and is Leicestershire's largest remaining area of semi-natural moorland, covering 850 acres (374 ha). It was established as a deer park in the 13th century (herds of Fallow and Red Deer still roam in a semi-wild state), and was given to the people of Leicestershire by Charles Bennion in 1928. Today it is managed, along with nearby Swithland Wood, by the Bradgate Park trustees on behalf of Leicestershire County Council.

The park vegetation is dominated by bracken, with a few small patches of wet heath and drier grassy areas. These consist mainly of purple moorgrass, and contain several locally rare plants including cross-leaved heath, lesser skullcap and lemon-scented fern. There are many scattered old oaks, and several newer plantations of mixed deciduous and coniferous trees. These are surrounded by drystone walls, creating undisturbed oases where many birds nest. The northern end of the park rises to around 600 ft (200 m) and has many rocky outcrops, one of which is the well known local landmark of Old John Tower. Several small ponds provide excellent habitat for dragonflies, amphibians and water plants.

The fast-flowing River Lin, fringed with alders, runs along the southern edge of the park, past the ruins of Bradgate House, and eventually into Cropston Reservoir. This drinking-water reservoir forms the eastern edge of Bradgate Park and is separated from it by a drystone wall. Public access is not allowed to the reservoir margins. The shallow southern end, which is easily watched from either the park or a public footpath to the east of the reservoir, usually has muddy areas in autumn, which are attractive to waders. The deeper water at the dam is favoured by diving ducks and grebes.

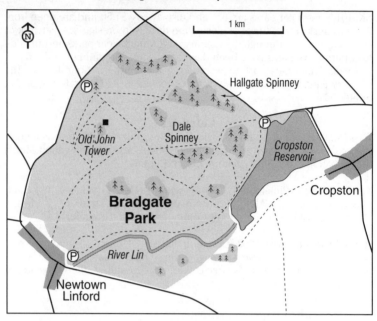

Species

BRADGATE PARK

The vast areas of bracken can often appear relatively birdless, even in summer; Yellowhammers and Meadow Pipits are the commonest breeding species, with a few Reed Buntings and Yellow Wagtails in the wetter areas. Several pairs of Tree Pipits also breed, and good views can be obtained as they perform their parachute song-flights from the oaks and the edges of the plantations. Unfortunately, the Whinchats, Common Redstarts and Wood Warblers that used to breed have all disappeared, but odd birds may still arrive on passage. Whinchats may occur anywhere in the park, while Common Redstarts used to favour the old oaks near the Newton Linford entrance and Wood Warblers still occasionally sing from the woods, with Hallgate Spinney and Dale Spinney being the favoured sites for this species. Northern Wheatears and Ring Ouzels sometimes appear on passage, with the latter favouring the rockier terrain similar to their upland breeding habitat. Grasshopper Warblers sometimes hold territory in the park; the scrubby area near the inflow of the reservoir is probably the best place to look and listen for this elusive species. All three species of woodpecker occur in the oaks and plantations, although Lesser Spotted is rarely seen. Green Woodpeckers can often be found feeding on the ant hills around the ruins. Nuthatches also like the old oaks, with their abundance of suitable nesting holes, while in the spring a number of Cuckoos are attracted to the park, where they often parasite the nests of Meadow Pipits.

Little Owl is another characteristic bird of the park, with several pairs breeding in most years; the enclosed area behind the ruins is one of the more reliable places to see them. Several pairs of Tawny Owls and Woodcocks also breed; the latter can be seen roding over the plantations at dawn and dusk in spring and summer, and are occasionally flushed from the wetter areas in the winter. Sparrowhawks may be seen hunting over the park at any time of the year, and several pairs breed in the plantations.

Common Buzzards are now well established in the area, and should be seen easily; a scan from one of the high points in the park (such as by Old John) should produce this species, and there is also a good chance of seeing Raven from here, especially in the early spring. Other raptors may occasionally appear, such as Merlin or Red Kite.

Grey Wagtails and Kingfishers can often be seen along the River Lin, and both usually breed in the area. Little Grebes have declined noticeably in recent years, but trilling birds may still be heard on the pond in the ruins enclosure and occasionally on the river itself. A recent addition to the avian scene on the river is Mandarin Duck, and several birds are now semi-resident along this stretch. They can sometimes be rather difficult to locate due to their habit of sitting in trees; on the other hand, they will sometimes join the resident Mallards, when they become very obvious. Spotted Flycatchers may be found in the late spring and summer in the oaks near the Newton Linford entrance, but are very unobtrusive.

The park is quiet in winter, but is a reliable site for European Stonechat, with up to four birds being present in most years from October through to March. The birds frequent the dead bracken and drystone walls, particularly around the ruins and the reservoir inflow. Mixed flocks of Siskins and Lesser Redpolls may be found feeding in the alders adjacent to the river.

Rarer visitors to the park in recent years have included White Stork, Honey Buzzard, Hen Harrier, Short-eared Owl, Great Grey Shrike and Leicestershire's only Richard's Pipit.

CROPSTON RESERVOIR
In winter, the reservoir holds reasonable numbers of most of the common ducks: Eurasian Wigeons, Mallards, Common Teal and a few Gadwall and Shovelers feed at the inflow end and around the edges, while Pochards, Tufted Ducks, Goldeneyes and Ruddy Ducks favour the deeper water off the dam. Up to 40 Great Crested Grebes and a few Little Grebes winter, and small numbers of Cormorants are usually present. As with any area of water, unusual visitors sometimes appear, particularly during hard weather, and recent scarce winter wildfowl have included Red-throated and Black-throated Divers, Slavonian and Red-necked Grebes, Scaup, Common Scoter, Long-tailed Duck, Common Eider and Red-breasted Merganser. The only waders usually present, apart from the ubiquitous Northern Lapwings, are small numbers of Common Snipe and the occasional Green Sandpiper and Jack Snipe. The trees behind the dam often contain a few Siskins during the win-

Ring Ouzel

ter months, and this is a good area to look for Common Crossbills if there has been an irruption of this species. The dam provides a fine view over Bradgate Park, and is a good place to scan from for raptors and Ravens. One or two Grey Wagtails are normally found on the stonework of the dam itself.

A gull roost usually forms on the reservoir, and is best viewed from the dam, although sometimes the site acts merely as a pre-roost assembly for the large gathering on nearby Swithland Reservoir; however, if shooting or other disturbance occurs at the latter site, the Cropston roost may number many thousands of birds. The rarer gulls are less likely to occur here than at Swithland Reservoir, but recent winters have produced several Mediterranean Gulls, along with the occasional Iceland and Glaucous Gull. Caspian Gulls have also been seen on a number of occasions in the winter.

The water level is often high in spring and the reservoir is therefore relatively quiet, although the occasional Black-necked Grebe or Garganey may brighten the day. Small numbers of ducks breed, including Gadwall and, more recently, one or two pairs of Mandarin Ducks. Little Ringed Plovers and a few pairs of Northern Lapwings may also nest if the water level drops sufficiently, but otherwise wader passage is usually poor and is restricted to the odd Common Sandpiper on the dam. Passage terns may appear during easterly winds in the spring; in contrast to nearby Swithland Reservoir, Cropston often has more Black Terns and fewer Arctics. Little Gulls are sometimes associated with these movements, and there have also been a few recent records of Little Tern at these times.

The reservoir is usually at its best in the autumn, when falling water levels can expose a large expanse of mud at the inflow end. This regularly attracts waders, of which the most numerous are Ringed and Little Ringed Plovers, Dunlin, Ruff, Common Snipe, Redshank, Greenshank and Green and Common Sandpipers. Of the scarcer species, Whimbrel and Wood Sandpiper are relatively frequent, while Knot, Sanderling, Little Stint, both godwits, Spotted Redshank and Turnstone have all been recorded occasionally. When water levels are low, many Grey Herons often feed along the shoreline, and there have been a number of recent records of Little Egret in July and August. Quite substantial numbers of moulting ducks are also usually present in late summer and may include one or two Garganeys. Hobbies may be seen hunting over the reservoir and the park, particularly in late summer, when family parties may be in evidence. Terns are regular on autumn passage, and occasional Little Gulls may drop in, while the late summer gull roost usually contains one or two Yellow-legged Gulls. Later in the autumn, the stonework of the dam is worth checking for Rock Pipits, which have been recorded on several occasions.

Inevitably, a reservoir of this size has attracted a few rarities over the years, and these have included Ferruginous Duck, Fulmar, Spotted Crake, Temminck's Stint, Purple Sandpiper and Arctic and Great Skuas.

Timing

Bradgate Park is by far the most popular recreational area in Leicestershire and is often very crowded, particularly on fine days in both summer and winter. Fortunately the birds using the reservoir do not seem to be unduly disturbed by the hordes of people, but bear in mind that parking may be difficult or impossible at weekends and on bank holidays.

Autumn is generally the best season for the reservoir, as the water level usually drops from July onwards, attracting waders. As with nearby Swithland Reservoir, the winter duck population can fluctuate markedly from day to day, and the gull roost can be a bit hit-and-miss.

Time of day seems to be unimportant with regard to migrant waders, and there is often evidence of continuing passage throughout the day, with a different mix of species present in the morning to the evening. To avoid the crowds in the park, early morning is preferable, although the best viewpoint from the park of the reservoir inflow faces directly into the morning sun; viewing at this time of day is better from the public footpath to the east of the reservoir.

Access

The park is open throughout the year and is served by three major pay-and-display car parks (£1.50 on weekdays, £2 at weekends and bank holidays), at Newtown Linford (SK523097), Hunt's Hill (SK523117) and Hallgates (SK543113). Park at any of these and explore the many pathways on foot. Hallgates is nearest to Cropston Reservoir; follow the main track through the park to view the inflow, which is the best area for waders. Alternatively, the inflow can be seen from the public footpath which runs through fields east of the reservoir; park sensibly at the end of Causeway Lane in Cropston (SK550107). The reservoir can also be watched from the dam; park in the lay-by on the B5330 (SK551111).

Calendar

Resident: Mute Swan, Mandarin, Tufted and Ruddy Ducks, Little and Great Crested Grebes, Sparrowhawk, Common Buzzard, Woodcock, Little and Tawny Owls, Kingfisher, all three woodpeckers, Meadow Pipit, Grey Wagtail, Nuthatch, Treecreeper, Raven, Yellowhammer, Reed Bunting.

October–March: Eurasian Wigeon, Gadwall, Common Teal, Shoveler, Pochard, Goldeneye, divers (rare), Jack and Common Snipe, Green Sandpiper, Mediterranean Gull (scarce), Caspian Gull (scarce), Iceland Gull (rare), Glaucous Gull (rare), European Stonechat, Fieldfare, Redwing, Siskin, Lesser Redpoll.

April–September: Garganey, Little Egret (scarce, July and August), Black-necked Grebe (scarce), Hobby, Little Ringed and Ringed Plovers, Dunlin, Ruff, Redshank, Greenshank, Green Sandpiper (July onwards), Wood Sandpiper (scarce), Common Sandpiper, Little Gull (scarce), Common, Arctic and Black Terns, Cuckoo, Tree Pipit, Yellow Wagtail, Common Redstart (now scarce), Whinchat, Northern Wheatear, Ring Ouzel (scarce), Grasshopper Warbler, Wood Warbler (scarce), Spotted Flycatcher.

13D. GROBY POOL

OS Landranger 140
OS Explorer 233

Habitat

At 38 acres (15.8 ha), Groby Pool is reputed to be the largest natural expanse of open water in Leicestershire, although there is some dispute over its exact origin – it was probably formed when a natural dam created a shallow lake, but may be an old Roman clay pit. The pool, which is owned by Hanson Quarry Products Ltd and managed on advice from English Nature, has been a Site of Special Scientific Interest since 1956. The western and northern margins are wooded, with areas of birch and alder, and there are some sizeable stands of reeds, mainly in the north-eastern corner. Thanks to the nearby rubbish tip, Groby Pool is now established as the best site locally to view scarce gulls at close quarters.

Species

Gulls are the principal attraction at this site, as birds feeding on the nearby tip regularly visit to bathe and loaf throughout the day, and then use the pool as a pre-roost assembly in the late afternoon before flying off to Swithland Reservoir. Observers can obtain much better views of gulls at Groby Pool than at the majority of inland roost sites, due to the pool's relatively small size and the fact that the light is usually much better. From late summer to early spring, large numbers of gulls can be found, and scarcer species are seen regularly. Yellow-legged Gulls are virtually ever-present from July to November, with peak numbers between August and October. Caspian Gulls tend to occur later in the year, from November to February, and in smaller numbers, but as many as ten different birds are usually identified during this period. Mediterranean, Iceland and Glaucous Gulls are all annual, the latter two often occurring during hard weather.

Mandarin Ducks are resident at Groby Pool, and the largest numbers (up to 25) are usually seen during the late autumn and winter. They can be difficult to find, as they often skulk under overhanging vegetation on the west and north sides of the pool. A drake Red-crested Pochard has been semi-resident since 1997, and often associates with the Mandarins. Good numbers of other ducks are present during the winter, particularly Pochard, and the occasional Goosander or Smew may appear. The alders and birches by the footpath along the northern edge of the pool are good for Siskins, Lesser Redpolls and Bramblings during the winter months, while Water Rails can be heard squealing in the reed swamp in this area. Several Bitterns have been recorded in the reedbed in recent winters, and one or two Little Egrets have taken to wintering at the site in the last few years.

Spring sees the arrival of a different selection of birds to the area. Warblers include plenty of Common Chiffchaffs, Willow Warblers, Blackcaps and Garden Warblers, while a good population of Reed Warblers exists in the reedbeds. Grey Herons breed on the small island in the middle of the pool, and Cormorants can usually be found sitting in the surrounding trees. Wandering Common Terns visit in the spring, and during periods of easterly winds in April and May the occasional Arctic Tern or Little Gull may put in an appearance. Due to the nature of the site, waders are very rare and are restricted to the odd Common Sandpiper feeding on the rocky shore on the eastern side, where Grey Wagtails are invariably seen too.

Autumn is notable for providing good views of Hobbies, and family parties can be watched hawking insects and chasing hirundines during August and September. Other raptors worth looking out for include Common Buzzard and Peregrine Falcon, both of which are regular in the area, while scarcities such as Honey Buzzard and Marsh Harrier have been noted flying over during the autumn. Ravens are also being seen with increasingly regularity.

Groby Pool is a well-watched site and, as such, a scattering of scarcities have been recorded, including Ring-necked Duck, Scaup, Black-necked and Slavonian Grebes and Great White Egret.

Timing

During the winter, late afternoon is the best time to see gulls, as they loaf on the pool before flying to roost at nearby Swithland Reservoir. In addition, Mandarins are often more visible late in the day. At other times of year timing is less important as, although the pool is popular with duck-feeding members of the public, little disturbance to the birdlife takes place.

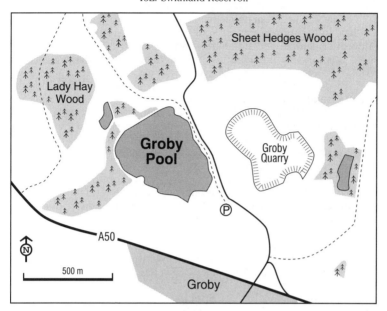

Access
The pool is 4 miles (6.4 km) north-west of Leicester off the A50 just north of Groby village. A free car park is located south of the pool by the minor road between Groby and Newtown Linford (SK525078), which is open from 8 am to 4.30 pm between October and March and 8 am to 8 pm between April and September. Car crime can be a problem here, so do not leave valuables on show. A footpath leads from the car park to the pool, skirting the eastern edge from where the whole area can be viewed. The footpath then continues along the northern edge of the pool, although the western shore is private.

Calendar
Resident: Mandarin Duck, Red-crested Pochard, Tufted Duck, Cormorant, Grey Heron, Sparrowhawk, Common Buzzard, Peregrine Falcon, Grey Wagtail, Marsh Tit.

October–March: Eurasian Wigeon, Gadwall, Common Teal, Pochard, Goosander (scarce), Smew (rare), Bittern (rare), Little Egret, Water Rail, Mediterranean Gull (scarce), Yellow-legged and Caspian Gulls, Iceland Gull (scarce), Glaucous Gull (scarce), Brambling, Siskin, Lesser Redpoll.

April–September: Hobby, Common Tern, Reed and Garden Warblers.

13E. SWITHLAND RESERVOIR

OS Landranger 129
OS Explorer 246

Habitat
Swithland Reservoir is approximately 1 mile (1.6 km) long by half a mile (0.8 km) wide, and lies at the eastern edge of Charnwood Forest. It is bisected by the Great Central Railway, and the northern and southern sections are

both easily watched from public roads. At the southern (inflow) end a shallow lagoon has formed, cut off from the rest of the reservoir by the road bridge; it is surrounded by reed-swamp and willow carr. The north-east shore was formerly bounded by Buddon Wood, but this has been sadly reduced to a narrow strip by the ever-expanding Mountsorrel granite quarry. This wood, originally oak, is now mainly composed of birch. There is, however, another small area of oak woodland on Brazil Island, connected to the banks by the railway viaduct, but this along with the rest of the reservoir grounds is private. There are several marshy areas around the reservoir, with stands of bulrush and reed canary-grass. The fields and hedges along Kinchley Lane are worth a look, particularly in autumn and winter, as is the railway embankment at Rabbit's Bridge (SK553143).

Swithland is now mainly used to top up nearby Cropston Reservoir, from where drinking water is taken; consequently the water level fluctuates considerably, although the shoreline is largely stony and thus disappointing for waders. The reservoir is relatively undisturbed; water sports have fortunately been resisted, and only a small amount of coarse fishing takes place. During the winter months, shooting in the reservoir grounds and surrounding fields can temporarily affect the number of wildfowl, which may then disperse to Cropston Reservoir or the Soar Valley Gravel Pits.

Species

One of the main attractions at this site is the gull roost, which during its heyday in the 1980s regularly attracted up to 15,000 birds. The closure of the nearby Mountsorrel tip in the early 1990s had a detrimental effect on the size of the roost, but since Groby tip has been opened about 3 miles (4.8 km) to the south-west, numbers have built up again. The roost can sometimes be difficult to watch as the best viewpoint, halfway along Kinchley Lane, faces directly into the setting sun; overcast evenings are therefore better. Mediterranean Gulls are frequently found between October and March, while Glaucous and Iceland Gulls are just about annual. The latter two species usually appear during hard weather in January and February although there have been several recent mid-March records, of birds presumably on spring passage. The occasional Kittiwake may join the roost, especially in March, while there is always the possibility of something outstanding; the first two county records of Ring-billed Gull occurred here, in 1988 and 1989 respectively. Sharp-eyed observers may pick out a Caspian Gull, especially during November or December, and this species is now occurring with some regularity during the winter months. Its close relative, Yellow-legged Gull, may also be encountered in the winter, but great care is needed with identification after December. Yellow-legged Gull is much more frequent during the late summer and autumn (from July onwards), when up to eight birds at a time have been present.

Large numbers of wildfowl winter at the reservoir, and there are nationally important populations of Gadwall, Shoveler and Little Grebe. Other species usually present in good numbers include Eurasian Wigeon, Common Teal, Tufted Duck, Pochard, Goldeneye and Ruddy Duck, along with the occasional Pintail and Goosander. Smew are infrequent visitors, and one or two Scaup are seen most winters. Rarer species of seaduck occur occasionally, usually during cold weather; Velvet Scoter, Long-tailed Duck, Common Eider and Red-breasted Merganser have all been noted in the past. Other hard-weather visitors may include Red-necked and Slavonian Grebes, or any of the three divers. The rarer wildfowl usually appear on the northern side of the reservoir, on the deep water near the dam.

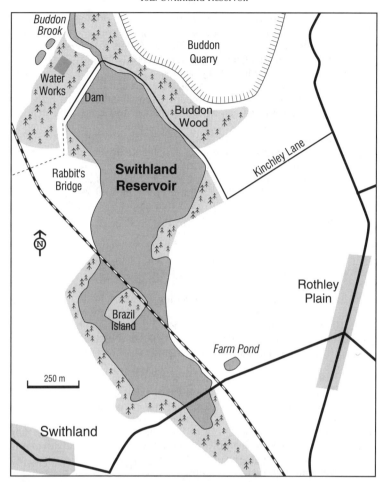

Water Rails can be found during the winter in reasonable numbers, the best sites being the inflow at the southern end or the marshy area along Kinchley Lane. A Bittern wintered every year from 1986 to 1991, and was most often seen from the causeway at the southern end. Buddon Wood and the trees around the dam hold woodpeckers (including Lesser Spotted), Marsh Tit, Siskin, Lesser Redpoll and Brambling, the latter being most frequent on passage in late March and April. Sparrowhawks are regular, and Peregrine Falcons are often seen from the dam perched in a prominent oak tree on the Buddon Wood skyline. Grey Wagtails are usually around the dam and Kingfishers may be seen anywhere around the reservoir, especially at the inflow lagoon and behind the dam.

Easterly winds in spring often bring a passage of terns, and Swithland is a particularly good site for Arctic Terns, especially in late April. Black Terns usually appear in May, but generally in smaller numbers, while two or three pairs of Common Terns nest on the special rafts. Little Gulls are sometimes associated with movements of terns, and Kittiwakes may also appear in March or April, especially after gales. Wader passage is light and dependent upon the water levels, but Common Sandpipers, Little Ringed Plovers and occasionally odd birds of other species turn up on the sloping stonework of the dam. The new farm pond just east of the railway bridge at the southern end of the reservoir may be worth checking, as waders have been seen here on occasions, including a Grey Plover in May 2000.

Breeding wildfowl include Greylag Goose, Mallard, Tufted and Ruddy Ducks, and there is a large colony of Grey Herons and Cormorants in trees on the south side of the reservoir. Pochard, Gadwall and Shoveler have also bred and Garganey is a scarce passage migrant, while Common Scoters are often encountered during the spring or early summer. Large gatherings of Common Swifts, Swallows and martins are well worth checking, as Swithland has developed something of a reputation in recent years for producing rare hirundines; the site shot to national fame in April 1999 with the finding of Britain's first twitchable Crag Martin, and Leicestershire's only two records of Red-rumped Swallow occurred here, in April 2003 and March 2004 respectively. These hirundine flocks may attract the attentions of hunting Hobbies. Rarer raptors have appeared on passage, including Osprey and Marsh Harrier, while wandering Common Buzzards or Red Kites may be seen at any time of year. Several pairs of Reed Warblers breed around the reservoir, along with Reed Buntings and the occasional pair of Sedge Warblers. Wood Warblers sometimes sing for a day or two on spring passage in Buddon Wood, but quickly move on.

Midsummer is often quiet. Post-breeding flocks of Northern Lapwings start to appear as early as June, and there is a regular flock of moulting diving ducks. Pochard and Tufted Duck predominate, but there have also been past records of the occasional summering Goldeneye. Black-necked Grebes are almost annual in late July and August and may stay for a week or more. Garganeys are more regular in autumn than spring, and usually favour the southern end of the reservoir. Passage waders are less numerous than at Cropston Reservoir but most of the regular species have been recorded; Ringed and Little Ringed Plovers, Dunlin, Greenshank and Common Sandpiper are the most frequent. The return passage of terns is not usually as large as in spring; small flocks of Black Terns may occur in the right weather conditions from July to October, although Arctic Terns are rare in autumn and usually involve juveniles. Migrant passerines can turn up in any area of cover around the reservoir and all areas of bushes and trees should be searched for warblers, chats and other species. It is also worth checking the stonework of the dam during October and November, as Rock Pipits have been noted on several occasions.

Swithland Reservoir is a well-watched locality and has amassed a good list of rare birds over the years, with the most recent being Ferruginous Duck, Lesser Scaup, Leach's Storm-petrel, White Stork, Spoonbill, Honey Buzzard, Killdeer, Pectoral Sandpiper, Red-necked and Grey Phalaropes, Great and Arctic Skuas, White-winged Black Tern, Crag Martin, Red-rumped Swallow, Firecrest and Great Grey Shrike.

Timing

Winter is the best time to see large numbers of birds, although spring and autumn probably offer better chances of finding something unusual. In winter, the gull roost assembles an hour or two before dusk, but as mentioned previously, pick an overcast afternoon for best viewing conditions. On really cold days, if the reservoir is frozen over, the gulls may be present all day.

Time of day for migrants is not too important, although early morning is usually best. Shooting occasionally takes place in the grounds during the winter months, causing temporary disturbance to ducks, which move to nearby Cropston Reservoir. The gull roost may also be disrupted and on some evenings may shift to Cropston. The shoots are mostly on Saturday mornings but times are irregular throughout.

Access
The south side of the reservoir can be watched from the minor road between Swithland and Rothley; park on the causeway at SK562132. The farm pond just east of the railway bridge is also viewable from the road, but parking here is limited; if viewing this area, walk from the causeway. To reach the north side of the reservoir, follow the minor road north from Rothley Plain cross-roads for half a mile (0.8 km) and turn left onto Kinchley Lane, which skirts the eastern shore and dam. Drive and park carefully as the lane is winding and narrow, and is often frequented by dog walkers and horse riders. The best views of the reservoir are obtained from the open wall halfway along the eastern shore, and from the dam itself. On no account enter the reservoir grounds, Buddon Wood or the railway line, as all are private.

Calendar
Resident: Greylag Goose, Gadwall, Tufted and Ruddy Ducks, Little and Great Crested Grebes, Cormorant, Grey Heron, Sparrowhawk, Common Buzzard, Peregrine Falcon, Tawny Owl, Kingfisher, Lesser Spotted Woodpecker, Grey Wagtail, Marsh Tit, Nuthatch.

October–March: Eurasian Wigeon, Common Teal, Pintail (scarce), Shoveler, Pochard, Scaup (scarce), seaducks (rare), Goldeneye, Smew (scarce), Goosander (scarce), divers (rare), Red-necked Grebe (rare), Slavonian Grebe (rare), Water Rail, Mediterranean Gull, Caspian Gull (scarce), Iceland Gull (scarce), Glaucous Gull (scarce), Kittiwake (scarce), Rock Pipit (scarce), Fieldfare, Redwing, Brambling, Siskin, Lesser Redpoll.

April–September: Garganey (rare), Pintail (scarce August and September), Black-necked Grebe (scarce), Osprey (scarce), Hobby, Little Ringed and Ringed Plovers, Dunlin, Greenshank, Common Sandpiper, Little Gull, Yellow-legged Gull (July onwards), Common, Arctic and Black Terns, Yellow-legged Gull (July onwards), Reed Warbler, Wood Warbler (scarce April).

13F. SWITHLAND WOOD

OS Landranger 129
OS Explorer 246

Habitat
Together with the adjacent private woodland known as The Brand, Swithland Wood forms the largest remaining area of the original Charnwood oak woodland, covering some 180 acres (72 ha) in total. Pedunculate and sessile oak predominate with stands of birch, small-leaved lime and alder, the latter particularly along the stream at the southern end of the wood. The shrub layer is mainly hazel with some holly but this has been much reduced by the effects of many visitors and their attendant dogs straying from the main pathways.

The woodland is very rich in wildlife, with over 250 plant species and 200 species of moths and butterflies having been recorded. A small herb-rich meadow at the northern end of the wood adds to the variety of habitats and in spring it is carpeted with common spotted orchids; it also holds the locally rare adder's tongue fern. Also within the wood are two very deep,

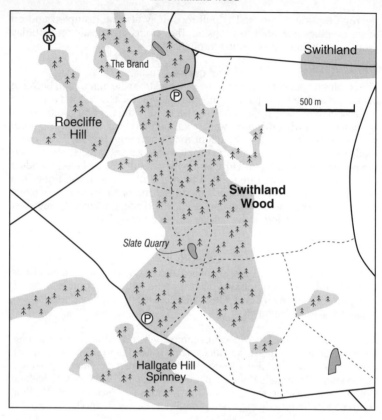

water-filled slate quarries, which provide a habitat for Mallard, Tufted Duck and Little Grebe and once hosted one of the county's most bizarre records, a Puffin!

Species

All three species of woodpecker are resident, and Swithland Wood is one of the best places in the county to see the secretive Lesser Spotted. Several pairs breed and the birds are most easily located in spring by listening for their distinctive calls. One of their favoured areas is around the car park at the southern end, although in winter they often join up with roving tit flocks. Nuthatch and Treecreeper are also easily seen and it is possible to compare the identification of Marsh and Willow Tits, the latter usually being found in the damper areas of the wood while the former are frequently attracted to small feeding stations in the southern car park.

A visit at dawn or dusk in spring is required to see Woodcocks roding, with one of the best places being the large spoil heap next to the southern-most quarry. From this vantage point the birds can be easily seen as they pass over the tree-tops at eye level.

Grey Wagtails breed in the steep-sided slate quarries and Little Grebe and Mallard have also done so in the past. More recently, Mandarin Ducks have been seen displaying in the quarries and may well breed in the area. Predators are represented by Common Buzzards, Sparrowhawks and Tawny Owls. The latter species may sometimes be found roosting during the day in the large holly trees at the southern end of the wood. Ravens are becoming more frequent in the general vicinity and on fine days, especially in early spring, may be seen soaring over the wood.

In spring the wood holds a good selection of warblers including Blackcap, Common Chiffchaff and Garden and Willow Warblers. In addition, this is the one of the more regular sites in Leicestershire for Wood Warbler, although in recent years their appearances have become more erratic, possibly because of the destruction of much of the shrub layer. Although Wood Warblers may sing from anywhere in the wood, the most regular sites are at the northern end near The Brand car park and in the fenced-off section at the eastern edge of the wood.

Spotted Flycatchers occur in reasonable numbers and there have been several recent spring records of Pied Flycatchers, some of which have involved long-staying singing males; this species could conceivably breed in the future, as they have also been seen inspecting nesting holes on more than one occasion. One former breeding species which may hold on in small numbers is the Hawfinch; although reported less than annually, usually from The Brand, it may still breed in that wood, which is private and therefore rather less disturbed.

The wood is relatively quiet in the winter, but tits and woodpeckers are perhaps easier to see at this time of year, and many birds of several species make use of the feeding stations in the southern car park. Lesser Redpolls and Siskins, the latter sometimes in good numbers, frequent the alders along the stream.

The wood has attracted several scarcities over the years, including European Nightjar, Dipper, Firecrest and Golden Oriole. In addition, one of the most unexpected species ever to appear in Leicestershire was found here in October 1997, when a Red-flanked Bluetail was trapped and ringed at The Brand.

Timing

Most of the warblers are present and singing by early May, but Wood Warblers may not arrive until mid-May in some years and have usually stopped singing by the first week of June. Early morning is definitely the best time of day in spring, as birds sing almost continuously for the first two hours after dawn but tend to be much less vocal later in the day. Woodcocks can be seen roding at dawn and dusk.

Access

The wood is about half a mile (0.8 km) south-west of Swithland village. There are car parks at the northern and southern ends of the wood at SK538129 and SK537117, charge £1. Keep to the main footpaths as erosion and trampling of the undergrowth are serious problems in the wood. The paths can be very muddy even in summer, and wellingtons are recommended.

Calendar

Resident: Sparrowhawk, Common Buzzard, Woodcock, Tawny Owl, all three woodpeckers, Grey Wagtail, Marsh and Willow Tits, Nuthatch, Treecreeper, Raven, Jay, Hawfinch (rare, possibly extinct).

October–March: Siskin, Lesser Redpoll.
April–September: Garden Warbler, Blackcap, Wood Warbler (now scarce), Common Chiffchaff, Willow Warbler, Spotted Flycatcher, Pied Flycatcher (scarce).

13G. THORNTON RESERVOIR

OS Landranger 140
OS Explorer 233

Habitat

Constructed in 1854, Thornton is one of Leicestershire's oldest reservoirs and lies just to the south-west of the Charnwood Forest district. Being situated in gently undulating countryside away from any major river valley, it does not attract the variety of waders and other passage migrants as some of the other waterbodies in the county, but is still worthy of exploration. The 76 acre (30.7 ha) reservoir is bordered on the eastern side by agricultural land, with mature gardens and Thornton churchyard on the western side. To the north is mainly coniferous woodland, along with a new plantation known as Brown's Wood.

Species

The reservoir attracts reasonable numbers of wildfowl in the autumn and winter, especially outside the fishing season when disturbance from boats is greatly reduced. Staple species are Eurasian Wigeon, Gadwall, Tufted Duck, Pochard and Great Crested Grebe, with smaller numbers of Common Teal, Goldeneye and Little Grebe. Large rafts of Cormorants can be seen at times of little disturbance. Mandarin Ducks are becoming fairly regular as this species expands away from the stronghold at nearby Groby Pool. Occasional scarcer wildfowl have appeared, including several Red-necked and Slavonian Grebes and the odd Smew. Water Rails are sometimes encountered in the marshy margins, particularly around the weir in the north-eastern corner. A small gull roost often forms and is easily viewable from the western car park; the majority of birds present are Black-headed Gulls, which in turn have attracted several Mediterranean Gulls. The area around the western car park and the churchyard usually holds flocks of tits and finches, which during the winter frequently include Siskins and Lesser Redpolls. The new plantation of Brown's Wood is a good site for wintering European Stonechats, and the boggy areas here attract Common Snipe and a few Jack Snipe.

During the spring Thornton has a peculiar attraction to Black Terns, which are more regular here than at any of the other Charnwood reservoirs. As everywhere, favoured conditions are east or south-east winds, weather which generally produces good numbers of Arctic Terns. Little Gulls are just about annual at this time of year and Ospreys are becoming more frequent. Small groups of Northern Wheatears and Whinchats pass through and favour the bare ground and new plantings at Brown's Wood, where Grasshopper Warblers may be heard reeling. Another notable summer visitor is the declining Spotted Flycatcher, several of which are usually present around the churchyard or the car park at the west end of the dam. Also in spring it is worth checking suitable areas of grassland, particularly the slope behind the dam, as there have been several recent records of passage Ring Ouzels.

A lack of suitable habitat means that migrant waders are few and far between in both spring and autumn. Occasional Common Sandpipers appear on the stonework of the dam but the majority of other species, which have included Bar-tailed Godwit and Knot in recent years, are only seen flying over. Curlews probably still breed in the surrounding fields, albeit in much reduced numbers than previously, and can often be seen flying over the reservoir any time between March and August.

Autumn sees the gradual build-up of wildfowl numbers, particularly after the end of the fishing season when disturbance is minimal. Black Terns are

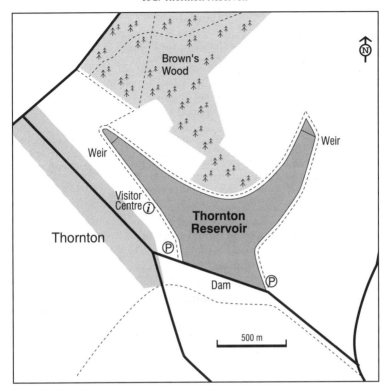

again regular at this time of year; although not usually seen in as large numbers as during the spring, they often remain for longer periods in the autumn.

Although not renowned as a site that produces rare birds, regular watching over the years has revealed Leach's Storm-petrel, Little Bittern, Great White Egret, Red-footed Falcon, Spotted Crake, Stone-curlew and Caspian Tern.

Timing
The main water can get very disturbed by large numbers of boats during the fishing season, while the car parks are only small and can soon become full at weekends. Therefore early morning and evening are the best times of day at any season.

Access
The reservoir is approximately 6.5 miles (10.4 km) north-west of Leicester and is easily reached via minor roads from Thornton and Markfield. There is a small parking area at the east end of the dam (SK475072) and a larger car park at the west end of the dam (SK470074). From either of these car parks a well-made path runs round the whole reservoir, although care should be taken when viewing from the dam as this is a rather narrow, deceptively busy road. A footpath leads off in a north-easterly direction from near the weir in the west arm, giving views over the new plantation of Brown's Wood.

Calendar

Resident: Great Crested and Little Grebes, Sparrowhawk, Common Buzzard, Kestrel, Little and Tawny Owls, Kingfisher, Grey Wagtail, Goldcrest, Willow Tit, Nuthatch, Bullfinch, Reed Bunting.

October–March: Eurasian Wigeon, Gadwall, Pochard, Tufted Duck, Cormorant, Water Rail, Common Snipe, Jack Snipe, European Stonechat, Fieldfare, Redwing, Siskin, Lesser Redpoll.

April–September: Osprey (scarce), Curlew, Common Sandpiper, Little Gull (scarce), Common, Arctic and Black Terns, Whinchat, Northern Wheatear, Grasshopper Warbler, Blackcap, Garden Warbler, Common Chiffchaff, Willow Warbler, Spotted Flycatcher.

14. EYEBROOK RESERVOIR

OS Landranger 141
OS Explorers 224 and 234

Habitat

Eyebrook Reservoir has a long record as an excellent inland locality for birdwatching and has attracted an impressive range of species over its 65-year history. Although recently somewhat overshadowed by Rutland Water, it remains one of the most important birding localities in Leicestershire and, indeed, the midlands.

This 400 acre (160 ha) reservoir, which was completed in 1940, was built to supply water for the steel industry in Corby. The site is relatively undisturbed; it is used for trout fishing in season, although anglers are not permitted at the shallow northern end, and watersports have thankfully been resisted. The reservoir occupies a sheltered position in the valley of the Eye Brook and has natural, gently shelving banks with a grassy fringe. The northern end is marshy and often grazed by cattle, with vegetation here including water mint, silver weed and amphibious bistort. A coniferous plantation stretches along much of the eastern shore and below the dam there is an avenue of European hardwoods. There are several small stands of willows around the reservoir. The surrounding land is mainly arable, with hawthorn hedges and scattered older trees.

A hide is located between the island and the bay at the south-western end of the reservoir, and a feeding station has been established a little further south by the track that leads to the dam.

Species

In winter the main attractions are the large numbers of wildfowl and the huge gull roost. The principal wildfowl are Eurasian Wigeon, Gadwall (in nationally important numbers), Common Teal, Shoveler, Pochard and Tufted Duck, with smaller numbers of Pintail, Goldeneye, Goosander and Ruddy Duck. Smew are regular, and numbers of this splendid little duck may reach double-figures. Of the rarer species, Slavonian Grebe and Scaup are annual, while hard weather may produce a diver or seaduck. Reasonably sized flocks of Bewick's Swans formerly wintered, although this species has declined markedly at Eyebrook over the last ten years and most records now are of transient birds in October and November. Large numbers of

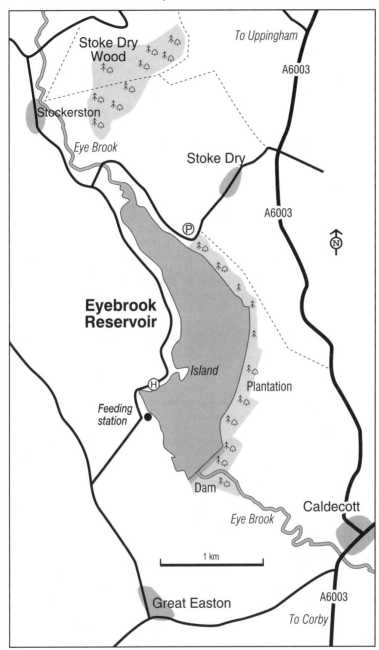

Canada and Greylag Geese may attract stray wild geese of other species, especially White-fronted. Waders congregate on the exposed mud at the northern end and include several thousand European Golden Plovers, up to 1,000 Northern Lapwings and as many as 150 Dunlin. One or two Ruff may be present throughout the winter months, and careful searching of the

European Golden Plover flock has produced two unseasonable Dotterels.

The gull roost is best observed from the road along western shore, although due to its size it is difficult to watch the whole roost from one spot. The large gulls tend to roost on the deep water between the island and the dam, while Common and Black-headed Gulls use the area north of the island. The Eyebrook roost is one of the best in the midlands, helped by the fact that there are several large rubbish tips only a few miles away in Corby. Mediterranean Gulls are regular between October and March, as are Caspian Gulls; for both of these species, November is the peak month, although small numbers usually remain throughout the winter. Both Iceland and Glaucous Gull are annual, with Iceland being the more frequent of the two; four or five individuals per winter of each is not uncommon. The occasional Kittiwake or Little Gull may also join the roost in the winter, while a Kumlien's Gull was seen in December 1995.

Passerine interest during the winter months is maintained by finch flocks which feed in the stubble fields around the reservoir; these flocks may contain good numbers of Tree Sparrows and Yellowhammers. The feeding station at the south-west end also attracts Tree Sparrows and sometimes Bramblings. Just to the south of the reservoir, the area around Great Easton is a traditional wintering ground for several Short-eared Owls.

The first signs of spring passage are often as early as February, when returning Shelducks, Oystercatchers, Ringed Plovers and Redshanks may arrive. Black-necked Grebes sometimes appear from late March onwards, while Garganey are regular in spring and Common Scoters are annual in March or April. Ospreys are now almost guaranteed at Eyebrook any time between late March and August and when not hunting will often perch in dead trees in the fields to the west of the reservoir. Other raptors in evidence may include Red Kites and Common Buzzards, both of which are resident in the general area, while Marsh Harriers usually pass through in small numbers during May. The northern end of the reservoir is a good place to watch hunting Hobbies from May onwards.

Spring wader passage can be unpredictable and is largely dictated by weather conditions and water levels. Eyebrook is often rather full of water during the spring, and if this is the case waders may be limited to the odd Little Ringed and Ringed Plover, Redshank or Common Sandpiper. However, when the water is lower, a range of species may be present, with Sanderling, Bar-tailed Godwit, Greenshank, Wood Sandpiper and Turnstone all being possible. Temminck's Stints have been seen on a number of occasions in mid-May over the years and this is certainly a species worth searching carefully for, although their habit of hiding in waterside vegetation can make them hard to locate. Little Gulls and Common, Arctic and Black Terns are all regular during late April and May, and in favourable conditions may appear in impressive numbers. Kittiwakes are annual spring visitors, usually in late March or early April. Late March also sees a noticeable movement of Meadow Pipits and Pied Wagtails; these flocks should be searched for White Wagtails, which are regular, and Water Pipits, which are scarce but possibly more frequent than believed. Yellow Wagtails are found in reasonable numbers on spring passage although appear to be declining significantly. A few Whinchats and Northern Wheatears usually pass through, while the hedgerows support a good population of Common Whitethroats.

Breeding birds on the reservoir include Mute Swan, Gadwall, Tufted Duck, Great Crested Grebe and one or two pairs of Common Terns. Sparrowhawks nest in the nearby woods and Little Owls sometimes hunt at dusk from telegraph poles along the road towards Stockerston. The plantation holds

Bewick's Swans

breeding Tawny Owls, Goldcrests, Spotted Flycatchers, Willow Tits and Treecreepers and has in the past attracted Common Crossbills during the summer months in irruption years.

Autumn brings probably the greatest variety of birds to the reservoir. Wader passage commences as early as July, and in addition to those which occur in spring, species may include Grey Plover, Knot, Little Stint, Curlew Sandpiper, Black-tailed Godwit and Spotted Redshank. The best area to look for waders is the northern end by the inflow, but in times of low water levels they can appear almost anywhere, particularly by the island. Wildfowl numbers begin to build up at this time of year, and can include significant flocks of Pintails. Red-crested Pochards are regular in August and September and can often be located among flocks of Coots. Groups of gulls are likely to contain small numbers of Yellow-legged Gulls, and by September there may be as many as 25 roosting at the reservoir. Little Egrets are annual from July to September.

Eyebrook has a good track record for producing rarities, especially waders. Over the years, these have included two Black-winged Stilts, Stone-curlew, Black-winged Pratincole, Killdeer, five Kentish Plovers, American Golden Plover, two Baird's Sandpipers and a Spotted Sandpiper. Rare wildfowl have included four American Wigeons, two Green-winged Teal, Blue-winged Teal, six Ring-necked Ducks and four Ferruginous Ducks, while other goodies have been Night Heron, Squacco Heron, two Great White Egrets, three Caspian Terns, Roseate Tern, five White-winged Black Terns, Shore Lark, Citrine Wagtail and Woodchat Shrike.

Timing

Excellent birdwatching can be enjoyed at this site throughout the year. Wildfowl numbers are at their highest from November to March, and this period is when the gull roost is usually at its best; to view the gull roost, arrive at least an hour before dusk. Passage migrants are present from April to early June and late July to October. If viewing from the western shore the light is better in the afternoons, and during inclement conditions much of the reservoir can be seen from a vehicle.

Access

The reservoir is 2 miles (3.2 km) south of Uppingham. Head south on the A6003 from Uppingham, turn right after 1.5 miles (2.4 km) on to the minor road signed to Stoke Dry and follow the road through Stoke Dry to the reservoir. The road then runs along the north-eastern shore of the reservoir, across the inlet at the northern end and then along almost the whole length of the western side. There is a small car park by the entrance to the plantation at SP852963, and many other places along the road where vehicles can be parked sensibly on the grass verge. The gull roost is best watched from the west shore near the island at SP850951, or if the gulls are loafing in nearby fields the gateway at the top of the hill near the feeding station at SP848947 is a good vantage point.

Access to the plantation, the dam and the hide is restricted to members of either the Leicestershire and Rutland Ornithological Society or the Rutland Natural History Society, but the vast majority of birds on the reservoir can be seen from various points along the road.

Calendar

Resident: Mute Swan, Gadwall, Tufted and Ruddy Ducks, Great Crested Grebe, Cormorant, Red Kite, Sparrowhawk, Common Buzzard, Little and Tawny Owls, Kingfisher, Goldcrest, Willow Tit, Tree Sparrow, Yellowhammer.

October–March: Bewick's Swan (scarce), Greylag Goose, Eurasian Wigeon, Common Teal, Pintail, Shoveler, Pochard, Scaup (scarce), Goldeneye, Smew, Goosander, divers (rare), Slavonian Grebe (scarce), European Golden Plover, Dunlin, Ruff, Common Snipe, Mediterranean, Caspian, Iceland and Glaucous Gulls, Kittiwake, Short-eared Owl, European Stonechat, Fieldfare, Redwing.

April–June: Shelduck, Garganey, Common Scoter (scarce), Black-necked Grebe (scarce), Marsh Harrier (scarce), Osprey, Hobby, Oystercatcher, Little Ringed and Ringed Plovers, Redshank, Common Sandpiper, Little Gull, Kittiwake (scarce), Common, Arctic and Black Terns, Yellow and White Wagtails, Whinchat, Northern Wheatear, Lesser and Common Whitethroats, Spotted Flycatcher.

July–September: Common Teal, Pintail, Garganey, Shoveler, Red-crested Pochard, Pochard, Black-necked Grebe (scarce), Little Egret, Marsh Harrier (scarce), Osprey, Hobby, Little Ringed and Ringed Plovers, Little Stint, Curlew Sandpiper, Dunlin, Ruff, Black-tailed Godwit, Curlew, Spotted Redshank, Greenshank, Green and Wood Sandpipers, Turnstone, Mediterranean, Little and Yellow-legged Gulls, Common and Black Terns, Yellow Wagtail, Whinchat, Northern Wheatear.

15. RUTLAND WATER

OS Landranger 141
OS Explorer 234

Habitat

Constructed as recently as 1975, Rutland Water is the largest man-made reservoir in Britain, with 3,100 acres (1,250 ha) of open water. It was formed by the construction of a dam at the eastern end and subsequent flooding of two shallow valleys of agricultural land. The surrounding area is thus one of gentle shelving natural banks given over to mainly arable farmland away from the immediate vicinity of the reservoir. The reservoir is under the ownership of

Osprey

Anglian Water, and is extensively used for recreational pursuits such as cycling, fishing and sailing. However, the whole of the western end of the reservoir is managed by the Leicestershire and Rutland Wildlife Trust (LRWT) as two nature reserves (at Egleton and Lyndon), and this area covers 555 acres (225 ha). Wildfowl numbers at the reservoir are particularly impressive, and an idea of its importance can be gained from the fact that it regularly holds over 15,000 birds during the winter months, with peaks in some years well in excess of 20,000. This has contributed to Rutland Water's designation as a Site of Special Scientific Interest, a Special Protection Area and a Ramsar Site.

The reserves consist of a range of habitats including three shallow lagoons with purpose-built islands, reedbeds, ancient meadows, hedgerows and small areas of scrub. Plantations created in the late 1970s include dense willow thickets and stands of oak, alder and ash, while the mature deciduous woodland at Lax Hill consists mainly of oak, beech, horse chestnut, sycamore and elm. The Anglian Water Birdwatching Centre at Egleton, which was opened in 1992 and upgraded in 2001, provides a viewing gallery, shop, toilets and educational facilities, and complements the other 21 hides which overlook the two reserves.

Away from the reserves, the LRWT now manage the three mature deciduous woods of Hambleton, Armley and Barnsdale. There are also plantations of young conifers and hardwoods at the base of the Hambleton peninsula. The dam is a good vantage point for looking over the eastern end of the reservoir and also provides a large area of stonework and open grassland as additional habitats.

Species

During the winter months the sheer number of wildfowl makes Rutland Water the single most significant inland site in the region, if not the entire country. Internationally important numbers of Gadwall and Shoveler occur, while the area is of national importance for a further ten species. To give an idea of the numbers involved, the following are the highest counts of 16 species of waterbird between 1999 and 2004: Mute Swan (526), Greylag Goose (340), Canada Goose (1,539), Eurasian Wigeon (3,630), Gadwall (1,529), Common Teal (1,876), Mallard (1,551), Shoveler (1,154), Pochard (742), Tufted Duck (7,496), Goldeneye (511), Ruddy Duck (1,345), Little Grebe (120), Great Crested Grebe (997), Cormorant (655) and Coot (4,021).

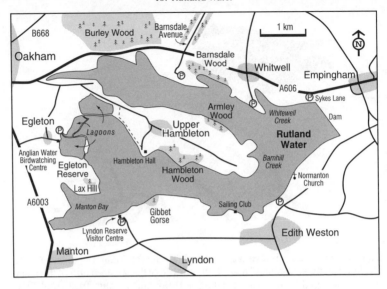

In addition, a wide range of other wildfowl occurs. Goosanders are the most frequent, and the wintering flock regularly numbers in excess of 50. Smew can be relied upon any time between November and March, and during January and February as many as 15 birds may be present, usually on the lagoons at the Egleton reserve. A small flock of Scaup often join the rafts of other Aythya ducks during the winter, and are best looked for on Lagoon III or off the dam. Hard weather sees arrivals of other seaducks, and species such as Long-tailed Duck, Common and Velvet Scoter and Red-breasted Merganser are virtually annual. The deep water off the dam is often where these vagrants are found, and this is also a favoured area for Great Northern Divers and Slavonian Grebes, both of which appear even in winters that are not particularly cold. Red-throated and Black-throated Divers are scarcer, as is Red-necked Grebe, and the area off the sailing club at Edith Weston has a peculiar attraction to the latter species. A few Bewick's Swans are sometimes present on the Egleton Reserve, and the resident flock of feral Greylag Geese may be joined by the occasional Brent Goose or groups of Pink-footed or White-fronted Geese.

Rutland Water has a large gull roost, but due to the size of the reservoir it is not easily watched. A large proportion of the birds roost in the south arm and are best viewed from either Goldeneye hide on the Egleton Reserve or Teal hide on the Lyndon Reserve. Yellow-legged Gulls are regular throughout the autumn and early winter, and numbers have exceeded 30 birds at any one time. Caspian Gulls are being identified with increasing regularity particularly between October and February, while Mediterranean Gulls are also regular in small numbers. Glaucous and Iceland Gulls are surprisingly rare considering the size of the roost, but this may be due to the lack of observers regularly watching the gulls at this site.

Large flocks of European Golden Plovers and Northern Lapwings winter on the Egleton Reserve, and up to 150 Dunlin can be found among them. A flock of Ruffs is often in evidence, usually on Lagoon I, and small numbers of Curlews remain throughout the winter. In recent years, one or two Little Stints and Black-tailed Godwits have overwintered. The secretive Jack Snipe is present in small numbers and a sharp-eyed observer may be lucky

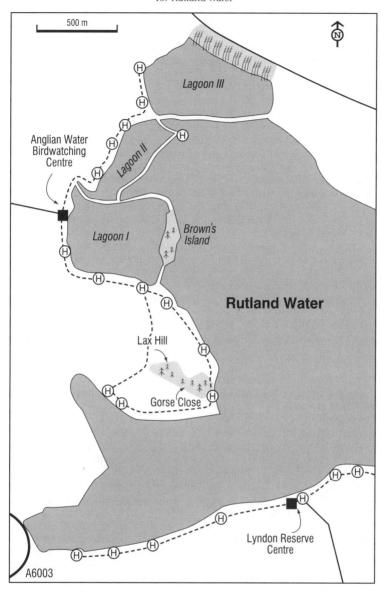

enough to find one at close range from one of the hides on the Egleton Reserve. Other waders to be seen at this time of the year include Common Snipe, Redshank and Green Sandpiper.

Water Rails winter around the Egleton Reserve, where Lagoon III offers an excellent opportunity to see this elusive species as birds are frequently seen feeding on the edge of the reedbed. Patient observers viewing from the hides overlooking this reedbed may be rewarded with a glimpse of a Bittern, a species that is now annual at Rutland Water. Cetti's Warblers and Bearded Tits are occasionally found in the reedbed, but are usually very difficult to see. Raptors include the resident Sparrowhawks, Common Buzzards and Kestrels, all of which can be seen over Burley Wood on fine days. Red Kites are now established in the area, and one or two Peregrine Falcons often visit the lagoons to terrorise ducks and waders during the winter months. Short-eared Owls are regular winter visitors in variable numbers, with the Brown's Island area of the Egleton Reserve being a favoured spot. Long-eared Owls are much scarcer although one or two birds are found most years, often on the Lyndon Reserve.

Wintering passerines are much in evidence around the Egleton Reserve. The feeding station close to the Anglian Water Birdwatching Centre attracts large numbers of Tree Sparrows and the occasional Brambling, while flocks of Siskins and Lesser Redpolls can be found in the alders by Lagoons II and III. Elsewhere around the reservoir, Barnsdale Avenue is a regular site for Bramblings, which feed on beechmast next to the road, while the short grass on the slope of the dam often holds flocks of Yellowhammers and Reed Buntings. This latter area has attracted several Snow and Lapland Buntings in the past, and any finch or bunting flock encountered should be scrutinised for such vagrants.

The first Little Ringed Plovers, Sand Martins and Northern Wheatears arrive from mid-March, and these are closely followed by Ospreys towards the end of the month. Following a reintroduction scheme at the reservoir, small numbers of this fish-eating raptor are now regular throughout the summer and a well-protected breeding population is slowly becoming established. While nest sites are obviously kept secret, birds can readily be seen around the reservoir, and the dead trees and specially erected platforms in Manton Bay are a good place to enjoy prolonged views. Another raptor worth keeping an eye out for during the spring is Marsh Harrier, which is regular during May. Hobbies can be seen hunting around the lagoons, sometimes in small groups.

Spring passage is at its peak from mid-April to late May, during which time an impressive selection of migrant birds for an inland site can be found. Much attention is focused on waders, and the shallow lagoons provide ideal feeding habitat for species such as Sanderling, Black-tailed and Bar-tailed Godwits, Whimbrel, Greenshank, Wood Sandpiper and Turnstone, all of which are frequent in small numbers, especially during the first few days of May. Rarer visitors which appear with some regularity include Temminck's Stint and Avocet, and a pair of the latter even attempted to nest on Lagoon I in 1996. The ideal weather for passage waders is easterly winds, and these conditions also produce Little Gulls and Arctic and Black Terns, all of which may appear in large flocks. Odd Sandwich and Little Terns are often associated with these movements. Other species which regularly appear on spring passage include Black-necked Grebes, which often favour the north arm or Lagoon III, and Garganeys, which invariably find the shallow water of Lagoon I to their liking. Northern Wheatears can be found on open grassy areas, with the dam being the most regular spot, and small numbers of Common Redstarts and Whinchats are found most springs.

The Egleton Reserve is the summer home to good populations of all the common warblers, with particularly notable totals of Reed and Grasshopper Warblers. Nightingales have declined in recent years, but several pairs still return to breed each summer; Barnsdale and Hambleton Woods are reliable sites, and most years there are one or two on both the Egleton and Lyndon Reserves. Nest-boxes in the plantation of ash trees close to the Anglian Water Birdwatching Centre hosts a thriving colony of Tree Sparrows, and among other summer visitors Sand Martins nest in the specially created wall next to Lagoon II and the declining Turtle Dove still hangs on in small numbers around the old meadows on the Egleton Reserve. The lagoons attract a good variety of breeding wildfowl and waders, including Egyptian Goose, Shelduck, Gadwall, Shoveler, Tufted Duck, Great Crested Grebe, Oystercatcher, Little Ringed Plover, Northern Lapwing and Redshank. A small colony of Black-headed Gulls, the only one in Leicestershire, has become established on the Egleton Reserve, where up to 50 pairs of Common Terns also breed. Cormorants nest on the lagoons and in the north arm and their numbers have increased dramatically over the last ten years to around 150 pairs.

Autumn passage begins in late June, when small numbers of Green Sandpipers appear on the lagoons. A recent development has been the regular arrival of large flocks of Black-tailed Godwits in July, which have numbered well in excess of 50 on several occasions. Wader passage continues until early November, peaking in August and September, and usually involves a greater variety of species than in the spring. Little Stints and Curlew Sandpipers can appear in reasonable sized flocks in good years, while birds such as Grey Plover, Knot and Spotted Redshank are regular. The largest numbers of waders in the autumn are usually found in Manton Bay, although in times of low water levels the exposed shore of the south arm around Hambleton Hall can be very productive. As in spring, easterly winds bring passage Black Terns, and occasionally flocks numbering several hundred may arrive; Little Gulls and Kittiwakes may often be found in similar conditions. Arctic Terns are much scarcer in the autumn and most records refer to juveniles.

Wildfowl numbers build up during the autumn and the peak counts of several species often occur in September. Up to 150 Pintails are present, while Garganey are regular on the lagoons and may involve as many as ten birds during August. Red-crested Pochards appear in small numbers during the autumn, as do Black-necked Grebes. Little Egrets are now an increasingly regular sight around the reserves from July to October, with a peak count of nine in 2004.

Migrant passerines during the autumn are usually restricted to a few Northern Wheatears and Whinchats, although easterly winds between late September and early November are likely to produce Rock Pipits, with the stonework of the dam being the most regular site. There is of course always the chance of a surprise, such as the Yellow-browed Warbler found in the Sykes Lane car park by the dam in October 2005.

Gales during the autumn, especially in September, often result in storm-driven seabirds appearing, and there have been several records of Fulmar, Manx Shearwater, Leach's Storm-petrel, Gannet and Arctic and Great Skuas. All four county records of Sabine's Gull have occurred at Rutland Water, along with Leicestershire's one and only Long-tailed Skua. Peculiarly, a large proportion of these seabirds have been seen in the north arm. Similar weather conditions during October often produce Grey Phalaropes, and a number of Little Auks have appeared in this month.

Rutland Water's inland location, away from any major river system, makes the occurrence of rarities unpredictable in spite of its large size, although some outstanding birds have been found since its construction. Associating with the vast numbers of wildfowl, rarities to have been found have included American Wigeon, four Green-winged Teal, Blue-winged Teal, five each of Ring-necked Duck and Ferruginous Duck, four Lesser Scaups and Europe's second Redhead. Scarce waders have been represented by Collared Pratincole, American Golden Plover, three White-rumped Sandpipers, several Pectoral Sandpipers, a Long-billed Dowitcher and a Lesser Yellowlegs.

Other exciting birds located over the years have included Night Heron, Cattle Egret, three Great White Egrets, Red-footed Falcon, three Ring-billed Gulls, two Caspian Terns, Roseate and Bridled Terns, nine White-winged Black Terns, Alpine Swift, Shore Lark, Red-throated Pipit, Bluethroat, two Savi's Warblers and six Arctic Redpolls.

Timing
Rutland Water is excellent at any time of the year, and the sheer size of the reservoir easily fills a full day's birdwatching. The eastern end of the reservoir around the dam is best visited early in the morning before the area becomes too disturbed with boats and windsurfers; the light is also better here at this time of day. In strong sunlight, viewing from some of the hides on the Egleton Reserve is difficult during the morning. The reservoir is very popular on sunny weekends and bank holidays, especially with cyclists, but the size of the area means that direct disturbance to birdlife is minimal.

Access
Rutland Water lies just to the east of Oakham and is easily reached from the Al via the A606 west of Stamford, and from the A47 along the A6003 north of Uppingham. The Anglian Water Birdwatching Centre and Egleton Reserve are accessed by turning east off the A6003 1 mile (1.6 km) south of Oakham towards Egleton and following the signposted road to the car park at SK878073. The staff at the Birdwatching Centre are very helpful and have up-to-date information about birds on the reserve. The reserve is open daily throughout the year between 9 am and 5 pm, closing at 4 pm from November to January. A permit is required and is available from the Centre, cost £4 for adults, £3 for senior citizens and £2 for children and students. This permit also gives access to the Lyndon reserve, which is reached by turning east off the A6003 2.5 miles (4 km) south of Oakham. Travel through Manton and then take the signposted minor road on the left after 1.2 miles (2 km) to the car park at SK894057. The reserve is open daily, excluding Mondays, from April to October and at weekends and bank holidays at other times of year.

The north arm is best viewed from the end of the track off the minor road 1 mile (1.6 km) west of Upper Hambleton at SK888085. It is worth scanning for raptors over Burley Wood to the north from here. Much of the south arm can be viewed from the track which leaves the minor road on the Hambleton peninsula half a mile (0.8 km) west of Upper Hambleton at SK892080; this track runs along the north shore of the south arm to Hambleton Hall and onwards through Hambleton Wood. Manton Bay, which is an excellent area for waders in the autumn, can be viewed from the A6003 at SK877052. However, parking here is difficult and the road is very busy, so caution should be exercised at all times.

To view the dam and adjacent areas of open water, park either in the Sykes Lane car park at the northern end of the dam (SK937081) or on the wide verge next to the minor road at the southern end of the dam (SK945072). Other parking areas are available around the reservoir which give views over the open water: on the north shore at Barnsdale (SK908088) and Whitwell (SK925081) and on the south shore at Normanton (SK929059).

Calendar
Resident: Mute Swan, Greylag and Egyptian Geese, Gadwall, Shoveler, Tufted and Ruddy Ducks, Little and Great Crested Grebes, Cormorant, Grey Heron,

Red Kite, Sparrowhawk, Common Buzzard, Kestrel, Woodcock, Barn and Tawny Owls, Kingfisher, Green and Great Spotted Woodpecker, Tree Sparrow.

November–March: Bewick's Swan (scarce), Eurasian Wigeon, Common Teal, Pintail, Red-crested Pochard, Pochard, Scaup, Long-tailed Duck (rare), Common Scoter, Velvet Scoter (rare), Goldeneye, Smew, Red-breasted Merganser (scarce), Goosander, Red-throated Diver (rare), Black-throated Diver (scarce), Great Northern Diver, Red-necked Grebe (scarce), Slavonian Grebe, Bittern (scarce), Peregrine Falcon, Water Rail, European Golden Plover, Dunlin, Ruff, Jack and Common Snipe, Curlew, Redshank, Green Sandpiper, Mediterranean, Yellow-legged and Caspian Gulls, Iceland Gull (rare), Glaucous Gull (rare), Kittiwake, Long-eared Owl (rare), Short-eared Owl, Fieldfare, Redwing, Siskin, Lesser Redpoll.

April–June: Garganey, Common Scoter, Black-necked Grebe, Marsh Harrier, Osprey, Hobby, Oystercatcher, Little Ringed and Ringed Plovers, Sanderling, both godwits, Whimbrel, Redshank, Greenshank, Wood and Common Sandpipers, Turnstone, Little Gull, Kittiwake, Common, Arctic and Black Terns, Turtle Dove, Cuckoo, Sand Martin, Yellow Wagtail, Nightingale, Whinchat, Northern Wheatear, Grasshopper, Sedge and Reed Warblers, Blackcap, Garden Warbler, Lesser and Common Whitethroats, Common Chiffchaff, Willow Warbler, Spotted Flycatcher.

July–October: Pintail, Garganey, Red-crested Pochard, Black-necked Grebe, Little Egret, Marsh Harrier, Osprey, Hobby, Little Ringed, Ringed and Grey Plovers, Knot, Sanderling, Little Stint, Curlew Sandpiper, Dunlin, Ruff, Black-tailed Godwit, Whimbrel, Spotted Redshank, Greenshank, Green, Wood and Common Sandpipers, Turnstone, Mediterranean, Little and Yellow-legged Gulls, Common and Black Terns, Rock Pipit (scarce), European Stonechat, Northern Wheatear.

16. SENCE VALLEY FOREST PARK

OS Landrangers 128 and 129
OS Explorers 232 and 245

Habitat

This 150 acre (60 ha) area, in the wide open valley of the River Sence, has been transformed from a disused opencast mine into a popular country park. Following the closure of the colliery several subsidence pools formed and the area reverted to rough grassland, and after being planted with over 98,000 trees the site was opened to the public in September 1998 as part of the National Forest. Other lakes have been created, bringing the total number of pools at the site to seven, while a wildflower meadow and some areas of rough grassland remain. A hide overlooks the Stonebridge Pool and wader scrape, and an artificial Sand Martin nesting wall has been constructed alongside Horseshoe Lake.

Species

Sence Valley Forest Park is one of the most important areas locally for wintering and breeding passerines, although the loss of large areas of rough grassland following the planting of thousands of trees has unfortunately had a detrimental effect on some species.

During the winter European Stonechats are regular visitors, with double-figures recorded on occasions. They can, however, be extremely mobile, and may be encountered anywhere, although the area between the main car park and Horseshoe Lake is often a good place. A pair remained throughout the summer in 2002 and raised four young, providing Leicestershire with its first breeding record of this species since the 19th century. A wintering finch and bunting flock is usually present somewhere near the hide and in the past contained small numbers of Corn Buntings; unfortunately, as with a number of other areas locally, this species now seems to have disappeared. More recently, with the continued growth of the many planted trees, flocks of Lesser Redpolls have become regular, particularly in the alder blocks to the west of the hide. Small numbers of Siskins often accompany these flocks, which are well worth scrutinising further as there have been several records of Mealy Redpoll, as well as an Arctic Redpoll in January 2006.

The site is not generally renowned for wildfowl, but reasonable numbers of Eurasian Wigeons, Common Teal and Pochards are usually present. A small wintering flock of Goosander can be found, often on the two most northerly pools in the park. Scarcer species such as Bewick's Swan, Red-crested Pochard, Scaup and Smew have all been recorded. Prior to the extensive tree planting at the site, the area proved attractive to wintering geese, and White-fronted and Brent were both seen, while in November 2004 a small flock of Pink-footed Geese was found feeding in winter wheat to the north of the park. In recent years, one or two Little Egrets have taken to wintering in the area. Common Snipe and Green Sandpiper can usually be seen on one of the pools, and one or two Jack Snipe lurk in the marshy areas.

Several species of raptor are possible during the winter months. As well as the resident Sparrowhawks and Kestrels, Common Buzzards are frequently seen flying over, Peregrine Falcon and Merlin are occasional visitors and there have been several records of Hen Harrier. Short-eared Owls are regular winter visitors in small numbers and can often be seen hunting at dusk around the sheep field at the north end of the park.

During the spring, the air resounds to the song of good numbers of otherwise declining species such as Grey Partridge, Skylark, Meadow Pipit, Linnet, Yellowhammer and Reed Bunting. Notable summer visitors include Sand Martins, which nest in the artificial wall adjacent to Horseshoe Lake, and Grasshopper Warblers, of which one or two can be heard singing from the areas of new plantings. Good numbers of Yellow Wagtails appear in April, with several pairs remaining to breed. Spring flocks of this species have occasionally been accompanied by Blue-headed Wagtails, while Water Pipit has also been recorded in early spring. The park is probably the best site in Leicestershire for finding passage Whinchats and Northern Wheatears, which appear in good numbers during the spring and autumn. Both species can occur anywhere, and may often be found on the paths and adjacent fence posts. Common Redstarts often associate with these two species, especially in the spring. The areas of rough grassland have proved attractive to Quails in recent springs, and this is one of the most regular sites in the county to listen for the distinctive call of this uncommon gamebird. Several Garganeys have been noted on both spring and autumn passage in recent years.

Spring mornings are good times to hear or see the local Curlews, which breed in nearby fields, and the site is slowly developing a reputation for producing passage waders. Little Ringed and Ringed Plover, Redshank and

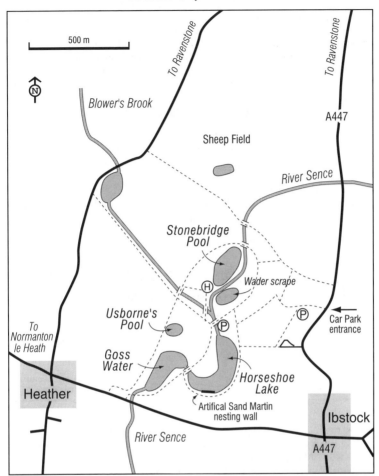

Green and Common Sandpiper are the most frequent, while Dunlin and Greenshank are regular. Other species of note recorded in recent years have been several Black-tailed Godwits and Wood Sandpipers, while rarities have included a Temminck's Stint in May 2000 and a Pectoral Sandpiper in October 2005. The best places to search for waders are either the scrape next to the hide or the shallow flash in the sheep field at the north end of the park.

Timing

The site is probably at its best in the winter months, when passerine flocks, raptors and wildfowl are all in evidence. However, the park can become extremely busy at weekends, and the general public and their associated dogs seem to be louder than average in this part of the world. Therefore, early mornings, evenings and weekdays are recommended.

Access

Sence Valley Forest Park is located between the villages of Ibstock and Heather, about two miles (3.2 km) south-west of Coalville. The main car park, which is open from 8 am until dusk every day, is signed off the A447 half a mile (0.8 km) north of Ibstock at SK405118, and from here several well-made footpaths criss-cross the park. Toilets and an information board can be found in the car park. Access is also possible on foot along the track which runs south-east from the minor road between Heather and Ravenstone at SK396122; this track gives views over the pool in the sheep field, but parking is extremely limited. Valuables should not be left in vehicles at any time, as the car park has a reputation for break-ins.

Calendar

Resident: Tufted Duck, Grey Partridge, Great Crested Grebe, Sparrowhawk, Common Buzzard, Kestrel, Curlew, Skylark, Meadow Pipit, Linnet, Yellowhammer, Reed Bunting.

October–March: Eurasian Wigeon, Common Teal, Pochard, Goosander, Little Egret (scarce), Merlin (scarce), European Golden Plover, Common Snipe, Jack Snipe, Green Sandpiper, Short-eared Owl (irregular), European Stonechat, Lesser Redpoll, Siskin.

April–September: Garganey (scarce), Quail, Little Ringed Plover, Redshank, passage waders, Sand Martin, Yellow Wagtail, Common Redstart (scarce), Whinchat, Northern Wheatear, Grasshopper Warbler.

17. SOAR VALLEY GRAVEL PITS

OS Landrangers 129 and 140
OS Explorers 233 and 246

The River Soar flows roughly south to north through Leicestershire, before joining the Trent on the Nottinghamshire border near Kegworth. Since the 1950s sand and gravel have been extracted from the Soar Valley for a distance of about 3 miles (4.8 km) north of Leicester, leaving a chain of flooded disused gravel workings from Cossington in the north to Watermead Country Park South, which lies just inside the city boundary, to the south. Although many of these pits are now used for leisure activities, particularly water sports, and others have been filled in, there are still relatively undisturbed areas to be found which provide suitable habitats for many species of birds. The stretch from Wanlip south to the city boundary has been a country park, controlled by Leicestershire County Council and Leicester City Council, for several years. Originally, this was something of a mixed blessing for wildlife, as although the habitats became protected, the benefits were countered by a large increase in disturbance from the growing numbers of visitors attracted to the site. However, two areas (at Cossington and Wanlip) have since been purchased by the Leicestershire and Rutland Wildlife Trust (LRWT) and are now managed as nature reserves, while further habitat improvement has been carried out in other areas of the valley, making the whole area one of the best birdwatching sites in Leicestershire.

The following sites are detailed in geographical order, from Cossington Meadows at the northern end of the valley to Watermead Park in the south.

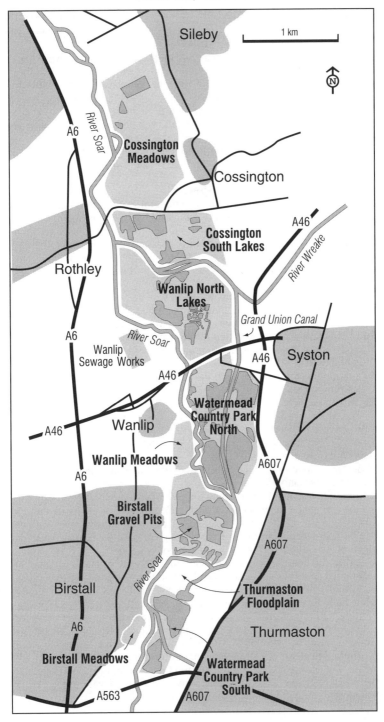

17A. COSSINGTON MEADOWS

Habitat

Following gravel extraction in this area, most excavated areas were back-filled with inert waste; parts were then covered with topsoil, while others developed into shallow pools. The site was purchased in 2004 by the Leicestershire and Rutland Wildlife Trust (LRWT) and developed as a nature reserve. This 173 acre (70 ha) area of riparian floodplain now contains a mosaic of valuable wetland habitats, with deep lakes, shallow pools, wet grassland and swamp. Various wetland creation projects are being undertaken at the reserve and new reedbeds are being planted. In addition, there are areas of hawthorn scrub and old hedgerows.

Species

During the winter months the main attraction at this site is Short-eared Owls, and over the last few years Cossington Meadows has become one of the most reliable sites in Leicestershire to see this fantastic species. Up to four birds may be present between November and April, with the rough vegetation around 'The Moor' being a favoured spot. A very obliging Hen Harrier wintered in the same area in 2002-03 and was often seen in close proximity to the owls.

The three lakes hold wintering wildfowl, with the dominant species being Eurasian Wigeon, Gadwall, Common Teal, Tufted Duck and Great Crested Grebe. Small numbers of other ducks such as Shoveler, Goosander and Ruddy Duck may be present, and a long-staying Velvet Scoter in the winter of 2002-03 provided observers with remarkable views and demonstrated the site's ability to attract vagrant species. Green Sandpipers winter in reasonable numbers (up to eight), with the 'Upper Marsh' being a good place to look. Common Snipe frequent the boggy areas and a few Jack Snipe lurk in the wet grasslands.

'The Moor' often has one or two wintering European Stonechats and there have been several recent records of Water Pipit, especially in the 'Upper Marsh' area. Roving tit flocks are worth checking as a Firecrest was seen with one such group in 2003.

Breeding species on the reserve include Gadwall, Tufted Duck, Great Crested Grebe, Little Ringed Plover and, most significantly, Redshank, while a pair of Oystercatchers and a few Ringed Plovers are usually present during the spring and may breed in the area. Common Terns are regular and in 2005 made use of the newly-installed rafts. Several Grasshopper Warblers can be heard singing from the areas of rough grassland and may occasionally provide extended views atop a tangle of bramble.

Spring and autumn passage periods can be interesting at this site, and the substantial areas of shallow pools and wet fields prove attractive to wildfowl and waders alike. Garganey are found most years, usually in April or August, while Little Egrets have become annual in July and August. Regular waders include Dunlin, Ruff, Greenshank, Green Sandpiper and Common Sandpiper, along with increasing visits by small flocks of Black-tailed Godwits and occasional Wood Sandpipers. Migrant Whinchats and Northern Wheatears are frequently encountered in spring and autumn, and White Wagtails are regular in April around the edges of the pools. Small parties of Hobbies are seen in late summer and autumn, when they can be watched hunting dragonflies over the pools.

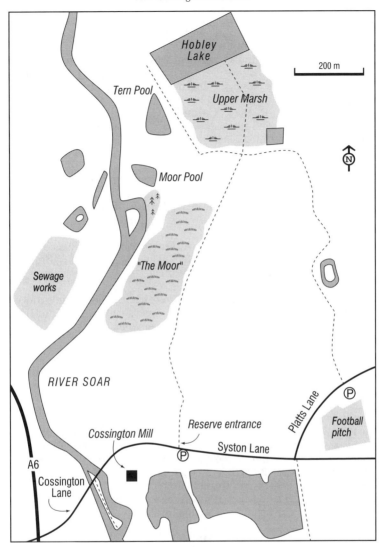

Timing

The site is worth a visit at any time of the year and timing is not too critical as there is very little disturbance in the area. If searching for Short-eared Owls, calm evenings between November and April offer the best opportunities. Passage waders may be present in spring and autumn depending on weather conditions. It is worth bearing in mind that, following heavy rain, large parts of the reserve will become inaccessible.

Access

The reserve lies 5.5 miles (8.8 km) north of Leicester and 5 miles (8 km) south-east of Loughborough. From the old A6 (Loughborough Road) in Rothley, turn east by the library on to Cossington Lane, crossing under the A6 bypass and then over the River Soar at Cossington Mill. Park in the lay-by on the left after 200 m at SK597131 and enter the reserve on foot via the obvious track by the information board. Alternatively, continue past the lay-by, turn left on to Platts Lane and park by the football pitch at SK603132; from here, a public footpath leads north to the site. The reserve is open at all times, but can become extremely wet following rain; wellingtons are therefore recommended. In times of flood, access to the area may be practically impossible.

Calendar

Resident: Gadwall, Tufted Duck, Red-legged Partridge, Great Crested Grebe, Sparrowhawk, Kestrel, Kingfisher, Great Spotted Woodpecker, Bullfinch, Reed Bunting.

November–March: Greylag Goose, Eurasian Wigeon, Common Teal, Shoveler, Goosander, Ruddy Duck, Cormorant, Jack Snipe, Common Snipe, Green Sandpiper, Short-eared Owl, Water Pipit (rare), European Stonechat, Fieldfare, Redwing, Lesser Redpoll.

April–June: Shelduck, Garganey (scarce), Oystercatcher, Little Ringed Plover, Ringed Plover, Redshank, Common Tern, White Wagtail (April), Northern Wheatear, Grasshopper Warbler, Sedge Warbler.

July–October: Garganey (scarce), Little Egret (scarce), Hobby, Little Ringed Plover, Dunlin, Ruff, Black-tailed Godwit, Greenshank, Green Sandpiper, Wood Sandpiper (scarce), Common Sandpiper, Whinchat.

17B. COSSINGTON SOUTH LAKES AND WANLIP NORTH LAKES

OS Landranger 129
OS Explorer 246

Habitat

This large area, bordered by the A607 to the east, the A46 to the south and the River Soar to the west, has huge potential but unfortunately much of the land is private and only visible with difficulty from certain spots. Cossington South Lakes contains three large pits which are given over for fishing, while Wanlip North Lakes has another three large pits which are extensively used for sailing, along with several smaller areas of water. Much of the surrounding area is grazing land which is subject to regular flooding. Areas of thick hawthorn scrub can be found at Wanlip North Lakes.

Species

As these two sites are more or less private they are paid little attention by local birdwatchers, although in the past certain individuals have obtained permission to enter the area and have provided an insight into what may be seen there.

The pits at Cossington South are quite deep and in the winter hold reasonable numbers of diving ducks including a few Goldeneye, and a Great Northern Diver spent a while here in January 1995. The grazing land and wet fields at Wanlip North attract good numbers of Eurasian Wigeons and Common Teal. The hawthorn scrub in this area was, for many years, a regular wintering roost site for up to ten Long-eared Owls, and it is to be assumed that birds are still present somewhere in the vicinity.

Notable breeding species include Grey Partridge and Barn Owl around Cossington South, while Oystercatcher, Little Ringed and Ringed Plover, Redshank and Common Tern have all bred at Wanlip North in the past.

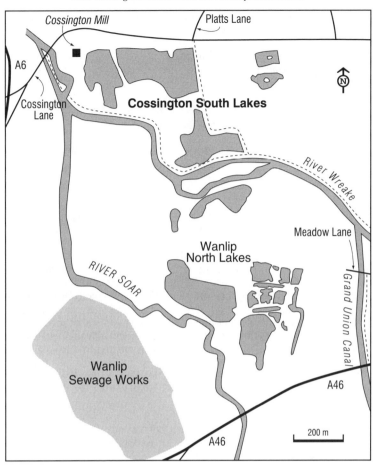

This area certainly deserves more attention, and to demonstrate its potential a Great White Egret was found in the Wanlip North area in November 2005.

Timing
Due to the access difficulties at these sites, timing is not a factor.

Access
Much of this area is private and as such viewing can be problematical. Cossington South Lakes are best accessed by turning east off Loughborough Road next to the library in Rothley on to Cossington Lane and following the road under the A6 and past Cossington Mill to the lay-by on the right at SK601130. From here, one of the pits can be viewed adequately. A public footpath runs south from this point and meets the River Wreake, passing another pit on the right. Continuing south alongside the Wreake provides distant views towards Wanlip North Lakes. The only other opportunities to watch the latter site are by parking at Cossington Mill (SK595130) and following the footpath south alongside the western bank of the River Soar, or by viewing from the verge of the A46 just north of Wanlip at SK603113; the latter option

should only be attempted with extreme care, as this is a particularly fast and busy stretch of road with no parking facilities.

Calendar

Resident: Mute Swan, Grey Partridge, Great Crested Grebe, Sparrowhawk, Kestrel, Barn Owl, Kingfisher, Reed Bunting.

October–March: Greylag Goose, Eurasian Wigeon, Gadwall, Common Teal, Pochard, Tufted Duck, Goldeneye, Long-eared Owl (scarce).

April–September: Oystercatcher, Little Ringed Plover, Ringed Plover, Redshank, Common Tern, Yellow Wagtail.

17C. WATERMEAD COUNTRY PARK NORTH AND WANLIP MEADOWS

OS Landranger 129
OS Explorer 246

Habitat

The northern section of Watermead Country Park, often referred to as Wanlip South Gravel Pits, consists of four large lakes and several smaller pools, and is managed by Leicestershire County Council. Of the largest lakes, one is used for sailing but the other three currently have no recreational use other than a small amount of fishing. A sizeable reedbed has become established to the west of the entrance track, with associated scrub of willows and sallows. Three hides have been erected in this area, along with a well-established artificial Sand Martin nesting bank. A new feature is the development of the excellent Wanlip Meadows Nature Reserve, which was purchased by the Leicestershire and Rutland Wildlife Trust in 2004. This 39 acre (16 ha) area appeared by accident; following gravel extraction the land was filled with inert waste and covered with topsoil, but this work was unsuccessful and the area reverted to a permanent scrape, providing the best piece of habitat in the Soar valley for waders. A large hide has been erected giving commanding views over the reserve.

Species

Wildfowl dominate the avian scene during the winter months, with the most notable feature being a large flock of Goosanders, numbers of which regularly reach over 60 birds. They prefer John Merrick's Lake, although can range widely over the whole area and beyond. The pits have the usual complement of diving ducks, including reasonable numbers of Goldeneye, and there are occasional visits by other species such as Scaup and Smew. Dabbling ducks are best looked for at Wanlip Meadows, where large numbers of Common Teal can be found, along with Eurasian Wigeons, Shovelers and sometimes a few Pintails.

Wanlip Meadows provides good habitat for wintering waders, and there are often up to 1,000 European Golden Plovers crammed on to the scrape. Numerous Common Snipe feed in the wet margins, although their true numbers are only usually revealed when the birds are flushed by a passing Sparrowhawk or Kestrel. Several Jack Snipe also hide in the wet vegetation, but as ever are difficult to locate.

Flocks of Siskins and Lesser Redpolls roam the site, but are best looked for around the reedbed, where good numbers of Water Rails winter. It is well worth keeping a listen out for Cetti's Warblers in this area, as there have been

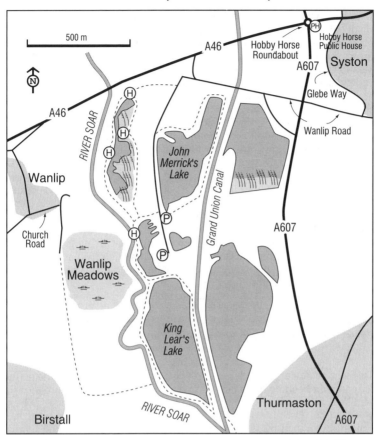

several recent winter records of this inveterate skulker. Easier to locate will be Common Chiffchaff, and up to five birds regularly winter in the reedbed. A small feeding station in the Sensory Garden, close to John Merrick's Lake, often attracts a few Bramblings.

By early spring, the first Oystercatchers, Ringed Plovers and Redshanks will have returned to Wanlip Meadows, and one or two pairs of each usually breed somewhere in the vicinity. A small heronry contains 10-15 nests and birds will be already on eggs by March. This is a good time of year to look for Lesser Spotted Woodpeckers, and the tall trees between the reedbed and the Wanlip Meadows hide are a reliable place to see drumming birds on calm days. The first spring migrants are invariably Sand Martins, which use the artificial nesting bank to good effect. A pair of Kingfishers often takes over one of the holes in the bank, and several other pairs nest in the area.

A selection of summer migrants breed in the country park, with the most noticeable being Reed Warblers, which nest at high density in the reedbed and other isolated stands of *Phragmites*. Sedge Warblers are also widespread, and the rough grassland around Wanlip Meadows usually attracts several singing Grasshopper Warblers. One or two Turtle Doves hang on in the area, but have declined over recent years. Among the resident breeding birds, Willow Tit is perhaps of most interest and several pairs can be found, particularly around the reedbed.

Easterly winds during late April and early May usually see the arrival of small parties of Arctic and Black Terns, with occasional Little Gulls associating with them. The larger areas of water, such as King Lear's Lake, are where these transients are usually found. Waders are restricted to Wanlip Meadows, but given suitable weather conditions and water levels a good variety may be found. Little Ringed Plover, Dunlin and Common Sandpiper are regular, and Black-tailed Godwit is becoming increasingly so, while species such as Grey Plover, Sanderling, Greenshank and Wood Sandpiper are recorded in most springs. In addition, the site is developing something of a reputation locally for producing Temminck's Stints during mid-May. Autumn wader passage usually involves much the same species, although Little Stint and Ruff are more likely at this time of year.

Late summer sees a pre-roost gathering of gulls at Wanlip Meadows, and between July and October there are regular records of Yellow-legged and Mediterranean Gull, the latter often involving pristine juvenile birds. Large numbers of Common Terns that have bred elsewhere in the valley bring their recently-fledged young here and join the gulls. Hobbies are regularly seen during the summer, often in the evenings, and sightings of Ospreys are becoming more regular. One or two Garganeys often join the returning Common Teal from August onwards, and there is a good chance of locating a Little Egret in the late summer and autumn.

This is the longest established and probably the most watched area of the Soar valley, and has inevitably attracted a number of scarcities over the years; these have included Great White Egret, Spotted Crake, Black-winged Pratincole, Pectoral Sandpiper and Marsh Warbler.

Timing

This section of the Soar Valley is worth visiting at any time of year. The country park can become quite busy at weekends, but generally disturbance to birdlife is minimal. Due to the position of the sun, Wanlip Meadows is best viewed from the hide in the mornings and from the west side in the evenings, although by summer it is often difficult to see on to the scrape from ground level as the surrounding vegetation tends to obscure much of the area; at these times, using the hide is the best option.

Access

This section of the Soar Valley is 4 miles (6.4 km) north of Leicester and immediately west of Syston. It is best reached by heading north from Leicester on the A607 and turning left 500 m south of the A46/A607 roundabout on to the minor road signed to Watermead Country Park next to the obvious large lake. Bear left at the small roundabout and the entrance to the country park is on the left at SK606113. An entry fee of £1.50 per vehicle is charged. The country park is open to vehicles from 8.30 am to dusk, although pedestrian access is possible at all times. The hides are open from 8.30 am to 4 pm.

Alternative access to Wanlip Meadows is possible from Wanlip village. Leave the A46 Leicester Western Bypass midway between the A46/A607 and A46/A6 roundabouts at SK600111 and head in to Wanlip. Turn left on to Church Road and at the end turn right on to an unmade road. Limited parking is available at the end of this track (SK601106), and a footpath gives views from the west side of the reserve.

Most footpaths around the area are well-made but, as with other parts of the Soar Valley, after heavy rain some paths may become inaccessible.

Calendar

Resident: Mute Swan, Greylag Goose, Gadwall, Tufted Duck, Little Grebe, Great Crested Grebe, Grey Heron, Sparrowhawk, Kestrel, Kingfisher, Green Woodpecker, Great Spotted Woodpecker, Lesser Spotted Woodpecker, Willow Tit, Reed Bunting.

October–March: Eurasian Wigeon, Common Teal, Pintail (scarce), Shoveler, Pochard, Goldeneye, Goosander, Water Rail, European Golden Plover, Jack Snipe, Common Snipe, Green Sandpiper, Cetti's Warbler (scarce), Brambling, Siskin, Lesser Redpoll.

April–June: Shelduck, Garganey (scarce), Osprey (scarce), Hobby, Oystercatcher, Little Ringed Plover, Ringed Plover, Grey Plover (scarce), Temminck's Stint (rare May), Dunlin, Black-tailed Godwit, Redshank, Greenshank (scarce), Wood Sandpiper (scarce), Common Sandpiper, Little Gull, Common Tern, Arctic Tern, Black Tern, Turtle Dove, Sand Martin, Yellow Wagtail, White Wagtail (April), Whinchat, Northern Wheatear, Grasshopper Warbler, Sedge Warbler, Reed Warbler.

July–September: Common Teal, Garganey, Shoveler, Little Egret, Osprey (scarce), Hobby, Little Ringed Plover, Ringed Plover, Little Stint (rare), Dunlin, Ruff, Common Snipe, Black-tailed Godwit, Redshank, Greenshank, Green Sandpiper, Wood Sandpiper (scarce), Common Sandpiper, Mediterranean Gull, Yellow-legged Gull, Common Tern, Black Tern (scarce), Turtle Dove, Sand Martin, Yellow Wagtail, Sedge Warbler, Reed Warbler.

17D. BIRSTALL GRAVEL PITS

OS Landrangers 129 and 140
OS Explorer 233

Habitat

This section of the Soar valley, which covers approximately 98 acres (40 ha) and contains nine small areas of water, has been designated as a nature reserve. Most of the pits are well-vegetated with reed and bulrush, although the two largest expanses of water, Key Lake and Worcester Lake, enjoy a more open aspect. With the exception of a large area of rough grassland adjacent to Worcester Lake, most of the surrounding land is thick with willow and hawthorn scrub, along with several good stands of alders. Two small hides, which are unfortunately often locked, overlook various areas of water.

Species

The principal attraction is wintering wildfowl; this is enhanced by the fact that the birds have become accustomed to large numbers of people and as such are often remarkably tame, making this site excellent for photography. The commoner ducks such as Eurasian Wigeon, Gadwall, Common Teal and Shoveler are joined by good numbers of Goosanders between November and April, which may number up to 60 birds. This is a reliable site for Smew, and up to four birds may be present between December and March, usually favouring the larger areas of water such as Worcester Lake. There have been occasional records of other scarce waterbirds such as Scaup, Red-breasted Merganser and Black-necked Grebe, although other sites in the Soar valley are usually more productive for species such as this. Water Rails are quite numerous during the winter months and, although usually only heard uttering their distinctive squeals, patient observers may be rewarded

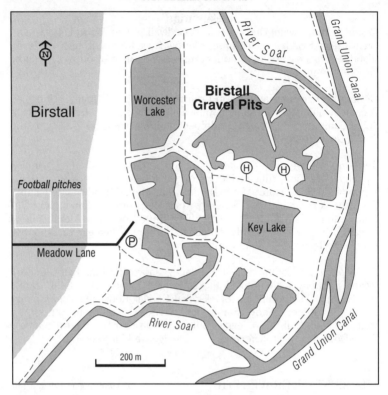

with close views from the hides. Between October and April, the stands of alders attract Siskins and Lesser Redpolls, often in reasonable numbers, and these flocks are worth checking for Mealy Redpolls, which have occurred on more than one occasion. The large rough field adjacent to Worcester Lake is a fairly regular site for European Stonechat during the winter months, and the thick vegetation around the pits, particularly near the hides, often harbours one or two wintering Common Chiffchaffs. A Long-eared Owl roost became established in the hawthorn scrub near the hides in the early 1990s and, although there have been no records of this species for several years, one or two birds may still persist in the area.

Breeding birds include Grey Heron, and around 50 pairs nest in the trees near the hide, making this the largest heronry in Leicestershire. Cormorants can be found roosting here, and it seems likely that this species will nest some time soon. This area has also attracted several Little Egrets in recent years, which more often than not join the roosting Cormorants and Grey Herons. Other resident species include Kingfisher and Willow Tit, both of which occur in reasonable numbers, while Tawny Owls usually nest in the more mature trees near the Meadow Lane car park and can sometimes be found roosting in the open during the day. Water Rails have bred and may do so regularly, although they are difficult to find among the thick vegetation. The resident species are augmented during the spring and summer by large numbers of warblers, and the areas of scrub are particularly good spots for Sedge Warbler and Lesser Whitethroat.

Wader passage is rather poor, due to a combination of lack of suitable habitat and human disturbance, and is much more productive in other parts of the Soar Valley. The occasional Common Sandpiper or Dunlin may drop in to Key Lake, while Oystercatchers and Little Ringed Plovers, both of which breed regularly in other parts of the Soar Valley, can often be found wandering the area. Likewise, migrant terns are more likely to be found elsewhere in the valley, although during favourable easterly winds in the spring Black Terns have appeared over Worcester Lake.

Timing
This section of the Soar Valley is very popular with dog walkers, especially at weekends, although direct disturbance to birdlife is minimal. However, any passage waders which may have taken up temporary residence on Key Lake are easily flushed, meaning an early morning visit is to be recommended.

Access
This area lies 3.5 miles (5.6 km) north of Leicester. From the A6/A563 roundabout south of Birstall (Red Hill Circle) take the minor road north-east signed to Birstall and at the next roundabout after 1.2 miles (2 km) take the second exit (Wanlip Lane). After half a mile (0.8 km) turn right on to Lambourne Road (next to a small row of shops), then first left on to Blenheim Road and first right on to Meadow Lane. A free car park can be found at the end of Meadow Lane (SK602096). From here, access is via several footpaths, which give good views over the pits.

Calendar
Resident: Tufted Duck, Great Crested Grebe, Cormorant, Grey Heron, Water Rail, Tawny Owl, Kingfisher, Great Spotted Woodpecker, Willow Tit.

October–March: Eurasian Wigeon, Gadwall, Common Teal, Shoveler, Pochard, Goldeneye, Smew, Goosander, European Stonechat, Common Chiffchaff, Siskin, Lesser Redpoll.

April–September: Oystercatcher, Little Ringed Plover, Common Sandpiper, Common Tern, Sedge and Garden Warblers, Lesser Whitethroat.

17E. WATERMEAD COUNTRY PARK SOUTH, THURMASTON FLOODPLAIN AND BIRSTALL MEADOWS

OS Landranger 140
OS Explorer 233

Habitat
This section of the Soar Valley was excavated in the early 1980s and now consists mainly of two sizeable flooded pits, one with a large island attractive to breeding terns and waders. As the area has matured some reasonable stands of *Phragmites* have developed around the edges of the lakes; much of the other vegetation is made up of willow and hawthorn scrub. The two lakes and surrounding land, which are within the Leicester city boundary, are managed by Leicester City Council as part of the larger Watermead Country Park. Immediately to the north, a further area of pits has now been filled in and has formed an extensive area of wet rough grassland known as Thurmaston Floodplain. Outside of the official country park boundary, between the River Soar and Birstall, a semi-permanent area of floodwater has developed in recent years, providing excellent habitat for waders and wildfowl; this area, which has great potential, is now referred to locally as Birstall Meadows.

Species

Winter sees good numbers of wildfowl at this site, attracted by the never-ending procession of bread-bearing members of the public. Large groups of Mute Swans and Canada Geese are immediately evident, with numbers in 2004 peaking at 251 and 508 respectively. The northern lake is favoured by diving ducks, with three-figure flocks of Pochard and Tufted Duck being regular, along with smaller numbers of Goldeneye, Goosander and Great Crested Grebe. This lake has produced records of Great Northern Diver and Red-necked and Slavonian Grebes in recent years. Dabbling ducks prefer the southern lake or Birstall Meadows, with the dominant species being Eurasian Wigeon, Gadwall, Common Teal and Shoveler. The growths of reeds around both lakes harbour a few Water Rails.

Thurmaston Floodplain is a regular wintering site for one or two European Stonechats, and in good years Short-eared Owls may be seen quartering the rough grassland. The boggy areas here contain large numbers of Common Snipe, with recent counts of up to 150 birds; several Jack Snipe are also usually present, but as ever are difficult to find.

Spring sees the arrival of several notable breeding birds. The island on the northern pit is home to a small colony of Common Terns, where breeding waders are represented by Oystercatcher, Little Ringed Plover, Northern Lapwing and occasionally Redshank. Every area of reed around the lakes resounds to the chuntering song of numerous Reed Warblers, while there is often a Grasshopper Warbler to be heard reeling on Thurmaston Floodplain. Other breeding species include Tufted Duck, Little Grebe and Kingfisher.

As the lakes are two of the largest areas of water in the Soar Valley, they regularly attract passage Arctic and Black Terns during the spring, with the occasional Little Gull accompanying them. Black-necked Grebes are almost annual in spring and autumn, and there have been a number of records of Common Scoter, mostly during early spring.

The two lakes do not provide much suitable habitat for passage waders but the semi-permanent floodwater of Birstall Meadows is ideal; small pools also often form on the floodplain, which may hold the occasional migrant. The commoner species such as Ringed Plover, Dunlin, Redshank, Green Sandpiper and Common Sandpiper are usually represented, while Black-tailed Godwit and Greenshank are not infrequent. Wood Sandpiper also turns up with some regularity. In addition, passage Garganeys have been noted on a number of occasions.

This section of the Soar valley has been one of the most regularly watched over the years, and has inevitably attracted a few scarcities, including Brent Goose, Common Eider, Bittern, Lesser Yellowlegs, White-winged Black Tern, Marsh Warbler and Snow Bunting.

Timing

This is a very popular area with dog-walkers and families, especially around the northern lake, although the majority of birds present seem to have become accustomed to screaming children and swimming canines and as such direct disturbance is not too much of a problem. However, warm sunny weekends are probably best avoided. When viewing Birstall Meadows, strong evening sunlight can be a problem. As with other sections of the Soar valley, some areas may become inaccessible after heavy rain.

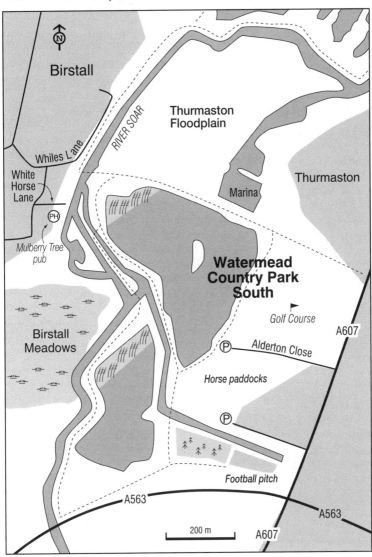

Access

This section of the Soar Valley lies on the northern edge of Leicester and immediately south-east of Birstall. The two large pits are best accessed by heading north-east out of Leicester on the A607, crossing over the A563 south of Thurmaston and turning left after a further 500 m on to Alderton Close (signed to Watermead Country Park South). A free car park is located at the end of this road adjacent to the largest lake (SK602086), and from here several well-made footpaths lead around the area. Thurmaston Floodplain can be reached via the path along the northern edge of the largest lake although may be inaccessible during times of flood. Birstall Meadows is viewable from the towpath of the River Soar which runs between the river and the southern lake (SK599086).

Calendar

Resident: Mute Swan, Canada Goose, Greylag Goose, Tufted Duck, Little and Great Crested Grebes, Sparrowhawk, Kestrel, Northern Lapwing, Tawny Owl, Kingfisher, Grey Wagtail, Reed Bunting.

October–March: Eurasian Wigeon, Gadwall, Common Teal, Shoveler, Pochard, Goldeneye, Goosander, Ruddy Duck, Water Rail, Jack Snipe, Common Snipe, Short-eared Owl (scarce), European Stonechat, Fieldfare, Redwing.

April–September: Shelduck, Garganey (scarce), Common Scoter (scarce), Black-necked Grebe (scarce), Hobby, Oystercatcher, Little Ringed and Ringed Plovers, Dunlin, Redshank, Green and Common Sandpipers, Common Tern, Arctic Tern (passage), Black Tern (passage), Yellow Wagtail, Grasshopper, Sedge and Reed Warblers.

LINCOLNSHIRE

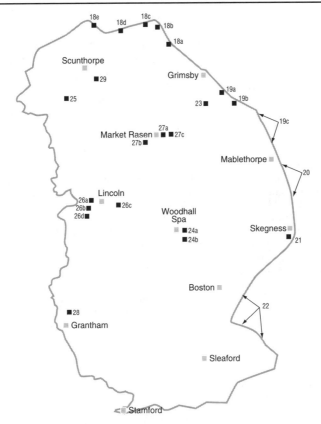

Coastal Lincolnshire

18. The Inner Humber
18A. Killingholme Haven Pits
18B. East Halton Skitter to Goxhill
     Haven
18C. Goxhill Haven to New Holland
18D. Barrow Haven to Barton-upon-
     Humber Clay Pits
18E. South Ferriby, Read's Island and
     Winteringham Haven
19. The north-east coast
19A. Cleethorpes to Humberston
     Fitties
19B. Tetney to Northcoates Point
19C. Donna Nook to Mablethorpe
20. The east coast: Sutton on Sea to
     Chapel St Leonards
21. Gibraltar Point
22. The Wash

Inland Lincolnshire

23. Covenham Reservoir
24. Kirkby on Bain area
24A. Kirkby Moor and Moor Farm
24B. Kirkby on Bain Gravel Pits
25. Laughton Forest
26. Lincoln area
26A. Boultham Mere
26B. Hartsholme Country Park and
     Swanholme Lakes
26C. North Witham Fens
26D. Whisby Nature Park and North
     Hykeham Pits
27. Market Rasen area
27A. Linwood Warren and
     Willingham and Walesby Woods
27B. Toft Newton Reservoir
27C. Wold Scarp
28. Marston Sewage Treatment
     Works
29. Messingham Sand Quarry

There is a pronounced change in the character of the River Humber from the largely sandy and gentle shelving open mudflats of the outer estuary south-east of Grimsby, to the less extensive but richer silt-laden intertidal shoreline of the upper reaches west of Skitter Ness. Areas of saltings are restricted in width, but some interesting short grass still exists in places where cattle are present to graze the sward. The sea defences are a mixture of natural grass-covered clay banks and man-made stone and tar constructions, with extensive tracks along the bank tops, offering the best viewpoints for birding at several localities. The areas of intertidal mud are in a constant state of flux within a dynamic estuary where the currents frequently change, moving vast amounts of silt and materials in short periods of time and quickly changing the local geography. The richest feeding areas for waders and wildfowl are found where the tides deposit the rich silt brought down by the Rivers Trent and Ouse from their confluence at Alkborough. As the nature of the estuary changes upriver from Grimsby so does the variety of birds which predominate, and to see the maximum number of species it is necessary to visit one of the outer estuary sites in addition to the Inner Humber.

Differences in substrate, even on a localised level, have effects on the bird communities which make use of them, with the more stony intertidal areas and extensive beds of seaweed attracting different species to the open soft silt areas, which again differ from the drier upper shoreline mud and tidal creeks.

18A. KILLINGHOLME HAVEN PITS

OS Landranger 113
OS Explorer 284

Habitat

This relatively small site, composed of three flooded clay pits and managed as a nature reserve by the Lincolnshire Wildlife Trust (LWT) has, over the last 35 years, proved to be one of the best spots in Lincolnshire for watching waders. The site, which has an enviable list of rare species to its credit, lies adjacent to the southern bank of the Humber estuary, with industrial areas to the north and west and agricultural fields to the south. The largest pit, adjacent to the Humber bank, is brackish and has a mix of shallow water, open mud, islands and beds of *Phragmites* and *Juncus* bordered with tall hawthorn hedgerows. A hide overlooks this pit, the water level of which is controlled to provide optimum conditions for waders. The two smaller freshwater lagoons are deeper and have extensive fringes of reed and sedge, along with areas of invading hawthorn and blackthorn scrub.

The adjacent Humber shore has a narrow stony fringe, with open mudflats at low tide. Some small stands of reeds have become established between the sea wall and the Humber itself. The open estuary can be of interest during rough weather, when seabirds and wildfowl may be seen, and the concrete sea wall offers a vantage point overlooking both the estuary and the main lagoon.

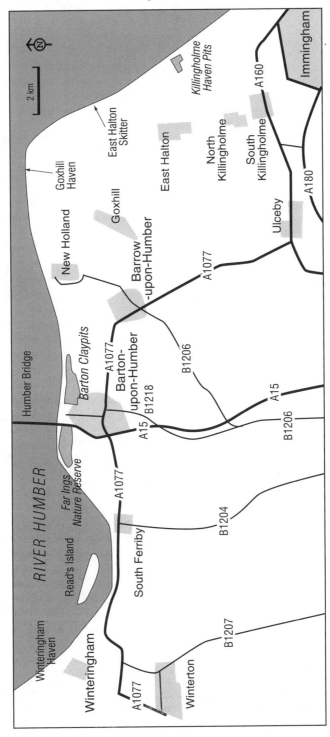

Species

In general the water levels are at their highest during the winter period, so birding interest centres mainly on wildfowl. The pits hold good numbers of Common Teal and Shovelers, with smaller numbers of Shelducks, Gadwall, Pochards and Tufted Ducks. One or two Smew are seen most winters, and during bad weather there have been records of Scaup, Red-throated Diver and Red-necked and Slavonian Grebes. Small parties of Bewick's and Whooper Swans occasionally appear, although their occurrences have become less frequent in recent years.

The variety of waders found during the winter does not compare to that of the spring and autumn, but a few species are present in good numbers. Northern Lapwings are usually the most numerous, closely followed by Redshanks, which can total up to 150 birds, and Dunlins. The shallow areas near the Humber bank may hold up to 100 Common Snipe, a few Jack Snipe are annual, and small numbers of Curlews and the occasional Bar-tailed Godwits are found. A wintering population of Black-tailed Godwits became established on the outer Humber in the mid-1990s and a few birds visit the area during the winter; however, a phenomenal count of 2,900 was made in December 2004.

Gulls often drop in to bathe on their way to roost on the Humber; Black-headed and Common are the most numerous, but a few large gulls appear from time to time with Glaucous in some winters. The expanding reedbeds hold reasonable numbers of Water Rails and occasional Bearded Tits, and one or two Bitterns are seen in most winters, sometimes giving good views to patient observers as they feed in the narrow reed fringes around the islands and pit edges. Long-eared Owls roost in the hawthorn scrub and Short-eared Owls are often seen over the grazing marshes to the north-west and south-east. Snow Buntings have sometimes wintered along the sea wall.

A recent feature of early spring has been the arrival of small numbers of Avocets at the pits, with up to 23 in March 2005 and 52 in April 2006. During April, the concrete sea walls provide attractive feeding areas for flocks of Yellow and Pied Wagtails, along with a few Northern Wheatears. In mid- or late May, hunting Long-eared Owls may be seen over adjacent rough grass fields well before dark, when they offer exceptional views. Marsh Harriers, which are increasing on the Humber, are usually seen several times during the spring, and Osprey is more or less annual on passage.

Breeding species include good populations of Sedge and Reed Warblers in the *Phragmites* and sedges around the pits, while Grasshopper Warblers are regular in rough grass areas among the industrial sites. A variety of other warblers occur in the hawthorns, with Lesser Whitethroats being numerous. Breeding wildfowl include Mute Swan, Greylag and Canada Geese and Little Grebe, while Ruddy Duck has nested in the past. Water Rails have bred in recent years and one or two pairs of Oystercatchers usually attempt to do so.

Waders occur in their greatest numbers and variety during the spring and autumn migration periods, which may in effect merge together with the last northbound waders passing in early June and the first returning Ruffs and Green Sandpipers appearing from mid-June. Regular passage species include Little Stint, Curlew Sandpiper, Ruff, Bar-tailed Godwit, Spotted Redshank, Greenshank and Green, Wood and Common Sandpipers. The adjacent shore attracts feeding Ringed Plover, Whimbrel and Turnstone. Numbers of Redshanks peak in August, with counts of 900 in 1995 and 600 in 2005, while Dunlin are at their most numerous in October, when over 1,000 may be present. Black-tailed Godwits arrive from July onwards and

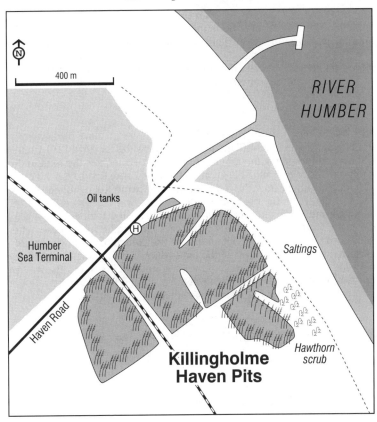

have shown a huge increase over the last ten years; in 1995, a flock of 178 in August was a record total, but in September 2004 and 2005 counts of 2,500 and 2,750 respectively were made. The list of vagrant waders is a long one, and includes no fewer than five Nearctic species: American Golden Plover, White-rumped, Baird's and Pectoral Sandpipers and two Lesser Yellowlegs, the more recent of which spent over a month on the main lagoon in the autumn of 2005. In addition, there have been records of Kentish Plover, Temminck's Stint, Sharp-tailed Sandpiper and Red-necked and Grey Phalaropes. Being a regularly watched site, other vagrants have been found over the years, including Ferruginous Duck, Purple Heron, Red-footed Falcon, White-winged Black Tern and Wryneck.

Spoonbills were regular visitors during the late 1970s but were then not seen for many years until six were recorded between May 2003 and June 2004. Wandering Little Egrets are becoming more frequent and may be encountered at any time of year, although spring and autumn are favoured.

Strong northerly to easterly winds and rain may force seabirds up the Humber, and the concrete sea wall offers a place from which to watch the estuary during such conditions. The range of species varies depending on the time of year, but can include seaducks, Arctic and Great Skuas, Kittiwakes, terns or Common Guillemots, any of which may occur in reasonable numbers.

Timing

Something of interest may be found throughout the year, but spring and autumn passage periods are the most productive. With the highest tides being early morning and early evening, these are the best times to see the largest numbers of waders. In strong sunlight, viewing is best from the sea wall in the morning and from the hide in the evening. Disturbance from the industrial areas is at its lowest in the evenings and on Sundays.

Access

The reserve lies on the Humber bank 3.1 miles (5 km) north-west of Immingham. From South Killingholme, travel east on the A160 for 1.2 miles (2 km) and turn left at the roundabout at TA170166. Follow the road under a railway bridge and after 100 m turn left on to Rosper Road. After 1.3 miles (2.2 km) turn right on to Haven Road (signed North Killingholme Haven) and the pits are on the right either side of the railway crossing at TA163198. Parking is rather limited, and it is not advisable to view the pits from a vehicle as the road can be very busy with heavy lorry traffic; in any case, better views can be obtained from either the sea wall, which runs along the north-eastern edge of the main pit, or the hide, which is next to the road halfway between the railway crossing and the haven mouth. The pit to the west of the railway line is only viewable from the road, and the increased amount of vegetation now present makes this difficult.

Calendar

Resident: Mute Swan, Little Grebe, Water Rail, Kingfisher.

October–March: Shelduck, Gadwall, Common Teal, Pintail, Shoveler, Pochard, Tufted Duck, Smew (scarce), vagrant seaducks and grebes, Cormorant, Bittern, Northern Lapwing, Dunlin, Jack and Common Snipe, Black-tailed Godwit, Curlew, Redshank, Long-eared and Short-eared Owls, European Stonechat, Bearded Tit.

April–September: Eurasian Wigeon, Common Teal, Garganey (scarce), Shoveler, Marsh Harrier, Oystercatcher, Avocet, Ringed Plover, Little Stint, Curlew Sandpiper, Dunlin, Ruff, both godwits, Whimbrel, Curlew, Redshank, Greenshank, Green and Common Sandpipers, Turnstone, Common Tern, Cuckoo, Long-eared Owl, Yellow Wagtail, Northern Wheatear, Grasshopper, Sedge and Reed Warblers, Lesser and Common Whitethroats.

18B. EAST HALTON SKITTER TO GOXHILL HAVEN

OS Landranger 113
OS Explorer 284

Habitat

From East Halton Skitter to Goxhill Haven, a formerly grazed area of foreshore has been allowed to revert to rough grassland and, being above the reach of even the highest tides, it is largely dry. The areas adjacent to East Halton Skitter are the wettest and are covered in sea aster, attracting flocks of finches and buntings later in the year. Several small stands of reed have become established on the saltmarsh, while inland from the sea wall the area is mainly a mixture of arable land and hawthorn hedges. A series of old borrow pits, with some open water and reedbeds, can be found against the sea defence banks; these include the Lincolnshire Wildlife Trust reserve of Dawson City Clay Pits at Skitter Ness, which consists of two disused clay pits,

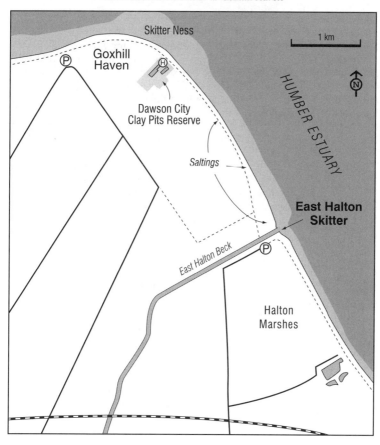

associated reedbeds and extensive areas of pasture and hawthorn scrub. A hide overlooks the two pits.

Species

Wintering Short-eared Owls are a speciality of this section of the Humber, with up to four birds usually hunting the foreshore; in good winters, such as in 2001, as many as ten may be present. Some birds linger well into May and have been seen displaying on occasions. Barn Owls are also regular, while Kestrels, Sparrowhawks and the odd Merlin hunt the area. The foreshore attracts flocks of Reed Buntings, Yellowhammers, Chaffinches and Tree Sparrows, with the occasional Twite, Lapland Bunting or Snow Bunting joining them. Rock Pipits are a common sight feeding on the rocky shoreline and among the flooded sea aster. They reach peak numbers in late October and early November when up to 40 birds may be present, but through the winter up to ten is a more usual total. European Stonechats are regular winter visitors in small numbers; up to three are usually seen, but eight were noted in November 2002.

During the winter months, waders on the foreshore consist mainly of Dunlin and Redshank, with a few Ringed Plovers, the odd Grey Plover or Turnstone and sometimes a group of Knot. The main flock of wintering Curlews, which may number up to 200, is usually to be found on the inland fields, particularly near the Dawson City Clay Pits reserve. These arable fields also contain large flocks of Northern Lapwings and European Golden Plovers, with numbers of the latter sometimes reaching 7,000. A walk across the rough foreshore may well flush a few Common Snipe and the odd Jack Snipe, which are also regular at the Dawson City reserve. The close-grazed saltmarsh at the Goxhill end of the section provides a roost site for waders at high tide, as well as a feeding area for a flock of Eurasian Wigeon. Small numbers of other wildfowl winter on the borrow pits, including Pochard, Ruddy Duck and Great Crested Grebe, while on the Humber itself rafts of Goldeneye may drift by on falling tides before flying back towards their favoured feeding area a little further west at New Holland.

Spring passage groups of Ringed Plovers, Grey Plovers, Sanderlings, Dunlins and Turnstones all occur along the shore from April to early June. Flocks of non-breeding Curlews are present throughout the summer, increasing during June with arrivals of continental birds. A few pairs of Redshank breed on the foreshore and one or two pairs of Oystercatchers and Northern Lapwings do likewise on the inland fields. Other breeding species include good numbers of Sedge and Reed Warblers, especially at the Dawson City reserve, where Water Rails also nest and Bitterns have done so in the past. Turtle Doves are regularly seen during the breeding season and Marsh Harriers are becoming increasingly frequent any time between April and August.

During the autumn, the exposed mud on the edges of the borrow pits attracts Ruff, Greenshanks and Green Sandpipers, with irregular visits from species such as Little Stint, Curlew Sandpiper, Spotted Redshank and Wood Sandpiper. The usual mix of Ringed Plovers, Dunlins, Bar-tailed Godwits, Curlews and Redshanks is found on the shore.

Although not a particularly well-watched area, a few rarities have been found over the years. These have included Green-winged Teal, Ferruginous Duck, two Little Bitterns, Spoonbill, Red-footed Falcon, Pectoral Sandpiper and Alpine Swift.

Timing

Winter is the peak season to visit this area in order to look for Short-eared Owls, with late afternoon usually providing the best opportunity for seeing them. Although there can be some good numbers of waders to search through, larger flocks can be found further west along the estuary. Even so, a knowledge of the tide times is useful, as closer views of the birds can be obtained just prior to high tide. Some shooting takes place by wildfowlers at East Halton Skitter, so these days are obviously best avoided.

Access

East Halton Skitter lies 5.6 miles (9 km) north-west of Immingham. The village of East Halton is reached via minor roads from either South Killingholme or Barrow upon Humber. In the centre of the village, just north of the Black Bull public house, the main road bends sharply at a right angle; from here, take the minor road east named Towles Corner, which immediately bears sharply to the left. After 400 m, bear right on to Townside and follow the road over a railway bridge. A minor road on the right leads to some reed-fringed pits (TA154212), while East Halton Skitter is reached by continuing north from the railway bridge for 1.6 miles (2.5 km) to the end of the road (TA146228). Park here and walk along the grass sea wall which runs north, watching for Short-eared Owls, pipits, finches and buntings on the saltmarsh.

The village of Goxhill, situated 5 miles (8 km) east of Barton-upon-Humber, is approached via minor roads from Barrow upon Humber. On entering the village follow signs to North End and continue north on Ferry Road to the Haven a further 1.9 miles (3 km) to the north-east (TA119252). Park on the roadside and walk east along the stone sea wall for 1 mile (1.6 km) to the Dawson City Clay Pits Reserve on the right at TA130253. The entrance is by the stile at the north-western corner and the hide is located along the waymarked route between the two pits. The sea wall continues to East Halton Skitter, a further 1.9 miles (3 km) to the south-east.

Calendar
Resident: Common Teal, Shoveler, Sparrowhawk, Kestrel, Water Rail, Northern Lapwing, Curlew, Redshank, Barn Owl, Skylark, Meadow Pipit, Yellowhammer, Reed Bunting.

October–March: Eurasian Wigeon, Pochard, Goldeneye, Ruddy Duck, Great Crested Grebe, Merlin, Ringed, European Golden and Grey Plovers, Dunlin, Jack and Common Snipe, Black-tailed Godwit, Turnstone, Short-eared Owl, Rock Pipit, European Stonechat, Tree Sparrow, Twite (scarce), Lapland Bunting (rare), Snow Bunting (scarce)

April–September: Marsh Harrier, Oystercatcher, Ringed Plover (passage), Grey Plover (passage), Sanderling (passage), Little Stint (scarce, August and September), Curlew Sandpiper (scarce, August and September), Dunlin (passage), Ruff, Bar-tailed Godwit, Spotted Redshank (scarce), Greenshank, Green Sandpiper, Turnstone (passage), Turtle Dove, Cuckoo, Sedge and Reed Warblers, Common Whitethroat.

18C. GOXHILL HAVEN TO NEW HOLLAND OS Landrangers 112 and 113
OS Explorers 281 and 284

Habitat
The sea wall between Goxhill Haven and New Holland pier is a barren stone construction, and the intertidal zone is quite restricted on all but the highest 'spring' tides. However, the presence of a grain and animal feed import and export terminal at New Holland Pier has inadvertently, through spillage, provided an important winter feeding resource for large flocks of wildfowl. A flooded clay pit (Fairfield Pit) just west of the pier is managed by the Lincolnshire Wildlife Trust as a nature reserve, and during the late summer the water level often falls to reveal a series of muddy islands attractive to waders and wildfowl.

Species
The winter period offers some exceptional birding along this section of the Humber. Large numbers of wildfowl gather to feed on the grain and animal feeds spilt from the old pier during shipping operations, which washes downriver towards Goxhill Haven. The diving duck flock is of most interest, with numbers building up from November and reaching a peak in January or February; the highest counts usually coincide with severe weather. Pochards predominate, and have peaked at over 2,000 in the past, with smaller flocks of Tufted Ducks and Scaup, of which numbers of the latter vary from about ten to over 260 in influx years. However, it is the impressive numbers of Goldeneyes which really catch the eye, and the site is of national

importance for this species: over 350 are counted most winters, and 584 were recorded in December 2000. November usually produces a flock of Common Scoters, which is often accompanied by a few Velvet Scoters and odd Long-tailed Ducks and Common Eiders, but all of these species depart by the end of December. A herd of up to 150 Mute Swans feed near the pier and are joined by small numbers of Whooper Swans most winters: these birds resort to Fairfield Pit during rough weather and at high tide. The Whoopers generally leave the area by March, although two immature birds summered in 1998. Fairfield Pit and the ski pit to the east of the grain terminal have good numbers of Little Grebes, with a variety of other ducks present in the winter.

Roosting waders at high tide include Ringed Plover, Dunlin, Redshank and Turnstone, while the fields immediately inland hold vast flocks of up to 4,000 European Golden Plovers and 2,000 Northern Lapwings. One or two Merlins are regular and there are occasional sightings of Hen Harrier and Peregrine Falcon. Flocks of Skylarks are a feature of frosty weather, feeding on the winter cereal fields, and small groups of Snow Buntings may be found along the sea wall, especially in November.

Spring and summer offer fewer rewards. Little Grebes and Ruddy Ducks breed on Fairfield Pit, where the non-breeding herd of Mute Swans summers and a pair of Oystercatchers usually attempt to nest. Good numbers of Sedge and Reed Warblers and Common Whitethroats can be found around Fairfield Pit, along with a few Grasshopper Warblers. During March and early April, it is worth looking on the stony shore of the Humber for Rock Pipits, which at this time of year are often of the Scandinavian subspecies *littoralis*. Marsh Harriers are being seen more regularly during the spring and summer.

If the water level drops on Fairfield Pit, there may be passage waders from late July onwards: Ruff, Black-tailed Godwit, Greenshank and Common Sandpiper are the most regular, with occasional Little Stints. On the fields and shore to the east the flock of European Golden Plovers increases to about 1,000 by late August, along with a similar number of Northern Lapwings, up to 200 Dunlins, 100 Redshanks and 80 Turnstones. In influx years, good numbers of Curlew Sandpipers may also be found in this area.

Timing

This site predominantly concentrates on wintering wildfowl, and therefore any time between October and March is the best period to visit. Numbers of most ducks are at their highest during January and February, especially during severe weather, although a greater variety of species is usually present during November. Calm days are best, as the Humber can become quite choppy due to the combined effects of wind and tide, making viewing difficult. The two or three hours around high tide are when the birds are most settled, and they will often drift closer to the shore. As the tide falls, parties of ducks drift off east towards Goxhill Haven, eventually flying back to the feeding area.

Access

For New Holland, leave the A1077 at Barrow upon Humber and take the B1206 north-east. On the southern outskirts of New Holland village, turn left at the roundabout and follow the bypass to a railway crossing. Immediately over the crossing turn left down a track between the railway and a warehouse, round a sharp right bend with a flooded clay pit (Fairfield Pit) to the left and park at the end of the track at TA080243. Fairfield Pit can be viewed from the track or the sea wall to the east of the car park. To obtain the best views of the

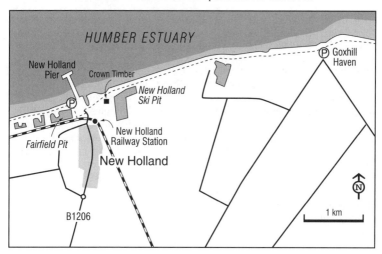

duck flock in the winter, walk back along the track to the railway crossing and then turn immediately left. Go through a green gate next to a red road barrier and follow the footpath signs between the warehouses to rejoin the sea wall after about 200 m next to Crown Timber. From here the Humber becomes visible, and views over New Holland ski pit are also possible.

Calendar

Resident: Mute Swan, Ruddy Duck, Little Grebe, Sparrowhawk, Curlew, Redshank, Kingfisher.

October–March: Whooper Swan, Pochard, Tufted Duck, Scaup, Common Eider, Long-tailed Duck, Common and Velvet Scoters, Goldeneye, Hen Harrier, Merlin, Peregrine Falcon, Ringed and European Golden Plovers, Northern Lapwing, Dunlin, Turnstone, Snow Bunting (scarce).

April–September: Marsh Harrier, Oystercatcher, Ringed Plover (passage), European Golden Plover (August onwards), Little Stint (scarce, August and September), Curlew Sandpiper (scarce, August and September), Dunlin (passage), Ruff, Black-tailed Godwit, Greenshank, Common Sandpiper, Turnstone (passage), Rock Pipit (April), Grasshopper, Sedge and Reed Warblers, Common Whitethroat.

18D. BARROW HAVEN TO BARTON-UPON-HUMBER CLAY PITS

OS Landranger 112
OS Explorer 281

Habitat

A series of abandoned clay pits lies inland from the Humber Estuary, between Barrow Haven and Chowder Ness. All of these were excavated in the heyday of the local brick and tile industry which flourished between 1850 and 1950. The pits, which lie mostly between the Humber bank and the Cleethorpes to Barton-upon-Humber railway line, form a complex of deep water areas interspersed with shallower sections and extensive reedbeds. The surrounding areas consist mainly of hawthorn and blackthorn scrub with invading willows and sallows in some of the drier reedbeds. Several of the pits are used for fishing and water sports but a significant proportion are managed by the Lincolnshire Wildlife Trust as nature reserves. At the eastern end of this section is the Barrow Haven Reedbed reserve, a 32 acre (12.7 ha) abandoned clay pit with extensive reedbeds, patches of hawthorn scrub and rough grassland, overlooked by a hide. The Pasture Wharf reserve is located halfway between Barrow Haven and the Humber Bridge, and is a 52 acre (21 ha) area of open water and reedbeds, along with 0.8 miles (1.3 km) of fore-shore. The jewel in the crown is the impressive Far Ings National Nature Reserve, between Barrow-upon-Humber and Chowder Ness, which was pur-chased in 1983 and expanded to 200 acres (81 ha) in 2004. Here, a total of eight hides overlook areas of open water, reedbed and scrub. In addition, the new Waters' Edge Country Park was officially opened in 2005, just to the east of the Humber Bridge; this developing 86 acre (35 ha) site contains lagoons, reedbeds and woodland walks. The intertidal zone of the adjacent Humber Estuary here comprises a rich mixture of silt and stony sections.

Species

During the winter, the flooded clay pits attract large numbers of wildfowl, with the dominant species being Pochard, Tufted Duck, Gadwall, Shoveler, Eurasian Wigeon, Ruddy Duck and Goldeneye. The latter may be present in particularly significant numbers during February and March, after the end of the shooting season, and a count of 135 was made in March 1999. Smew are regular winter visitors, preferring the pits to the west of the town, while small numbers of Pintail and Goosander are seen at this time of year. Of the scarcer species, Scaup is regular and there have been records of as many as 50 on the pits during rough weather, while Red-necked, Slavonian and Black-necked Grebes appear with some frequency. Any of the three divers may occur in hard weather, with Red-throated the most likely.

The extensive reedbeds contain large numbers of wintering Water Rails, with up to 80 estimated in the area in December 2001. A few Bearded Tits can also be found during the winter months, and several Bitterns lurk in the reedbeds, giving views to patient observers. One or two Marsh Harriers usu-ally remain in the area at this time of year. One species that has appeared in a few recent winters is Cetti's Warbler but, as ever, getting good views of the birds can prove difficult.

The hawthorn and blackthorn scrub which surrounds the pits occasion-ally harbours roosting Long-eared Owls in winter, when the berry crop sustains flocks of Fieldfares and Redwings for a few weeks. Willow Tits and Tree Sparrows both regularly visit feeding stations at Far Ings and Waters' Edge Country Park. Small flocks of Siskins and Lesser Redpolls may be encountered and are worth checking for Mealy Redpolls, which have occurred on a number of occasions.

The foreshore has in recent years become more important for feeding waders and there are good numbers of several species to be seen at low tide. Dunlin is the most numerous, with midwinter peaks sometimes reach-ing 2,000, while significant numbers of Redshanks, Ringed Plovers and Turnstones are all present. These large gatherings attract the occasional Grey Plovers or Bar-tailed Godwits. Jack Snipe winter in the area in small numbers, but are more likely to be found around the clay pits.

Spring sees the arrival of large numbers of warblers to the clay pits, and the reedbeds hold significant breeding populations of Reed Warblers (over 300 pairs) and Sedge Warblers (over 130 pairs). Lesser and Common Whitethroats and Garden Warbler are all widespread in the scrubby areas,

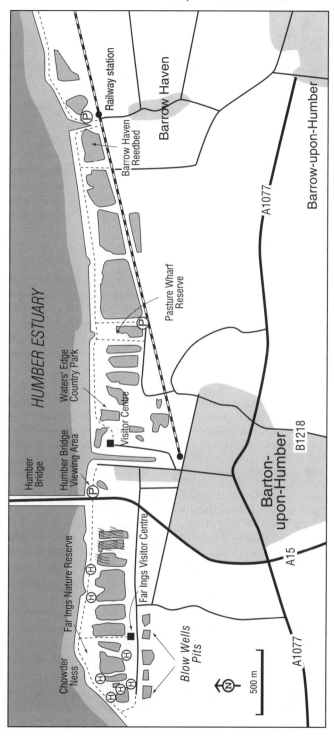

Bittern

and are joined by singing Grasshopper Warblers in April and May, some of which may remain throughout the summer. The reedbeds also contain breeding Water Rails, which can be heard singing from March to June, and Marsh Harriers are a regular sight during the spring and summer. A few pairs of Bearded Tits nest in these areas, but numbers have unfortunately been declining of late from a peak of 35 pairs in 1983. A major success story, however, has involved Bitterns; thanks to appropriate management of the reedbeds, the species bred in the area in 2000 after an absence of 21 years. The reserves here and elsewhere on the south bank of the Humber are now one of the national strongholds of this enigmatic bird.

A good selection of wildfowl breeds on the clay pits, including Greylag Goose, Gadwall, Shoveler, Pochard, Tufted and Ruddy Ducks and Little and Great Crested Grebes. Common Terns make use of specially provided rafts at Waters' Edge Country Park and Far Ings. A reasonable population of the declining Willow Tit still exists in the area; 11 territories were located in 1999, although numbers may have dropped a little since. Other notable breeding species include Barn and Tawny Owls, Kingfisher and Tree Sparrow.

The spring and autumn migration periods always produce a good variety of birds. Common, Arctic and Black Terns are regular at both seasons, often being seen on the Humber in preference to the pits, and small groups of Little Gulls are often associated with arrivals of terns. Garganeys appear most springs and have bred in the area on occasions. Hobbies are now regular in both spring and autumn but Osprey remains a scarce transient.

Northbound migrant waders are a feature of May. Good numbers of Ringed Plover, Sanderling, Dunlin and Turnstone occur, with less frequent appearances by Avocet, Grey Plover, both godwits and Greenshank. Autumn sees a wider variety of species, and Knot, Little Stint, Curlew Sandpiper, Spotted Redshank and Wood Sandpiper may all be seen in favoured conditions.

Strong north to south-easterly winds in the autumn can force a variety of seabirds into the estuary as far as the Humber Bridge. Most turn back east, but a significant proportion passes on westwards. Gannets and Arctic Skuas are the most regular species, with Fulmar and Manx Shearwater being about annual. Parties of Kittiwakes may appear, although they are as likely to be seen in May or June as in the autumn. Scarcer seabirds have been noted in the most severe weather, including Leach's Storm-petrel, Pomarine, Long-tailed and Great Skuas and Sabine's Gull. Gales in late October or November may bring Little Auks up the Humber; between 29 October and 4 November

1995 a remarkable total of 282 was recorded. Seaducks are more regular from mid-October, when flocks of Common and Velvet Scoters, Common Eiders and Red-breasted Mergansers may be seen, and North Sea gales may produce large influxes of Goldeneyes.

As the estuary acts as an east-west guiding line for migrants there is often a good visible passage to be seen from the Humber bank on early mornings in autumn, with the main birds involved usually being Woodpigeons, hirundines, Skylarks, Meadow Pipits, wagtails and finches. The sea wall and the areas of scrub around the pits may also harbour a few migrants at this time of the year; Northern Wheatears are regular, and other species such as Black Redstart, Whinchat and Ring Ouzel are found occasionally. October sees the arrival of a few European Stonechats, some of which may remain to winter in the area, and this time of year often brings small irruptive flocks of Bearded Tits moving along the Humber. Rock Pipits are on the move in October and November, and the latter month is a good time to locate Snow Buntings.

This is a well-watched area with a wide variety of habitats, and as such has attracted a number of rarities over the years. The most memorable have been two Lesser Scaup, Little Bittern, Night Heron, Red-footed Falcon, Black-winged Stilt, Great Snipe, Laughing Gull, White-winged Black Tern, Little Swift, two Red-rumped Swallows, Penduline Tit and Arctic Redpoll. Other scarcities within the last five years have included several Green-winged Teal and Ring-necked Ducks, Ferruginous Duck, Purple Heron, Common Crane, Temminck's Stint, three Pectoral Sandpipers, Richard's Pipit and Yellow-browed Warbler.

Timing

The clay pits are worth visiting at any time of year. Spring and autumn probably offer the greatest variety of species and provide the opportunity of finding something out of the ordinary, while cold winter conditions may force impressive numbers of wildfowl on to the pits. As with all reedbeds, to fully appreciate the volume of birdsong during the spring, a warm, calm day is needed with an early start.

Seabirds and seaducks on the Humber are most likely to be seen on a rising tide following northerly to south-easterly winds. With the tide drifting birds westwards towards the Humber Bridge they often give repeated views as they fly back east to avoid passing under the bridge and are then again drifted back by the flowing tide.

Access

Barrow Haven: From Barrow-upon-Humber take the minor road north signed to Barrow Haven and follow this for 1.2 miles (2 km) to a railway crossing. There is a car park on the right immediately over the crossing by the Old Ferry Wharf (TA062236). Walk across the bridge next to the railway over the Haven and follow the footpath onto the sea bank to view the pits to the west. A set of wooden steps just through the gate to the left leads to a hide overlooking the Lincolnshire Wildlife Trust reserve pit of Barrow Reedbed (TA080242). The grass sea-bank path continues west to Barton-upon-Humber, with flooded clay pits to the left and the Humber foreshore to the right.

Barton-upon-Humber: The clay pits to the east of the town have numerous tracks and footpaths around them which allow easy exploration. The majority can be seen from the Humber bank, which is best accessed from the Humber Bridge viewing area (TA027234); there is a large car park here which is signposted from the town centre. To reach Pasture Wharf Reserve, take the A1077 towards Barrow-upon-Humber and turn left on to Falkland Way. After 1 mile (1.6 km) the road passes over a railway crossing and leads to a car park at the eastern end of this road (TA042229). Waters' Edge Country Park is found by heading north out of Barton-upon-Humber towards the Humber Bridge viewing area and turning right just after the railway station by Proudfoot Food Store on to Maltkiln Road and following the signs to the car park.

Far Ings National Nature Reserve lies to the west of the town. To reach the visitor centre, head north out of the town towards the Humber Bridge viewing area and turn left just north of the railway station (signposted to Far Ings). Follow this road for 1 mile (1.6 km) and the car park is on the right at TA011230. From here, access is possible to the eight hides on the reserve. The visitor centre has toilets and a shop, and up-to-date information on the birds present on the reserve can be obtained. In addition, the pits on the west side of Barton-upon-Humber can be viewed from the Humber bank.

Calendar

Resident: Shelduck, Gadwall, Shoveler, Pochard, Tufted and Ruddy Ducks, Little and Great Crested Grebes, Bittern, Marsh Harrier, Sparrowhawk, Kestrel, Water Rail, Ringed Plover, Northern Lapwing, Curlew, Redshank, Barn and Tawny Owls, Kingfisher, Great Spotted Woodpecker, Bearded and Willow Tits, Tree Sparrow, Reed Bunting.

November–March: Pink-footed Goose, Eurasian Wigeon, Common Teal, Pintail, Scaup, Common Eider (scarce), Common Scoter, Velvet Scoter (scarce), Goldeneye, Smew, Red-breasted Merganser, Goosander, Red-throated Diver (scarce), Black-throated Diver (rare), Red-necked Grebe (scarce), Slavonian Grebe (scarce), Black-necked Grebe (scarce), Peregrine Falcon, Grey Plover, Dunlin, Jack Snipe, Turnstone, Little Auk (scarce, October and November), Rock Pipit, European Stonechat, Fieldfare, Redwing, Siskin, Lesser Redpoll, Snow Bunting.

April–June: Greylag Goose, Garganey, Hobby, Oystercatcher, Avocet, Little Ringed Plover, Sanderling, both godwits, Whimbrel, Greenshank, Common Sandpiper, Turnstone, Little Gull, Kittiwake, Common, Arctic and Black Terns, Turtle Dove, Cuckoo, Yellow Wagtail, Northern Wheatear, Grasshopper, Sedge and Reed Warblers, Lesser and Common Whitethroats.

July–October: Eurasian Wigeon, Common Scoter, Gannet, Hobby, Little Ringed Plover, Knot, Little Stint, Curlew Sandpiper, Dunlin, both godwits, Whimbrel, Greenshank, Green and Common Sandpipers, Arctic Skua, other skuas (scarce), Little Gull, Kittiwake, Common, Arctic and Black Terns, Yellow Wagtail, European Stonechat (October onwards), Northern Wheatear.

18E. SOUTH FERRIBY, READ'S ISLAND AND WINTERINGHAM HAVEN

OS Landranger 112
OS Explorer 281

Habitat

The remnants of Read's Island and the rich mudflats of South Ferriby basin are some of the best feeding areas for waders and wildfowl on the upper Humber estuary. Read's Island supposedly formed around the wreck of a sunken ship in the 16th century and gradually grew in size to a maximum of 500 acres (220 ha). For many years there was a house on the island with

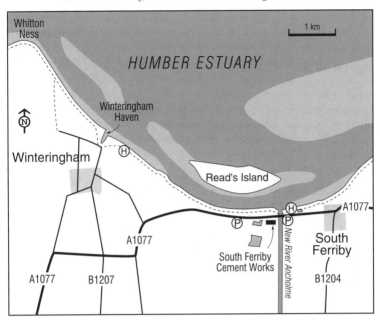

a resident stock man and, latterly, gamekeeper. It was grazed with cattle and sheep until the 1970s when it was stocked with Fallow Deer, a few of which remain today. Tidal erosion is a major threat and has accelerated over recent years, reducing the island's size to approximately 135 acres (60 ha). It is now mainly dominated by rough grass and hemlock and provides a high-tide roost site for waders. The RSPB has recently become involved in the management of the site, particularly the three lagoons on the island, which are now home to large numbers of breeding waders.

To the north-west of Read's Island is the Lincolnshire Wildlife Trust reserve of Winteringham Foreshore, a 52 acre (21 ha) area of saltmarsh with extensive reedbeds and stands of sea aster, which has been designated as a Site of Special Scientific Interest. A hide at this site overlooks large areas of mudflats at low tide, as does another hide at South Ferriby.

Species

During the winter months, the main attraction in this area is the large population of Pink-footed Geese. This species has enjoyed a remarkable upturn in its fortunes since 1995, and the count of 5,150 in November 2003 was the highest on the Humber for over 40 years. The birds, which are generally present between October and February, roost on Read's Island at night and feed on the fields inland during the day. These large flocks inevitably attract other stray geese, with small numbers of White-fronted being seen in most winters and Tundra Bean Geese having occurred on several occasions. Large wintering flocks of Eurasian Wigeon and Common Teal frequent the area around Read's Island, and one such group attracted a vagrant Green-winged Teal in January 2006, while good-sized flocks of Pintail may be seen off Winteringham/Whitton. Small parties of Bewick's and Whooper Swans appear in October and November, sometimes remaining for the winter.

The whole of the upper estuary is a nationally important area for wintering European Golden Plovers (up to 20,000) and Northern Lapwings (up to

10,000), significant numbers of Dunlins, Curlews and Redshanks are present, and the odd Greenshank may winter in the area. The best places for observing waders at all seasons are the muddy basin to the east of South Ferriby sluice and the mud on the southern edge of Read's Island. In addition, a walk along the foreshore may well flush Common and Jack Snipe. The winter months usually produce a few Short-eared Owls, with the salt-marsh around Winteringham Haven being particularly favoured. This area also attracts fairly regular Marsh and Hen Harriers, Merlins and Peregrine Falcons, along with one or two wintering European Stonechats.

There is a major gull roost off Winteringham Haven, which in midwinter holds tens of thousands of Black-headed, Common and Great Black-backed Gulls, along with up to 1,500 Herring Gulls. Unfortunately the birds are usually too far offshore to be properly visible in the failing light of winter afternoons, although odd Glaucous and Iceland Gulls may accompany the other large gulls and can sometimes be seen on the sand banks off Winteringham before flying to roost.

Most of the interesting breeding birds are confined to the inaccessible Read's Island, where Shelduck, Oystercatcher, Northern Lapwing, Curlew and Redshank all nest. However, it is the colonisation by Avocets of this site which provides the most interest and represents a fantastic success story; nesting only commenced here in the late 1990s, but by March 2004 there were 350 birds present, making Read's Island one of the largest breeding sites for this species in Britain. Due to the absence of ground predators on the island, the colony is also very productive. Other breeding species in the area include a few pairs of Ringed Plovers on stony parts of the sea defences, Meadow Pipits and Reed Buntings on areas of saltmarsh and Yellow Wagtails on the inland fields.

The spring and autumn passage periods bring an increasing variety of waders, and 'spring' tides from July to September can produce some spectacular movements of waders searching out high-tide roosting sites. Large flocks of Dunlins (up to 2,500) and Ringed Plovers (up to 600) are features of April and May, with autumn peaks for Ringed Plover again reaching 600 in August. These are supplemented by regular appearances of small parties of Grey Plovers, Knot, Little Stints, Curlew Sandpipers, both godwits, Whimbrels, Greenshanks, Common Sandpipers and Turnstones.

Marsh Harriers are now a regular sight at all times of year, with peak numbers of adults and young in late August and September. Hobbies are being seen more frequently along the Humber and even Peregrines have occurred in July, which is also when the first Merlins return. Parties of Bearded Tits sometimes frequent the foreshore reedbeds during September and October, when irrupting flocks may be located along the Humber banks.

Seabirds and seaducks do not regularly pass the Humber Bridge and as such are quite scarce on this section of the estuary. However, there are a few autumn records of Arctic Skua, while ducks such as Common Scoter and Common Eider may appear in November.

Given the number of waders using this area it is not surprising that rarities have been found and these have included two each of American and Pacific Golden Plovers and White-rumped and Broad-billed Sandpipers, as well as one Black-winged Stilt. In addition, this part of the estuary has attracted Spoonbill and Common Crane in recent years.

Timing

The principal consideration on this part of the estuary is the time of the tides and their relative heights. The highest 'spring' and lowest 'neap' tides coincide and occur every four weeks in relation to lunar cycles, with the highest of all the annual tides in April, May, August, September and October. A set of tide tables is thus essential before planning a visit. For waders on the extensive mudflats at South Ferriby and Read's Island, a visit commencing two to three hours before high tide will produce the closest views of birds as they move nearer to the shore by the rising tide. On the highest tides, however, most birds will be forced off the shore and into inaccessible roosts on Read's Island up to two hours before high tide.

Pink-footed Geese are best looked for as they leave or return to their roost site on Read's Island at dawn and dusk. Large flocks feed on the inland fields during the day but are easily disturbed and may move considerable distances in search of safer areas.

Some shooting by wildfowlers is permitted at Winteringham Foreshore during the winter months, and obviously these times are best avoided.

Access

South Ferriby and Read's Island: The A1077 Barton-upon-Humber to Scunthorpe road passes through South Ferriby village and alongside the Humber opposite Read's Island where two lay-bys (SE968212) provide a convenient parking spot for viewing the island. In addition, a small car park is located just south of the road opposite the Hope and Anchor public house (SE975211). From there cross the road, cross a bridge over a drain to the right and then bear left over a stile onto the grass bank. Follow this to view the mudflats and gain access to the hide which overlooks the best areas for waders in the basin.

Winteringham Haven: Heading west on the A1077 take a right turn to Winteringham and in the village centre turn right on to Low Burbage Road down a gentle hill. After half a mile (0.8 km) the road bears sharply to the left and crosses a drainage channel. Park on the roadside verge here (SE935228) and climb the stile on the right to follow the grass sea-bank path to a hide which overlooks the saltmarsh and mudflats. Alternatively, go over the bridge and bear right down the track where the riverbank footpath continues north-west or go through the kissing gate on the right and down the track between the high hawthorn hedges to a viewpoint over the estuary.

Calendar

Resident: Shelduck, Marsh Harrier, Northern Lapwing, Curlew, Redshank, Meadow Pipit, Reed Bunting.

October–March: Bewick's and Whooper Swans, Tundra Bean Goose (rare), Pink-footed Goose, White-fronted Goose (scarce), Eurasian Wigeon, Common Teal, Pintail, Hen Harrier, Merlin, Peregrine Falcon, European Golden Plover, Dunlin, Jack and Common Snipe, Short-eared Owl, European Stonechat, Bearded Tit.

April–September: Hobby, Oystercatcher, Avocet, Ringed and Grey Plovers, Knot, Little Stint (August and September), Curlew Sandpiper (August and September), Dunlin (passage), Ruff, both godwits, Whimbrel, Greenshank, Common Sandpiper, Turnstone, Yellow Wagtail.

19. THE NORTH-EAST COAST

OS Landrangers 113 and 122
OS Explorers 283 and 284

For the purposes of this guide, this section of the Lincolnshire coast has been divided in to three parts. The sites detailed are presented from north to south.

19A. CLEETHORPES TO HUMBERSTON FITTIES

OS Landranger 113
OS Explorers 283 and 284

Habitat

The busy seaside resorts of Cleethorpes and Humberston would appear to have little to offer the birdwatcher, but a combination of large intertidal mudflats, attractive saltmarsh and easily worked areas of migrant cover make the area worthy of exploration, especially during passage periods and in the winter months. To the north of the pier, low tide reveals large expanses of sandy shore, with extensive areas of rock and beds of cockles attractive to waders and gulls. Further south, a large, expanding area of saltmarsh runs from the leisure centre south to Buck Beck outfall, and is flanked by mudflats and an outer sand bank on the seaward side and a strip of sea buckthorn on the landward side. The Buck Beck outfall itself provides a roosting area for gulls and waders at high tide. Just inland, the boating lake sometimes attracts scarce wildfowl while the surrounding ornamental plantings can attract migrants, as can the areas of mature trees and bushes by both the pumping station and the area known as the 'old tip' close to the Buck Beck outfall.

Further south, Humberston Fitties is mainly occupied by caravan sites, but many of the semi-permanent chalets have sycamores and sallows in the gardens, and a belt of young pines along the sea defences also offers some cover for migrants.

Species

One of the main attractions of this area is the exceptional approachability of birds which in other localities are usually wild and flighty. Owing to the regular presence of large numbers of people walking along the beach and seafront, the waders and gulls feeding on the mudflats can become very tame. In addition, there is an easily watched high-tide roost, best viewed either from the leisure centre car park or Buck Beck outfall, which means that close study of most birds is possible with a minimum of effort.

The high-tide wader roost is worthy of attention throughout the year, although it is at its best from August to April. In winter the roost is dominated by thousands of Knot, Dunlins, Oystercatchers, Sanderlings and Bar-tailed Godwits, with reasonable flocks of Turnstones and Ringed Plovers. In addition, huge numbers of European Golden Plovers and Northern Lapwings feed and rest in the area from November to January, often flying out onto the beach to bathe. Redshanks are quite numerous, feeding in the creeks, and increasing numbers of Black-tailed Godwits are being recorded at this time of the year. The occasional Spotted Redshank or Greenshank may winter in the area and small groups of Ruffs are sometimes present. The latter species is encountered more often a little further south around the yacht club pools at Humberston Fitties, where Jack Snipe are also regular winter visitors. A

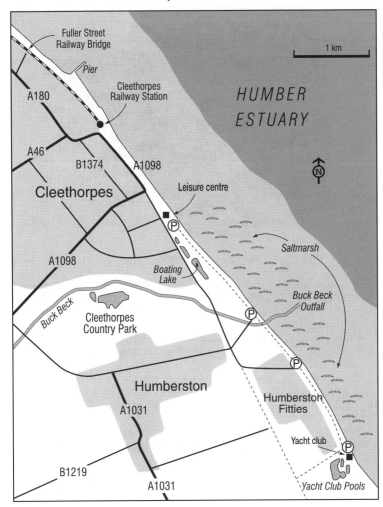

speciality of the area is Purple Sandpiper, and one or two winter on the rocky shore to the north of Cleethorpes opposite Fuller Street railway bridge.

Inevitably, the huge numbers of waders regularly attract the attentions of Peregrine Falcons and one or two are seen daily, often loafing on the outer sand banks. Merlins are usually present, and the occasional Hen Harrier may be located over the saltmarsh, particularly around Humberston Fitties. One or two Short-eared Owls can usually be seen hunting in the latter area between October and April.

The expanding area of saltmarsh has encouraged increasing numbers of Dark-bellied Brent Geese to winter in the area south of the leisure centre, with up to 500 present in January 2005. These flocks are well worth scrutinising thoroughly, as small groups of Pale-bellied Brents have been seen in recent winters and the rarer Black Brant has been located on a couple of occasions. Little Egrets are now regular in the area in small numbers, and may be found at any time of year.

143

Oystercatchers

On winter afternoons, as high tide approaches, gulls feeding further up the estuary gather to bathe in the freshwater creek and roost on the sand bar at Buck Beck outfall. The most numerous are Common and Black-headed, with variable numbers of Herring and Great Black-backed Gulls. Both Glaucous and Mediterranean Gulls are regularly found, and the latter species is often encountered at other sites along the seafront, where they can often be attracted to bread.

The boating lake is worth checking during the winter months, if only to look at the ornamental wildfowl collection. Occasionally wild birds join the tame ones, and Bewick's Swan, Common Eider, Long-tailed Duck and Red-breasted Merganser have all appeared.

Small flocks of Snow Buntings are usually present in the winter months, either around the Buck Beck car park or near the yacht club at Humberston Fitties. The latter area regularly produces records of Lapland Buntings, particularly in November, and has also attracted Shore Larks in recent years. Rock Pipits winter on the saltings, where a flock of Twites can often be found. Around the pumping station, species such as Water Rail, Willow Tit, and Tree Sparrow can be seen.

The species composition of waders in the spring is much the same as during the winter months, but counts of northward-bound Ringed Plovers and Sanderlings may be higher in May. Other passage visitors such as Whimbrel and Greenshank occur at this time of year, while in the autumn a few Curlew Sandpipers and Little Stints add to the variety. The rarer waders are more likely in autumn, and records have included Lesser Yellowlegs and several Grey Phalaropes. From July onwards, large numbers of terns come in to roost at high tide; the most numerous is Common Tern, with recent counts of up to 500, with smaller numbers of Little and Sandwich and occasional Arctic and Black Terns. These gatherings also sometimes attract Little Gulls. Offshore, a few Arctic Skuas may be seen harassing the feeding terns and occasionally Gannets and other seabirds may pass up the Humber.

The trees and shrubs around the boating lake and adjacent pumping station may hold a few migrants in spring and autumn such as Common Redstart, Lesser Whitethroat, Common Chiffchaff, Willow Warbler and

Spotted and Pied Flycatchers, and have in the past produced Wryneck, Icterine, Barred and Yellow-browed Warblers, Firecrest, Red-breasted Flycatcher and Serin. Nearby, the area of mature trees and shrubs close to the Buck Beck car park has held both Red-backed and Great Grey Shrikes in the autumn, and the golf course just inland from here regularly hosts passage Ring Ouzels. The narrow belt of Scots pines along the edge of the Humberston Fitties holiday camp is badly disturbed, but even so it is always worthy of a look in the early mornings during spring and autumn. The same can be said of the gardens of the chalets in the caravan park where stunted sycamores and shrubs offer some cover. Long-eared Owls, Black Redstarts, Northern Wheatears and Firecrests are often seen in March, April, October and November, and the location has had several Richard's Pipits, Subalpine Warbler, Arctic Warbler and three Parrot Crossbills, as well as two spectacular White-tailed Eagles. The whole area's coastal location, immediately across the Humber from Spurn Point, means that scarce migrants can turn up anywhere: recent examples have included a Red-backed Shrike by Grimsby Town Football Club's ground, a Pallas's Warbler on waste ground by the Pleasure Island complex and a Yellow-browed Warbler by Cleethorpes library.

Timing

The period up to three hours before high tide is the peak time to visit the wader roost; a late afternoon or evening tide is best as the sun will be behind the observation point. The highest 'spring' tides can be quite spectacular, as this area is the Humber Estuary's main wader roosting site.

During the spring and autumn, early morning can produce a few migrants, which may be disturbed later in the day; winds with an easterly component to them are obviously the best conditions to bring in the scarcer species. The area can be inundated with holidaymakers during the summer and this time of year is best avoided.

Access

The foreshore at Cleethorpes is easily viewed from a number of locations on the seafront between the pier (TA303097) and the Buck Beck outfall (TA328067). The leisure centre car park (pay and display) at TA315080 is one of the best spots as it overlooks the northern end of the high tide roost ridge, while the free car park at Buck Beck (TA327068) is another good area from which to view. Wintering Purple Sandpipers are usually to be found on the rocky foreshore adjacent to Fuller Street railway bridge at TA297100; this area is about 400 m north-west of Cleethorpes Pier.

The boating lake is midway between the leisure centre and the Buck Beck outfall at TA318073; there are several car parks along this stretch of road, from where it is a short walk through the boating lake area to the foreshore.

To reach Humberston Fitties, follow the minor road south from the boating lake for half a mile (0.8 km), go straight across at a roundabout and continue to a car park adjacent to the sea wall (TA332061). Access to the Fitties is along the dune ridge to the south through the belt of small pines to the yacht club.

There is open access to the beach and foreshore throughout the area, but remember that tidal creeks can fill remarkably quickly on a rising tide; if walking out towards the water's edge it is best to follow a falling tide and be constantly aware of the dangers of the location.

Calendar

Resident: Little Grebe, Little Egret, Sparrowhawk, Ringed Plover, Curlew, Barn Owl, Meadow Pipit, Willow Tit, Tree Sparrow, Reed Bunting.

November–February: Pink-footed and Brent Geese, Eurasian Wigeon, Pintail, Long-tailed Duck (scarce), Merlin, Peregrine Falcon, Water Rail, Oystercatcher, European Golden and Grey Plovers, Knot, Sanderling, Purple Sandpiper, Dunlin, Ruff, Jack and Common Snipe, both godwits, Turnstone, Mediterranean Gull, Glaucous Gull (scarce), Short-eared Owl, Kingfisher, Rock Pipit, European Stonechat, Twite, Lapland Bunting (scarce), Snow Bunting.

March–June: Osprey (scarce), Grey Plover, Knot, Sanderling, Dunlin, Bar-tailed Godwit, Whimbrel, Turnstone, Sandwich, Common, Arctic and Little Terns, Turtle Dove, Cuckoo, Long-eared Owl (March and April), Black Redstart (March and April), Common Redstart (April and May), Whinchat, Northern Wheatear, Ring Ouzel (April), Lesser and Common Whitethroats, Common Chiffchaff, Willow Warbler, Spotted Flycatcher, Pied Flycatcher (April and May).

July–October: Gannet, Marsh Harrier, Grey Plover, Knot, Sanderling, Little Stint (August and September), Curlew Sandpiper (August and September), Dunlin, Ruff, both godwits, Whimbrel, Spotted Redshank, Greenshank, Turnstone, Arctic Skua, Mediterranean and Little Gulls, Sandwich, Common, Arctic, Little and Black Terns, Long-eared Owl (October), Short-eared Owl, Wryneck (scarce, August and September), Black Redstart (October), Common Redstart (August to October), Northern Wheatear, Ring Ouzel (September and October), Icterine Warbler (scarce, August to October), Barred Warbler (scarce, August to October), Lesser Whitethroat, Common Whitethroat, Yellow-browed Warbler (scarce, September and October), Common Chiffchaff, Willow Warbler, Firecrest (October), Spotted Flycatcher, Red-breasted Flycatcher (scarce, September and October), Pied Flycatcher (August and September), Red-backed Shrike (scarce, August and September), Great Grey Shrike (scarce, October).

19B. TETNEY TO NORTHCOATES POINT

OS Landranger 113
OS Explorer 283

Habitat

South of Humberston Fitties a wide area of saltmarsh stretches south to Northcoates Point (rather confusingly spelt differently from the nearby village of North Cotes) and forms a major part of the RSPB's Tetney Marshes reserve, the latter of which covers 3,335 acres (1,350 ha) of intertidal mudflats and saltmarsh. Criss-crossed with tidal creeks, this is a dangerous area and is best viewed from the sea wall. Inland, the arable fields are worth checking for passage waders in spring and raptors in winter. The sea-bank path at Tetney follows the outside edge of a large reclaimed area of former saltmarsh now mostly turned over to arable farmland, with the grassy banks still being grazed by cattle. A series of large hawthorn bushes form the principal migrant habitat at Northcoates Point, but unfortunately a large hedgerow in this area has recently been destroyed. The MOD pools, which are both brackish, can prove useful in spring and summer but sometimes dry out in hot weather before autumn passage commences. The disused airfield inland of Northcoates Point has now been converted from pasture to unattractive arable fields.

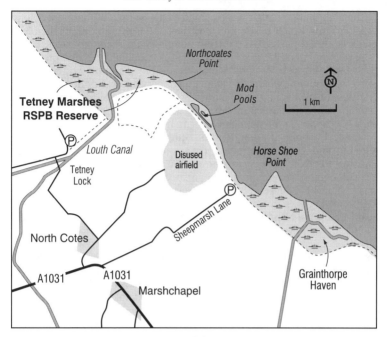

Species

In the winter months, large flocks of Oystercatchers, Grey and European Golden Plovers, Northern Lapwings, Knot, Dunlins and Bar-tailed Godwits feed on the mudflats at low tide, while Redshanks frequent the creeks. Small numbers of Jack Snipe regularly winter in the marshy areas, and a few Ruff can be found on the reclaimed fields. Up to 700 Brent Geese may be present in the area, often feeding on inland winter wheat fields; this flock regularly contains several Pale-bellied Brents and has on recent occasions hosted Black Brants. Groups of Pink-footed Geese occasionally pause in the fields, but this species is more usually seen flying over. One or two Little Egrets frequent the pools and creeks; in line with many other places, this delightful heron is on the increase and may be encountered at virtually any time of year.

Wintering raptors are represented by regular Hen Harriers, Merlins and Peregrine Falcons; the latter can often be found loafing on the mudflats. Several Short-eared Owls may be present in good years, with odd birds lingering well into the spring.

A few Lapland Buntings are usually present around the sea banks, and small flocks of Snow Buntings appear regularly, especially in November. Twites can be found in good numbers between October and March, with a recent count of 260 in January 2004 being particularly notable. It is also worth keeping an eye out for Shore Larks, which are found along this section of coast with some regularity. Rock Pipits are common in the creeks and on the saltmarsh, while a few Water Pipits have wintered in recent years, including up to eight in early 2004; they often favour the area around the canal at Tetney Lock. One or two European Stonechats may be encountered, although this species is more frequent on passage in October and March.

The main summer interest is provided by the nationally important colony of Little Terns, which nest on a stony part of the shore north of the MOD pools. Up to 80 pairs have bred, but numbers and breeding success vary from year to year as the species suffers losses from high tides and predation by Foxes, Kestrels and Merlins. Yellow Wagtails breed around the grass banks of the reclamation, which also attract migrants such as Northern Wheatear and Whinchat in spring and autumn. The inland fields have proved to be something of a traditional site for small groups of Dotterel in late April and early May, although their appearance can never be guaranteed.

Marsh Harriers are frequent on migration, particularly during the autumn, and other raptors are occasionally seen flying over: Honey Buzzard, Red Kite, Montagu's Harrier, Rough-legged Buzzard and Osprey have all been noted on more than one occasion, and a Red-footed Falcon was seen in 1976. Several Common Cranes have also been seen in the area.

The MOD pools dry out with regularity in late spring but are flooded again by summer 'spring' tides. Being shallow they attract passage waders such as Spotted Redshank, Greenshank and Green and Wood Sandpipers, and over the years have attracted rarities such as Black-winged Stilt and Greater Sand Plover. The pools have also been visited on several occasions by Spoonbills. Passage periods bring good numbers of Ringed Plovers, European Golden Plovers, Knot, Sanderlings, Dunlins and Turnstones to the foreshore, where they are best observed from the bank by Horse Shoe Point car park. Regular searching produces records of Curlew Sandpiper, Little Stint and Black-tailed Godwit and rarities have included Broad-billed Sandpiper. The saltmarsh and creeks at Tetney have good numbers of Whimbrels in April, May, July and August, and one creek held a unique 'double' of American and Pacific Golden Plovers in July 1986; another of the latter was also found in July 2002.

This is not a good spot for seawatching as most birds pass well offshore, cutting across the estuary mouth to Spurn Point, although the odd Gannet or Arctic Skua can sometimes be seen. During the late autumn, species such as Common Eider, Common Scoter, Red-breasted Merganser and Red-throated Diver may be offshore. There is usually a sizeable resting flock of Sandwich and Common Terns on the beach during late July and August, sometimes numbering up to 200 of each species. The highest numbers of terns roost during evening 'spring' tides in this period.

Available habitat for passage migrants is limited to a few hawthorn bushes on the sea embankment, and there are much better sites to search for these species further south along the coast. However, the usual range of common migrants appears in favourable conditions and the scarcer species such as Richard's Pipit, Red-backed Shrike, Firecrest and Icterine, Barred and Yellow-browed Warblers appear every now and again. In addition, recent records of Rustic Bunting and Marsh, Great Reed, Dartford, Subalpine, Arctic, Pallas's and Dusky Warblers show the area has potential.

Timing

This is a good area at any time of year. Visits to coincide with high 'spring' tides in the early morning or late evening produce the best viewing conditions for waders and terns. As with any east coast locality, the appearance of passage migrants depends on the prevailing weather conditions, with easterly winds needed to produce falls of the commoner migrants and the chance of something rarer.

Access

It is possible to walk along the grass-covered sea wall from Humberston Fitties as far as Tetney Marshes RSPB, a distance of about 2 miles (3.2 km), checking the scattered hawthorn bushes, the saltmarsh to the east and the fields on the inland side.

The main entrance to Tetney Marshes RSPB is reached by following minor roads from the A1031 at either Tetney village or North Cotes to Tetney Lock, where another minor road runs east alongside the Louth Canal. About 400 m further on the road turns sharply left. There is limited parking here on the roadside (TA345025), from where a path heads north-east along the bank of the canal for 1.25 miles (2 km). It is then possible to take a circular walk around the reclamation embankments, viewing the saltmarsh and creeks to the north, the borrow pits on the southern side and the reclaimed fields. At the north-eastern extremity of the reclamation a wooden gate gives access to the sea bank, which runs alongside the old air-field fence south to Horse Shoe Point. From this path a sandy track leads off east across the saltmarsh between the two larger MOD pools to the shore. Breeding Little Terns can be seen from the point where this track passes through the dunes.

Alternative access is via Sheepmarsh Lane, a minor road signed to Horse Shoe Point which leaves the A1031 just north of Marshchapel at TA352001. After 2.5 miles (3 km) the road reaches the sea wall where there is a car park (TA381018). To reach North Cotes Point and Tetney Marshes RSPB, walk north along the sea embankment or the beach.

Calendar

Resident: Little Egret, Sparrowhawk, Northern Lapwing, Curlew, Barn Owl, Kingfisher, Meadow Pipit, Tree Sparrow, Reed Bunting.

November–February: Pink-footed and Brent Geese, Shelduck, Pintail, Common Eider, Common Scoter, Red-throated Diver, Hen Harrier, Merlin, Peregrine Falcon, Oystercatcher, European Golden and Grey Plovers, Knot, Dunlin, Ruff, Jack and Common Snipe, Bar-tailed Godwit, Redshank, Short-eared Owl, Shore Lark (scarce), Water and Rock Pipits, European Stonechat, Twite, Lapland and Snow Buntings.

March–June: Marsh Harrier, Hobby, Ringed Plover, Dotterel (scarce late April and May), Knot, Sanderling, Dunlin, Whimbrel, Greenshank, Green and Wood Sandpipers, Little Tern, Turtle Dove, Short-eared Owl, Water Pipit (scarce, March and April), Yellow Wagtail, Common Redstart (April and May), Whinchat, Northern Wheatear, Common Whitethroat, Reed Warbler.

July–October: Gannet, Marsh Harrier, Hobby, Ringed Plover, European Golden Plover, Knot, Sanderling, Little Stint (August and September), Curlew Sandpiper (August and September), Dunlin, Black-tailed Godwit, Whimbrel, Spotted Redshank, Greenshank, Green and Wood Sandpipers, Turnstone, Arctic Skua, Sandwich, Common and Little Terns, Short-eared Owl, Yellow Wagtail, Common Redstart (August to October), Whinchat, Northern Wheatear, Ring Ouzel (September and October), Icterine Warbler (scarce, August to October), Barred Warbler (scarce, August to October), Yellow-browed Warbler (scarce, September and October), Firecrest (October), Pied Flycatcher (August and September), Red-backed Shrike (scarce, August and September).

Habitat

This section of the Lincolnshire coast has a well-preserved natural sand dune system which, combined with extensive sand and mudflats beyond an ever expanding saltmarsh, make the area one of national importance. Most of the coastline is made up of the 2,841 acre (1,150 ha) Donna Nook National Nature Reserve and the 2,349 acre (951 ha) Saltfleetby-Theddlethorpe Dunes National Nature Reserve. These two sites adjoin at Saltfleet Haven, meaning there is over 10.6 miles (17 km) of coastline with generally open access.

The Donna Nook reserve consists of dunes, slacks and intertidal areas. Coastal processes, particularly sand and mud accretion, alter the natural features from year to year, and sand from the beach and offshore sand banks is blown inland by easterly winds to form dune ridges. The dune system here varies in width but is generally narrower than that further south. It is dominated by marram and sand couch, with patches of elder and some encroaching sea buckthorn which forms dense clumps. North of Stonebridge car park the dunes lead to the site of the old Pyes Hall where a small group of sycamores and a block of elders and hawthorns are a magnet for migrants. Between the advancing dunes and the sea bank there are areas of saltmarsh, which have gradually become less saline. Open lagoons originally formed by excavation work for the sea bank are also found and their muddy margins attract waders in spring and autumn. However, by far the largest part of the reserve consists of sandflats, which support breeding terns and waders as well as large numbers of Grey Seals.

The Saltfleetby-Theddlethorpe Dunes reserve consists mainly of tidal mudflats, salt- and freshwater marshes and sand dunes. On the foreshore, accreting mudflats and saltmarsh in the north give way to a narrower sandy beach at the southern end. The sand dunes are also much wider in the north and there is an extensive freshwater marsh between two dune ridges, which converge into a narrower ridge south of Churchill Lane at Theddlethorpe. The principal vegetation in the dunes is sea buckthorn, although there are some large areas of elder and hawthorn scrub. Open areas of marram and long rough grasses are grazed into short turf by the abundant Rabbit population and managed with winter cattle grazing. Clumps of sallows and willows occur in the freshwater areas, which are covered in marsh orchids during the summer. Stands of sycamore trees attractive to migrants are found at Rimac and Sea View Farm as well as at Paradise, where the Lincolnshire Wildlife Trust own a 2 acre (0.8 ha) lagoon known locally as Paradise Pool.

From Mablethorpe a line of dunes runs north and has pockets of elder and hawthorn scrub among the sea buckthorn which can harbour migrants, especially in autumn. A concrete shelter adjacent to the tourist information centre offers protection from bad weather for seawatching and also looks out over the outfall which runs down the centre of the beach.

Species

Over the last 40 years this part of the Lincolnshire coast has received frequent attention from birdwatchers and has a creditable list of migrant and vagrant species to its name. Its prime east coast location ensures a good supply of migrants but the extensive areas of habitat and low numbers of birdwatchers make the discovery of rarer species less frequent than more well-watched localities elsewhere on the east coast of Britain. The area,

Shore Larks

however, probably offers some of the greatest potential for finding your own rare birds within the region.

During the winter months, the saltmarsh areas at Theddlethorpe, Saltfleet and Donna Nook provide some exceptional birding. Four key wintering passerines are of most interest: Shore Lark, Snow Bunting, Lapland Bunting and Twite. Shore Larks were formerly a much more frequent visitor, with flocks of up to 120 recorded at Donna Nook in the 1960s, but are sadly now rather scarce; however, a small group usually winters somewhere along this stretch of coastline, with favoured sites being the saltings at Rimac and Donna Nook. The birds are often found at the latter site among the colony of grey seals, where the largest flock of recent times, of up to 38 birds, wintered in 2003-04. Snow Buntings are frequently found in association with Shore Larks, although may occur anywhere; they are most regular on the saltings at Rimac, Theddlethorpe and from Pyes Hall south to Donna Nook. Flock sizes vary through the winter months, with the peak numbers often to be found early in November and December. Three-figure flocks are not uncommon, with recent examples including 400 in December 2003 (Donna Nook) and 300 in December 2004 (Donna Nook, Rimac and Theddlethorpe). Numbers of Lapland Buntings are generally small, although reasonably large flocks have been found in two recent winters, when peak counts were 63 at Pyes Hall in January 2003 and 45 at Rimac in November of the same year. These two areas are probably the best places to look for this species, although their habit of skulking in long grass rather than taking to flight makes them difficult to find. Flocks of Twites may be encountered anywhere along the coast in areas of rough wet grass, particularly at Donna Nook where there were 200 in December 2003. Other wintering passerines on the saltmarsh include groups of Skylarks, Linnets and Rock Pipits, the latter of which may number up to 60 at favoured sites such as Rimac. Water Pipits sometimes winter, although they usually prefer freshwater pools. The extensive cover of sea buckthorn provides a source of food for large flocks of Fieldfares, Redwings and Blackbirds from November to early January, but the winter scene in the dunes can be a rather barren one, with just a few Woodcocks, Blackcaps and Yellowhammers present.

The outer foreshore from Rimac northwards is the haunt of large flocks of Northern Lapwings, European Golden Plovers, Knot, Redshanks, Mallards, Eurasian Wigeons and Shelducks, and a few Jack Snipe usually winter in the area, with others seen on passage from September onwards. Little Egrets, which now breed locally, are regular along this stretch of coast at all times of year. Dark-bellied Brent Geese, which peak at 1,500 to 2,000 birds in

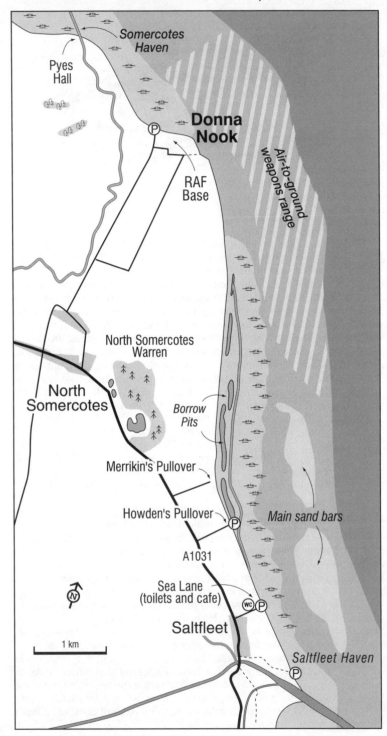

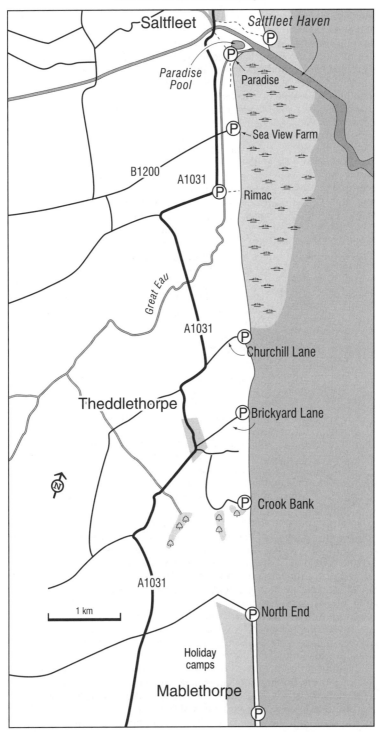

Saltfleet

Saltfleet Haven

Ⓟ

Ⓟ

Paradise Pool

Paradise

Ⓟ Sea View Farm

B1200

A1031

Ⓟ Rimac

Great Eau

A1031

Ⓟ Churchill Lane

Theddlethorpe

Ⓟ Brickyard Lane

Ⓝ

Ⓟ Crook Bank

A1031

1 km

Ⓟ North End

Holiday camps

Mablethorpe

Ⓟ

January, can also be found, with the areas around Howden's Pullover, Rimac and Sea View Farm being especially favoured. Occasional groups of Pink-footed Geese rest in the inland fields, particularly south of Rimac, although this species is more usually noted flying over in large flocks, generally going south in October and November and north-west in January and February. Likewise, parties of Bewick's and Whooper Swans may appear, more often than not on passage in November.

With such an abundance of food the area inevitably attracts concentrations of raptors, and Hen Harriers, Sparrowhawks, Merlins and Peregrine Falcons all winter along this stretch of coast. A few Short-eared Owls are also regular, although numbers vary year to year. Flocks of gulls, consisting mainly of Herring and Great Black-backed, gather to rest at the mouth of Saltfleet Haven, and are joined on occasions by Glaucous Gulls from January onwards. Kittiwakes are frequent but the sea is often rather quiet in midwinter, although there are always Red-throated Divers and a few Common Guillemots offshore. Small wintering flocks of Common Scoter are sometimes joined by other species of seaduck such as Long-tailed Duck, Common Eider and Velvet Scoter. One of the best places for watching these birds is the higher dunes just north of Mablethorpe, where a sunken forest offshore seems to attract feeding birds.

The usual scatter of scarce early spring migrants can be expected anywhere with suitable habitat. Finding Firecrests in the sea buckthorn is mainly a matter of luck and good hearing, while migrant Ring Ouzels in late March and April can also be elusive in areas of scrub, but Black Redstarts, European Stonechats and Northern Wheatears are easier to locate as they favour manure heaps or close-grazed grassy and sandy areas. The Scandinavian subspecies of Rock Pipit is a regular early spring migrant on the foreshore, where passage Short-eared Owls are often seen in March and April. Visible migration along the dunes in April and May involves Turtle Doves, Skylarks, Meadow Pipits, hirundines, Goldfinches and Linnets. Several raptors can normally be seen during the spring, with Marsh Harrier regular in April and May (and again from July to October) and the rarer Montagu's Harrier a distinct possibility in May. Hobbies are frequently noted in spring and Osprey is virtually annual at this time of year.

Spring falls of migrants are mostly drifted in on east or north-east winds, often with associated mist or rain; however, the numbers of birds are never as impressive as in autumn and most arrivals involve only a few individuals of a limited number of species. Falls are dominated by Northern Wheatears, Whinchats, Common Redstarts, Willow Warblers and Spotted Flycatchers, with smaller numbers of Yellow Wagtails and Pied Flycatchers and the occasional Wood Warbler. The more sought-after species, such as Hoopoe, Wryneck, Golden Oriole and Red-backed Shrike, are unpredictable in their appearance, although the latter is virtually annual somewhere along this stretch of coastline in the spring. These scarcer species are usually found from mid-May onwards; this is also the peak time for arrivals of Bluethroats, males of which have been found singing and briefly holding territory. Common Rosefinch and Ortolan Bunting are two other species which may appear in these conditions, and there is always the chance of a singing Marsh Warbler from late May to mid-June.

The sandy foreshore plays host to significant flocks of summer-plumaged Ringed Plovers, Dunlins and Sanderlings, the latter numbering up to 300 in most years. The sandy fields inland of the sea bank at Donna Nook are a regular spring stop-over point for groups of Dotterels; the best fields vary from year to year with the stage of cultivation. The freshwater areas at Donna

Nook, Rimac and Paradise Pool attract a variety of passage waders during both the spring and autumn, with the more regular species such as Ruff, Black-tailed Godwit, Whimbrel, Greenshank and Green and Common Sandpipers being joined occasionally by scarcer migrants like Avocet, Little Stint, Curlew Sandpiper, Spotted Redshank and Wood Sandpiper. Paradise Pool provided records of both Temminck's Stint and Red-necked Phalarope in 2004, while overshooting southern migrants such as Night Heron, Purple Heron and Spoonbill have all been recorded on the freshwater areas in the past.

Willow Warblers and Common Whitethroats are easily the most numerous breeding warblers, with lesser numbers of Sedge Warbler, Reed Warbler and Blackcap and a few pairs of Grasshopper Warblers at Rimac. Territory-holding Nightingales have been occasional in recent years, with passage birds in April and May often joining them in song. Other breeding species in the dunes include Red-legged Partridge, Skylark, Tree Sparrow, Linnet and Yellowhammer, while the freshwater lagoons have nesting Little Grebes along with substantial populations of Meadow Pipits and Reed Buntings.

A colony of Little Terns is present on the beach, but suffers from disturbance by human visitors, flooding by 'spring' tides and predation from Foxes, Kestrels and early autumn Merlins. Feeding birds are best seen at the mouth of Saltfleet Haven, where they also rest on the beach. Keep well away from the well-signed breeding areas where a few pairs of Shelducks, Oystercatchers, Ringed Plovers and Redshanks also nest.

From July onwards the terns and gulls which feed offshore gather to rest on the sand bars at Theddlethorpe beach and the mouth of Saltfleet Haven. Sandwich Terns may number several hundred birds, with a recent count of 1,100 in July 2001. Smaller groups of Common Terns, often with a few Arctic and Black Terns, Little Gulls and Kittiwakes, are also present and the gathering of birds has attracted vagrants such as a Lesser Crested Tern in 1993 and a number of Sabine's Gulls over the years. Arctic Skuas loaf offshore and frequently fly up the beach, chasing food-carrying adult terns. Later in the autumn, skuas may rest on the shore and offer excellent opportunities for study; as an example, up to 20 Pomarine Skuas were seen on the beach daily in September 1987.

This stretch of the coast is not, in general, good for seawatching as the shore is exposed and rough seas make locating birds in the swell difficult. However, some height and shelter can be found at Mablethorpe and interesting seawatching can be carried out here in favourable conditions; for instance, strong northerly winds on September 11th 2001 produced totals of 17 Sooty Shearwaters, 11 Manx Shearwaters, one Pomarine Skua, 321 Arctic Skuas, nine Long-tailed Skuas and 96 Great Skuas. Later in the year, mainly November, small numbers of Little Auks may be seen after northerly gales.

Most of the autumn passerine interest is related to falls of migrants, which may occur any time from early August to early November. The ideal weather conditions consist of easterly winds and rain and, although such weather patterns seem to be becoming less frequent, some spectacular numbers of birds may be involved. Falls in late August and September are usually dominated by species such as Common Redstart, Whinchat, Northern Wheatear, Garden Warbler, Common Whitethroat and Willow Warbler, all of which may be widespread, but specialised feeders such as Pied and Spotted Flycatchers become concentrated in favoured stands of sycamores, willows and sallows. These arrivals in the early part of the autumn may include Wood Warblers, while of the scarcer species Wryneck, Icterine and Barred Warblers and Red-backed Shrike are more likely in August and early

September. Wrynecks are often found on open sandy areas among the dunes, and both Icterine and Barred Warblers are best searched for in berry-laden elders, with Pyes Hall being a favoured site. Red-backed Shrikes are often associated with hawthorn and elder bushes; Rimac and Donna Nook are probably the two best places to look.

Falls in October produce the largest numbers of birds and are usually dominated by Goldcrests, which may arrive in their thousands; good numbers of thrushes (with a few Ring Ouzels) and Bramblings may also be involved, along with a few Firecrests and the odd Woodlark or Great Grey Shrike. This time of year offers the best chance of finding eastern vagrants, with the most regular being Richard's Pipit, Yellow-browed and Pallas's Warblers and Red-breasted Flycatcher. This section of the coast is particularly noted for Richard's Pipits and up to ten birds occur in some years; the dunes to the north of Rimac and the freshwater marsh, dunes and fields north from Howden's Pullover to Pyes Hall are regularly frequented spots. Red-breasted Flycatchers and the rarer *Phylloscopus* warblers are usually found in stands of sycamores, with the most obvious places to look being Pyes Hall, Saltfleet village (particularly Sea Lane), Sea View Farm, Rimac and Theddlethorpe village (especially Churchill Lane).

There is a prominent passage of Rock and Meadow Pipits and Reed Buntings during October, and small numbers of Shore Larks and Lapland and Snow Buntings may also be encountered; Lapland Buntings sometimes frequent the inland stubble fields with flocks of Skylarks. Arrivals in late October and November usually bring Long-eared Owls, Black Redstarts and Firecrests along with good numbers of Woodcocks.

Regular ringing at Theddlethorpe dunes over the years gives an indication of what vagrants may be skulking in the sea buckthorn scrub, and records from here have included Thrush Nightingale, Red-flanked Bluetail and Blyth's Reed, Booted, Subalpine, Arctic and Radde's Warblers. Observations at Donna Nook and Saltfleetby give an even better hint of what there is to be found by birders willing to put the effort in. An enviable list of passerine rarities is headed by an Alpine Accentor in November 1994 and a Lanceolated Warbler in September 1996, with other goodies including Great Spotted Cuckoo, Scops Owl, Alpine Swift, European Bee-eater, Tawny Pipit, Olive-backed Pipit, Thrush Nightingale, Red-flanked Bluetail, three Desert Wheatears, Savi's, Booted, Subalpine, Greenish, Arctic, Radde's and Dusky Warblers, Isabelline Shrike, Lesser Grey and Woodchat Shrikes, Arctic Redpoll, Parrot Crossbill and Rustic and Black-headed Buntings. Rare waders are also well represented, with the highlight being Britain's second Lesser Sand Plover at Rimac in May 2002; other records have involved Collared Pratincole, American Golden Plover, Broad-billed Sandpiper, Great Snipe and a Long-billed Dowitcher. Additional rarities over the years have included Red-breasted Goose, Blue-winged Teal, Great White Egret, Glossy Ibis, White-tailed Eagle, Red-footed Falcon, Laughing Gull and Caspian, Lesser Crested and White-winged Black Terns.

Timing

This area has lots to offer during the spring and autumn migration periods, as well as throughout the winter. Easterly or south-easterly winds are the peak conditions for producing falls of migrants, particularly if they are associated with rain or fog. Seabirds are best looked for during or after northerly gales. Within these general confines the foreshore at Saltfleet village is best viewed early in the morning before holidaymakers and dog walkers cause disturbance.

The foreshore at Donna Nook is an RAF bombing range with access only possible to the shore at weekends and when the red warning flags are not flying. On weekdays, the area north from Stonebridge car park to Pyes Hall is best looked at before bombing starts at about 8 am, as the incoming planes fly low over the dunes and cause real noise problems. At weekends there are usually no difficulties, except the perennial problem of disturbance by dog walkers.

An added attraction at Donna Nook in November and December is provided by the Grey Seals, which pup on the upper reaches of the beach near the Stonebridge car park. This is a very popular event and the site is wardened throughout this period. Please heed all instructions relating to reducing disturbance to these mammals.

Access

This section of coastline has plenty of public access points which are detailed here. Other tracks and roads leading to the sea are usually private and visitors should only use the well signed official car parks. All of the area is accessed from the main A1031 Cleethorpes to Mablethorpe coast road.

For Donna Nook and Pyes Hall follow the minor roads north from North Somercotes village signed to Donna Nook. Once through the village the road runs straight for 2 miles (3.2 km) to the Stonebridge car park (TF422998). There is restricted access to the beach and foreshore from Pyes Hall south to Howden's Pullover on weekdays when the RAF uses the bombing ranges. A series of marker boards are situated at all public access points, with red flags flying to indicate that the shore is in use, and these boards should not be passed. The attractive migrant habitat at Pyes Hall is a 1 mile (1.6 km) walk north-west along the dunes or beach (TA408007). The Donna Nook reserve proper can be reached by walking south for about 1.5 miles (2.4 km) along the beach before entering the dunes south of the coastguard tower.

Public access is possible along an unmetalled road at Merrikin's Pullover, 0.8 miles (1.3 km) south-east of North Somercotes village at TF445958, although there are no parking facilities here.

Howden's Pullover is signed from the A1031, 1.5 miles (2.4 km) south of North Somercotes village. An unmetalled road leads to the sea bank where there is a car park (TF449952). It is then possible to walk north to Donna Nook along the sea bank, dunes or foreshore, or south to Saltfleet village.

In Saltfleet village turn north-east on to Sea Lane where a car park with toilets and a cafe, open in summer, is found after 400 m (TF456944). The raised sea defences here offer good views over the extensive saltmarsh, which is particularly interesting in the winter, and a stand of sycamores by the amusement arcade is attractive to migrants. Tracks lead north towards Howden's Pullover and south to Saltfleet Haven.

Moving south through Saltfleet, take the left turn immediately before the sharp bend and an uneven track follows the bank of the Haven to a small car park adjacent to a line of dunes (TF467935). From here, footpaths head north on either side of the dune ridge and offer views of the scrub, saltmarsh and inland fields. It is possible to walk out to the mouth of the Haven to look for seabirds, gulls and waders but the tidal creeks are very dangerous and vigilance is necessary.

Between Saltfleetby and Theddlethorpe Dunes there are six entrance points, all of which have small car parks and offer access to the dune system, foreshore and beach. Travelling south on the A1031 through Saltfleet village, the road bends sharply right over the Haven, and here a track leads straight on to the Paradise car park at the northern end of the reserve (TF459933). Paradise Pool is situated just south-east of this car park. Moving further south along the A1031, a metalled track opposite the B1200 turning to Louth leads off left to Sea View Farm (TF46492). This small car park is adjacent to a group of old sycamore trees, which prove attractive to passage flycatchers and warblers. About half a mile (0.8 km) further south the A1031 turns sharply right, and a track to the left leads to the Rimac car park, which is reached via the tarmac road over a wooden bridge which spans the Great Eau (TF467917). A saltmarsh viewpoint, with an 800 m disabled access trail, has been constructed straight out from this car park.

Continuing south, the A1031 takes a sharp left-hand bend, then after 1.5 miles (2.4 km) it turns right. A left turn here leads down Churchill Lane to another car park (TF478901). Two further car parks can be accessed from the village of Theddlethorpe St Helen. After the church a left turn off the A1031 splits into two metalled tracks; the northern one leads to Brickyard Lane (TF483893) and the southern one winds about 1 mile (1.6 km) to Crook Bank (TF489882).

A number of car parks are found at Mablethorpe giving access to the dunes and beach, with the most useful being at North End (TF498870) and on the dune top 1 mile (1.6 km) further south (TF505858). These are accessed by taking the minor road north-east off the A1031 1.5 miles (2.4 km) south of Theddlethorpe St Helen, signed to Mablethorpe North End. From the southern of these two car parks, a seawatching shelter is a further 200 m south along the dunes or beach.

Calendar

Resident: Shelduck, Red-legged Partridge, Little Grebe, Little Egret, Sparrowhawk, Redshank, Barn Owl, Skylark, Meadow Pipit, Tree Sparrow, Linnet, Yellowhammer, Reed Bunting.

November–February: Bewick's and Whooper Swans, Pink-footed and Brent Geese, Eurasian Wigeon, Shoveler, Common Eider, Long-tailed Duck (scarce), Common and Velvet Scoters, Red-throated Diver, Hen Harrier, Merlin, Peregrine Falcon, Water Rail, Ringed and European Golden Plovers, Northern Lapwing, Knot, Sanderling, Jack and Common Snipe, Woodcock, Glaucous Gull (scarce), Kittiwake, Common Guillemot, Short-eared Owl, Shore Lark, Water Pipit (scarce), Rock Pipit, European Stonechat, Fieldfare, Redwing, Twite, Lapland and Snow Buntings.

March–June: Common Scoter, Quail (scarce, May and June), Red-throated Diver (March), Marsh Harrier, Hen Harrier (March and April), Montagu's Harrier (scarce, May), Osprey (scarce, April and May), Merlin (March and April), Hobby, Peregrine Falcon (March and April), Oystercatcher, Ringed Plover, Dotterel (scarce, late April and May), Grey Plover, Knot, Sanderling, Dunlin, Ruff, Jack Snipe (March and April), Bar-tailed Godwit, Whimbrel, Curlew, Greenshank, Green Sandpiper, Wood Sandpiper (scarce, May), Common Sandpiper, Turnstone, Little Gull, Glaucous Gull (scarce, March), Sandwich, Common, Arctic and Little Terns, Turtle Dove, Cuckoo, Short-eared Owl (March and April), Shore Lark (March and April), Rock Pipit (March and April), Yellow Wagtail, Nightingale (scarce), Black Redstart (March and April), Common Redstart (April and May), Whinchat, European Stonechat (March), Northern Wheatear, Ring Ouzel, Grasshopper, Sedge and Reed Warblers, Common Whitethroat, Wood Warbler (scarce), Firecrest (March), Spotted Flycatcher, Pied Flycatcher (April and May).

July–October: Brent Goose (September onwards), Common Scoter, Velvet Scoter (September onwards), Red-breasted Merganser, Red-throated Diver, Sooty Shearwater (August and September), Manx Shearwater, Leach's Storm-petrel (scarce, September and October), Gannet, Marsh Harrier, Hen Harrier (September onwards), Merlin, Hobby, Water Rail, European Golden Plover, Knot, Sanderling, Little Stint (scarce, August and September), Curlew Sandpiper (scarce, August and September), Ruff, Jack Snipe (September onwards), Woodcock (October), Black-tailed Godwit, Whimbrel, Spotted Redshank, Greenshank, Green and Wood Sandpipers, Pomarine Skua (scarce), Arctic Skua, Long-tailed Skua (scarce), Great Skua, Mediterranean and Little Gulls, Kittiwake, Sandwich, Common, Arctic and Little Terns, Common Guillemot, Long-eared Owl (October), Short-eared Owl (October), Wryneck (scarce, August and September), Woodlark (scarce, October), Shore Lark (October), Richard's Pipit (scarce, September and October), Rock Pipit (September onwards), Black Redstart (October), Common Redstart (August to October), Whinchat, European Stonechat (October), Northern Wheatear, Ring Ouzel (October), Icterine Warbler (scarce, August to October), Barred Warbler (scarce, August to October), Pallas's Warbler (scarce, October), Yellow-browed Warbler (scarce, September and October), Wood Warbler (scarce, August), Firecrest (October), Spotted Flycatcher, Red-breasted Flycatcher (scarce, September and October), Pied Flycatcher (August and September), Red-backed Shrike (scarce, August and September), Great Grey Shrike (scarce, October), Brambling (September and October), Twite (September onwards), Lapland Bunting (September onwards), Snow Bunting (September onwards).

20. THE EAST COAST: SUTTON ON SEA TO CHAPEL ST LEONARDS

OS Landranger 122
OS Explorer 274

Habitat

The coastline south of Mablethorpe sprang to fame during the east coast floods of 1953, when large sections of the sea defences were destroyed and huge areas of countryside flooded. Since then much of this section of the coast has been protected with man-made sea defences of clay, stone and concrete, with large areas being rebuilt and strengthened during the 1990s. Some natural dunes still exist south of Huttoft Car Terrace to Chapel St Leonards, where the sea wall is again concrete. It is ironic that the destruction of the natural coastline led to the creation of the valuable bird-rich clay pits at Chapel, Wolla Bank, Huttoft and Sandilands, which were all excavated to provide materials for the rebuilding of the sea defences following the 1953 floods. These pits, consisting of areas of deep water with reedbeds and willow/sallow scrub, are now managed as nature reserves by the Lincolnshire Wildlife Trust.

Four main types of habitat of interest to the birdwatcher are to be found along this stretch: the strip of sea defences and its associated vegetation, which is of value at times of migration; the open beach and sea; the low-lying rich arable fields just inland which, during the winter months, can be attractive to wildfowl and some waders; and the clay pits themselves.

Those sand dunes which remain, between Huttoft Car Terrace and Anderby Creek, are mostly covered in sea buckthorn scrub and are, in general, rather unattractive to birds. Immediately north and south of Anderby Creek are several small gardens with sycamores, willows, hedgerows and lawns which provide ideal habitat for migrant passerines. There is also an extensive area of young sycamores to the north of the creek beyond the bungalows. Further south there are extensive areas of sallows and willows at Chapel Six Marshes, while open grazed dune and longer grass can be found adjacent to Chapel Pit. A car park at Chapel coastguard lookout also has some scrub surrounding it. This spot provides a good vantage point for seawatching as the coast turns slightly south-west here, and the raised concrete sea wall provides a degree of elevation useful along this low-lying coastline. Other areas of sallows, willows and sycamores are found around the outfall at Chapel St Leonards, again often in gardens, and have proved to be attractive to migrants.

Inland from the sea defences, the arable fields between Anderby Creek and Huttoft Bank often hold wintering wildfowl and can be viewed from the coast road. Towards Chapel St Leonards some small areas of permanent pasture remain, although the acreage has been greatly reduced in recent years. A golf course south of Sandilands provides a large area of short grass with rougher patches of longer vegetation, and recent work on the sea defences has left areas of short grass with open sandy areas adjacent to the concrete sea wall. A large, slightly elevated concrete car terrace at Huttoft provides a convenient seawatching point and also allows watching to be carried out from a vehicle in inclement weather.

Species

The sea off the Lincolnshire coast is rather unpredictable with regard to the birds that may be seen, but in winter there will always be something to look at. Red-throated Divers are usually present, although may be quite distant; numbers vary, but during good feeding movements up to 500 may be seen in a couple of hours, flying north or south offshore. Other divers are real rarities and if they do occur are just as likely to be seen on the clay pits. Flocks of Common Scoters and a few Common Eiders are regular, but the best variety of species is found during or after periods of strong northerly oriented winds. In these conditions, Scaup, Red-breasted Merganser, Long-tailed Duck and Velvet Scoter become likely and auks, mainly Common Guillemots, may be numerous. Periods of northerlies in late October or November usually produce movements of Little Auks, with birds flying north on days after the strongest winds. Similar weather conditions in midwinter often give rise to a southerly passage of large gulls; the majority will be Herring and Great Black-backed, but good movements usually include a few Glaucous and odd Iceland Gulls. Small feeding flocks of Little Gulls are often a feature of the sea off Huttoft Bank in midwinter.

The clay pits can attract a vagrant Red-necked or Slavonian Grebes, Long-tailed Duck or Scaup, while Smew is fairly regular. Bitterns are seen in most winters but as everywhere are elusive; the hide overlooking Huttoft Pit is the best bet for locating one. Water Rails are common in the reedbeds surrounding the clay pits and Bearded Tits are regular visitors in the same areas. Cetti's Warblers are being recorded with increasing frequency during the winter months.

The arable fields either side of the coast road hold large flocks of Northern Lapwings and European Golden Plovers, and small parties of Bewick's and Whooper Swans are usually present. In winters when influxes

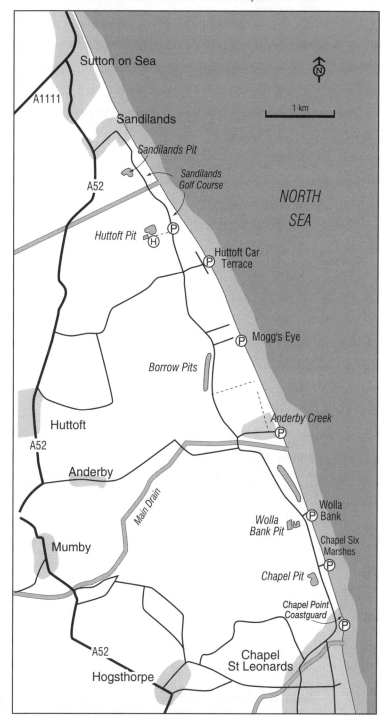

of geese from the continent take place, the same fields may attract flocks of White-fronted, Barnacle, Tundra Bean and Pink-footed Geese. Raptors such as Hen Harrier, Merlin and Peregrine Falcon are often found in this area, as well as a few Short-eared Owls.

Waders are not particularly numerous in the winter, but parties of Sanderling may be found along with small numbers of Ringed Plovers, and a few Purple Sandpipers are usually present somewhere between Trusthorpe and Chapel St Leonards. Rock Pipits are widespread along the sea embankments, and small flocks of Snow Buntings are often present, though they can be rather mobile.

Spring migration begins with Northern Wheatears appearing along the sea embankments, with a few European Stonechats and Black Redstarts joining them from late March. Firecrests are regularly encountered at this time of year at Anderby Creek and Chapel St Leonards. Early spring also often sees a marked passage of Short-eared Owls. Later, during April, scarcer migrants such as Whinchat, Common Redstart and Ring Ouzel may be numerous during periods of easterly winds, and older stands of trees often attract passage Spotted and Pied Flycatchers and the occasional Wood Warbler.

The reedbeds of the clay pits are enlivened with singing Reed and Sedge Warblers, while Grasshopper Warblers can be relied upon along the stretch from Anderby Creek south to Chapel Six Marshes. Marsh Harriers are frequent visitors to the clay pits and sometimes breed in the area, and the coastal location of the reedbeds has produced a number of rarities over the years, including Little Bittern, Purple Heron, Spoonbill, Marsh Warbler and two Great Reed Warblers. Similarly the coastal scrub can be productive, evidenced by the Great Spotted Cuckoo which appeared at Anderby Creek in May 1971. The golf course at Sandilands attracts passage Yellow Wagtails and sometimes waders such as Whimbrel, Ruff and Black-tailed Godwit, and Dotterels have put in an appearance on a few occasions. Breeding birds are fairly limited; Reed, Sedge and Grasshopper Warblers are present along with Common Whitethroats and Willow Warblers in the scrub, and a few ducks breed on the pits, where Water Rails and Bearded Tits sometimes summer.

By July, Sandwich, Common and Little Terns and Arctic Skuas are regularly present offshore, and the gull roost off Huttoft Bank often contains small numbers of Mediterranean Gulls. A good autumn seawatch is possible any time from August to November but the key factor is the weather. A good strong blow lasting a day or more, from the north, north-east or east, will bring a marked passage of several species of seabirds, which can be observed from any of the locations mentioned along this stretch of coast. Most species usually move south in the strongest winds and return north as the wind abates, when they are best observed as they are generally moving slower and closer to the shore. Gannets are usually the most numerous species in the early autumn (August to September), with smaller numbers of Fulmars, Arctic and Great Skuas, Kittiwakes, Little Gulls and Common, Arctic, Sandwich and Black Terns. The two rarer skuas, Pomarine and Long-tailed, are slightly more erratic in their appearances, although may be seen in reasonable numbers in some years. Strong northerlies bring small groups of Manx and Sooty Shearwaters and, especially in September, Leach's Storm-petrels, when there is also the chance of something out of the ordinary like a Sabine's Gull. Later in the autumn (October to November) the species composition changes, with more seaducks such as Common and Velvet Scoters, Red-breasted Mergansers and Long-tailed Ducks, along with Kittiwakes, Common Guillemots, Little Auks and greater numbers of Great and Pomarine Skuas.

Pallas's Warbler

If water levels are low at Huttoft Pit it attracts the usual variety of migrant freshwater waders; Greenshank, Spotted Redshank, Common and Jack Snipe and Green, Wood and Common Sandpipers are the most frequent, with a few Curlew Sandpipers and Little Stints. Black-tailed Godwits are a regular feature of the autumn, as are flocks of juvenile Ruffs, and both species feed on Sandilands golf course. Flocks of Whimbrels and the occasional Dotterel also drop in sometimes. Rarer waders found at Huttoft over the years have included Black-winged Stilt, American Golden Plover, Pectoral Sandpiper and Lesser Yellowlegs, while Wilson's Phalaropes at both Anderby Creek and Chapel St Leonards demonstrate that vagrant waders can turn up elsewhere. Huttoft has also produced Blue-winged Teal and Laughing Gull at this time of year.

Visible migration is often quite pronounced along this stretch of the coastline as the dune system is narrow and the stream of birds more concentrated. The August passage of Common Swifts, hirundines and Yellow Wagtails is joined in September by flocks of Meadow Pipits and a few Grey Wagtails. By late September and throughout October, Skylarks, Chaffinches, Goldfinches and Linnets predominate, with smaller numbers of Bramblings and Siskins. When there is an easterly element to the wind, falls of Willow Warblers, Common and Lesser Whitethroats, Whinchats, Northern Wheatears, Common Redstarts and Spotted and Pied Flycatchers may take place, and there is always the chance of a Wryneck, Icterine or Barred Warbler or Red-backed Shrike from early August onwards. Such migrants can appear almost anywhere, although the sycamore trees at Anderby Creek and Chapel St Leonards are favoured, especially by Icterine Warblers. From late September through October, Firecrest, Yellow-browed Warbler, Red-breasted Flycatcher and Great Grey Shrike become more likely, while Sandilands golf course and the grassy areas south of Anderby Creek have proved attractive to Richard's Pipits. Black Redstarts frequent the stonier areas of the banks in late October and early November, when Woodcocks, Long-eared and Short-eared Owls and incoming flocks of thrushes can be found in any of the localities mentioned.

This section of the coastal strip is not extensively watched but records of Greenish, Pallas's, Hume's and Dusky Warblers, Penduline Tit and Isabelline Shrike show the potential of the area to attract eastern vagrants during the autumn.

Timing

As there is a limited intertidal area along this section of the coast the times of high and low tide are not important for seawatching. During the winter a calm clear day will offer the best views of divers and seaducks, but onshore gales bring more chance of a passage of ducks, divers, gulls and auks. Spells of easterly or south-easterly winds are the most productive conditions in spring and autumn for migrant passerines, while the heaviest visible migration usually occurs in periods of light south-westerly winds when the birds move into the wind.

For seabirds a day or two of strong north to north-easterly winds, preferably with rain or reduced visibility, followed by a day of lighter winds is the ideal scenario but there will be some birds to see at most times during the autumn. As this is an east-facing coast, the sun can be a problem while seawatching in the early morning; however, in fine settled conditions skuas and terns may move south in the late evening when the light is at its best, being behind the observer.

The coastal car parks can become congested on warm weekend days during the summer, although midweek is still fairly quiet.

Access

All sites mentioned in this section are accessed from the coast road between Sutton on Sea and Chapel St Leonards. Head north-east off the A52 just south of Sutton on Sea onto a minor road signposted to Sandilands; this road passes a large hotel on the right and then turns sharply right before running alongside the sea wall to the entrance to the golf course. A small parking area on the right at TF531802 adjoins the entrance to Sandilands Pit, a Lincolnshire Wildlife Trust reserve. About 0.75 miles (1.2 km) further south a small pull-in on the right at TF533793 is the car park for Huttoft Pit, another Lincolnshire Wildlife Trust reserve. A path leads along the side of the field south of the pit to a hide. Another 750 m south a left turn signposted to the sea leads to Huttoft Car Terrace (TF542787), where it is possible to park right next to the sea at high tide. Even at low tide the coast here is fairly steeply shelved and the tide edge is never far out.

Travelling south again on the minor road, tracks lead off left to car parks adjacent to the dunes at Moggs Eye and Marsh Yard. There are borrow pits to the west of the road and the extensive wide open fields should be scanned for wildfowl and waders in the winter.

Three miles (4.8 km) south of Sandilands is Anderby Creek. Turn left into the village where there is a car park at the end of the road adjacent to the dunes (TF552761). Walk up the sand track over the dunes and a small shelter is useful for seawatching in bad weather but unfortunately has a somewhat restricted perspective. Again from the car park, a track runs northwards along the edge of some small gardens and eventually passes an open-air sports complex backed with young sycamores. An obvious pathway leads into the trees while the main path continues north through another small copse. By walking south from the car park and crossing the creek at its mouth another area of scrub with some sycamores and elders is reached.

Continue south on the coastal road and tracks off to the left lead to car parks at Wolla Bank (TF556749) and Chapel Six Marshes (TF559742). Both car parks are set adjacent to the dunes, with some extensive but largely impenetrable areas of marshland, willows, sallows and bramble, and at Chapel Six Marsh a small conifer plantation. The dunes between the two car parks are grazed by donkeys, forming a nice open area of short grassland.

The entrances to the Lincolnshire Wildlife Trust reserves of Wolla Bank Pit and Chapel Pit are on the west side of the coast road at TF556749 and TF558740 respectively.

As the coast road reaches the northern outskirts of Chapel St Leonards the coastguard lookout car park at Chapel Point is on the left at TF562732. There is some scrub around the car park and across the road. Walk south on the sea wall past a row of holiday chalets to the mouth of the Willoughby High Drain, a fairly wide drainage channel, and then walk down the side of the drain and turn left onto a narrow residential road which runs south parallel with the dunes. The gardens and scrub around the channel mouth and farther south are good for migrants.

Calendar

Resident: Bittern, Sparrowhawk, Barn Owl, Bearded Tit, Reed Bunting.

December–February: Bewick's and Whooper Swans, Pink-footed and White-fronted Geese, Eurasian Wigeon, Shoveler, Scaup, Common Eider, Long-tailed Duck, Common and Velvet Scoters, Smew (scarce), Red-breasted Merganser, Red-throated Diver, Red-necked Grebe (scarce), Slavonian Grebe (scarce), Hen Harrier, Merlin, Water Rail, Ringed and European Golden Plovers, Northern Lapwing, Sanderling, Purple Sandpiper (scarce), Ruff, Jack and Common Snipe, Mediterranean and Little Gulls, Iceland Gull (scarce), Glaucous Gull, Common Guillemot, Short-eared Owl, Rock Pipit, European Stonechat, Cetti's Warbler (scarce), Twite, Snow Bunting.

March–May: Shoveler, Marsh Harrier, Merlin, Water Rail, Ruff, Whimbrel, Short-eared Owl, Yellow Wagtail, Black and Common Redstarts, Whinchat, European Stonechat, Northern Wheatear, Ring Ouzel, Grasshopper, Sedge and Reed Warblers, Common Whitethroat, Wood Warbler (scarce), Firecrest, Spotted and Pied Flycatchers.

July–November: Brent Goose (September to November), Common Eider, Long-tailed Duck, Common and Velvet Scoters, Red-breasted Merganser, Red-throated Diver, Fulmar, Sooty Shearwater (August to October), Manx Shearwater, Leach's Petrel (September to October), Gannet, Marsh Harrier (to October), Hen Harrier (September onwards), Merlin, Hobby, Water Rail, European Golden Plover, Sanderling, Little Stint (scarce), Curlew Sandpiper (scarce), Ruff, Jack Snipe (October onwards), Common Snipe, Woodcock (October to November), Black-tailed Godwit, Whimbrel, Spotted Redshank (scarce), Greenshank, Green, Wood and Common Sandpipers, Pomarine Skua (irregular), Arctic Skua, Long-tailed Skua (irregular), Great Skua, Mediterranean and Little Gulls, Kittiwake, Sandwich, Common, Arctic, Little and Black Terns, Common Guillemot, Little Auk (October to November), Long-eared Owl (October and November), Short-eared Owl, Wryneck (scarce, August to October), Richard's Pipit (scarce, September to October), Rock Pipit (September onwards), Yellow Wagtail, Black Redstart (October to November), Common Redstart, Whinchat, European Stonechat, Northern Wheatear, Ring Ouzel, Icterine Warbler (scarce, August to September), Barred Warbler (scarce, August to October), Pallas's Warbler (scarce, October to November), Yellow-browed Warbler (September to November), Firecrest (October to November), Spotted Flycatcher, Red-breasted Flycatcher (scarce, September to November), Pied Flycatcher, Red-backed Shrike (scarce, August to October), Great Grey Shrike (scarce, October to November), Twite (September onwards), Snow Bunting (September onwards).

21. GIBRALTAR POINT

Habitat

Gibraltar Point is situated on the Lincolnshire coast 3 miles (4.8 km) south of Skegness. It has mostly developed over the last 500 years through the accretion of a series of sand dune ridges separated by saltmarsh. The reserve covers over 1,112 acres (450 ha) and is an integral part of the Wash, representing its north-western extreme. The extensive foreshore and beach habitats lead south into the River Steeping Haven which demarcates the southern boundary of the reserve.

Saltmarsh and sand dunes demonstrate all stages of succession and plant colonisation from bare mud and sand. Much of the stable dune area has been colonised by a dense cover of sea buckthorn with mixed elder, hawthorn and privet. In addition to open dune grassland and dune slack, there is an extensive freshwater marsh and a small woodland. The natural habitats have merited designation as a Site of Special Scientific Interest and National Nature Reserve and international recognition has been received through designation as a Special Protection Area, Candidate Special Area of Conservation and Ramsar site. The recent addition to the site, Croftmarsh, is a Local Nature Reserve.

Gibraltar Point's geographical position and habitats make it an important migration staging post for thousands of birds. The Lincolnshire Wildlife Trust set up one of the first bird observatories here in 1948 and ringing commenced using Heligoland traps, one of which still exists today, although mist-netting is now more widely practiced.

The frontline coastal habitats here are dynamic, with embryo dunes forming and subsequently eroding in certain areas and shingle ridges building to stand proud of the highest 'spring' tides before being smothered by sand and early dune vegetation. Where pockets of mud are deposited, pioneer halophytes such as samphire may give rise to saltmarsh development. Such annuals provide an important seed supply for winter passerines. As marsh matures, the tussocky vegetation becomes an important nesting ground for Skylarks, Meadow Pipits and small numbers of Redshanks.

Active management of the stable dunes has concentrated on the clearance of areas of scrub to restore floristically rich dune grassland and dune slacks which support southern marsh orchid and Natterjack Toad. Where dune slack is left unmanaged, small patches of reed eventually succumb to shading by sallows providing excellent cover for insect-dependant migrants from early spring to late autumn.

Much of the East Dunes were used by the military in two world wars and the resulting disturbed ground allowed vast swathes of rosebay willowherb to establish, requiring management intervention. Sheep grazing on the dunes suppresses scrub, rosebay and other problem plants as well as maintaining a fine dune turf, benefiting plant communities, invertebrates and birds. Rabbits play an important role too, maintaining short lawns on the strip saltings for pipits, larks and wagtails.

At the turn of the 1900s, the northern section of the old saltmarsh was claimed from tidal waters through the instatement of a large earth bank. The resulting freshwater marsh has developed a rich flora. The borrow pits here provide a mix of open water, sea club rush and reed. Other water bodies of various sizes were created during military occupation and provide refuges for dragonflies, amphibians and Water Voles. The freshwater

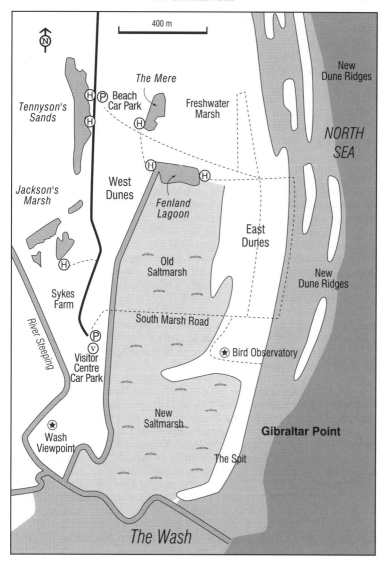

mere was excavated in the early 1970s to provide a permanent water body for wintering and nesting waterbirds and autumn waders, for which it has an impressive list. The Fenland Lagoon was created to provide a saline habitat between the freshwater marsh and saltmarsh.

To the west of Gibraltar Road lies the historic Sykes Farm area. Evidence of most of the buildings has long since disappeared, however the derelict 1830 barn has been converted into the reserve office. The old orchard and surrounding stands of sycamores remain. Old stands of elm along the boundaries have mostly succumbed to dutch elm disease, but some remain on the approach track to the nature reserve office. The main wooded block known as the Plantation consists of mixed deciduous and coniferous trees, planted in 1966 when the spread of caravan parks across the coastal belt was becoming a cause for concern. Today, most of the non-native pines have been thinned out and replaced with ash, field maple, hazel and hawthorn.

Until the late 1990s the reserve hinterland to the north of Sykes Farm was under intensive arable production. Since then, the Lincolnshire Wildlife Trust has purchased 120 acres (48.5 ha) up to the Cowbank Drain. This area, including Jackson's Marsh and Tennyson's Sands, has been designated the Croftmarsh Local Nature Reserve. Habitat creation work has involved the excavation of a series of brackish lagoons of varying depth, strips of reedbed and a large tract of grazing marsh with seasonally flooded areas.

Species

During the winter months the bleakness of the site becomes apparent, but so too does the dependence of many birds on the varied coastal habitats. Most sought after are the waders, wildfowl and birds of prey, and this leads the visitor to the saltmarsh and mudflats at the south end of the reserve. En route to the estuary small groups of Redshanks can be encountered on the saltmarsh, while wintering Rock Pipits secrete themselves within the clumps of sea couch and sea purslane unless flushed by a passing raptor. Water Pipits can also occur in the salt and freshwater marsh. Little Egret is a conspicuous winter bird on the marsh and in tidal creeks, tending to accumulate on Jackson's Marsh before flying to roost in the late afternoon.

The estuary is best scanned from the Wash Viewpoint. At low tide, waders are spread out across the mudflats and although many are distant, the sheer scale of numbers can be appreciated. Oystercatcher, Grey Plover, Dunlin, Bar-tailed Godwit, Curlew and Redshank are usually all well represented, although the most numerous species is Knot: up to 10,000 may attend the high tide roost during midwinter. Parties of Sanderlings can be found on the sandy foreshore. Cold weather periods push more Northern Lapwings and European Golden Plovers to the coast and, in such conditions, several thousand of each can occur. Inevitably, with so many waders in the area, raptors are usually in close proximity; a scan over the sand and shingle ridges may provide views of a resting Merlin or Peregrine Falcon.

The reserve supports over 2,000 Brent Geese annually, with peak numbers in January and February. They commute between the estuarine mudflats and saltmarsh and inland fields, often pausing on the Croftmarsh lagoons to bathe. This is the best opportunity to check for any vagrants within the flock; Black Brant and Pale-bellied Brents have become annual visitors, and a Red-breasted Goose was noted in February 1985. Also commuting to and from the estuary are flocks of dabbling ducks such as Eurasian Wigeon, Common Teal and Mallard. The Croftmarsh lagoons provide an excellent refuge for these, along with some Gadwall, Shovelers and Pintails. Shelducks are common on the mudflats through the winter. Wintering Water Rails are more often heard than seen, although the Mere is a good place to glimpse this elusive bird. Woodcock is another winter visitor, sometimes flushed from underfoot, but more easily seen as birds leave the dune scrub at dusk and fly onto Croftmarsh.

Large numbers of gulls roost on the flats or offshore during the winter months. The morning exodus from The Wash often sees sizeable gatherings taking the pickings from a falling tide. There is a chance of a Glaucous or Iceland Gull, although Mediterranean Gulls are more likely. At sea Red-throated Divers can usually be seen in moderate numbers, although during January and February numbers can build to several hundred. Black-throated and Great Northern Divers are occasional visitors at this time of

Bluethroat

year, as are Slavonian Grebes. In some years, a wintering flock of scoters becomes established offshore, which may contain up to 1,000 Common Scoters and 60 Velvet Scoters. Otherwise, seaducks are generally unpredictable; small numbers of Common Eiders and Red-breasted Mergansers are regular, although Long-tailed Ducks are scarce. Winter gales can produce significant movements of Kittiwakes and Fulmars and maybe the odd skua or Little Auk.

The reserve has become known as one of the few reliable sites in Britain to find wintering Shore Larks, with a revival during the 1990s when 60-90 were seen. In more recent winters, however, numbers have been much lower. Twite is no longer guaranteed, but single Arctic Redpolls visited in January 1996 and 1984. One or two Lapland Buntings are present most winters but are elusive in the remotest saltmarsh. Flocks of Snow Buntings may be encountered, although these have become harder to find in recent years. As with most sites, large flocks of wintering passerines have dwindled, although parties of Greenfinches, Linnets and Goldfinches can still be found. The wintering flock of Corn Buntings is very much a prominent feature though; up to 60 birds may assemble close to the visitor centre car park during the late afternoon. Also here at this time, Barn and Short-eared Owls may be hunting over the Old Saltmarsh and Hen Harriers will be making their way to roost, although these are best looked for from the Wash Viewpoint. Up to five birds can be seen, with Merlin and Sparrowhawk also in attendance. The latter part of winter is marked by movements of Pink-footed Geese, and skeins move to the north-west coast of England from north Norfolk on the first leg of their journey to Iceland.

The onset of spring migration can be heralded by the call of an errant Rook on the move in early March, coinciding with a light build-up of Robins, Song Thrushes, Redwings, Starlings or Goldcrests preparing for departure. Passage Woodlarks are another indication of spring. The real classic signs though are the trio of European Stonechat, Black Redstart and Northern Wheatear which often turn up between the Wash Study Centre and the Wash Viewpoint along 'Rock Ridge' in mid-March. Ring Ouzels may also arrive with this first migrant wave. Major rarities during March have included a Snowy Owl which moved north from nearby Wainfleet in 1991, a Pine Bunting in 1995 and, most unexpectedly, a Sora in 2006.

The passage of continental finches can involve hundreds of birds, particularly Chaffinches, with usually a good representation of Bramblings. Anything can get caught up in these movements and it is not uncommon to see Blue and Great Tits and corvids all pouring south over the dunes on a good passage day. Firecrests are regular from March to May with up to six in a day. The first hirundines are to be expected by late March and are usually heading south, as are all migrants in spring; this is an east-coast phenomena thought to relate to the reorientation of overshooting migrants.

Spring migration through most of April can be quite subtle, but excitement is always provided by passage raptors including Sparrowhawks, Marsh Harriers, Common Buzzards and one or two Ospreys and Red Kites. Rough-legged Buzzard is a strong possibility, Black Kite has been recorded three times but Honey Buzzard is more likely. In addition, spring sightings of Common Crane are now annual.

Another highlight of this period is the spring wader passage. The build-up of Knot and Grey Plovers averages about 8,000 and 2,000 respectively, with many birds exhibiting striking summer plumage. Dunlin and Bar-tailed Godwit occur in lower numbers. Sanderling flocks peak in late May, when over 2,000 can assemble. Little Stint and Curlew Sandpiper may be concealed within these wader flocks and parties of Whimbrels become a common sight and sound as they head north. On the Croftmarsh lagoons, waders may include Ruff, Black-tailed Godwit, Greenshank and Common Sandpiper. The best chance of Water Pipit is also here in early April with up to five having been seen on occasions. Temminck's Stint, Wood Sandpiper and Garganey are virtually annual in spring and there has been a series of Purple Heron records.

Marked falls of birds can occur during late April and May, mostly involving wagtails, chats and warblers. The Rabbit-grazed strip saltings are good for Yellow and White Wagtails and Northern Wheatears, and have also hosted Stone-curlew, Dotterel and Tawny Pipit on more than one occasion. The dune edge seaward of the bird observatory can be particularly rewarding and is a good bet for Common Redstart, Whinchat, Wood Warbler, Firecrest or Pied Flycatcher during suitable weather in May. If classic fall conditions prevail then Scandinavian migrants may be displaced by north-easterly winds, before being forced to make landfall under rain, drizzle or fog. Red-backed Shrike, Wryneck and Bluethroat have been grounded at this time, with Golden Oriole and Common Rosefinch perhaps more likely these days. Red-throated Pipit, Thrush Nightingale and River Warbler have all paid spring visits, and buntings have been represented by Ortolan, Rustic and, more exceptionally, Yellow-breasted.

Visible migration provides interest on a daily basis, but particularly into a south-westerly wind. Later in the spring, Goldfinch and Linnet are the predominant finches, with flocks of the latter often pausing to feed on the seeds of early annuals. Linnet is the preferred carrier species for Serin, one of several species which can be expected to overshoot from the Mediterranean on spring migration from time to time. Red-rumped Swallows have become increasingly regular, with an exceptional record of four together over the Mere in April 2003. Other flavours of a southerly airstream have included Night Heron, European Bee-eater, Woodchat Shrike and Subalpine Warbler. Movements of Common Swifts are typical of late spring and can attract a Hobby or two, while Alpine Swift has been seen dashing through on some four occasions. The number of species involved in visible migration scales down during early June, however the chance of a scarce migrant is still high in the form of Honey Buzzard, Golden Oriole,

Red-backed Shrike or Common Rosefinch, and it is probably the best month for Quail. June has also produced the odd Red-footed Falcon and several European Bee-eaters and Marsh Warblers, but exceptional rarities have been Little Swift in 2002 and long-staying Sardinian Warblers in 1979 and 1986. During most summers, small parties of irruptive Common Crossbills arrive, although an exceptional influx brought 110 in June 1991.

In the dunes, Common Whitethroats are the most numerous breeding bird. Willow Warblers are common too, along with a sprinkling of Lesser Whitethroats and Sedge Warblers. In most years, one or two Grasshopper Warblers hold territory along the Mill Pond Road. Small colonies of Linnets can be encountered in the dunes, although Lesser Redpoll has declined from a common to rare breeding bird. Turtle Doves can usually be found from late May; small parties feed on the seeds of spring beauty while nesting is restricted to the denser, older scrub stands.

The saltmarsh hosts a lower diversity of breeding species but populations of Skylarks and Meadow Pipits are significant. Reed Bunting and Redshank breed in lower numbers on the marsh. On the shore, shingle ridges host important populations of Little Terns and Ringed Plovers; the terns can be seen fishing close inshore or using various lagoons and tidal pools in rough weather. Breeding colonies of Black-headed Gulls on the Fenland Lagoon and Croftmarsh occasionally attract immature Little and Mediterranean Gulls. In recent years, the newly created lagoons of Jackson's Marsh and Tennyson's Sands have been colonised by Avocets; nesting alongside may be Oystercatchers, Little Ringed and Ringed Plovers and Common Terns, while the grazing marsh beyond has started to attract breeding Northern Lapwings. Marsh Harrier and Hobby are increasingly seen during the summer months, and non-breeding Montagu's Harriers will often linger in the area for several days.

Back on the lagoons, Spoonbills often pause for long spells; four birds summered here in 2002. More unexpected were June records of Wilson's Phalarope in 1987 and Lesser Yellowlegs in 1990. Continuing on the rare wader theme, July has produced its share, with Broad-billed Sandpiper in 1990, Long-billed Dowitcher in 2004 and Terek Sandpiper in 2005; in addition, the first Great White Egret for the reserve arrived in July 1993. The routine return of northern waders commences early with Green Sandpipers in evidence by mid-June. Black-tailed Godwits, Greenshanks and Ruffs arrive slightly later on the freshwater pools, while on the estuary numbers of Grey Plovers and Knot are building by mid-July; up to 8,000 of the latter may be present in the high tide roost by the end of the month. Also on the beach, up to 1,000 Sandwich Terns become a feature as pairs arrive with their young from east-coast colonies on the first leg of their southbound migration. A roost of large gulls usually contains Yellow-legged Gull, during the latter part of the summer.

A more truly autumnal spectacle is provided by the first skuas which are attracted in to harass the feeding terns, and by August Arctic Skuas are offshore on a daily basis. Other seabirds can be concentrated into this sector of the North Sea following strong northerly winds – Pomarine and Long-tailed Skuas are seen annually in such conditions and passages of Sooty Shearwaters have included 358 on September 16, 2005. Smaller numbers of Manx Shearwaters occur too. Leach's Storm-petrel is annual, there has been a good run of Sabine's Gulls in recent years, and European Storm-petrel and Balearic Shearwater are possible. The majority of these seabirds are heading north, alongside often hundreds of Gannets. Northerlies can still produce interesting passage into November; Little Auks and Great and Pomarine

Skuas are a good bet this late in the year and Grey Phalarope is a distinct possibility.

August and September are key months for passage waders; Greenshank build up to 50 or more, roosting on the Fenland Lagoon and Black-tailed Godwit number over 100 at their roost on Croftmarsh. An autumn roost of Common Sandpipers can develop on Croftmarsh and involve up to 50 individuals, along with up to ten Green Sandpipers. Ruff, Spotted Redshank and Wood Sandpiper add to the wader composition and the occasional Red-necked Phalarope and Pectoral Sandpiper have been seen. This period usually brings Little Stints and Curlew Sandpipers to the lagoons and estuary; most are juveniles, but a flock of 73 adult Curlew Sandpipers moulting out of summer plumage on 10 August 2004 was exceptional. Any of the 'spring' tide sequences from August to October will provide impressive wader flocks. It is not uncommon for over 50,000 Knot to be present in the roost, further augmented by up to 5,000 each of Grey Plover, Bar-tailed Godwit and Dunlin. The peak wader count of the year may be close on 100,000 birds.

The freshwater habitats should also be checked for wagtails, and a Citrine Wagtail was a nice find in September 1983. A scan of the reeds may reveal the first autumnal Water Rails and perhaps a Spotted Crake. The Mere traditionally hosts Jack Snipe in front of the hide and Garganey can be found with patience.

In common with spring, the onset of easterly winds raises the prospects of an arrival of landbirds. The first fall of migrants usually occurs from mid-August and doubtless involves many British breeding birds such as Common Redstarts, Whinchats, Northern Wheatears, Lesser Whitethroats, Willow Warblers and Pied Flycatchers, but evidence that continental birds are involved can be proven by the arrival of the occasional Hoopoe, Wryneck, Barred and Icterine Warbler or Red-backed Shrike. During the largest falls, over 480 Common Redstarts and 200 Pied Flycatchers have been seen in a day. Overhead, Meadow Pipits, finches and hirundines can move south on a broad front; up to 35,000 Swallows have been estimated passing over during a single afternoon! The potential for raptor passage is also high, but somewhat unpredictable. Sparrowhawks are regularly seen heading south, but on 11 September 1998, 46 Kestrels moved south, along with six Marsh Harriers, four Hobbies and an Osprey. Perhaps the most impressive raptor movement occurred in late September 2000 when 34 Honey Buzzards passed through in groups of up to six.

Towards the end of September, the autumn period takes on a distinctly different feel. Migrant Willow Warblers, Common and Lesser Whitethroats are replaced by Common Chiffchaffs and Blackcaps, and tit flocks are worth checking for straggling warblers, Firecrests and the odd Treecreeper. Visible migration of passerines becomes dominated by finches, particularly Greenfinch and Goldfinch, but Siskins are often prominent and parties of Chaffinches harbour newly arrived Bramblings. Of the rarer finches, 'northern' Bullfinch and Hawfinch have paused during this period and Common Rosefinches have associated with Linnets. Rock Pipits are now taking over from Meadow Pipits, with Skylarks and small numbers of sparrows and buntings caught up in the movement during October. The first Lapland and Snow Buntings may also be located. Perhaps the most significant species which can arrive en masse are Goldcrests and thrushes; a fall during mid-October 1990 produced over 1,000 Goldcrests, 9,500 Fieldfares and 6,200 Redwings. With these come smaller numbers of Song Thrushes, Robins and Ring Ouzels, while peak Blackbird arrivals can be witnessed in early November; an estimated 100,000 arrived on 5 November 1961! Waxwing and

Great Grey Shrike are typical scarce migrants at this time of year, but with the 1990 fall came three Parrot Crossbills. From further east, Red-breasted Flycatcher is a regular visitor and Yellow-browed Warbler is to be expected annually; up to ten have been recorded in a single day. Pallas's Warbler is the later counterpart of Yellow-browed and with luck can be found most Octobers. Greenish, Arctic and Radde's Warblers have all occurred, but the Hume's Warbler of 2003 was the first county record. Richard's Pipits are almost annual and there have been a handful of Olive-backed Pipits and Little Buntings.

Passerine migrants, particularly thrushes, Starlings and Skylarks, can be seen arriving off the sea, but more unusual sights may include a Woodcock or Short-eared or Long-eared Owl coming in low over the waves, or a displaced Little Auk accompanying a flock of landbound Starlings. Offshore wildfowl movements can include Eurasian Wigeon, Common Teal and Common Scoter in good numbers with a few Scaup and Goldeneyes, as well as skeins of Pink-footed Geese heading to the Norfolk coast.

This is the time to expect the unexpected in respect of numbers of birds or rarities. Pied Wheatear, Lesser Grey Shrike and Nutcracker have all occurred, but the Red-flanked Bluetail of 2002 was a particular star. Beyond mythical, however, were two Nearctic passerines; an American Redstart in 1982 and a Northern Waterthrush in 1988. The former showed to many in the Plantation during November and, remarkably, birders there were also treated to an Isabelline Shrike in close proximity. This simultaneous demonstration of the extremes of eastern and western vagrancy is what makes Gibraltar Point one of the most exciting sites in Britain for bird migration.

Timing

Although there is plenty to see at all times of year, May, September and October are perhaps the most exciting months for the numbers of birds on migration and the chance of scarce species, which usually arrive following winds anywhere between south-easterly and north-easterly. Visible migration of passerines and hirundines is best seen from late April through May and again from August into November; a south-westerly wind produces the greatest movements.

Migration periods are more protracted for waders, for which spring passage commences in March and goes through to early June and autumn from late June to mid-November. 'Spring' tides occur on a monthly basis (check the relevant tide tables for full details), forcing more waders out of The Wash to roost on the outer ridges of the reserve. A suitable vantage point should be selected at least an hour before the larger tides (7 m or above) to watch the arrival of thousands of waders. The highest tides fall during the early mornings or evenings.

Sea passage is generally light in spring, but from August the number and diversity of seabirds increases. Strong northerly winds are the key to sea-watching success; find a high vantage point in the dunes, where scrub will provide shelter. Early morning seawatching can be somewhat hampered by the rising sun. Conversely, Croftmarsh is best viewed from the hides early in the day before the sun swings round to the west.

Access

Situated 3 miles (4.8 km) south of Skegness, the reserve is approached via a minor road signposted to Gibraltar Point from the town centre. There is limited public transport to the reserve, thus the majority of visitors will arrive at one of two car parks. There are large information boards with orientation maps in both car parks, and links directly onto the main track network. Seasonal car park charges apply and any organised parties are requested to book in advance.

The south car park is adjacent to the visitor centre, which is open throughout most of the year and houses an exhibition, café, toilets and gift shop. Reserve leaflets, maps and other information can be provided by the Lincolnshire Wildlife Trust volunteers at the centre. The adjacent field station, the 'Wash Study Centre', hosts residential educational groups and courses and is an ideal base for birdwatching parties.

Formal visitor access is focused on the southern half of the reserve and there is a circular route of approximately 2.3 miles (3.7 km) which takes in most of the key habitats. The main route is surfaced to a reasonable standard, allowing wheelchair use. Access through the saltmarsh is possible via the South Marsh Road; visitors should remain on the paths to reduce damage and keep disturbance to a minimum. While access onto sensitive areas such as Croftmarsh and the Freshwater Marsh cannot be permitted, there are good opportunities to view over such areas. There are hides overlooking the Fenland Lagoon, Freshwater Mere and lagoons at Tennyson's Sands and Jackson's Marsh, the latter being a very spacious hide suitable for birdwatching parties.

A visit to the Wash Viewpoint at the southern extreme of the reserve gives a view south into the vast estuarine plain of the northern Wash. During the highest tides, wader flocks can be observed moving north out of the wash from here, as well as from the Bird Observatory viewpoint or Mill Hill. Roosting and feeding waders can easily be disturbed and visitors are requested not to approach too closely.

During the summer months, the beach is zoned to protect breeding shorebirds at the south end. Elsewhere, some areas of dunes are fenced on a large scale to retain grazing cattle and Hebridean sheep. Here, gated access points are provided.

The boundary of the Gibraltar Point National Nature Reserve runs west to east at Seacroft Esplanade, but the dune and marsh habitat continues north for a further 0.6 miles (1 km) and is designated as an SSSI up to the boat compound on South Parade; several avenues off Drummond Road give access to the SSSI. Some of the large gardens here have hosted a range of migrants, but these are connected to private residences. However there is more open access via a network of unofficial tracks through the dunes. Large stands of mature sycamores create a backdrop to the dunes, with patches of elm, poplar and sallow, providing a tract of 'dune woodland' which offers some excellent birding. Access to the outer dunes across the saltmarsh is difficult due to the presence of a large tidal creek which can only be crossed a fair way to the north. In any event, the blocks of scrub over much of the outer dune system are extremely dense and bird finding can be hard work. The mix of rough grassland, grazed areas and tidal pools has plenty of potential for breeding, wintering and passage species, although this area is heavily populated by dog walkers and there are perennial problems with off-road vehicles. Patches of relict dune habitat can be found fronting the holiday and amusement infrastructure along the Skegness seafront and there are some good migrant hotspots. The best of these is around the North Parade car park where Sardinian Warbler and Red-flanked Bluetail have occurred. Migrant finding in these areas can be easier than in the SSSI habitats to the south, but the surroundings are much less attractive.

Calendar

Resident: Little Grebe, Cormorant, Little Egret, Sparrowhawk, Oystercatcher, Northern Lapwing, Curlew, Redshank, Skylark, Meadow Pipit, Linnet, Lesser Redpoll, Yellowhammer, Reed Bunting.

November–February: Pink-footed and Brent Geese, Black Brant (scarce), Shelduck, Eurasian Wigeon, Gadwall, Common Teal, Pintail, Shoveler, Common Eider, Long-tailed Duck (scarce), Common and Velvet Scoters, Goldeneye, Red-breasted Merganser, Red-throated Diver, Black-throated Diver (scarce), Great Northern Diver (scarce), Slavonian Grebe (scarce), Fulmar, Hen Harrier, Merlin, Peregrine Falcon, Water Rail, European Golden and Grey Plovers, Knot, Sanderling, Dunlin, Common Snipe, Woodcock, Bar-tailed Godwit, Turnstone, Mediterranean Gull, Iceland Gull (scarce), Glaucous Gull (scarce), Kittiwake, Little Auk (scarce, November), Barn and Short-eared Owls, Shore Lark (scarce), Water and Rock Pipits, European Stonechat, Fieldfare, Redwing, Lapland, Snow and Corn Buntings.

March–June: Brent Goose (March and April), Garganey, Spoonbill (scarce, May and June), Honey Buzzard (scarce, May and June), Red Kite, Marsh Harrier, Hen Harrier (March and April), Montagu's Harrier (scarce, May and June), Common Buzzard, Osprey, Merlin (March and April), Hobby, Peregrine Falcon (March and April), Common Crane (scarce), Avocet, Little Ringed Plover, Ringed Plover, Grey Plover, Knot, Sanderling, Temminck's Stint (scarce), Dunlin, Ruff, Jack Snipe (March and April), both godwits, Whimbrel, Greenshank, Green, Wood and Common Sandpipers, Turnstone, Mediterranean and Little Gulls, Sandwich and Common Terns, Turtle Dove, Cuckoo, Long-eared Owl (March and April), Short-eared Owl (March and April), Hoopoe (rare), Wryneck (scarce), Woodlark, Water Pipit (March and April), Yellow Wagtail, White Wagtail (March and April), Bluethroat (scarce), Black Redstart (March and April), Common Redstart (April and May), Whinchat, European Stonechat, Northern Wheatear, Ring Ouzel, Grasshopper, Sedge and Reed Warbler, Lesser and Common Whitethroats, Wood Warbler (scarce), Firecrest, Pied Flycatcher (April and May), Golden Oriole (scarce, May and June), Red-backed Shrike (scarce, May and June), Brambling, Common Crossbill (irregular, June), Common Rosefinch (scarce, May and June).

July–October: Pink-footed Goose (September onwards), Brent Goose (October onwards), Eurasian Wigeon, Gadwall, Common Teal, Garganey, Scaup (October onwards), Common Eider, Common and Velvet Scoters, Goldeneye (October onwards), Red-breasted Merganser, Red-throated Diver, Sooty Shearwater (August and September), Manx Shearwater, Leach's Storm-petrel (scarce, September and October), Gannet, Honey Buzzard (scarce, September), Marsh Harrier, Hen Harrier (September onwards), Common Buzzard, Merlin, Hobby, Peregrine Falcon, Water Rail, Ringed and Grey Plovers, Knot, Sanderling, Little Stint, Curlew Sandpiper, Dunlin, Ruff, Jack Snipe (October onwards), Common Snipe, Woodcock (October), both godwits, Spotted Redshank, Greenshank, Green, Wood and Common Sandpipers, Pomarine and Arctic Skuas, Long-tailed Skua (rare), Great Skua, Mediterranean, Little and Yellow-legged Gulls, Kittiwake, Sandwich, Common, Arctic and Little Terns, Common Guillemot, Little Auk (October onwards), Long-eared Owl (October), Short-eared Owl (October), Wryneck (scarce, August and September), Shore Lark (scarce, October), Richard's Pipit (scarce, September and October), Rock Pipit (September onwards),

Yellow Wagtail, Waxwing (scarce, October), Black Redstart (October), Common Redstart (August to October), Whinchat, European Stonechat, Northern Wheatear, Ring Ouzel (October), Fieldfare (September onwards), Redwing (September onwards), Icterine Warbler (scarce, August to October), Barred Warbler (scarce, August to October), Pallas's Warbler (rare, October), Yellow-browed Warbler (September and October), Wood Warbler (scarce, August), Firecrest (October), Spotted Flycatcher, Red-breasted Flycatcher (scarce, September and October), Pied Flycatcher (August and September), Red-backed Shrike (scarce, August and September), Great Grey Shrike (scarce, October), Brambling (September onwards), Siskin, Common Rosefinch (scarce, August to October), Lapland Bunting (September onwards), Snow Bunting (September onwards).

22. THE WASH

OS Landrangers 122 and 131
OS Explorers 249, 261 and 274

Habitat

The Wash is the largest and numerically most important estuary in the British Isles for combined wader and wildfowl totals, and has been designated as a Ramsar site and a Special Protection Area. Situated half in Norfolk and half in Lincolnshire, it presents an exceptional area for watching huge numbers of birds within the East Midlands region. Stretching from Gibraltar Point in the north-east to Terrington, east of the mouth of the River Nene, the Wash drains three major rivers in the Lincolnshire section, the Witham, Welland and Nene.

Huge areas of intertidal mud and sandflats provide ideal feeding and roosting areas for a large variety of waders and wildfowl, while saltmarshes, grazing marsh and reclaimed arable fields just inland of the sea defences attract different waders, wintering passerines and hunting owls and raptors. The surrounding farmland is privately owned, but the RSPB and English Nature manage some large sections of saltmarsh and grazing marsh. There are numerous points of public access to the estuary embankments and the whole area is best explored from these banks by scanning over the salt-marsh, mudflats, grazing marsh and inland fields.

The geography of The Wash differs little around its perimeter, with subtle differences in substrate and vegetation accounting for the varying propor-tions of species using different areas. Typically, a raised sea bank gives way abruptly to a wide expanse of saltmarsh vegetation, dominated by sea aster and various rough grasses; this then fades into an open expanse of mud, silt and sand, intersected by tidal creeks which drain these flats at low tide. 'Spring' tides usually inundate the saltmarsh, with the highest of the year lap-ping up to the base of the sea defences, especially if backed by a strong northerly wind. Neap tides rarely reach as high as the outer edge of the salt-marsh and it is important to know the times and heights of local tides to make the most of birding in this area.

Historically, The Wash has been subjected to regular land claim around its edges, which has resulted in a gradual loss of areas of saltmarsh and an extension of the rich arable farmland around its periphery. In their early stages land claim schemes usually involve throwing up a clay bank around an area of saltmarsh, which is then seeded with grass for a few years to help

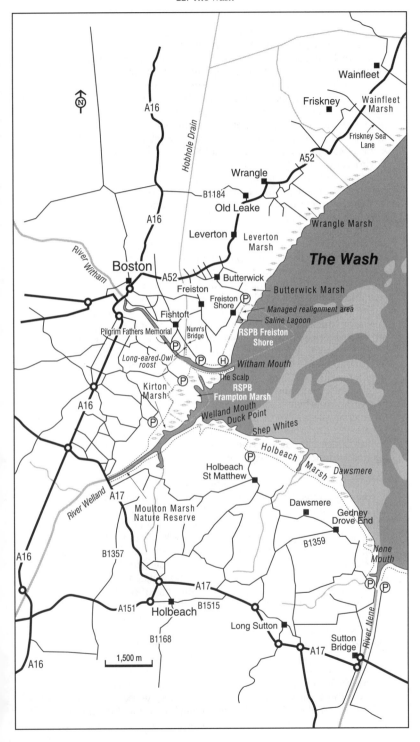

dry out the salts before it is turned over to cultivation. In such periods, these new seeded banks and grass enclosures can be beneficial to various species of birds, but in the long term the loss of valuable natural habitat is of far greater consequence. However, in recent years the folly of these land claims has become apparent. Saltmarsh has always acted as a buffer between the sea and the land, and the erosion of this habitat has threatened the integrity of the sea defences. In order to rectify this, the Environment Agency has identified managed realignment as a solution. This involves the inner sea bank being strengthened, and the outer sea bank being breached to allow the sea to flood the land. This land quickly reverts to saltmarsh, and a good example can now be seen at RSPB Freiston Shore. The RSPB and the Environment Agency are also in the process of converting approximately 420 acres (170 ha) of arable land into wet grassland and coastal grazing marsh at both Freiston Shore and Frampton Marsh.

The construction of the sea defence embankments created a string of borrow pits inland of the defences, with small linear reedbeds soon becoming established. More recent excavations may be shallow and during dry spells can provide feeding habitat for those migrant waders which prefer smaller pools to the open expanses of the main estuary. Drainage ditches dissecting the agricultural fields may also have reedbeds and rough grass banks and provide hunting grounds for raptors and owls throughout the year and nesting sites for Marsh Harriers.

The mouths of the three major rivers, where the essentially fresh water meets the brackish water of the estuary, prove attractive to diving ducks, and are also recognised spots for watching seabirds during the right weather conditions in the autumn. The Lincolnshire Bird Club hide at Cut End at the mouth of the River Witham provides welcome shelter from the worst of the weather in this open and windswept locality.

In such a generally flat and barren landscape there are few trees or hedgerows, so where these do occur they can be of interest as spots to look for migrant passerines or as roost sites for raptors and owls. One famous Long-eared Owl roost is located on the banks of the Hobhole Drain at Nunn's Bridge, although this has declined in recent years and may now have been abandoned completely.

Species

In some locations, dramatic scenery combines with the presence of certain birds to provide a rich birding experience. The scenery of the Wash could hardly be described as dramatic, but the flat, open vistas have an enchantment of their own and the spectacle of vast flocks of waders and wildfowl using the estuary provides a memorable experience. Quoting figures from the regular monthly estuary counts demonstrates just how many birds are present and why the area presents such a magnificent birdwatching opportunity. Unless stated otherwise, all counts given are the five-year mean between 1999 and 2004 from the entire estuary.

In common with many parts of Britain, the number of Little Egrets around the Wash has increased dramatically. A roost of 138 was located in the winter of 2005-06, and some pairs now stay on to breed in the area. One of the great success stories of the winter months has been the dramatic increase in Dark-bellied Brent Geese, flocks of which are found around the estuary; the peak winter count in 1999-2000 was an impressive 28,811. Probably the best site to get close, prolonged views of these geese is on the lagoon at RSPB Freiston Shore. There is a steady decline in numbers through to the spring but flocks can still be seen into May at favoured sites such as Kirton

Marsh. A regular flock of Pink-footed Geese winters in the Holbeach Marsh area and other flocks fly over en route to and from their north Norfolk wintering areas. The totals of other wildfowl are dominated by Shelduck (8,928), Common Teal (2,117) and Mallard (2,484), and an increasing number of Pintails are wintering in the Wash. Historically, a large flock has wintered on the eastern side of the Nene Mouth, mostly on the Norfolk side of the county boundary at Terrington, but with sometimes considerable numbers by the Nene Mouth itself. More recently, Pintails have become regular at RSPB Freiston Shore.

Of the seaducks, Common Eiders are present all year but reach their highest totals from January to March. The five-year mean of 1,244 represents an increase in recent years. The best locations for seeing Common Eider are to the north-west of the Witham Mouth, towards Freiston and Friskney. Other seaducks occur in smaller numbers, with Red-breasted Merganser, Long-tailed Duck, Common and Velvet Scoters and Scaup all being annual in midwinter. Most records come from the Witham and Welland Mouths but Holbeach Marsh produces records at high tide. A flock of Goldeneyes winters off the Witham Mouth, where up to 150 birds have been recorded, and this locality is a favoured site for turning up occasional Red-throated and Black-throated Divers and Red-necked, Black-necked and Slavonian Grebes. The saline lagoon at RSPB Freiston Shore has also started to produce these species with a couple each of Long-tailed Duck and Red-throated Diver and a single Black-throated Diver all being recorded since 2001.

At low tide, the vast flocks of Knot (62,823), Dunlins (36,414), Bar-tailed Godwits (17,738), Oystercatchers (14,795), Grey Plovers (8,309) and Curlews (4,449) feed way out on the open mudflats. As high tide approaches, the flocks move to safe roosts either on the upper shore during neap tides or on the fields immediately inland of the sea defences during higher tides. Their massed movements and constant calling makes an impressive spectacle and the roosts on the fields and lagoons usually offer good views of the birds during the high-tide period. The hide and sea bank at RSPB Freiston Shore offer unrivalled opportunities on the Lincolnshire side of the Wash to get close to flocks of roosting waders without disturbing them.

Redshanks (3,508) tend to feed closer to the estuary walls in the higher saltmarsh and tidal creeks, along with a flock of Black-tailed Godwits which is found throughout most of the year at Holbeach Marsh. Increasingly, Black-tailed Godwits have started to use the lagoon and foreshore at RSPB Freiston Shore; peak counts of over 2,000 were made there in the autumn of 2005, with a five-year mean of 4,073 birds in The Wash. Another welcome development in recent years is the colonisation of RSPB Freiston Shore by Avocets, which first nested there in 2001; by 2005 there were 31 breeding pairs.

Returning migrants, many still in fine breeding plumage, are back by July/August and Greenshank and Spotted Redshank can be numerous on passage, with up to 100 of both species in some July and August counts; indeed, there were 336 Greenshanks recorded around The Wash in July 2003. Ringed Plovers reach their peak during the spring and autumn migration peak periods, with up to 1,000 in May and August. Recent mild winters have seen an impressive build up in the numbers of wintering Northern Lapwings (46,775) and European Golden Plovers (23,103) which are usually to be found on the fields adjacent to the estuary, although both fly to feed on the outer flats on lower tides. The European Golden Plover peak counts, however, occur in the late summer as returning migrants flood into the east coast estuaries to moult. Three American Golden Plovers have been found in recent years among these flocks at RSPB Frampton Marsh. Other species occur on migration, notably Whimbrel (April to September) and small numbers of Curlew Sandpipers, Little Stints and Green, Wood and Common Sandpipers, but locating them in among the hordes of other waders can be difficult. Borrow pits around the estuary banks may dry out to reveal muddy margins in the late summer and autumn and these are the best places to look for the scarcer species like Curlew Sandpiper, Little Stint and Wood Sandpiper. The strip of borrow pits at Holbeach Marsh has turned up three star rarities: White-rumped and Sharp-tailed Sandpipers and Long-billed Dowitcher. Other rare waders found around the Lincolnshire coast of The Wash over the years have include Marsh Sandpiper at the Witham Mouth, Spotted Sandpiper at Shep Whites and Lesser Yellowlegs, two Pectoral Sandpipers and several Temminck's Stints at RSPB Freiston Shore.

With the amount of available prey on offer, it is no surprise that The Wash holds a good population of raptors at all seasons. In winter, Merlins and Hen Harriers are regularly seen, their true numbers usually only revealed by coordinated counts of roosting birds. Such counts have revealed that up to 20 Hen Harriers may be using the area in midwinter, but the exact number of Merlins is more obscure; up to 15 birds are recorded most years. Single birds may be seen anywhere over the saltmarsh and adjacent fields during the day, but the area between the Witham Mouth and Gedney is the best site to look for roosting birds. Merlins often use small copses or shelterbelts near the estuary banks and sometimes share their roosts with Sparrowhawks, which are a regular sight over The Wash throughout the year. Winter also brings small numbers of Peregrine Falcons, but they are seldom tied to a particular locality and tend to roam widely. Kestrels are resident, reaching their highest numbers in August when recently fledged juveniles join adults hunting butterflies over the sea aster on the saltmarsh.

From April to September a visit to The Wash is likely to provide sightings of Marsh Harriers, as a number of pairs now breed in the area and several immature non-breeding birds are present through the summer months. Males can be seen displaying from early April when their appearance overlaps with that of departing Hen Harriers. A small population of Montagu's Harriers continues to struggle to establish itself around The Wash, with the result that there are sporadic sightings of a few birds, often first-summer individuals, from late April through to August. Other large raptors occasionally pass by, and these have included Black Kite, White-tailed Eagle and Honey Buzzard.

Short-eared Owls winter in variable numbers, and a pair or two may stay to breed on the saltings in some years. Their communal roosts may be situated in long grass areas on the banks or the edges of the saltmarsh. Birds can often be seen hunting the embankments or rough dyke edges around the inland fields during the day in midwinter, where Barn Owls may also be seen hunting at dusk. The same habitat, between Wainfleet and Friskney, memorably played host to a Snowy Owl during the winter of 1990–91. Declining numbers of Long-eared Owls return each winter to their favoured roost in the hawthorns on the bank of the Hobhole Drain near Nunn's Bridge.

Huge numbers of gulls roost in the Wash but they are seldom in suitable locations to offer good views. However, one such opportunity is slightly inland at Boston Tip, where large flocks may gather to bathe on the Witham adjacent to the tip – they can then be viewed from the footpath on the northern side of the river. The Herring and Great Black-backed Gulls are occasionally joined by Glaucous or Iceland Gulls in the early part of the year.

Dark-bellied Brent Geese

Passerines do not figure highly on The Wash species list but there are some interesting wintering birds and the extensive lengths of grass embankments with scattered bushes, all within easy reach of the east coast, attract a few passage migrants. Rock Pipits are particularly numerous in winter, although making any sensible estimate of their total population is far from easy. During the early spring, examples of the Scandinavian race may be seen in their distinctive breeding plumage. Water Pipits are likely to be overlooked, but one field adjacent to RSPB Frampton Marsh held up to six birds in December 2005, along with a vagrant Buff-bellied Pipit. Twite flocks are scattered in their distribution, often being found with Lapland Buntings where work has disturbed the banks and given rise to a growth of seeding plants. Lapland Buntings may be common in some winters but maximum numbers (up to 350 in January 1986) occurred at Butterwick when a land-claim project led to the construction and seeding of new banking; since then the favoured site has been at RSPB Frampton Marsh. Stubble fields adjacent to the banks remain a good bet for this species. In the fens inland, Corn Buntings remain fairly common and winter feeding flocks may be encountered around the Wash embankments, along with small parties of Snow Buntings.

During the spring and autumn migration periods a scattering of migrants frequent the grassy banks, including Whinchat, European Stonechat, Northern Wheatear and Ring Ouzel. There are occasional records of other species in patches of scrub, small copses and hedgerows; species such as Common Redstart, Common Chiffchaff, Willow Warbler and Spotted and Pied Flycatchers all occur infrequently. Also, rarities normally associated with coastal sites, like Wryneck, Barred and Pallas's Warblers, Red-breasted Flycatcher and Red-backed, Woodchat and Lesser Grey Shrikes have all been found by persistent observers. The bushes along the banks of the Witham Mouth, around the hide on the northern side and along the southern bank from RSPB Frampton Marsh towards Tab's Head, can both be worth checking in suitable conditions; October 1998, for example, produced two Richard's Pipits and up to seven Great Grey Shrikes.

Looking for seabirds can be profitable in the correct weather conditions, when northerly gales force birds down the North Sea and into The Wash to take shelter. At such times, most birds fly around the edges of The Wash, returning out to sea again at Gibraltar Point. Skuas, however, may not return out to sea but head off high inland down the River Nene in particular, but also the Welland, on an overland migration route. Although Common Terns are regular throughout the summer, there is a pronounced passage of birds from August, when small numbers of Arctic, Little and Black Terns and Little Gulls also appear. The best locations for seeing these birds seem to be at the Witham Mouth, where the Lincolnshire Bird Club hide offers shelter from the weather, and along the shore at Holbeach Marsh. The period of two hours either side of high tide is best; at other times the birds may be too far offshore to identify. The principal seabirds involved are Gannets, Fulmars and Arctic and Great Skuas, with lesser numbers of Pomarine and Long-tailed Skuas, Manx Shearwaters and Leach's Storm-petrels, but rarities such as Sabine's Gull have been noted on a few occasions. In the late autumn, Little Auks and Common Guillemots can be pushed into The Wash by gales and a Black Guillemot, a very rare bird for Lincolnshire, spent a few days at the Witham Mouth in the 1977-78 winter.

Timing

To make the most of a visit to The Wash, at least part of the time there should coincide with high tide and the period either side of this, to see the spectacular wader roosts as well as seaducks and seabirds. In the spring and autumn, early morning and late evening high tides will be the higher ones and are the best, as most of the birds present will be affected. In winter, with restricted hours of daylight, a late morning high tide will offer the best opportunity for seeing wildfowl and waders. Remember in winter that walking along the exposed embankments can be very cold so it is best to wear too much rather than too little clothing, and be prepared for bad weather. Obviously avoid days with fog and reduced visibility, and on hot summer days heat haze will make observations difficult, if not impossible, over the saltmarsh and mudflats.

On weekdays the RAF bombing ranges at Holbeach St Matthew and Wainfleet may be in use, and noise from the aeroplanes can be considerable; at such times disturbance to birds may occur.

Access

Because the land adjacent to The Wash has a system of minor roads resembling a spider's web, it is strongly recommended that the relevant Ordnance Survey map be consulted when making visits to the specific sites mentioned here. OS Landranger 131 covers most of the sites, with the section north of Wrangle covered by Landranger 122. Access in all cases is limited to walking along the sea defences and grass-covered earth banks, and watching over the surrounding inland fields, the saltmarsh and mudflats. The sites listed below are in geographical order from south to north.

Nene Mouth: Take the minor road north off the A17 immediately east of the river bridge at Sutton Bridge (TF483210) and continue for 3 miles (4.8 km) to a car park by the old lighthouse (TF493255). From here the sea bank leads out to the edge of the saltmarsh and the mouth of the river.

Gedney Drove End: The village of Gedney Drove End, which is signed from the A17, is north of Long Sutton 5 miles (8 km) along the B1359. In the village the road bears to the right, and after 1.2 miles (2 km) there is a car park by the sea bank (TF478283), from where footpaths lead onto the sea bank.

Holbeach Marsh car park: The village of Holbeach St Matthew is signed from the A17 between Long Sutton and Holbeach and is reached by following a series of minor roads. In the village a minor road heads north from by a telephone box to a car park adjacent to the sea wall (TF408338).

Kirton Marsh: Leave the A16 at Kirton 3 miles (4.8 km) south of Boston (TF309384) onto a minor road that runs south-east for 3.5 miles (5.6 km) to a small car park by the sea wall.

RSPB Frampton Marsh: From the A16 in Kirton take the minor road signposted to Frampton village and continue along this road (passing through Frampton village) for about 3.5 miles (5.6 km) until reaching a sharp left-hand bend. Turn right here (signposted RSPB Frampton Marsh) and follow the road to a car park (TF363385), from where a public footpath leads onto the sea wall.

Nunn's Bridge and Witham Mouth: In Boston follow signs to the docks and then signs to Fishtoft. In the centre of Fishtoft, turn right towards Nunn's Bridge. Immediately after crossing the Hobhole Drain at Nunn's Bridge (TF367415) take a sharp right up a slope onto the bank of the drain and the Long-eared Owl roost is usually in the hawthorns across the drain after about 200 m. The mouth of the Hobhole Drain and the Pilgrim Fathers monument are found by continuing to the end of this track. For the Witham Mouth car park, continue along the minor road from Nunn's Bridge, ignoring the right turning for the Long-eared Owl roost, to the car park at the end of the road (TF380391). The actual river mouth, with a hide for seawatching, is another 2 miles (3.2 km) east along the riverbank.

RSPB Freiston Shore: Head east from Boston on the A52 Skegness road and turn right at Haltoft End (signposted to RSPB Freiston Shore). Follow the minor road through Freiston and then to Freiston Shore. The reserve car park is accessed over a steep concrete ramp adjacent to the Plummers guest house (TF397424).

Butterwick Marsh: Leave Boston on the A52 Skegness road and turn right into Butterwick village. From the village head east on one of the minor roads that lead to a small parking area (TF408437).

Friskney: Leave the A52 5 miles (8 km) north of Wrangle (TF480552) and turn south-east onto a minor road that leads to an RAF observation tower. Continue to the next raised bank; a small copse is half a mile (0.8 km) to the north along this bank.

Wainfleet: From the A52 at Wainfleet St Mary a road runs south-east from a sharp bend on the A52 for 2 miles (3.2 km) to the sea bank (TF528561).

Calendar

All year: Shelduck, Common Eider, Cormorant, Little Egret, Kestrel, Oystercatcher, Ringed and Grey Plovers, Northern Lapwing, Knot, Sanderling, Dunlin, both godwits, Curlew, Redshank, Turnstone, Barn Owl, Skylark, Meadow Pipit, Reed Bunting.

November–March: Bewick's and Whooper Swans, Pink-footed and Brent Geese, Eurasian Wigeon, Common Teal, Pintail, Scaup, Long-tailed Duck, Common and Velvet Scoters, Goldeneye, Red-breasted Merganser, Red-throated Diver, Red-necked and Slavonian Grebes, Hen Harrier, Merlin,

Peregrine Falcon, European Golden Plover, Ruff, Common Snipe, Iceland Gull (scarce), Glaucous Gull (scarce), Common Guillemot, Long-eared and Short-eared Owls, Water Pipit (scarce), Rock Pipit, European Stonechat, Tree Sparrow, Twite, Lapland, Snow and Corn Buntings.

April–June: Brent Goose (April and May), Marsh Harrier, Montagu's Harrier (scarce), Hobby, Avocet, Dotterel (scarce, April and May), Whimbrel, Spotted Redshank, Greenshank, Common Sandpiper, Little Gull, Common Tern, Arctic Tern, Little Tern, Turtle Dove, Cuckoo, Yellow Wagtail, Whinchat, Northern Wheatear, Ring Ouzel.

July–October: Pink-footed Goose (September onwards), Brent Goose (September onwards), Eurasian Wigeon, Common Teal, Pintail, Common and Velvet Scoters, Fulmar, Manx Shearwater, Leach's Storm-petrel (scarce, September and October), Gannet, Marsh and Hen Harriers, Merlin, Hobby, Peregrine Falcon, European Golden Plover, Little Stint, Curlew Sandpiper, Ruff, Whimbrel, Spotted Redshank, Greenshank, Green and Common Sandpipers, Pomarine Skua (scarce), Arctic Skua, Long-tailed Skua (scarce), Great Skua, Mediterranean and Little Gulls, Sandwich, Common, Arctic, Little and Black Terns, Long-eared and Short-eared Owls, Rock Pipit, Whinchat, European Stonechat, Northern Wheatear, Twite, Lapland, Snow and Corn Buntings.

23. COVENHAM RESERVOIR

OS Landranger 113
OS Explorer 283

Habitat

Constructed in 1969, this 200 acre (81 ha) concrete-sided reservoir is owned by Anglian Water and used for a variety of water sports, with a small section in the south-eastern corner being maintained as a disturbance-free area. As the reservoir is raised high above the surrounding low-lying farmland it stands as a landmark visible from several miles away on a clear day. The wide path around the top of the reservoir banks provides a good vantage position to scan the surrounding fields, which are largely arable with inter-secting dykes and occasional hawthorn hedgerows.

The reservoir itself has steeply sloping inner banks of concrete with a low protecting concrete wall. The open water is dotted with buoys used for water sports, which provide perches for gulls and terns. The grassy outer banks are also steep sided, and in places close-grazed by sheep, with some well established small areas of mainly deciduous trees. Other plantations exist around the bottom of the banks where an open flat area is also grazed. A small linear shelter-belt on the southern edge of the reservoir is composed mainly of ash trees.

Species

Winter interest is concentrated mainly on wildfowl, with typical fare including Mallard, Pochard, Tufted Duck, Goldeneye (which sometimes peak at over 100 birds), Little and Great Crested Grebes and Cormorant. There are also regular appearances by small numbers of Eurasian Wigeons, Gadwall, Common Teal, Pintails, Shovelers, Smew and Goosanders. Being so close to

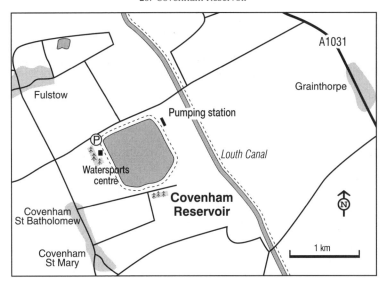

the east coast, Covenham is a in a good position to attract vagrant seaducks: Scaup and Common Scoter are annual visitors, Long-tailed Ducks have wintered in small numbers in several years, and Velvet Scoters are occasional. There are also frequent records of Red-necked and Slavonian Grebes and all three divers; some of these individuals may stay for lengthy periods. Small flocks of Whooper Swans are sometimes seen during the winter months, usually on the adjacent fields, and occasional White-fronted, Pink-footed and Brent Geese are encountered.

There is a large gull roost on the reservoir, which consists mainly of Common and Black-headed Gulls with a few Herring and Great Black-backed Gulls. In addition there is a constant stream of mostly Common Gulls, which feed inland on the Wolds during the day and fly to roost on the coast, pausing to bathe on the reservoir from mid-afternoon in the autumn and winter months. These gulls usually gather on adjacent fields to preen, where they can be scanned for the increasingly regular Mediterranean Gull and vagrant Glaucous and Iceland Gulls.

The fields surrounding the reservoir have flocks of Northern Lapwing and European Golden Plover in midwinter, while the rough grass on the dyke banks attracts hunting Short-eared and Barn Owls. The latter species is particularly common in the area and birds can be seen drifting over their hunting territories throughout the year. A good-sized flock of Yellowhammers and Chaffinches is often attracted to the farmyard and field in the south-east corner of the reservoir, and these are joined by a few Tree Sparrows and the occasional Brambling. Sparrowhawks are a daily sight, wintering Merlins can usually be located on the surrounding fields and Peregrine Falcons are not infrequent at this time of year.

Adult Mediterranean Gulls are fairly regular in late March; this is also a good time to see Iceland and Glaucous Gulls, which often drop in during the day rather than being seen in the evening roost. Migrating flocks of Common, Arctic and Black Terns and Little Gulls pass through from mid-April but seldom linger for long in the spring. In favoured conditions of easterly winds, Little Gulls in particular can be seen in impressive numbers, such as the flock of 47 in April 2005.

In spring, the reservoir walls and banks are exceptionally good for migrant Yellow and White Wagtails due to the abundance of insects. Peak April counts of Yellow Wagtails may exceed 100 birds, and individuals showing the characteristics of Blue-headed, Grey-headed and Ashy-headed Wagtails have been identified. Late March is a good time to search for Rock Pipits, and several birds at this time of year have been of the Scandinavian subspecies. A few migrant Northern Wheatears occur on the banks and occasional Black Redstarts appear, often around the pumping station in the north-east corner. The grassy banks attract late passage flocks of Fieldfares and Redwings in April, which are sometimes joined by migrant Ring Ouzels. The path around the top of the bank has a good growth of weeds, which brings feeding Goldfinches, Greenfinches, Linnets and Yellowhammers. Large flocks of Common Swifts feed over the reservoir all summer, with good numbers of hirundines during April, May, August and September.

The concrete banks offer little habitat for waders but Common Sandpipers are frequent while small flocks of Sanderling and Turnstone also appear in May. Other species may arrive in spring during suitable weather conditions: for instance, Avocet, Whimbrel, Spotted Redshank and Wood Sandpiper were recorded in May 2005. The site has something of an attraction to Temminck's Stints, with the peak time for this scarce migrant being mid-May.

Meadow Pipits breed in areas of rougher grass, with attendant Cuckoos always present, and a few pairs of Tree Sparrows survive in the ash plantation on the south side of the reservoir. In addition, small numbers of Turtle Doves may be present during the summer but, in general, the range of breeding species is rather limited.

Autumn migration brings a wider range of passage waders; Common Sandpipers are the most regular but may be outnumbered by influxes of species such as Ruff, Little Stint or Curlew Sandpiper. A wide variety of other waders including Grey Plover, Black and Bar-tailed Godwits, Spotted Redshank and Wood Sandpiper have been recorded feeding on the impenetrable concrete banks, while Purple Sandpipers have appeared in early November on a number of occasions. Both Red-necked and Grey Phalarope are regular vagrants and are often remarkably tame; the latter usually appears following strong winds later in the autumn, in October or November. In addition, rarities such as Black-winged Stilt, Pectoral Sandpiper, Lesser Yellowlegs and Wilson's Phalarope have all occurred.

Parties of Black Terns and Little Gulls arrive following easterly winds, particularly in August, although Arctic Terns are much scarcer at this time of year than during the spring. The occasional Kittiwake or Sandwich Tern may also be noted. Autumn gales sometimes bring seabirds onto the reservoir, although being within easy sight of the coast few remain long unless exhausted. There have been records of Manx Shearwater, Leach's Storm-petrel, Shag and Pomarine, Arctic and Great Skuas, while in the late autumn even Little Auks may put in a brief appearance. Slavonian and Black-necked Grebes often make lengthy stays during the autumn as do vagrant seaducks such as Scaup, Long-tailed Duck or Velvet Scoter, which arrive from October onwards. A recent feature of late autumn has been the presence of small numbers of Snow Buntings, which are often very confiding and may remain for a few days feeding on the concrete shoreline.

Raptors seem to be attracted by large bodies of water, although the immediate habitat would appear to offer little in the way of suitable feeding for most species. Migrant Marsh Harriers and Ospreys are regular in spring and autumn, the winter months may produce a few Hen Harrier records and vagrants such as Honey Buzzard, Red Kite and Montagu's Harrier have been recorded.

As you would expect, this well-watched reservoir within easy flying distance of the east coast has turned up a good crop of rare birds over the years. In addition to the waders already mentioned, the site has an impressive selection of scarce terns to its credit, including a long-staying Gull-billed in 1972, a Whiskered in 1987 and no fewer than seven White-winged Black Terns since 1974. Red-breasted Goose, American Wigeon, Ring-necked Duck and Ferruginous Duck head the list of rare wildfowl. Despite its inland location, the reservoir has played host to Shore Lark, Lapland Bunting, three spring Ortolan Buntings and, in November 2004, a Barred Warbler.

Timing
Although some birds will be present at any time of year, the best periods are winter and the spring and autumn migration periods. As there is open access to all banks of the reservoir, it is possible to compensate for the position of the sun at any time of day. With extensive use of the reservoir for a variety of water sports, early morning visits are recommended as the birds will be more settled.

Access
Covenham Reservoir is situated 5 miles (8 km) north of Louth and is accessed via a minor road which runs north-east from the A16 0.6 miles (1 km) south of Ludborough. A car park is located at the north-western corner of the reservoir at TF340962, from where a series of steps leads up to the reservoir bank. It is then possible to walk all the way around the reservoir.

Calendar
Resident: Sparrowhawk, Barn Owl, Meadow Pipit, Tree Sparrow, Yellowhammer.

October–March: Whooper Swan (scarce), Eurasian Wigeon, Gadwall, Common Teal, Pintail, Pochard, Tufted Duck, Scaup, Long-tailed Duck, Common Scoter, Velvet Scoter (scarce), Goldeneye, Smew (scarce), Goosander, divers (scarce), Little, Great Crested, Red-necked and Slavonian Grebes, Cormorant, Merlin, Peregrine Falcon (scarce), European Golden Plover, Northern Lapwing, Redshank, Green Sandpiper, gull roost including Mediterranean Gull (scarce) and Iceland and Glaucous Gull (rare), Short-eared Owl, Rock Pipit (scarce), Grey Wagtail, European Stonechat, Fieldfare, Redwing, Brambling, Snow Bunting (scarce), Reed and Corn Buntings.

April–September: Black-necked Grebe, Marsh Harrier (passage), Osprey (passage), Sanderling, Dunlin, Ruff, Common Sandpiper, Turnstone, other passage waders, Little Gull, Kittiwake (scarce), Common, Arctic and Black Terns, Turtle Dove, Cuckoo, Yellow Wagtail, White Wagtail (April and May), Black Redstart, Northern Wheatear, Ring Ouzel (scarce).

24. KIRKBY ON BAIN AREA

This district in central Lincolnshire is composed of a number of relict and working gravel pits in the valley of the River Bain, along with some impressive areas of heathland and woodland on the sand and gravel deposits to the west of the river.

24A. KIRKBY MOOR AND MOOR FARM

Habitat

The heathlands at Kirkby Moor and nearby Moor Farm are both Lincolnshire Wildlife Trust reserves; together they contain an extensive area of open sandy warren. A large percentage of the heath is made up of very short Rabbit-grazed turf and bare sand around the warrens, with patches of heather and bracken around the periphery. Shelter-belts of pine, some old Scots pines and birch scrub make up most of the rest of the reserves, although Moor Farm has a good acidic bog and a pond at Kirkby Moor is surrounded by older conifers and oaks. The adjacent Forestry Commission-owned Ostler's plantation is mostly coniferous, with Scots pine predominating, but recent clear-felling and subsequent replanting has opened up some of the area adjacent to Kirkby Moor itself.

Species

Roving flocks of finches and tits, Goldcrests and odd woodpeckers make up the staple winter species mix on these heathland sites, which are at their best when the fruiting of the birch and pine trees coincides with a winter influx of northern finches. Reasonable sized flocks of Lesser Redpolls and Siskins will then predominate in most winters but Common Crossbills may also be in evidence, especially at Moor Farm and Ostler's plantation. During one such influx winter, in 1990-91, a flock of up to 44 Parrot Crossbills frequented the old Scots pines by the roadside. At the same time a large flock of Lesser Redpolls at Kirkby Moor contained several Mealy Redpolls and at least three Arctic Redpolls. Occasional Firecrests have also wintered in the area. Woodcocks feed on the wet woodland floor but are seldom seen during the day unless flushed accidentally. In spring and early summer males can be seen at dusk and dawn as they rode above the trees. Sparrowhawks and Kestrels are common, there have been records of Common Buzzard and Goshawk, and Rough-legged Buzzards have been seen during the winter months on several occasions. Kirkby Moor was formerly a traditional wintering site for Great Grey Shrike but, although the habitat remains excellent for the species, recent records have been few and far between.

All three species of woodpecker breed in the area, and Green Woodpeckers are particularly in evidence when they feed on the open sandy warrens. Jays are also common at both sites. Northern Wheatears appear regularly on passage, especially in spring, along with the occasional Black Redstart. Woodlarks are present at both reserves and in recent years Common Redstarts have bred at Kirkby Moor. In spring Hobbies can be seen displaying over the Forestry Commission plantation, while rarer still was a female Red-footed Falcon in May 1994. In most summers there are a few Common Crossbills in the vicinity, suggesting that they may nest occasionally. Cuckoos

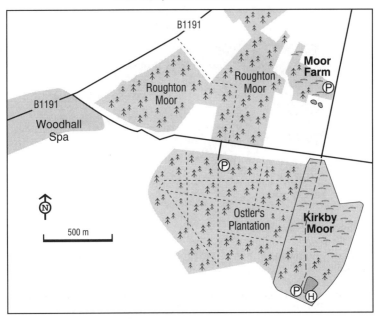

are common at Kirkby Moor and can be seen in reasonable numbers in some years. Tawny and Little Owls can be found in Ostler's plantation where, in suitable clearings on warm summer evenings, European Nightjars are sometimes heard and seen, but sadly the Tree Pipits and Nightingales that formerly occurred at Kirkby Moor have all but disappeared.

Timing
The most productive time of year is spring and summer, when most birds are in song and the heathland flora is at its best. On mild spring days there is a reasonable chance of seeing a Grass Snake or Adder on the heaths. Warm evenings during the late spring and summer are the best conditions for hearing and seeing European Nightjars. Wintering finch flocks are usually present from November to February and arrivals of Common Crossbills often take place in June.

Access
Kirkby Moor and Moor Farm, which are both Lincolnshire Wildlife Trust reserves, lie just east of Woodhall Spa. From the B1191 on the north-eastern outskirts of Woodhall Spa, take the minor road eastwards signed to Kirkby on Bain. There is a public car park on the right after 0.8 miles (1.3 km), at TF216628, for the Forestry Commission Ostler's plantation walks. To reach Moor Farm, turn left after a further 0.6 miles (1 km) onto the minor road just before a large house. The entrance is on the left after 500 m, at TF226634. The Kirkby Moor reserve entrance is opposite the aforementioned left turn at TF225629, down a track leading across open heath to the marked trails around the pools and woodland. Entrance to both reserves is by permit only.

Calendar
Resident: Sparrowhawk, Kestrel, Woodcock, Little and Tawny Owls, all three woodpeckers, Skylark, Goldcrest, Willow Tit, Treecreeper, Jay, Lesser Redpoll,

Woodlark

Bullfinch, Yellowhammer.
October–March: Common Buzzard, Rough-legged Buzzard (scarce), Fieldfare, Redwing, Firecrest (irregular), Brambling, Siskin, Common Crossbill.

April–September: Hobby, Turtle Dove, Cuckoo, European Nightjar, Woodlark, Common Redstart, Northern Wheatear, Reed Warbler, Lesser and Common Whitethroats, Garden Warbler, Blackcap, Common Chiffchaff, Willow Warbler, Spotted Flycatcher, Common Crossbill (irregular).

24B. KIRKBY ON BAIN GRAVEL PITS

OS Landranger 122
OS Explorer 273

Habitat

Sand and gravel is still being extracted at Kirkby on Bain and several of the pits are being actively worked. However, some of the worked-out pits have been replanted with trees and a reserve has been created, which is managed by Lincolnshire Wildlife Trust. One large pit, which forms part of the reserve and is just to the south of the rubbish tip, is maintained as a shallow water habitat, with gravel and sand islands and spits appearing when the water level is lowered. There is little encroaching vegetation to date and the steep-sided banks mean that reed growth is limited, but the other older pits to the west of the road now support a dense cover of willows, sallows and birch scrub on the surrounding banks. Two of the pits at the northern end of the workings are presently in use as a rubbish tip, and inevitably attract large numbers of gulls and corvids. The old River Bain runs along the eastern edge of the reserve and can be accessed from the public footpath.

Species

Great Crested and Little Grebes are present throughout the year, while Black-necked Grebes are regularly recorded in the spring and have bred in the area in recent years. A number of species of wildfowl are present throughout the year, with highest totals in the winter months. Key species are Gadwall, Shoveler, Pochard, Tufted Duck and Ruddy Duck, all of which breed in most years or at least are present throughout the summer. Eurasian Wigeon, Common Teal and Goldeneye are regular autumn/winter visitors, and Pintail and Garganey are seen most years. There are occasional winter records of Smew and Goosander. Gulls, mainly Black-headed but with smaller numbers of Common, Lesser Black-backed, Herring and Great Black-backed, feed on the nearby rubbish tip and use the pits to bathe. There have been records of Glaucous and Iceland Gulls in the late winter (usually February or March), while in January 2006 a Hooded Crow joined the mass of scavenging corvids on the tip. In most years a Green Sandpiper winters in the area, and occasional Rough-legged Buzzards do likewise.

Spring brings early records of Sand Martin, and there is a small breeding colony of this species around the pits; this could explain the regular visits by Hobbies during the summer months. Other raptors are represented by regular records of passage Marsh Harrier and Osprey, while Common Buzzards can frequently be seen over Tumby Woods to the east and the area occasionally turns up a wandering Red Kite. Little Ringed Plovers breed among the gravel workings and other waders such as Ringed Plover, Northern Lapwing and Redshank formerly nested and may do so again. Grey Wagtails have also bred nearby in recent years. The reserve pit holds a

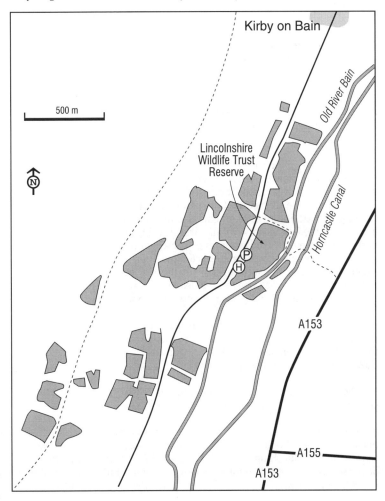

few pairs of breeding Common Terns and there is a thriving colony of Black-headed Gulls, which has sometimes attracted Mediterranean Gulls during the summer months. Lincolnshire's first breeding record of Lesser Black-backed Gull occurred here in 1993, and large numbers of non-breeding birds of this species present during the summer attract Yellow-legged Gulls, with up to ten regular during July and August. Spring migration often brings a few Little Gulls and Black Terns, and first-summer Little Gulls may linger for long periods.

When the water levels are lowered in spring and autumn the site attracts a good variety of migrant waders, which may include species such as Knot, Sanderling, Bar-tailed Godwit and Turnstone. More regular are Greenshank, Spotted Redshank, Green, Wood and Common Sandpipers, Ruff, Little Stint and Curlew Sandpiper, while rarities in the wader department have included Red-necked Phalarope, Temminck's Stint, Pectoral Sandpiper and, more exceptionally, a fine Sociable Lapwing in spring 1993 and a Baird's Sandpiper in September 2005. Other good birds found at this site in recent years have included White-tailed Eagle in 2005, both Laughing and Franklin's Gulls in 1998 and White-winged Black Tern in 2001.

Timing
The best times to visit are from mid-March to September for migrant and breeding birds. Winter is less productive as a rule, but can be good for wildfowl and gulls.

Access
Access to the whole area is restricted but most of the pits can be viewed from the minor road which runs north–south from Kirkby on Bain to Coningsby. Approaching from the north the first pits are situated either side of the road about 1 mile (1.6 km) south of Kirkby on Bain. A little further on, it is possible to park carefully opposite the entrance to the landfill site (TF238613) and view the reserve pit on the left and the mature workings on the right. From here a public footpath leads off to the left, crossing the old River Bain and the Horncastle Canal and ending at the A153 Horncastle to Coningsby road. The reserve pit can also be viewed from a hide, accessed from within the Lincolnshire Wildlife Trust (LWT) car park. Continuing south past Bain Aggregates leads to further pits which must be viewed from the roadside, although suitable parking is limited. There is also a public footpath which runs along the western side of the site from Kirkby on Bain to Tattershall Thorpe, a distance of 2.5 miles (4 km). From this footpath it is possible to view some pits which cannot be seen from the road.

Calendar
Resident: Greylag Goose, Gadwall, Shoveler, Pochard, Tufted and Ruddy Ducks, Little and Great Crested Grebes, Cormorant, Sparrowhawk, Common Buzzard, Kestrel, Stock Dove, Grey Wagtail.

October–March: Eurasian Wigeon, Common Teal, Pintail, Goldeneye, Goosander, Green Sandpiper, Iceland Gull (rare), Glaucous Gull (rare).

April–September: Shelduck, Pintail (scarce), Garganey (scarce), Black-necked Grebe, Marsh Harrier (irregular), Osprey (irregular), Hobby, Oystercatcher, Little Ringed and Ringed Plovers, Northern Lapwing, Little Stint (scarce), Curlew Sandpiper (scarce), Dunlin, Ruff, Common Snipe, Black-tailed Godwit, Redshank, Greenshank, Green, Wood and Common

Sandpipers, Mediterranean Gull (rare), Little Gull, Black-headed Gull (colony), Lesser Black-backed and Yellow-legged Gulls, Common and Black Terns, Turtle Dove, Cuckoo, Kingfisher, Sand Martin (colony), Sedge Warbler, Reed Warbler, Garden Warbler, Common Whitethroat, Common Chiffchaff, Willow Warbler, Spotted Flycatcher.

25. LAUGHTON FOREST

OS Landranger 112
OS Explorer 280

Habitat

Laughton Forest is a large, mainly coniferous, woodland planted by the Forestry Commission on what was the open sandy heathland known as Scotton Common. The forest forms part of the extensive blown-sand region of north-west Lincolnshire, which overlies the ironstone-bearing sandstone that gave rise to the steel industry of Scunthorpe and led to the destruction of most of the natural heathland of the area. The heathland today is a complex mosaic of dry and wet areas, and many of these wet acidic bogs remain as SSSIs within the forest. Along the western edge of the forest are the remnants of an inland sand dune system; work to enhance this has been going on for ten years and the area at Tuetoes Hills was notified as an SSSI a few years ago.

Conifers began to be introduced in the 1920s; these early plantings reached maturity from 1980, and extensive clear-felling and replanting has taken place on a rotational basis since then. Most of the forest is composed of Corsican and Scots pine, with a few plantations of oak, beech, sycamore and larch and small areas of birch, willow, hawthorn and blackthorn scrub. The acid bogs within the forest consist of reed-fringed open water, surrounded by willow and birch scrub and the odd Scots pines. In addition, there are areas of birch woodland and some older oak woodland to the south of the forest proper. Recent developments have seen heathland restoration work being carried out on a large area of the eastern side of the forest, along with other areas throughout the forest as a whole, with the eventual aim of linking these to form a continuous heath of 988 acres (400 ha). Grazing is targeted at modifying the ground flora in a positive way, with scrub regeneration being controlled through the direct application of herbicides.

To the east of the main block of forest lies the 158 acre (64 ha) Lincolnshire Wildlife Trust reserve of Scotton Common. This low-lying tract of land is covered in its drier parts by developing oak, birch and pine, while the wetter areas contain much purple moor-grass and cross-leaved heath; rarer species of plant such as bog asphodel and marsh gentian also occur. Extensive areas of invading birch and pine have been felled to maintain the open heathland habitat and grazing by Hebridean sheep is carried out at appropriate times to prevent birch re-growth. A 40 acre (16 ha) area of heathy fields to the north was added to the reserve in 1988.

The whole area is surrounded by mainly arable farmland but there are further pockets of heathland to the north around Scotton village, some of which have been converted to golf courses. The River Trent is a short distance to the west and flood management 'washes' at Susworth and Scotterthorpe can attract flocks of wildfowl during the winter and spring.

Species

Winter can sometimes appear rather quiet in blocks of coniferous forest such as this, although an encounter with a roving flock of small birds may brighten the day. These flocks inevitably consist mainly of tits, usually with a few Goldcrests and Treecreepers accompanying them. Common Crossbills have become more frequent in recent years, and breeding is now fairly regular, while Siskin and Lesser Redpoll are more erratic, with good numbers in some winters and hardly any in others. A favoured area for these three species, particularly Common Crossbills, is the old trees by the southern car park. Such flocks of these irruptive visitors have contained rarer species on several occasions; in the winter of 1990-91, up to 19 Parrot Crossbills favoured the car park trees, while at the same time an Arctic Redpoll was found in a large flock of Lesser Redpolls feeding in birch scrub. More recently, two Parrot Crossbills were located in March 1995, and in the winter of 1995-96 as many as seven Arctic Redpolls associated with a flock of 450 Mealy Redpolls. Other finches may be in evidence during the winter months, and large flocks of Chaffinches, Greenfinches and Goldfinches may contain a few Bramblings.

The areas of wet heath attract good numbers of wintering Common Snipe, with a few Jack Snipe often also present. Woodcocks may be encountered at this time, although they are more easily observed during the spring when they carry out their roding display above the treetops. Raptors include several Sparrowhawks, which are often displaying by February, and Common Buzzards, which have increased in the area over recent years. Occasional Hen Harriers are seen between the western edge of the forest and the river, and Rough-legged Buzzard has wintered in the past.

From mid-February onwards, Woodlarks return to the forest and can be seen singing above the areas of clear-fell on calm days. This is a species which is faring particularly well, and census results showed a 50 per cent increase in breeding pairs between 1997 and 2000. Early spring is also a good time to see the resident Green and Great Spotted Woodpeckers, both of which are common, while the local Grey Herons, which are unfortunately declining, will already be sitting on their nests.

Spring and summer offer the best birding in the forest, with several notable species being relatively common and easy to see. Summer visitors include impressive numbers of Garden Warblers, Common Chiffchaffs and Willow Warblers, and the clear-fells resound to the songs of Tree Pipits,

European Nightjar

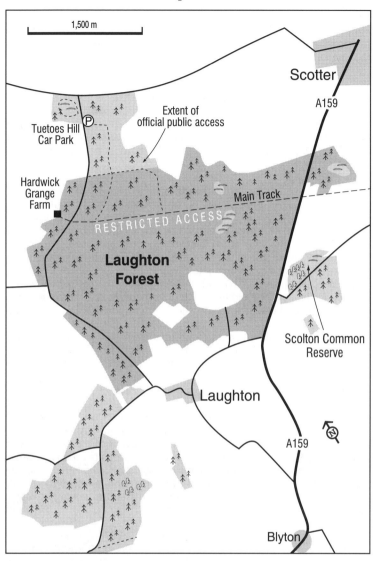

which perform their parachute displays from mid-April right through the summer. Common Crossbills may linger in some years and there is often a further arrival of birds in June and July along with Siskins. Lesser Redpoll was formerly a not uncommon breeding bird, but as with many areas has declined significantly in recent years; one or two pairs may still hang on in suitable habitat though. Warm summer evenings from late May can be highly productive, with the singing Tree Pipits and warblers being gradually replaced in the late evening by roding Woodcocks and churring European Nightjars. Up to 30 singing males of the latter species are regularly located each spring, and by standing on the tracks adjacent to the clear-fells exceptional views can be had of the males' wing-clapping display-flight; the birds will also often come close to investigate human intruders. The squeaky-gate call of young Long-eared Owls is usually evident as dusk approaches, and adults are often out hunting early during late May and June, when they can be seen drifting over the clear-fells or perched in trees around the edges of the open areas.

Timing

As with most woodland sites, the greatest bird activity is in the early morning and to a lesser extent the late evening. Woodlarks usually arrive back to the forest from late February, and they are at their most vocal on calm sunny days in March and April. An evening visit in similar weather conditions from late May to August is the time to hear and see Woodcocks and European Nightjars.

Access

Laughton Forest is approximately 7.5 miles (12 km) south-west of Scunthorpe town centre. The only official access currently is from the Tuetoes Hill car park, which is reached by leaving the A159 at Scotter west on to a minor road which then effectively encircles the forest; the car park is on the east side of the minor road at SE847011. From here, informal public access is allowed to the extreme northernmost block of the forest (see map). In addition, the SSSI land to the west of the road has public access, but due to the sensitive nature of the dune habitats and the presence in summer of grazing livestock, visitors should act responsibly and avoid straying from paths.

A further mile (1.6 km) south of the Tuetoes Hill car park, a track opposite Hardwick Grange Farm leads in to the forest (SE840000). Members of the public often use this area, which is not actually a car park but has by default become one. This track continues eastwards through the forest, joining the A159 after 1.9 miles (3 km), and gives views over various areas of clear-fell.

To reach Scotton Common reserve, turn east off the A159 1.9 miles (3 km) south-west of Scotter on to a minor road signed to Scotton. After 300 m there is a footpath on to the reserve on the left (SK866981); parking here is restricted and vehicles should not be left on the protected roadside verge. A further 0.6 miles (1 km) along the minor road is the main entrance where a gate gives access to a car park (SK873985). Once on the reserve, take special care to avoid disturbance to nesting birds and trampling of fragile habitats.

Calendar

Resident: Sparrowhawk, Common Buzzard, Woodcock, Tawny Owl, Green and Great Spotted Woodpeckers, Mistle Thrush, Willow Tit, Goldcrest, Treecreeper, Bullfinch, Yellowhammer.

October–March: Hen Harrier (scarce), Jack and Common Snipe, Woodlark (February onwards), Fieldfare, Redwing, Brambling, Siskin, Lesser Redpoll, Common Crossbill.

April–September: Grey Heron, Hobby (scarce), Turtle Dove, Cuckoo, Long-eared Owl, European Nightjar, Tree Pipit, Garden Warbler, Common Chiffchaff, Willow Warbler, Spotted Flycatcher, Common Crossbill (irregular).

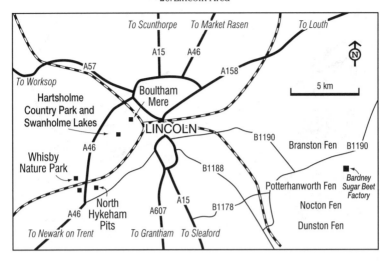

26. LINCOLN AREA

OS Landranger 121
OS Explorers 272 and 273

The area around the city of Lincoln offers an attractive range of birdwatching localities, all within easy reach of one another. The city lies in a gap cut through the ridge of the limestone heights by the River Witham on its course to the Wash. Sand and gravel deposits lie to the west and south of the city, while the broad valley of the Witham to the east forms an important habitat. The sites detailed here are listed in alphabetical order.

26A. BOULTHAM MERE

OS Landranger 121
OS Explorer 272

Habitat

Known formerly as Skewbridge Ballast Pit, this Lincolnshire Wildlife Trust reserve covers 47 acres (19 ha) in total. As its old name suggests, it was originally excavated as a source of ballast for construction of the nearby railway, and has since developed into an attractive lake with large beds of reed and sedge. Mature trees and shrubs, mainly willow and sallow, flank the railway. A tern raft has been built at the northern end of the mere, and the whole area is overlooked by a hide on the western shore.

Species

Boultham Mere is one of the most regular sites for wintering Bitterns in Lincolnshire. Up to three birds have been seen most years since 1979, generally arriving in late October and remaining into March. Patience is usually required, but with luck a visitor should be rewarded with views towards dusk as the birds fly to roost in the reedbed. If the mere is frozen, the birds may well be seen standing out in the open on the ice. The reedbed is also attractive to Bearded Tits in the winter months, and up to five birds have been seen in recent years, while Water Rails may be heard squealing from

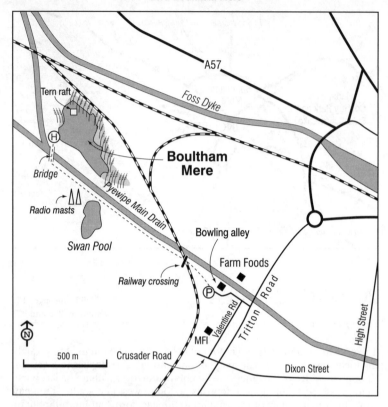

the same area. Reasonable numbers of wildfowl visit at this time of year, with the main species being Eurasian Wigeon, Common Teal, Shoveler and Tufted Duck. Smaller numbers of Goldeneyes and Goosanders may be present, and the odd Pintail or Smew may add variety to the scene. Pink-footed Geese often pass overhead in large numbers, particularly in January when they will be heading north-west en route from north Norfolk to Lancashire. Loafing groups of gulls are worth checking through, as there have been a few records of Mediterranean, Iceland and Glaucous Gull in recent years.

Spring sees the arrival of good numbers of warblers, particularly Sedge and Reed, with over 20 pairs of each utilising the reedbed. Other breeding species on the reserve include Little and Great Crested Grebes, Common Tern and Kingfisher. In addition, Barn, Little and Tawny Owls are all resident, as are Tree Sparrows. During spring and autumn passage periods Marsh Harriers are regularly seen, while Hobbies are not infrequent and the occasional Osprey may pass overhead. Groups of Arctic Terns move north during favourable conditions in the spring, particularly in late April and early May, and there are occasional visits by other transient species such as Little Gull, Kittiwake and Sandwich and Black Tern. Garganeys are regular during both spring and autumn.

As with most large areas of water, several scarcities have been recorded in recent years, including Green-winged Teal, Purple Heron, Spotted Crake, Red-necked Phalarope, Caspian Tern, Savi's Warbler and Marsh Warbler.

Timing

Although the reserve lies within the city of Lincoln, it is comparatively quiet and therefore for a general visit timing is not too critical. Wintering Bitterns are best seen in the evenings, any time up to two hours before dark.

Access

The reserve lies 1.2 miles (2 km) west of Lincoln city centre. From Lincoln High Street (B1262) head west along Dixon Street, cross Tritton Road on to Valentine Road and follow this to the bowling alley, where vehicles should be parked (SK964705). On foot, follow the dirt track from the bowling alley car park westwards alongside the Pyewipe Main Drain, crossing the railway at a gated crossing. After a further 0.6 miles (1 km) cross the drain using the bridge at SK956712 to enter the reserve. The hide is 100 m north of this point.

Calendar

Resident: Little and Great Crested Grebes, Barn, Little and Tawny Owls, Kingfisher, all three woodpeckers, Tree Sparrow.

October–March: Pink-footed Goose, Eurasian Wigeon, Common Teal, Pintail (scarce), Shoveler, Goldeneye, Goosander, Bittern, Water Rail, Mediterranean Gull (scarce), Bearded Tit.

April–September: Garganey (scarce), Marsh Harrier, Hobby, Little Gull (scarce), Common and Arctic Terns, Northern Wheatear, Sedge, Reed and Garden Warblers, Common Whitethroat, Willow Warbler, Common Chiffchaff.

26B. HARTSHOLME COUNTRY PARK AND SWANHOLME LAKES

OS Landranger 121
OS Explorer 272

Habitat

On the south-western outskirts of Lincoln lie Hartsholme Country Park and Swanholme Lakes Nature Reserve, two adjacent areas both owned and managed by the City of Lincoln Council. Hartsholme is dominated by its Victorian reservoir and is surrounded by the old gardens and woodlands of what used to be a private estate. The woodlands are planted with a mixture of both native and non-native species. In addition, there are areas of open grassland, which increases the diversity of vegetation.

Swanholme Lakes is the site of former sand and gravel extraction; excavation ceased in the 1960s, leaving deep flooded pits. Areas of heathland, grassland and woodland exist between the pits. As Swanholm is locally important for its dragonflies, damselflies and scarce aquatic plants, it was designated as a Site of Special Scientific Interest in 1985 and a Local Nature Reserve in 1991.

Species

This locality offers a good range of species typically found in the habitats represented. Winter brings flocks of Lesser Redpolls and Siskins, which complement the more usual Blue, Great, Coal and Long-tailed Tits. This time of year also offers perhaps the best chance of locating species such as Goldcrest, Willow Tit and Treecreeper, and these roving tit flocks have attracted the occasional wintering Firecrest. Wildfowl that can be seen include

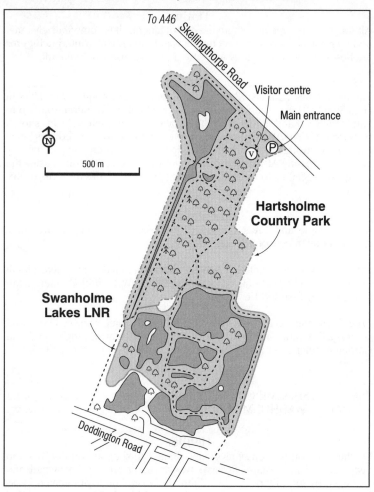

Eurasian Wigeon, Common Teal, Shoveler, Pochard, Tufted Duck and Ruddy Duck, while Gadwall can reach locally important numbers of up to 150. Egyptian Goose and Red-crested Pochard are also likely, and occasional scarce waterbirds such as Smew and Red-necked Grebe has been recorded. However, it is the regular flock of Goosander, mostly on the Swanholme side of the area, which attracts most interest, with numbers peaking at around 40 birds in most winters. Another feature at this time of year is the roost of thousands of Carrion Crows, Rooks and Jackdaws that occupy the denser woodland at Hartsholme.

Resident birds such as Sparrowhawk, Tawny Owl, Green and Great Spotted Woodpeckers and Jay are joined in the summer months by a good range of warblers, including Blackcap, Common Chiffchaff, Garden and Willow Warblers In common with many other sites, the national decline of Lesser Spotted Woodpecker means that this species no longer occurs, at least not on a regular basis.

Although not noted for rarities, up to four Arctic Redpolls occurred at Swanholme during the famous invasion in the winter of 1995-96.

Timing
Being so close to the centre of Lincoln this site unsurprisingly attracts crowds, especially as weekends. Therefore, early morning, evening and weekday visits are recommended.

Access
Although there are several access points, the main entrance is located off the Skellingthorpe roundabout on the A46 Lincoln bypass about 3 miles (4.8 km) west of the city centre. Take the Birchwood turn south-eastwards from the roundabout and follow the road for a mile (1.6 km); the car park for Hartsholme is on the right at SK946697 and is well signed. A visitor centre, when open, gives a list of recently seen birds, while a Countryside Ranger should also be on hand for advice. From here, Swanholme Lakes are a further half a mile (0.8 km) to the south.

Calendar
Resident: Mute Swan, Greylag and Canada Geese, Tufted Duck, Great Crested Grebe, Cormorant, Grey Heron, Sparrowhawk, Stock Dove, Tawny Owl, Kingfisher, Green and Great Spotted Woodpeckers, Goldcrest, Willow Tit, Jay.

September–March: Eurasian Wigeon, Gadwall, Common Teal, Shoveler, Red-crested Pochard, Pochard, Ruddy Duck, Goosander, Redwing, Siskin, Lesser Redpoll.

April–August: Egyptian Goose, Common Swift, hirundines, Blackcap, Garden Warbler, Common Chiffchaff, Willow Warbler.

26C. NORTH WITHAM FENS

OS Landranger 121
OS Explorers 272 and 273

Habitat
To the east of Lincoln the broad open valley of the River Witham, once regularly subject to flooding, has now been transformed through drainage into a rich, mainly arable, landscape of huge open fields dotted with scattered old willow trees. Wide drainage channels, some with small reedbeds along their inner sides, cross the fens at regular intervals. These former fens, named after the villages of Branston, Potterhanworth, Nocton, Dunston, Blankney and Martin, still attract large numbers of wildfowl and a good selection of raptors, so are worthy of scrutiny. Adjacent to the River Witham at Bardney, the settling ponds of the sugar-beet factory attract passage waders and wildfowl and, although access is prohibited, the pools can be viewed from the river bank.

Species
Some excellent birdwatching can be experienced during the winter months, although at first glance the fens may appear rather bleak and desolate. However, by scanning the fields from different points along the roads that cross the area, the regular wintering flock of wild swans should be located; these herds usually comprise mainly Bewick's Swans, with smaller numbers of Whoopers often present. Parties of Pink-footed Geese sometimes appear, and any group of geese encountered is worth checking thoroughly as other species have occasionally been recorded, including seven Tundra Bean Geese in December 2003. Another speciality of the area

is raptors; sightings of Kestrel, Sparrowhawk, Merlin, Peregrine Falcon and Common Buzzard are regular, while up to three Hen Harriers usually winter and are best located during the late afternoon just before they go to roost. A recent development is the occasional wintering of one or two Marsh Harriers, Red Kites are also being seen more frequently and there have been at least two records of Rough-legged Buzzard in recent winters. Barn Owls, which are a relatively common breeding bird in the area, can be seen during the late afternoon at this time of year, and these may be joined by the occasional Short-eared Owl. A Common Crane was a surprise visitor to the fens in January 2005. There are often good-sized flocks of finches and buntings roaming the fields, and these may include reasonable numbers of Bramblings. Corn Buntings still hang on in some numbers during the winter months, with the area north of the B1190 around Branston Fen and Bardney Lock being a good place to look. Another species worth searching for is European Stonechat, which occasionally frequent the area.

Spring and summer are rather quieter, although Marsh Harriers are regularly seen and Barn Owls often hunt during the daytime when they are feeding young. Common Buzzard and Hobby both now breed in the general vicinity and are seen frequently over the fields and woodland edges. Other breeding birds include Marsh Tit, Nuthatch and all three woodpeckers in Potterhanworth Wood, and in some years Quail can be heard singing from the fields. Spotted Flycatchers frequent Bardney village and a few Turtle Doves are seen.

By autumn, large flocks of European Golden Plover and Northern Lapwing are found on the harvested fields, and migrant Ruff and Dotterel have been found associating with them in August. The most notable feature at this time of year, however, is the roost of Marsh Harriers, which at its peak in late August or September may number over 15 birds. They seem to prefer sugar-beet fields for their roost sites.

The lagoons at Bardney sugar-beet factory are at their best during spring and autumn when, subject to suitable water levels, many passage waders drop in. Green and Common Sandpipers, Dunlins and Greenshanks are seen in good numbers, especially during the autumn, and these are regularly joined by smaller groups of Ruffs and Black-tailed Godwits. The scarcer species such as Little Stint, Curlew Sandpiper, Wood Sandpiper, Bar-tailed Godwit and Spotted Redshank are less predictable, but most are annual in their appearances. A Pectoral Sandpiper graced the pools in 2005, while past glories have included Long-billed Dowitcher, Marsh Sandpiper and Baird's Sandpiper. In addition, Lincolnshire's only Solitary Sandpiper occurred here in 1963. Passage periods also see the regular appearance of Black Terns and Little Gulls in small numbers, and there have been two records of the rarer White-winged Black Tern. During the winter months wildfowl are attracted to the lagoons, with species such as Eurasian Wigeon, Common Teal and Shoveler dominating. Goosanders can often be encountered on the adjacent River Witham, and the herds of Bewick's and Whooper Swans from the surrounding fens frequently fly in to bathe on the pools. Water Pipits have occasionally wintered, but can be difficult to see due to the lack of access to the site. One or two Peregrine Falcons regularly roost on the sugar-beet factory roofs.

Timing

The winter months, between late October and March, offer the best birdwatching on the fens, and late afternoon is usually the best time to look for raptors and owls. Timing of spring and autumn visits is not too critical,

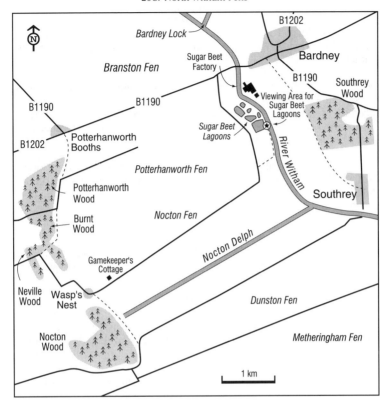

although again evenings are more likely to produce Marsh Harrier sightings. Passage waders on the sugar-beet factory lagoons generally arrive during periods of easterly winds.

Access

The fens are located approximately 6 miles (9.6 km) east of Lincoln. The best views are obtained by heading west out of Bardney village on the B1190 for 0.8 miles (1.4 km) and turning left on to the minor road signed to Wasp's Nest at TF105691. This uneven road runs around Potterhanworth and Nocton Fens and allows the area to be watched from a vehicle. Good viewing spots are close to the sugar-beet factory lagoons at TF107683 and 1.2 miles (2 km) east of Wasp's Nest at TF101661. Continuing through Wasp's Nest, a series of sharp bends leads to Neville Wood, where a bridleway leads off to the right at TF070657. This bridleway joins a footpath and runs along the eastern edge of Potterhanworth Wood, from where more good views over the fens can be obtained. Woodland species can also be seen here, but the woodlands themselves are strictly private. Another footpath runs south from Wasp's Nest alongside the eastern edge of Nocton Wood and past the end of Nocton Delph, again allowing views of woodland birds and over the fens. Other minor roads cross Blankney and Martin Fens a little further to the south.

Access to Bardney sugar-beet factory is prohibited, but the lagoons can be viewed from the bank of the River Witham. Park by the minor road between Bardney and Wasp's Nest at TF115673, follow the obvious track from here to the river bank and then turn left to view the lagoons.

Calendar

Resident: Red-legged and Grey Partridges, Sparrowhawk, Common Buzzard, Kestrel, Barn Owl, Kingfisher, all three woodpeckers, Skylark, Marsh Tit, Nuthatch.

October–March: Bewick's and Whooper Swans, Pink-footed and Greylag Geese, Eurasian Wigeon, Common Teal, Shoveler, Goosander, Red Kite (scarce), Marsh Harrier (scarce), Hen Harrier, Merlin, Peregrine Falcon, European Golden Plover, Northern Lapwing, Short-eared Owl, Water Pipit (rare), European Stonechat, Tree Sparrow, Brambling, Corn Bunting.

April–September: Quail, Marsh Harrier, Hobby, European Golden Plover, Northern Lapwing, Little Stint (scarce), Curlew Sandpiper (scarce), Dunlin, Ruff, Black-tailed Godwit, Greenshank, Green and Common Sandpipers, Common and Black Terns, Turtle Dove, Spotted Flycatcher.

26D. WHISBY NATURE PARK AND NORTH HYKEHAM PITS

OS Landranger 121
OS Explorer 272

Habitat

To the south and west of Lincoln, extensive sand and gravel deposits have given rise to a large-scale aggregate extraction industry. This has left abandoned workings that have subsequently flooded, and the whole area has become very attractive to birds. The site is bisected north/south by the A46 Lincoln bypass and east/west by the Newark to Lincoln railway line. To the west of the A46, the majority of the pit complex now forms Whisby Nature Park, a Local Nature Reserve managed by the Lincolnshire Wildlife Trust. Noted for its bird interest as long ago as the 1960s, Whisby comprises a complex of small, medium and large flooded gravel pits, while redundant settlement lagoons form wet willow scrub or clay grassland. Natural succession has allowed large areas of birch woodland and a variety of native scrub species to develop on ground between the pits. A small, semi-natural oak woodland lies alongside the railway, and an agricultural drain of some local importance runs through the reserve.

To the east of the A46 lie North Hykeham Pits. This area is still mostly in the ownership of the aggregate companies, with the exception of the waterbody known as Millennium Green, which is owned and managed by a Charitable Trust. Although the majority of the area has been excavated, there are still small-scale operations currently being undertaken, particularly on Apex Pit. The area here is generally more open with less scrub, although some amenity tree planting has taken place. Apex Pit is by far the largest waterbody and is used by two sailing clubs and an angling club.

Species

As would be expected from such a well-watched and long established site, Whisby and North Hykeham Pits offer some of the best birding in the Lincoln area. The place becomes alive in the spring and early summer months, and it is the return of Nightingales to Whisby that draws in many birdwatchers. Nightingales are a local speciality and with patience can show exceptionally well. Coot Lake has always traditionally been the best place to connect with this species, although birds can be seen and heard elsewhere; the population is slowly increasing, with 12 singing males recorded in 2005.

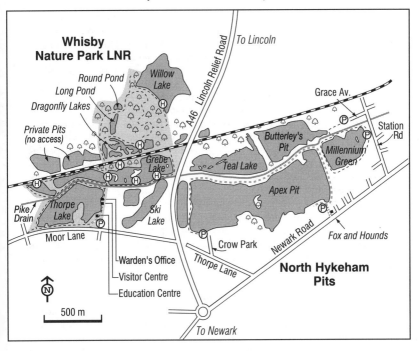

Warblers are well represented, with Sedge, Reed and Garden Warblers and Lesser Whitethroat occurring along with the commoner species; in addition, a few Grasshopper Warblers can be heard reeling. Other summer migrants that usually breed include Little Ringed Plover, Turtle Dove (at low density) and Cuckoo, while the area is home to colonies of Black-headed Gulls, Common Terns and Sand Martins. Hobbies are becoming commoner and Osprey, Little Gull, Arctic Tern and Black Tern are more or less annual at this time of year. Scarcer birds recorded in the spring recently have included Black-necked and Slavonian Grebe, Little Egret, Common Scoter and Marsh Harrier. Late spring and early summer sees the appearance of large flocks of Lesser Black-backed Gulls at Apex Pit, which also include small numbers of Yellow-legged Gulls.

Autumn marks the end of the breeding season and the gradual departure of the summer migrants. Small numbers of waders pass through but rarely stay long; Greenshank, Common Sandpiper and Green Sandpiper are the most regular, while Ruff, Black-tailed Godwit and Wood Sandpiper are all just about annual. Past records have included Curlew Sandpiper and both Temminck's and Little Stints. As autumn progresses duck numbers start to build up, with Eurasian Wigeon, Gadwall, Common Teal, Shoveler, Pochard and Goldeneye all easily seen. Pintails are occasionally recorded, as are Goosanders and Red-crested Pochards. If the Common Terns have had a successful breeding season, good numbers of juvenile birds will be on the wing in late August prior to their departure. Come October, Common Snipe and Woodcocks make an appearance, frequenting the damper areas.

Winter months bring variable numbers of Lesser Redpolls and Siskins to the woodlands. These areas are also frequented by small roving parties of tits and Goldcrests and in 2005-06 attracted a wintering Firecrest. Although not as common as a few years ago, Water Rails can still be heard or occasionally seen at this time of year. Apex Pit has long been known as a winter gull roost, and regular watching over the last few years has produced the five commoner species, regular Mediterranean Gulls, smaller numbers of Glaucous Gulls and the occasional Iceland Gull. As the taxonomic status and identification of the larger gulls becomes better understood, it comes as no surprise to find recent winter sightings of Caspian Gull as well. Odd surprises sometimes appear, evidenced by the two records of both Ring-billed and Kumlien's Gulls.

Resident species are well represented with perhaps the most important of these being Willow Tit. Although not as common as formerly, Whisby still offers one of the best places locally to see this nationally declining species. Other resident birds of note include Little and Great Crested Grebes, Sparrowhawk, Kestrel, Stock Dove, Green and Great Spotted Woodpeckers, Mistle Thrush and Bullfinch.

With such a well-watched site, there is always the chance at any time of year of finding a good bird, although the spring and autumn months perhaps offer the best opportunity. Rarities in the past have included a Laughing Gull in 1984, a Cattle Egret in 1986, two Caspian Terns, American Wigeon, Woodlark, Wryneck and, exceptionally for an inland site, a singing White-spotted Bluethroat which remained on territory for several days in June 1987.

Timing

Whisby can get very busy, particularly at weekends and on bank holidays, and as the site develops and becomes more attractive to visitors, is set to become ever more popular. North Hykeham Pits tend to be quieter and used more by locals, but Apex Pit is popular with anglers and the two sailing clubs are used extensively during the summer months. Therefore, early mornings, evenings and weekdays are likely to be the most productive times to visit. To view the Apex Pit gull roost, arrive at least an hour before dark and preferably two hours prior to dusk in the winter months.

Access

Whisby Nature Park is approximately 4.3 miles (7 km) south-west of Lincoln and is well signed off the A46 Lincoln bypass. The main car park is at SK914661, where there is a visitor centre run by Leisure Connection Ltd on behalf of the local authority. Maps of Whisby and general advice can be obtained here. Adjacent to the visitor centre is the warden's office and workshop, from where more detailed information on birds and other wildlife, and the best places to currently observe them, can be obtained. From the car park, there are a number of walks that can be undertaken, with those on the southern side of the railway suitable for wheelchair users. There are seven hides altogether overlooking the various water-bodies, providing excellent viewing and photographic opportunities.

The North Hykeham Pits are a little trickier to access. Apex Pit is best reached off Newark Road from the end of Crow Park at SK922660 (small parking area for anglers) for the western end, and down a track next to the Fox and Hounds pub at SK933663 for the eastern end, which is also the best spot to observe the gull roost. Please be aware that a lockable barrier has just been installed at the entrance to this track, so park sensibly in the vicinity of the pub and walk in. Millennium Green is easily accessed from Station Road (SK937668), or with careful parking from the end of Grace Avenue (SK935672). Butterly's Pit and Teal Lake currently have no official access, but it is possible to partially observe these two waterbodies from the northern side of Apex Pit.

Calendar

Resident: Mute Swan, Greylag Goose, Gadwall, Tufted Duck, Red-legged Partridge, Little and Great Crested Grebe, Cormorant, Grey Heron, Sparrowhawk, Kestrel, Stock Dove, Barn and Tawny Owls, Green and Great Spotted Woodpeckers, Skylark, Mistle Thrush, Willow Tit, Treecreeper, Jay, Linnet, Bullfinch, Reed Bunting (scarce in winter).

October–March: Eurasian Wigeon, Common Teal, Pintail (scarce), Shoveler, Red-crested Pochard (scarce), Pochard, Goldeneye, Goosander (occasional), Water Rail (scarce), European Golden Plover, Northern Lapwing, Dunlin, Common Snipe, Woodcock, Green Sandpiper, large gull roost with regular Mediterranean Gulls and occasional Glaucous Gulls, Little Owl, Kingfisher, Grey Wagtail, Fieldfare, Redwing, Goldcrest, Tree Sparrow, Siskin, Lesser Redpoll.

April–September: Egyptian Goose, Shelduck, Ruddy Duck, Hobby, Oystercatcher, Little Ringed and Ringed Plovers, Greenshank, Common Sandpiper, Little Gull (occasional), Black-headed Gull (colony), Lesser Black-backed Gull, Yellow-legged Gull, Common Tern (colony), Arctic Tern (small passage), Black Tern (scarce), Turtle Dove (scarce), Cuckoo, Sand Martin (colony), Nightingale, Grasshopper Warbler (scarce), Sedge and Reed Warblers, Blackcap, Garden Warbler, Lesser and Common Whitethroats, Common Chiffchaff, Willow Warbler.

27. MARKET RASEN AREA

OS Landrangers 112, 113 and 121
OS Explorers 281, 282 and 284

Market Rasen is situated on an area of blown sands in the valley of the River Race, which rises from the scarp slope of the Wolds above Tealby to the west, and flows down to join the River Ancholme at Bishopbridge. The principal sites of interest are the woodlands and remnants of the old heathland along with the western scarp of the Wolds, and the small but interesting Toft Newton Reservoir.

27A. LINWOOD WARREN AND WILLINGHAM AND WALESBY WOODS

OS Landrangers 113 and 121
OS Explorer 282

Habitat

Few spots could be said to be typical of the old heathland which covered much of this district in the 19th century, but the small Lincolnshire Wildlife Trust reserve at Linwood Warren is a good example. Although subject to increasing encroachment by birch and pine scrub, recent management work has opened up extensive areas and rejuvenated the heather and acidic-bog vegetation which characterises the reserve. Adjacent to the reserve is a golf course, with the typical variety of short-turf fairways and rough patches of grass, birch and pine scrub.

The largest tracts of the old sandy warrens were converted to coniferous woodland, the present day Willingham and Walesby Forests, and are now

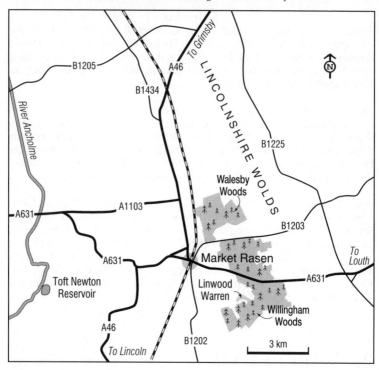

reaching maturity and becoming subject to a system of clear-felling. Replanting with more consideration for wildlife potential is a welcome development and looks set to enhance the value of the site. Within the forest, which consists mainly of Scots and Corsican pines, there are areas of larch and some stands of alders and poplars along the watercourses which dissect the woodland.

Species

During the winter, contact with a roving mixed-passerine flock may produce an exciting encounter. The interface between conifer and deciduous woodland, or pockets of birch scrub, can be good spots to bump into these flocks, which are dominated by Coal, Long-tailed, Blue and Great Tits and may include variable numbers of Goldcrests and Treecreepers, as well as the odd Lesser Spotted or Great Spotted Woodpecker. Fruiting birches and alders attract feeding flocks of Siskins and the increasingly scarce Lesser Redpoll. A small field in the centre of Willingham Forest, planted with brassicas and with an abundant growth of seed-bearing weeds, proves a magnet for Chaffinches, Bramblings, Greenfinches and Dunnocks and, in the winter of 1992–93, played host to a White-throated Sparrow for several weeks.

Stands of larch are the best place to look for feeding Common Crossbills, which can be extremely quiet and elusive when feeding. The Scots pines by the picnic site held a flock of up to 17 Parrot Crossbills in the winter of 1990–91, and two Arctic Redpolls joined a flock of Common and Lesser Redpolls at Linwood around the same time. Bullfinches are quite numerous and favour the blocks of blackthorn scrub, moving to growths of hazel in the spring to feed on catkins.

By March, Sparrowhawks will be displaying over the woodlands and Mistle Thrushes singing at full volume, and all three woodpeckers will be drumming or calling as they establish breeding territories. Lesser Spotteds are often found in boggy patches of old birch with rotten and broken trees. Summer is enriched by the song of many Willow Warblers, Common Chiffchaffs, Blackcaps and Garden Warblers, while the clear-fells echo to the distinctive lilt of Tree Pipits and the purring of Turtle Doves, although the latter two species are, unfortunately, becoming increasingly scarce. Spotted Flycatchers are common around the forest edges, and occasional singing Wood Warblers pause for a few days in May in the older deciduous areas of the woodland. Siskins are sometimes present through the summer and Common Crossbills may breed in small numbers, but the best time to look for this species is from June onwards during irruption years, when vibrant flocks are to be seen and heard over the tree-tops. Roding Woodcocks can be heard on late spring evenings as they drift over the tree-tops, and the increasing areas of clear-fell have provided perfect habitat for two recent colonists, European Nightjar and Woodlark, both of which are now breeding throughout the area.

Timing

Winter walks are best on calm, sunny days, when locating calling flocks of birds is easier. Although the Willingham Woods walks are popular with the general public, disturbance is not usually a problem, except in the area

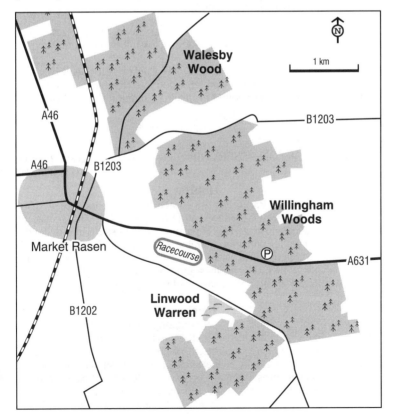

immediately adjacent to the main car park. To make the most of birdsong in spring an early start is recommended on a warm morning. The hour before dark on warm calm evenings is the time to listen for European Nightjars and roding Woodcocks.

Access

Access to Linwood Warren reserve is restricted to Lincolnshire Wildlife Trust permit holders only. Leave the A631 in Market Rasen on a minor road sign-posted to Linwood and the race course, and the reserve entrance is on the right after 1.5 miles (2.4 km) at TF129879. A marked trail leads around the reserve taking in the different habitats.

Willingham Forest has a well-signed, short red trail which starts from the main car park and picnic area. This is situated beside the A631 2 miles (3.2 km) west of Market Rasen at TF138884. The Forestry Commission allows open pedestrian access to all their woods, and there are several good forest paths and rights of way which go through a variety of habitats. However, during the shooting season from 1 September to 1 February, access is closed or restricted to some areas. Notice of such closure or restrictions are posted in the car park picnic site.

Calendar

Resident: Sparrowhawk, Kestrel, Woodcock, Stock Dove, Tawny Owl, all three woodpeckers, Mistle Thrush, Goldcrest, Long-tailed, Willow and Coal Tits, Treecreeper, Jay, Bullfinch, Yellowhammer.

October–March: Common Buzzard, Common Snipe, Fieldfare, Redwing, Brambling, Siskin, Lesser Redpoll, Common Crossbill, Reed Bunting.

April–September: Woodcock, Turtle Dove, Cuckoo, European Nightjar, Woodlark, Tree Pipit, Garden Warbler, Wood Warbler (scarce), Common Chiffchaff, Willow Warbler, Spotted Flycatcher, Common Crossbill (irregular but increasingly common).

27B. TOFT NEWTON RESERVOIR

OS Landrangers 112 and 121
OS Explorer 281

Habitat

To the west of Market Rasen lies the 40 acre (16 ha) concrete-sided Toft Newton Reservoir, which is managed as a trout fishery. The outer banks and periphery are all sheep-grazed short pasture, while the surrounding land is mostly very flat, rather uninspiring arable. As the reservoir is only sizeable water area for many miles around and lies at the upper end of the Ancholme valley, which runs north–south from the Humber Estuary, it is an attractive stopover location for a variety of passage species.

Species

Toft Newton holds a good range of wintering wildfowl, although if disturbance by anglers becomes too severe the birds will often move to the upper stretches of the River Ancholme north of Bishopbridge. A mixed flock of Pochards and Tufted Ducks is the staple fare, with smaller numbers of Gadwall and Goldeneyes. There are occasional records of Scaup, Common Scoter and Goosander, while seaducks such as Common Eider, Long-tailed Duck and Velvet Scoter have all appeared. A drake Smew regularly winters,

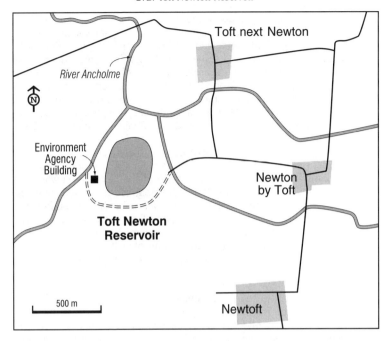

although often goes missing for extended periods; it is occasionally joined by others, and up to seven were seen in December 2002. A varying sized flock of Great Crested Grebes is present, and the reservoir has an uncanny ability to attract Slavonian and Red-necked Grebes and the odd Black-throated or Great Northern Diver. Small parties of Bewick's and Whooper Swans occur in some years, and generally feed on the surrounding fields and fly to the reservoir to bathe and rest. The usually coastal Brent Goose has been found on a number of occasions, including a notable flock of 16 in March 2005. A winter gull roost is composed mainly of Black-headed and Common Gulls, but has attracted the ever-increasing Mediterranean Gull at times. Passerine interest is maintained by flocks of Yellowhammers which feed around the grassy perimeter. It is worth searching for Snow Buntings on the concrete shoreline as there have been a number of sightings of this winter visitor, including a flock of 25 in December 2004; they can often be very confiding.

The spring and autumn migration periods produce a good variety of species but many birds do not linger for long due to the constant disturbance. The insect-rich concrete walls attract Northern Wheatears and White and Yellow Wagtails during the spring, with a few pairs of the latter remaining to breed on the surrounding fields. Small numbers of Rock Pipits may appear in the autumn, mainly during October. Common, Arctic and Black Terns are fairly regular in late April and early May, along with the occasional Little Gull. Ospreys are becoming increasingly frequent spring visitors, attracted to the reservoir by its plentiful supply of trout. Black-necked Grebes are sometimes found during spring passage periods but are more frequent in autumn, especially August, when most records refer to juveniles. Slavonian Grebes are also passage visitors but are usually found later in the autumn, particularly in October.

A few waders appear each autumn and feed on the algae and weed washed up on the concrete banks. As most of the birds at this time of year are juveniles, they quickly adapt to the disturbance from anglers and can become very tame. Numbers are usually low, but regular species include Ringed Plover, Dunlin, Ruff, Greenshank and Common Sandpiper, along with virtually annual Little Stint and Curlew Sandpiper. There are also records most years of one or two other scarcer waders such as Grey Plover, Knot, Sanderling, Bar-tailed Godwit, Wood Sandpiper or Turnstone. There is always the chance of something much rarer: recent records have included three Temminck's Stints in May 1999, Pectoral Sandpiper in September 2004, Red-necked Phalarope in September 2005 and Grey Phalarope in October 2003.

Timing

The principal problem at this location is the extensive use of the reservoir for trout fishing; anglers walk all around the inside of the reservoir walls and boats are scattered over the water. While disturbance to birdlife is obviously not intentional it is considerable, but it is surprising how tolerant some species become. There is no real way around the problem as even early mornings and late evenings are busy, but the site is quieter in the winter months and on weekdays. Spring and autumn offer the best chance of a scarce passage migrant but winter has a good selection of wildfowl and the possibility of a diver or scarce grebe.

Access

Toft Newton Reservoir is 5 miles (8 km) west of Market Rasen. From the A631 1.2 miles (2 km) west of Middle Rasen, take the minor road jus south of West Rasen signed to Toft next Newton and follow the signs to the reservoir. Follow the track to the west side and park at the end by the Environment Agency building at TF033874. There is usually no problem with access to the reservoir banks, but it is courteous to ask permission from the water bailiff first.

Calendar

Resident: Sparrowhawk, Kestrel, Stock Dove, Barn Owl, Skylark, Meadow Pipit,

October–March: Whooper Swan (scarce), Gadwall, Pochard, Tufted Duck, Scaup, Goldeneye, Smew, Great Crested Grebe, Red-necked Grebe (scarce), Slavonian Grebe (scarce), Cormorant, European Golden Plover, Northern Lapwing, gull roost, Rock Pipit (October and November), Fieldfare, Redwing, Tree Sparrow.

April–September: Black-necked Grebe, Osprey (scarce), Hobby, Ringed Plover, Little Stint, Curlew Sandpiper, Dunlin, Ruff, Greenshank, Common Sandpiper, Little Gull, Common, Arctic and Black Terns, Turtle Dove, Cuckoo, Yellow Wagtail, White Wagtail (April and May), Northern Wheatear, Yellowhammer.

27C. WOLD SCARP

OS Landranger 113
OS Explorers 282 and 284

Habitat

Increasingly large tracts of land between the eastern side of the forest and the Wolds are being put down to long-term set-aside which, combined with the rough grassland slopes of the Wold scarp, produces an extensive area of wild habitat. The fields, bordered by short hawthorn hedgerows, are large, whereas the Wold edge is often a mosaic of cattle- and sheep-grazed pasture and rougher grassland on the steeper slopes, with some small deciduous

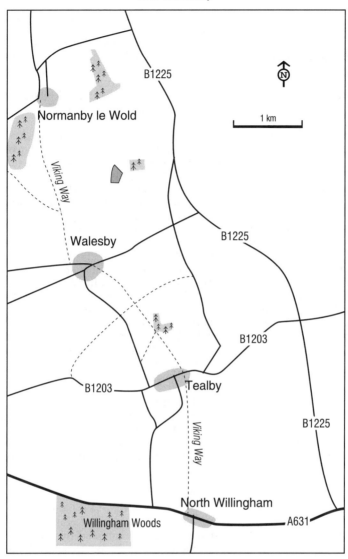

copses around the isolated farms. Much of the steeper slope is wet, with *Juncus* and rough grasses dominating the vegetation; patches of gorse and broom are most in evidence during the spring when their yellow flowers dot the green hillsides. The cultivated fields on the Wold summits are mostly put down to cereals, sugar beet and oilseed rape.

Species

The Wolds and adjacent fields are probably at their best in the winter, but with wide open fields and large areas of suitable habitat the good birds can take some finding. Woodpigeons are incredibly numerous, and their abundance attracts wintering Peregrine Falcons, but a chance encounter with one on the wing marks a lucky day. Skylarks also form good-sized flocks and sometimes become mixed in with flocks of Meadow Pipits feeding in the rougher grass fields on the scarps.

The set-aside fields and stubbles provide winter feeding for flocks of Yellowhammers, Reed Buntings, Linnets and Goldfinches, which in turn attract the occasional Corn Bunting. Grey Partridges are still quite common and coveys are easily seen in the bare winter fields. Stock Doves also form feeding flocks in the winter months and are a regular sight on the scarps, where they will often mingle with large feeding flocks of Rooks, Jackdaws, Carrion Crows and Magpies.

Birds of prey are probably the key interest group in this habitat. Barn Owls take advantage of the rough set-asides and the Wold scarps, and can often be seen hunting in daylight in midwinter. They are joined by varying numbers of Short-eared Owls from September to April. In the winter, Merlins roam the tops and valleys and Common Buzzards are regular, while odd Rough-legged Buzzards are found on some part of the Wolds in most winters and occasional wandering Red Kites have been seen over the last 15 years.

Good numbers of Skylark and Meadow Pipit breed, with a few pairs of Northern Lapwing still holding their own. Scrubby areas have breeding Linnets, Yellowhammers, Common Whitethroats, Turtle Doves and, in some of the damper spots, Grasshopper Warblers. Small numbers of Corn Buntings are present in cereal fields on the Wold tops. The short grass slopes often have a few pairs of Yellow Wagtails and may play host to migrant Northern Wheatears in the spring. Local breeding Kestrels hover over the scarp slopes and the inland valleys, where Sparrowhawks breed in the small copses and hunt over the open fields and hedgerows. In addition to these two common species there are increasing summer reports of Hobbies, which may well be breeding in the area. Set-asides have also proved attractive to calling Quail in the spring and summer.

Timing

For raptors and owls, October to March is the best period for this area, with the additional interest of wintering passerine flocks. March is a good month for seeing local Sparrowhawks and any other lingering raptors in display. Summer is quieter, but the area is not looked at much at this time of year and could repay further investigation.

Access

Good views of the western scarp of the Wolds are possible from several localities. The best vantage points are along a minor road which runs north–south from the A631 Market Rasen to Louth road, to the village of Walesby. A minor road, signposted to Tealby, runs north from the A631, 2.75 miles (4.2 km) west of Market Rasen. The scarp and valley of North Willingham are visible on the right. On reaching Tealby village, turn left onto the B1203 for 250 m then right again onto a minor road signed to Walesby. This again offers views up the Wold scarp to the right, with a nice plantation in the valley by Castle Farm, and also views over the set-aside fields to the left. At the T-junction in Walesby, turn left to return to Market Rasen through another block of Willingham Forest or turn right and then left onto another minor road which runs west towards Usselby.

From Walesby three public footpaths lead north across the valley of the youthful Kingerby Beck up the Wold scarp towards Normanby le Wold. The views over the forest and surrounding area are magnificent on a clear day. Further north, another excellent walk follows the Viking Way through Nettleton Valley, rich pasture grazed by cattle and sheep on the sandstone outcrop. From the A46, 1 mile (1.6 km) south of Caistor, turn east into Nettleton village and follow the road to an obvious right-hand bend (TF113997). Here a track leads off to the left and is well signed. It is 2.5 miles (4 km) up the valley to a minor road, which runs along the Wold top, and by turning right and following this road down the hill a circular route brings you back to the starting point.

There are now a number of Stewardship schemes in the area which allow access. These are well signed with appropriate maps adjacent to the existing public footpaths,

Calendar

Resident: Grey Partridge, Sparrowhawk, Kestrel, Stock Dove, Barn Owl, Green Woodpecker, Skylark, Meadow Pipit, Mistle Thrush, Yellowhammer.

October–March: Hen Harrier, Common Buzzard, Rough-legged Buzzard (scarce), Merlin, Peregrine Falcon, European Golden Plover, Northern Lapwing, Short-eared Owl, Fieldfare, Redwing, Tree Sparrow, Brambling, Reed Bunting, Corn Bunting.

April–September: Hobby, Quail, Turtle Dove, Cuckoo, Northern Wheatear, Grasshopper Warbler.

28. MARSTON SEWAGE TREATMENT WORKS

OS Landranger 130
OS Explorer 247

Habitat

Marston Sewage Treatment Works lies just under 4 miles (6 km) north-west of Grantham, bordered by the River Witham to the north and abutting the Great Northern Railway to the east. Marston is one of the few 'old style' sewage farms left operating in the country, and in its heyday between 1920 and 1970 attracted vagrants such as Black-winged Stilt, Great Snipe and White-winged Black Tern. Although subsequently much reduced in size, it still retains settling lagoons and flooded grassland along with rotating settling beds. Many of the settling lagoons are rapidly becoming encroached by willow scrub and can only be viewed from the road, but some are at least occasionally inundated. The remaining three grass plots that extend from the sewage works compound (SK906426) towards the parish of Marston are flooded in rotation and the site's productivity is heavily dependent on water levels and extent of available mud. Viewing conditions can be difficult in summer owing to tall vegetation but the fields are usually cut in late summer. Anglian Water have been quite pro-active in creating a small (screened) wader scrape overlooked by a hide, and have also provided another observation tower at the eastern end of the site near the works compound as well as various owl/Kestrel nest-boxes. The recent addition of a *Phragmites* reedbed had added to habitat diversity and the site is encircled by both arable and pastoral farmland. Scrub alongside the railway line is also attractive to migrants at both ends of the year and this area can be viewed inadequately from the bridleway (the Viking Way) that runs towards the River Witham. Access is prohibited to both Frinkley (mixed) and Jericho (primarily coniferous) Woods to the east and south respectively, but Frinkley can be viewed from the Viking Way alongside the River Witham and Jericho may be viewed distantly from the main access road to the sewage works.

Species

Waders are the primary attraction at Marston and are themselves highly dependent on water levels. Green Sandpipers are practically resident at Marston: one or two birds usually winter there and spring passage lasts from late March to early May. Autumn migration commences from the second or third week of June with numbers peaking in late August and trailing off into October. Wood Sandpipers are annual in early June and August/September. Of the larger *Tringa* sandpipers, Redshanks bred up until 1997 but are now more scarce than Greenshanks on passage; Spotted Redshanks are irregular in both migration seasons. Dunlin, Ruff and Little Ringed Plover are typical migrants in spring and autumn, with up to 50 Ruffs recorded in August. Scarcer waders such as Little Stint and Curlew Sandpiper are highly dependent not only on the vagaries off the site's conditions but also on predation rates on the Arctic tundra and numbers vary annually. Mid-May is sometimes characterised by the arrival of 'shore-waders' such as Turnstone with northbound flocks of Ringed Plovers of the subspecies *tundrae*. Curlews are also near-resident at Marston; the few remaining breeding pairs in south Lincolnshire use the site to feed in summer and up to 40 are present in winter. Common Snipe is another former breeder; hundreds may be present in winter, although they are difficult to observe in the long grass. A few Jack Snipe are also present at this season.

A sizeable flock of Eurasian Wigeons is present in winter and has hosted a drake American Wigeon on two occasions. Common Teal and Mallard are both abundant in winter along with a few Shovelers, Gadwall and occasional Pintails. Garganeys are recorded occasionally on passage, but diving ducks and other deepwater species such as grebes are unsurprisingly scarce, although the scrape once held a Black-necked Grebe and the river attracts Goosanders in some winters. Overhead skeins of transient Pink-footed Geese are a regular winter feature en route to or from north Norfolk, and a Snow Goose was once observed with such a group. On rare occasions odd birds or even sizeable skeins may stage briefly on neighbouring arable land. Wild swans are occasionally present in winter, although their occurrence is unpredictable; as with many of these scarcer wildfowl species, periods of hard weather are often most productive. Gulls are often conspicuous by their absence at Marston; a small Black-headed/Common Gull flock is usually present in winter and has attracted odd Mediterranean Gulls. An interesting, if brief development, catalysed by a drainage 'accident' leading to exceptionally high water levels in 1999, was the resurgence of the Black-headed Gull colony that the site used to be famous for. Large gulls are scarcer but there are single records of both Yellow-legged and Glaucous Gulls.

Sightings of raptors are usually fairly predictable at all times of year. Aside from the near-ubiquitous Sparrowhawks and Kestrels, Common Buzzards now visit daily on hunting forays, and are best looked for soaring over Frinkley and Jericho Woods. Hobbies and Marsh Harriers are regular visitors during the summer months, with juveniles of the latter often remaining for several weeks in autumn. Peregrine Falcon and Merlin are regular winter visitors, although Hen Harrier is exceptional here. A single Honey Buzzard was recorded during the September 2000 influx, circling over Jericho Wood together with an Osprey; the latter species is also annual in occurrence along the River Witham. Owls are also a feature of Marston: Barn, Tawny and

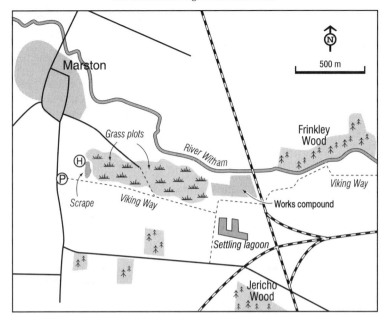

Barn, Tawny and Little are all resident, while Short-eared Owls were former-ly more regular in winter but should still be searched for quartering over the grass plots in the late afternoon. Long-eared Owls nest in the extensive conifer plantations of Jericho Wood and can sometimes be seen hunting over the lagoons and grass plots in midsummer when their normal noctur-nal hunting regimes are constrained by day length.

Winter passerines of note include the regular presence of a pair or two of European Stonechats on the grass plots and small numbers of Grey Wagtails along the drainage channels (often with Water Rails for company). Water Pipits have occurred in at least three different winters and should be looked for both in the grass plots and around the sewage works compound. Beware confusion with occasional Rock Pipits of the subspecies *littoralis* in early spring. Common Chiffchaffs are regular winter visitors with two recent records of very pale birds of the subspecies *tristis* or 'fulvescens'. A sizeable flock of Pied Wagtails in normally present in winter and a Yellow Wagtail wintered successfully in 1993-94. This latter species is a regular feature of the summer months, albeit in ever-decreasing numbers. Large flocks of over 200 birds formerly occurred in spring around the sewage works compound but recent gatherings have been more modest. Blue-headed Wagtails are annual in occurrence and Grey-headed Wagtail has occurred once. Gatherings of over 2,000 Common Swifts and equal numbers of hirundines may occur over the sewage works in May during periods of inclement weather. Summer warblers include breeding Reed and Sedge, with odd reeling Grasshopper Warblers in some years; early autumn can see significant passage of the reg-ular *Phylloscopus* and *Sylvia* warblers. Whinchats are fairly predictable in their occurrence in August and September in the grass plots and along the hedgerows, and small groups of Northern Wheatears are sometimes encountered in both spring and autumn in the fields on the south side of the Viking Way. The hedgerow bordering the Viking Way also attracts occa-sional Common Redstarts and acts as a leading line for migrant warblers.

Early mornings in mid-late autumn may be productive for visible migration; hundreds of Skylarks, Meadow Pipits and finches may be seen heading south-west on the Wash-Severn route.

Marston has received a highly variable amount of coverage over the last 80 years with past glories including Red-footed Falcon, Black-winged Stilt, Great Snipe, Red-necked Phalarope, White-winged Black Tern and Bluethroat. More recent finds have included American Wigeon, Honey Buzzard, Corncrake, Spotted Crake, Pectoral Sandpiper, Twite and Snow Bunting.

Timing

Late April to mid-May and August/early September are best for migrant waders and passerines. Easterly winds are best for both scarce waders and chats. Midsummer can be quiet but has produced odd records of good waders. Dabbling duck numbers tend to peak in midwinter but are strongly tied to prevailing weather conditions, the colder the better. Time of day is not critical but early morning usually sees the peak of passerine activity.

Access

The site is located just under 4 miles (6 km) north-west of Grantham, just south-east of the parish of Marston. There is a small car park at SK893437 signposted on the east side of the unclassified road 400 m south of the village. Leave the car here and walk east along the Viking Way to reach the Viking Hide (accessible to wheelchair users). After checking the scrape here continue walking west checking the fields to the north of the bridleway until you reach the access road to the sewage works compound. Walk right to check the lagoons (if any are flooded) and the hedge for Tree Sparrows. Retrace your steps back left to check around the sewage works for wagtails and warblers (best viewed from close to the railway line at SK910427) and then continue on under the railway if time permits to check the river and the periphery of Frinkley Wood.

Calendar

Resident: Tufted Duck, Little Grebe, Sparrowhawk, Common Buzzard, Curlew, Common Snipe, Barn, Long-eared and Little Owls, Kingfisher, Grey Wagtail, Blackcap, Common Chiffchaff, Marsh Tit, Tree Sparrow.

October–March: Bewick's Swan (scarce), Whooper Swan (rare), Pink-footed Goose (scarce), Eurasian Wigeon, Gadwall, Common Teal, Pintail (scarce), Shoveler, Goosander (scarce), Merlin, Peregrine Falcon, Water Rail, Jack Snipe (scarce), Green Sandpiper, Short-eared Owl, Water Pipit (rare), European Stonechat, Lesser Redpoll.

April–September: Garganey (rare), Marsh Harrier (scarce), Osprey (rare), Hobby, Oystercatcher, Little Ringed and Ringed Plovers, Ruff, Dunlin, Little Stint (scarce, August onwards), Curlew Sandpiper (scarce, August onwards), Black-tailed Godwit (scarce), Spotted Redshank, Greenshank, Green Sandpiper, Wood Sandpiper (scarce), Common Sandpiper, Turnstone (rare), Turtle Dove, Yellow Wagtail, Common Redstart (rare), Whinchat, Northern Wheatear, Grasshopper Warbler (scarce), Sedge and Reed Warblers.

29. MESSINGHAM
SAND QUARRY

Habitat

This Lincolnshire Wildlife Trust reserve has been created following the extraction of sand, which left a series of lagoons of differing depths. These are now in the later stages of succession, with reed fringes, willow and sallow clumps and birch scrub on the surrounding sandy spits and ridges. There is a small area of remnant heath supporting heather and other heathland flora, while woodland, grassland and marsh add to the variety of habitats. Three hides overlook the largest areas of water.

Species

Wintering wildfowl include good totals of Eurasian Wigeons, Gadwall, Common Teal, Pochards and Tufted Ducks, with smaller numbers of Shoveler and Goldeneye and fairly regular appearances by groups of Goosanders. Small parties of Whooper Swans are irregular, but increasing, visitors. A few winters have brought Bitterns but they are usually very difficult to catch up with even in such a restricted area of reedbeds. The marshy areas have a few Common Snipe and odd Jack Snipe, which as always are very elusive.

The plantations and birch woodland have the usual feeding tit flocks, with resident Willow Tits being of interest, and there have been several records of Common Chiffchaffs and Firecrests wintering with these flocks. Groups of Lesser Redpolls and Siskins feed in the alders and birch. Long-eared Owls are elusive residents, but in some winters an easily viewable roost may become established, such as in November and December 2005 when up to 12 were visible from the hides.

The site is good for watching raptors over the heaths and woods to the west or over the fields around the reserve. Winter sightings usually include a few Peregrine Falcons, with occasional Hen Harrier and Merlin, while Sparrowhawks, Common Buzzards and Kestrels are resident in the area. Spring and autumn bring passage Marsh Harriers and Ospreys, both of which are being seen more frequently, and Hobbies are regular throughout the summer months.

Sand Martins

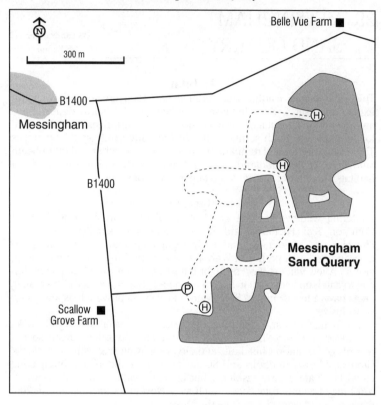

Migrant waders in spring and autumn are attracted to the muddy areas around the pits and also to flooded areas on the grass fields to the west and north of the reserve. The most frequent are Dunlin, Ruff, Greenshank and Green and Common Sandpipers, but Black-tailed Godwit, Whimbrel and Wood Sandpiper are virtually annual and a wide range of other species has appeared including Avocet, Temminck's Stint, Pectoral Sandpiper and Red-necked Phalarope. Little Ringed and Ringed Plovers often breed, as do a few pairs of Northern Lapwings, Common Snipe and Redshanks if suitable conditions exist. Migrating parties of Arctic and Black Terns make brief visits in the spring and autumn and a few Little Gulls are recorded most years, usually in April and May.

The flooded pits have a thriving breeding colony of Black-headed Gulls, and in the early 1990s a male Mediterranean Gull paired with a Black-headed Gull, rearing several hybrid young. Other breeding birds include Shelduck, Shoveler, Pochard, Tufted and Ruddy Ducks, Little and Great Crested Grebes, Common Tern, Kingfisher and Sand Martin. Turtle Doves are regularly seen during the summer months.

The combination of a wide range of habitats and an area of open water in an isolated location has brought a variety of rarities to the site in recent years. Messingham has proved to be particularly attractive to vagrant herons, with the highlight being Britain's fourth Green Heron in September 2001; Little Bittern, Squacco Heron, Cattle and Great White Egrets and Purple Heron have also appeared. In addition, there have been records of American Wigeon, Green-winged and Blue-winged Teal, Ring-necked Duck,

White-tailed Eagle, Spotted Crake, Common Crane, three Caspian Terns, White-winged Black Tern, Alpine Swift, Red-rumped Swallow, Marsh Warbler and Red-backed Shrike.

Timing
This is a good all-year reserve and a visit is worthwhile at any time, although spring offers the greatest variety of species and the best chance of a scarce migrant.

Access
Messingham Sand Quarry is 3.1 miles (5 km) south-east of Scunthorpe. The entrance to the reserve car park (SE908032) is off the B1400 half a mile (0.8 km) south of the T-junction from the B1400 at Messingham, opposite Scallow Grove Farm. Part of the northern section of the reserve can be viewed from the minor road between Messingham and Scawby opposite Belle Vue Farm (SE917042).

Calendar
Resident: Greylag Goose, Gadwall, Shoveler, Pochard, Tufted and Ruddy Ducks, Little and Great Crested Grebes, Sparrowhawk, Common Buzzard, Kestrel, Tawny Owl, Long-eared Owl, Kingfisher, Green and Great Spotted Woodpeckers, Lesser Spotted Woodpecker (scarce), Meadow Pipit, Willow Tit, Jay, Bullfinch, Yellowhammer, Reed Bunting.

October–March: Whooper Swan (scarce), Eurasian Wigeon, Common Teal, Goldeneye, Goosander, Bittern (rare), Peregrine Falcon, Jack Snipe, Common Snipe, Siskin, Lesser Redpoll.

April–September: Shelduck, Marsh Harrier, Osprey (scarce), Hobby, Oystercatcher, Little Ringed Plover, Ringed Plover, Dunlin, Ruff, Black-tailed Godwit (scarce), Whimbrel (scarce), Redshank, Greenshank, Green Sandpiper, Wood Sandpiper (scarce), Common Sandpiper, Little Gull, Common, Arctic and Black Terns, Turtle Dove, Cuckoo, Yellow Wagtail, Sedge, Reed and Garden Warblers.

NORTHAMPTONSHIRE

30. Daventry area
30A. Badby Wood and Fawsley Park
30B. Borough Hill
30C. Daventry Reservoir Country Park
31. Fermyn Woods Country Park
32. Fineshade Wood, Wakerley Great Wood and Blatherwycke Lake
33. Hollowell Reservoir
34. Nene Valley Gravel Pits
34A. Thrapston Gravel Pits and Titchmarsh Nature Reserve
34B. Stanwick Lakes Country Park
34C. Ditchford Gravel Pits
34D. Earls Barton Gravel Pits and Summer Leys Nature Reserve
34E. Clifford Hill Gravel Pits
35. Pitsford Reservoir
36. Salcey Forest
37. Stanford Reservoir

30. DAVENTRY AREA

The town of Daventry, in west Northamptonshire, has three interesting sites within close proximity, and these are presented in alphabetical order.

30A. BADBY WOOD AND FAWSLEY PARK

Habitat

Badby Wood is one of the few natural-looking woodlands in Northamptonshire, comprising mainly mature deciduous trees. The wood grows on a sandy soil and in May the floor is carpeted with bluebells. There are many footpaths criss-crossing the area, allowing extensive exploration, while an obvious high point, called Hazeley Knob, seems to attract woodland species more usually associated with the western side of Britain. Large oak, ash, sweet chestnut, sycamore and cherry trees are scattered throughout the wood, in addition to which one or two clearings and a plantation of conifers at the south-east end add to the variety of habitats and increase the number of bird species attracted to the woodland.

Adjoining the wood is Fawsley Park, an area of ancient parkland encircling the church. A large number of mature oaks are spread across the open grassland of the park, which is grazed by sheep and horses. This habitat is almost unique within Northamptonshire in as much as the whole area is open to the public. Within the park are three small lakes, two of which have *Phragmites* reedbeds and are surrounded by alders and other species typical of this type of habitat. Coarse fishing is allowed on two of the lakes from mid-June to mid-March, with trout fishing on the third, although none of the lakes are heavily fished.

Species

The woodland is alive with birdsong in spring, and this is the best site to see Common Redstart and Wood Warbler in Northamptonshire, although neither is guaranteed. Common Redstarts prefer the older trees, especially the oaks, but the male's habit of delivering its song from high in the canopy makes locating birds quite troublesome. Spotted Flycatchers are relatively common in the woodland and parkland and its cousin the Pied Flycatcher, a county rarity, appears every couple of years or so in either area. Great Spotted Woodpeckers are common and there are still one or two Lesser Spotted Woodpeckers to be found but they can be very difficult to find in the tops of the old trees. Green Woodpeckers prefer the open parkland; this is also a good spot to listen for the loud ringing call of the Nuthatch, which can be found in either habitat although favours the older trees with dead branches and holes for nesting.

The common warblers such as Blackcap, Garden Warbler, Common Chiffchaff and Willow Warbler are widespread, with Common Chiffchaffs being particularly attracted to the rhododendrons. Tawny Owls frequently call at dusk but the lack of a developed scrub layer makes the wood unsuitable for Nightingales. In recent years Common Buzzards have returned and are seen daily and Ravens have been reported in the area on a fairly regular basis.

The largest lake next to the church has a reedbed which attracts Reed Warblers during the summer, and Water Rail has bred. Other resident birds on the lakes include Mute Swan, Tufted Duck and Great Crested Grebe. The

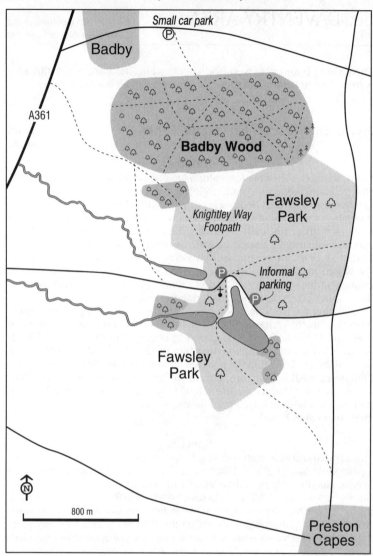

alders sometimes hold feeding flocks of Siskins and Lesser Redpolls in the winter, during which time Grey Wagtails are often found, preferring the fast-flowing overflows of the lakes. In the spring and summer they are replaced by Yellow Wagtails which like the damper areas of grassland. The summer abundance of insects attracts feeding flocks of Common Swifts and hirundines, which can be seen swooping over the woodland canopy as well as around the parkland.

Timing

Early morning in early to mid-May is the best time to visit as all the summer visitors will have arrived; with the territorial males in full song establishing their breeding territories, they will be much easier to locate in the oaks which are still relatively open at this time. As the canopy closes and bird-song diminishes later in the breeding season there is still plenty of activity but the birds are harder to pinpoint. In the winter months fine days with lit-tle wind offer the best chance of bumping into the mixed feeding flocks of tits, Goldcrests, Nuthatches and Treecreepers which characterise the wood-land. The parkland and lakes can be interesting at any season.

Access

Leave Daventry southwards on the A361 and after 2 miles (3.2 km) turn left into Badby village 100 m south of the B4037. Pass through the village towards Everdon and after 200 m there is a small parking area on the right surrounded by horse chestnut trees (SP564589). Walk up the dirt track to the wood, which is 200 m from the road, from where a mass of footpaths enables ample exploration. To reach Fawsley Park continue along the road towards Everdon and turn right after 0.7 miles (1.1 km) to enter the parkland. The road passes close to all three lakes and there are plenty of places to pull in and footpaths to follow.

Calendar

Resident: Mute Swan, Tufted Duck, Great Crested Grebe, Sparrowhawk, Common Buzzard, Kestrel, Water Rail, Moorhen, Coot, Tawny Owl, all three woodpeckers, Goldcrest, Marsh Tit, Willow Tit, Nuthatch, Treecreeper, Jackdaw, Raven (rare).

October–March: Pochard, Grey Wagtail, Siskin, Lesser Redpoll.

April–September: Common Swift, Sand Martin, Swallow, House Martin, Yellow Wagtail, Common Redstart, Reed Warbler, Blackcap, Garden Warbler, Wood Warbler (scarce), Common Chiffchaff, Willow Warbler, Spotted Flycatcher, Pied Flycatcher (rare), Reed Bunting.

30B. BOROUGH HILL

OS Landranger 152
OS Explorer 222

Habitat

Borough Hill is the highest point in the Daventry area, rising to 650 feet (200 m). An ancient hill fort occupies the summit, and the BBC used the hill for the site of the BBC World Service Radio Station until 1992. Now only one of the 14 transmission masts remains and the area was opened to the public in 1995.

The area is grazed by sheep, with some rather unkempt hedgerows attrac-tive to migrants. A circular walk of 2 miles (3.2 km) around the 140 acre (56 ha) summit offers spectacular views over the surrounding countryside.

Species

Although Borough Hill was only opened to the public in 1995, it has already earned a reputation as one of the best sites for observing migration in Northamptonshire. Its elevation above the surrounding countryside makes it an obvious place for attracting migrant passerines and for witnessing pas-sage raptors.

During the spring and autumn, Northern Wheatears can sometimes be present in double figures, with a peak day count of 27 in April 1997. Common Redstart, Whinchat and Pied Flycatcher are all just about annual

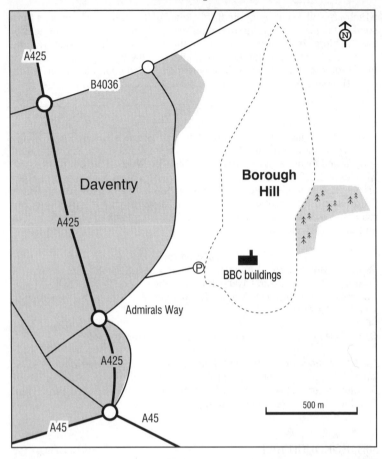

in both passage periods, and multiple occurrences are not unusual. A speciality of the hill is Ring Ouzel, a species which is regularly located in small numbers each spring between mid-March and late April. Tree Pipits are sometimes seen on migration, as are Black Redstarts, while scarcer visitors have included Woodlark, Richard's Pipit, several Wood Warblers, Twite and Lapland Bunting.

The site has a good record for producing migrant raptors, with records of county rarities including Honey Buzzard and Goshawk. Marsh Harrier and Merlin are more frequent, as is Peregrine Falcon, while Common Buzzards can be seen at any time of year.

Borough Hill has a number of locally important breeding birds, such as Skylark and Tree Sparrow. Green Woodpeckers are resident and Ravens are being noted with increasing regularity.

Timing

Spring and autumn are the peak times to visit Borough Hill, and it is worthy of exploration any time between early March and late May, and again from August to early November. Migrant passerines usually appear when the wind has an easterly component to it, although surprises are possible during any weather conditions. Raptors are best observed on calm sunny days.

226

Access

Borough Hill is 1 mile (1.6 km) south-east of Daventry Reservoir. Leave the A45 on the south-eastern outskirts of Daventry northwards on the A425 and after 500 m turn right on to Admirals Way. After a further 300 m turn right at the base of the hill and follow this road to a small car park (SP586621). A footpath of 2 miles (3.2 km) encircles the top of the hill.

Calendar

Resident: Common Buzzard, Green Woodpecker, Skylark, Meadow Pipit, Raven, Tree Sparrow.

October–March: Merlin (scarce), Peregrine Falcon, European Stonechat, Fieldfare, Redwing, Brambling.

April–September: Marsh Harrier (scarce), Hobby, Tree Pipit (scarce), Black Redstart (scarce), Common Redstart, Whinchat, Northern Wheatear, Ring Ouzel, Wood Warbler (scarce), Spotted and Pied Flycatchers.

30C. DAVENTRY RESERVOIR COUNTRY PARK   OS Landranger 152
OS Explorer 222

Habitat

Daventry Reservoir, which covers 130 acres (52 ha), was constructed as long ago as 1804. It is used to supply water to the nearby Grand Union Canal and, as such, the water levels fluctuate outside of normal environmental factors. Apart from the dam at the northern end, the reservoir is surrounded by a narrow belt of mature deciduous woodland with some willows, which grow to the water's edge. The immediate surroundings also encompass small areas of both short-mown and rough grassland. The land to the north and east of the dam is arable farmland, although a large housing estate is planned on the eastern edge.

The area was designated as a country park in 1978, and is managed by Daventry District Council, which leases the reservoir from British Waterways. There is an information centre, toilets (including facilities for the disabled), a café along the path to the dam and an adventure play-ground for children by the car park. Coarse fishing is allowed in some areas between mid-June and mid-March, with the dam being the most popular site with anglers. A footpath of 2 miles (3.2 km) encircles the reservoir and provides an attractive walk.

Species

Winter wildfowl numbers reach about 1,000, with Mallard (200), Common Teal (185), Pochard (135) and Shoveler (45) being the most obvious species, along with Eurasian Wigeon, Tufted Duck, a few Goldeneye and up to 20 Goosanders. Of the scarcer species, Scaup is the most likely and records often involve long-staying individuals. Other seaduck to have been found include Common Eider, Long-tailed Duck, Velvet Scoter and Red-breasted Merganser, while there have also been winter sightings of Slavonian Grebe and Red-throated, Black-throated and Great Northern Divers, one of the latter of which lingered for over five months. Cormorants are often present in good numbers, and Shags have visited the site on several occasions in recent years. Depending on water levels, flocks of European Golden Plovers and Northern Lapwings, with smaller numbers of

Wryneck

Common Snipe and the odd Green Sandpiper, can be seen at the water's edge, particularly on the south and west banks.

There is a small gull roost usually holding a few hundred birds, although much larger numbers form a pre-roost gathering before leaving to spend the night elsewhere. These birds are best viewed from the site of the former Carvell hide, which it is hoped will be rebuilt soon. Mediterranean Gulls are recorded on an annual basis, with the majority of records being of juveniles in autumn (particularly August) and adults in the early spring. Yellow-legged Gulls are regular during the autumn, when they accompany Lesser Black-backed Gulls, while both Ring-billed and Caspian Gulls have also visited the site.

The scrubland to the south of the car park is often where winter flocks of Siskin and Lesser Redpoll feed, and reasonable sized flocks sometimes occur. Such flocks are always worthy of careful scrutiny, as there have been several records of Mealy Redpoll, as well as an Arctic Redpoll which arrived during the famous influx in the winter of 1995-96.

Spring brings a profusion of insects and hence an abundance of food for migrant passerines, with a variety of warblers being numerous and occasional Common Redstarts and Ring Ouzels being noted. The scrub and rough grassland areas have Blackcap and Common and Lesser Whitethroats, along with occasional Grasshopper Warblers, and singing Wood Warblers have occurred on passage more than once in the mature trees. The reservoir itself has breeding Great Crested Grebes and Canada Geese, while Gadwall, Common Teal, Shoveler and Tufted Duck have all nested in the past. Up to ten pairs of Common Terns make use of the purpose-built rafts on the water.

During periods of easterly winds in the spring, small parties of Black Terns and Little Gulls often make an appearance. Arctic Terns are annual in occurrence, and during favourable conditions large flocks have been recorded, including 570 in May 1998. Both Little and Sandwich Terns occur every two or three years, although their visits are usually rather brief. Small groups of Common Scoters are sometimes encountered, especially in April, and this is a good time of year for Black-necked Grebes. In addition, there is a spring record of a pair of displaying Red-necked Grebes. Ospreys now pass through with increasing regularity and other interesting birds at this time have included a Honey Buzzard which provided many observers with excellent views for over a week in June 2002.

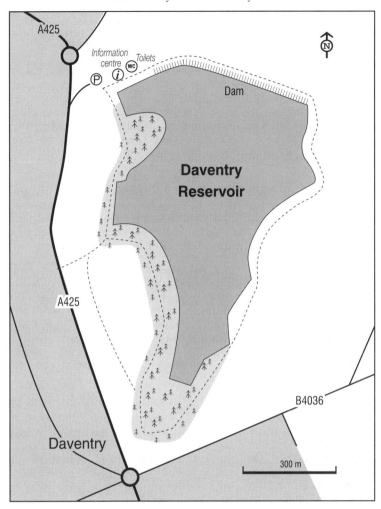

With increased recreational use of the canal system during the summer, the reservoir level often falls considerably as water is required to top up the canal. It is in these conditions that waders occur in the largest numbers. Species such as Dunlin, Ruff, Greenshank and Green and Common Sandpipers are the most numerous, although there is always the chance of something scarcer at this time, with Little Stint, Curlew Sandpiper and Spotted Redshank being the most likely. Rarer still, Pectoral Sandpipers have been recorded on several occasions, and there have also been sightings of Avocet, Kentish Plover, Temminck's Stint, Purple Sandpiper and Red-necked Phalarope. Autumn has also proved to be a favoured time for Little Egrets, which are being noted with increased regularity.

A total of 206 species of bird have been found in this relatively small area, including several notable rarities, the most extraordinary of which was Britain's third Pacific Swift which showed to one fortunate observer in July 1995. Another remarkable occurrence was in September 1996, when a Baird's Sandpiper was joined the following day by a Wilson's Phalarope. In addition, there have been records of Green-winged Teal, Ferruginous Duck, Spoonbill, Sabine's Gull, White-winged Black Tern, Wryneck and Red-rumped Swallow.

Timing

The area will repay a visit at any time of year, but the autumn period (which offers the chance of passage waders) and winter (when the highest totals of wildfowl are recorded and the possibility of scarce species is greater) are the best two times. As the reservoir is viewable from the footpath which skirts the whole site, it is possible to compensate for varying light conditions. The evening pre-roost gathering of gulls is best viewed from the site of the old Carvell hide, from three hours or so prior to dusk.

Access

Daventry Reservoir Country Park is on the north-eastern edge of Daventry, with a well-signed car park off the A425 Northern Way in the north-western part of the reserve (SP577642). A footpath runs right round the reservoir. A new hide is planned to replace the four destroyed by vandals. A pay-and-display car park is in operation, charge 60p for an hour or £1.20 all day.

Calendar

Resident: Canada Goose, Great Crested Grebe, Sparrowhawk, Common Buzzard, Kestrel, Great Spotted Woodpecker, Nuthatch.

October–March: Eurasian Wigeon, Common Teal, Shoveler, Pochard, Tufted Duck, Goldeneye, Goosander, European Golden Plover, Northern Lapwing, Common Snipe, Green Sandpiper, Mediterranean Gull (scarce), Caspian Gull (rare), Rock Pipit (scarce, mainly October and March), Fieldfare, Redwing, Siskin, Lesser Redpoll.

April–September: Common Scoter (scarce), Black-necked Grebe (scarce), Little Egret (scarce, July onwards), Osprey (scarce), Dunlin, Ruff, Greenshank, Green and Common Sandpipers, Mediterranean Gull (scarce, August onwards), Little Gull, Yellow-legged Gull (August onwards), Sandwich Tern (rare), Common Tern, Arctic Tern (mainly April and May), Little Tern (rare), Black Tern, Common Redstart (scarce), Northern Wheatear, Ring Ouzel (rare April), Grasshopper Warbler (scarce), Blackcap, Lesser and Common Whitethroats, Wood Warbler (rare).

31. FERMYN WOODS COUNTRY PARK

OS Landranger 141
OS Explorer 224

Habitat

This area changed its name from Brigstock Country Park when a large part of the adjacent Fermyn Wood was added, making it the largest in the county. The original part of 37 acres (15 ha) is a former sandpit and was acquired by Northamptonshire County Council 30 years ago. It has been well-managed and has developed into an attractive area of meadow and hilly scrub with a number of small pools which border the ancient mixed woodland of oak, ash and conifers.

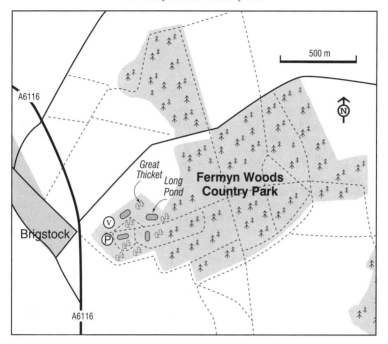

Species

This is the best site in Northamptonshire for Hawfinch in winter, with up to 24 present in early 2006, although in some years they are scarce or absent. The attraction for them are the numerous blackthorn and hawthorn bushes with their crop of sloe and haws offering a food supply, which lasts into the new year. They are most easily seen from the high ground above the fishing pool, which affords good views of the eastern edge of the scrub where it joins the mature woodland in the Great Thicket and Long Pond area. Willow Tits are not uncommon and in winter both these and the similar Marsh Tit visit the bird feeders near the ranger station. Winter finches such as Siskin and Lesser Redpoll find the whole area to their liking and sizeable parties of Fieldfares and Redwings are often present as long as the berries last. Meadow Pipits, Reed Buntings and Yellowhammers are often in evidence at this time of the year.

In spring or summer, a walk into the mixed oak and ash woodland can be rewarding. Both Nuthatch and Jay give themselves away with their loud, distinctive calls and all three species of woodpecker are present, although Lesser Spotted is the hardest to find. Warblers are very vocal with Blackcaps, Garden Warblers, Common Chiffchaffs and Willow Warblers inside the woodland where Wood Warbler has occurred. Common and Lesser Whitethroats favour the scrubland, as do Linnets and Bullfinches. This area has attracted a Ring Ouzel on passage and even a visiting Red-backed Shrike.

Sparrowhawks, Red Kites, Common Buzzards and Kestrels are seen over-head daily at any time of the year, and an evening walk could be rewarded with a roding Woodcock between March and June or a Nightingale singing during the summer.

Timing
Early mornings are best before dog walkers from the local village arrive, but Hawfinches can be present at any time of day and are occasionally even seen in the car park.

Access
Fermyn Woods Country Park is 4.3 miles (7 km) south-east of Corby and 5 miles (8 km) north-west of Thrapston. The main car park is signed off the A6116 Thrapston to Corby road just east of Brigstock village at SP952850. The country park is open all day every day; the car park is pay and display (£1.20 for up to an hour, £2 all day), with an annual ticket available for £20 or for £28 covering all parks. There are toilets open from 9 am to 5 pm and a visitor centre open 11 am to 5 pm at weekends and during school holidays, and at other times if the Ranger is on site. Hot drinks and snacks are available, there are information boards, a feeding station, children's play area, picnic area and one pool where coarse fishing is allowed in season. The various tracks around the reserve and the adjacent woodland are mainly hard-packed and are well marked. Nature trails and woodland walks vary in length from half a mile (0.8 km) to 2.2 miles (3.5 km).

Calendar
Resident: Red Kite, Sparrowhawk, Common Buzzard, Kestrel, Woodcock (scarce), Tawny Owl, Long-eared Owl (rare), Green and Great Spotted Woodpeckers, Lesser Spotted Woodpecker (scarce), Goldcrest, Marsh and Willow Tits, Nuthatch, Treecreeper, Jay, Goldfinch, Linnet, Bullfinch, Yellowhammer.

October–March: Meadow Pipit, Fieldfare, Redwing, Siskin, Lesser Redpoll, Hawfinch.

April–September: Nightingale (scarce), Blackcap, Garden Warbler, Lesser and Common Whitethroats, Common Chiffchaff, Willow Warbler, Spotted Flycatcher.

32. FINESHADE WOOD, WAKERLEY GREAT WOOD AND BLATHERWYCKE LAKE

OS Landranger 1410S
Explorers 224 and 234

Habitat
These close neighbours, part of the once vast Rockingham Forest royal hunting area, are Forestry Commission woodlands of 600 acres (243 ha) and 900 acres (364 ha) respectively, and are two of the four largest remaining patches of ancient forest in Northamptonshire. The woodlands both have plantations of various coniferous and deciduous species, with pine, oak, sycamore, ash, birch and larch, the latter particularly in Wakerley. Forestry practice has become more wildlife-conscious in recent years, and as the

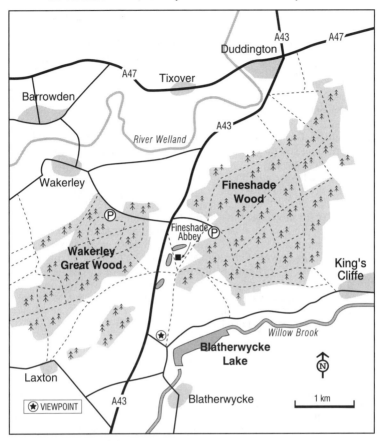

blocks are thinned, felled and re-planted in rotation, a rich network of trees of all ages develops, providing feeding and breeding areas for a range of species. There are a few pools dotted around both sites.

Species

Rarely a year goes by without these two woodlands hosting a flock of Common Crossbills, most often in the mature larches by the Wakerley car park. This is the best site in Northamptonshire for this species, and in the winter of 1990-91 a large flock contained a couple of Parrot and Two-barred Crossbills. One or two Hen Harriers have roosted in winter in the past; the area chosen depends on tree height and density, with the low, less disturbed plantations being favoured. The mixed woodland, especially the birches and larches, often attract flocks of Lesser Redpolls, and these groups have included a small number of Mealy Redpolls and, during the influx in the winter of 1995-96, the much rarer Arctic Redpoll.

Spring sees the arrival of a number of species that are rather localised in Northamptonshire. European Nightjars have occurred in the more open areas created after felling has been carried out, and the young plantations have proved particularly attractive to Grasshopper Warblers; large numbers have been trapped and ringed in Fineshade in recent years. Visitors may be lucky enough to hear Nightingales and Turtle Doves in song though both have declined; likewise, Tree Pipits bred until a few years ago, but may still occur on passage.

Long-eared Owl, Lesser Spotted Woodpecker and Hawfinch are all rare residents and Woodcocks are present in low numbers. Mandarin Ducks have often been seen on the small ponds dotted through the woods and have bred in nestboxes erected for them.

Rockingham Forest is perhaps best known today for its population of Red Kites. Seventy birds from Sweden and Spain were released in the area between 1995 and 1998 as part of the scheme to reintroduce this species into England. This has proved a great success; 99 young were tagged in the 2005 breeding season and the population now stands at about 200. Most carry plastic wing-tags on the upper surface of both wings; these tags vary in colour each year and bear letters, numbers or symbols readable in the field. The Rockingham Red Kite Project office is adjacent to the Fineshade car park and during the breeding season houses an exhibition and, usually, a live web-cam showing a local Red Kite (or Common Buzzard) nest.

Blatherwycke Lake provides a good vantage point to look for Red Kites and Common Buzzards, both of which should be seen easily here. During the summer, Ospreys are fairly regular visitors from nearby Rutland Water. A small colony of Grey Herons is situated in the pines and Shelducks sometimes breed. The lake attracts a variety of wintering wildfowl including Eurasian Wigeon, Gadwall, Common Teal, Pintail, Tufted Duck and Pochard, along with one or two Goldeneye and many Greylag and Canada Geese. Occasional rarer visitors have included American Wigeon and Ferruginous and Long-tailed Ducks.

Timing

As with most woods, early mornings tend to be the best time for a visit, especially during the breeding season when birds are in full song. Spring evenings can also be productive, when Woodcocks may be seen roding and the possibility of hearing Nightingales or even a European Nightjar increases. The area is very popular with orienteers, walkers and cyclists along some tracks at weekends, and Sundays in particular, but the woods are large enough for anyone to find quieter areas.

Access

The woodlands straddle the A43 7.5 miles (12 km) north-east of Corby. Wakerley Great Wood is west of the A43; turn west off the A43 miles 1.8 miles (3 km) south-west of Duddington on to a minor road signed to Wakerley and the car park and picnic area are located on the left after 0.6 miles (1 km) at SP963987. There are toilets and information boards explaining the history of the Rockingham Forest. Fineshade Wood is east of the A43 and the car park is reached by turning east off the A43 opposite the minor road to Wakerley (SP978983). It is here that the Red Kite Project has its information office and guided walks are available on Sunday mornings. There are numerous tracks, some of which are hard-packed, around both woodlands, and a hide overlooks a pond just off the main track through Fineshade.

For Blatherwycke Lake, travel south along the A43 from either the Wakerley or Fineshade car parks for 1.2 miles (2 km) and turn east towards Blatherwycke village. A pull-off on the left on a small bend after 400 m at SP971965 offers views over the lake, which is private. From this point Red Kites and Common Buzzards are consistently in view. The lake itself can be watched over the low drystone wall bordering the road along the western bank.

Calendar

Resident: Greylag Goose, Grey Heron, Red Kite, Goshawk (rare), Sparrowhawk, Common Buzzard, Kestrel, Woodcock, Long-eared Owl (scarce), Green and Great Spotted Woodpeckers, Lesser Spotted Woodpecker (scarce), Marsh and Willow Tits, Nuthatch, Treecreeper, Hawfinch (scarce).

October–March: Eurasian Wigeon, Gadwall, Common Teal, Pintail, Pochard, Tufted Duck, Goldeneye, Cormorant, Hen Harrier (rare), Peregrine Falcon (scarce), Fieldfare, Redwing, Siskin, Lesser Redpoll, Common Crossbill.

April–September: Shelduck, Mandarin Duck (scarce), Osprey, Turtle Dove (scarce), Tree Pipit (rare), Nightingale (scarce), Grasshopper Warbler, Blackcap, Garden Warbler, Wood Warbler (rare), Common Crossbill (scarce).

33. HOLLOWELL RESERVOIR

OS Landranger 141
OS Explorer 223

Habitat

Owned by Anglian Water, this 140 acre (57 ha) reservoir was opened in 1938 and is used for domestic water storage. The site nestles in a narrow, sheltered valley surrounded mainly by wheat fields and sheep-grazed pasture. Along the west bank there is a margin of sedges and reeds, and within the perimeter of the reservoir grounds there are several mature plantations, some of pine and some mixed. If the water level falls in late summer, the Guilsborough bay on the western bank provides a good expanse of mud, attractive to waders and wildfowl.

A sailing club is based at the west end of the dam, and yachts can be very much in evidence on Sunday afternoons. There is also coarse fishing, with an open season from mid-June to mid-March. Most anglers prefer to fish from the dam.

Species

The late autumn wildfowl counts at Hollowell Reservoir have topped 2,700 birds, making this the seventh most important site in Northamptonshire for this group of species. Eurasian Wigeon is the most numerous dabbling duck, with up to 850 birds being present, followed by Mallard (215), Common Teal (160), Gadwall (140), Shoveler (45) and often a few Pintails. The shallower water at the northern end is most attractive to the dabbling ducks. Conversely, diving ducks prefer the deeper water near the dam; the most numerous is usually Tufted Duck (up to 200), with smaller numbers of Pochard (120), Goosander (30) and Goldeneye (20). Smew are virtually annual during the winter months, and Red-crested Pochard, Scaup and Common Scoter are not infrequent. Of the scarcer species, there have been records of American Wigeon, Green-winged Teal, Ring-necked and Ferruginous Ducks, Common Eider, Long-tailed Duck and Velvet Scoter, as well as Red-throated and Great Northern Divers and Red-necked, Slavonian and Black-necked Grebes.

There is a winter gull roost, with the main species being Black-headed, Common, Lesser Black-backed and Herring Gulls, but inevitably

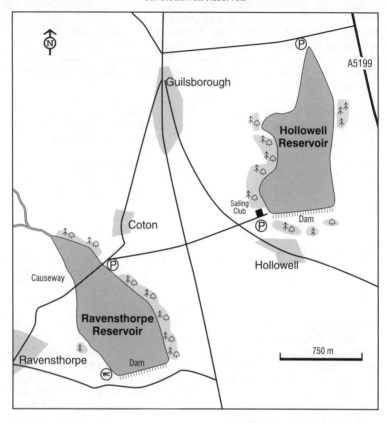

Mediterranean, Yellow-legged and Caspian Gulls have occurred with some regularity in recent years. A few Iceland and Glaucous Gulls have also been located, although they remain rare.

In the woodlands, flocks of tits and finches may include a few Siskins and Common Crossbills in good years for these species, while the hedgerows and grass fields contain groups of wintering Redwings and Fieldfares. The wealth of wildfowl and passerines brings in hunting Peregrine Falcons and Merlins on occasion during the winter months. The resident Common Buzzards can often be seen hunting during the winter days.

There is often a good spring passage of the three commoner inland tern species, with sizeable totals of Common, Arctic and Black being recorded in suitable weather conditions; Sandwich and Little Tern have also occurred. The regular waders pass through in small numbers, with Greenshank and Common Sandpiper the most frequent, but anything is possible and both Avocet and Collared Pratincole have paid spring visits in the past. Passage raptors include Osprey, which is almost annual, and increasingly regular Marsh Harriers. Garganey is a scarce visitor at this season.

Nesting waterbirds are relatively few in variety, with Mute Swan, Canada Goose, Great Crested Grebe, Moorhen and Coot the principal species. The plantations hold a selection of breeding birds such as Sparrowhawk, Kestrel, Green and Great Spotted Woodpeckers and Treecreeper, and the hedgerows and areas of scrub hold Blackcap, Garden Warbler, Lesser and Common Whitethroats and Yellowhammer.

A drop in the water level during the early autumn will reveal areas of mud which may attract passage waders. The most frequent are Ringed Plover, Dunlin, Ruff, Redshank, Greenshank and Green and Common Sandpipers, but most years a few scarcer species also appear, such as Black-tailed Godwit, Whimbrel, Spotted Redshank and Wood Sandpiper. Pectoral Sandpiper has occurred on several occasions and Temminck's Stint and Grey Phalarope have also been recorded.

In total, 209 species have been recorded at Hollowell Reservoir, including such rarities as Little Bittern, Spoonbill, White-winged Black Tern, Hoopoe and Dartford Warbler.

Timing

Autumn is probably the best time to visit, as wildfowl are arriving for the winter and, if the water levels have dropped, there is a chance of a few waders. These will most likely be at the northern feeder stream end or in Guilsborough bay on the west bank. Wildfowl are present all winter but numbers begin to fall by late February. Winter is also the time to see the small gull roost. The light conditions mean that the reservoir is best viewed from the east bank in the morning and the west side in the afternoon.

On Sunday afternoons sailing activities may disturb wildfowl, which will either become concentrated at the quieter northern end of the reservoir or move to nearby Ravensthorpe Reservoir.

Access

The reservoir is 10 miles (16 km) north of Northampton. To gain access to the whole reservoir a permit is necessary, available from The Fishing Lodge, Pitsford Reservoir, Brixworth Road, Holcot, Northamptonshire. Otherwise, viewing is limited to just two spots: (1) the car park by the feeder stream at the northern end; head south-west off the A5199 3.5 miles (5.6 km) north-west of Creaton and the car park is on the left after 500 m (SP683738); (2) the car park at the southern end by the access road to the sailing club; turn west off the A5199 at Creaton on to a minor road signed to Hollowell and the access road and car park are just o the west of Hollowell village (SP686722).

Ravensthorpe Reservoir is 1 mile (1.6 km) south-west of Hollowell Reservoir and can be viewed from the causeway at its northern end (SP675711). The southern section of this reservoir is heavily fished for trout;

Garganey

in spite of this, Pied-billed Grebe, Glossy Ibis, Purple Heron, Alpine Swift and Great Reed Warbler are among the 197 species which have occurred at this small site.

Calendar

Resident: Mute Swan, Greylag and Canada Geese, Great Crested Grebe, Sparrowhawk, Common Buzzard, Kestrel, Tawny Owl, Green and Great Spotted Woodpeckers, Treecreeper, Yellowhammer.

October–March: Eurasian Wigeon, Gadwall, Common Teal, Pintail (scarce), Shoveler, Red-crested Pochard (scarce), Pochard, Tufted Duck, Scaup (scarce), Goldeneye, Smew, Goosander, Ruddy Duck, Little Grebe, Common Snipe, Mediterranean Gull (scarce), Caspian Gull (scarce), Iceland Gull (rare), Glaucous Gull (rare), Fieldfare, Redwing, Siskin, Common Crossbill (scarce).

April–September: Garganey (scarce), Marsh Harrier (scarce), Osprey (scarce), Little Ringed and Ringed Plovers, Dunlin, Ruff, Black-tailed Godwit (scarce), Redshank, Greenshank, Green and Common Sandpipers, Little Gull, Yellow-legged Gull (July onwards), Common, Arctic and Black Terns, Yellow Wagtail, Northern Wheatear, Blackcap, Garden Warbler, Lesser and Common Whitethroats.

34. NENE VALLEY GRAVEL PITS

OS Landrangers 141, 152 and 153
OS Explorers 207, 223 and 224

The River Nene runs roughly south-west to north-east through Northamptonshire, before ultimately draining into The Wash in Lincolnshire. There are several extensive areas of old gravel pits along its course, and the sites detailed here are arranged geographically from north to south.

34A. THRAPSTON GRAVEL PITS AND TITCHMARSH NATURE RESERVE

OS Landranger 141
OS Explorer 224

Habitat

This locality consists of a chain of former gravel pits stretching a distance of nearly 3.5 miles (5.6 km) along the River Nene north-eastwards from Thrapston, with the most recently excavated pits at either end.

Part of the complex is the 180 acre (73 ha) Titchmarsh Nature Reserve, managed by the Northamptonshire Wildlife Trust. The reserve contains two lakes, the largest of which (Aldwincle Lake) was flooded in 1986 and has several islands which are managed to keep the vegetation in check, enabling ducks, waders and Common Terns to breed. This lake is surrounded by rough grassland and there is a *Phragmites* reedbed at the western end. A former duck decoy has been the site of an important heronry for many years and is surrounded by willows, alders, silver birches and Scots pines, which were planted by Lord Lilford in 1885. The lake at the north-east end of the complex has become a carp fishery, with a resultant increase in

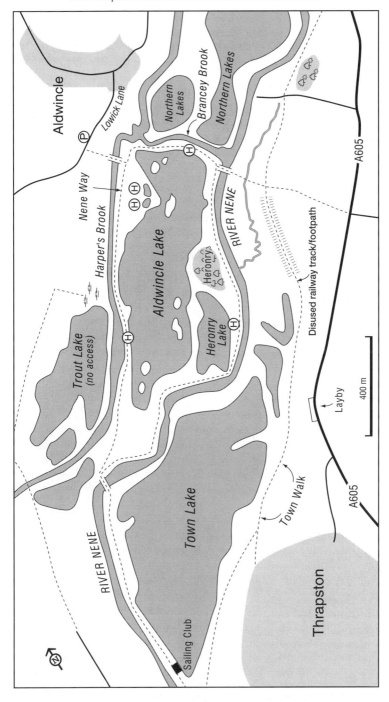

disturbance. There are young deciduous plantations at intervals around the reserve, along with areas of grassland and scrub. There are five hides, two of which give views over Aldwincle Lake and two which overlook purpose-built scrapes. The fifth hide is adjacent to a small lake next to the heronry (Heronry Lake).

The lake closest to Thrapston village (Town Lake) is the largest and deepest, and is home to an active sailing club, but at the eastern end of the pit there are several narrow islands covered in mature trees which offer a safe haven for nesting waterbirds. Coarse fishing is allowed on this lake from mid-June to mid-March. The track of the former railway line running north-east out of Thrapston is a popular footpath (Town Walk), affording good views of Town Lake but not Titchmarsh Reserve, although access can be gained to the reserve from it. The mature trees and associated scrub which have grown up along this track attract an interesting range of woodland bird species. To the east and north of Harper's Brook are three smaller lakes, one of which is a private trout lake with few surrounding trees, the others being encircled by a variety of trees, predominantly willows.

Species

This area has consistently been the second most important site in Northamptonshire for wildfowl, hosting over 5,000 individuals in December 1999. Eurasian Wigeon is the most numerous, with sometimes over 1,250 birds present, but there have been peaks of 1,400 Coots, 350 Tufted Ducks, 250 Pochards, 250 Common Teal, 95 Shovelers, 30 Little Grebes, 150 Cormorants, 240 Mute Swans and 670 Gadwall. This site is of national importance for the latter species and is ranked the tenth best in Britain. Goldeneye usually reach their peak numbers in February with over 120 in 2001. Smew are recorded annually in small numbers but numbers of Goosanders have decreased steadily over the past ten years and rarely total over 30. Greylag and Canada Geese are prolific breeders and both regularly number over 300 birds by the end of the summer. As many as 180 Great Crested Grebes are present in the autumn months, with up to 50 throughout the year. The Grey Heron colony fluctuates in number, but over 40 nests have been regular since the 1990s.

The small reedbeds visible from the hide overlooking the Heronry Lake have in recent years been the best place in Northamptonshire for observing Bitterns. Up to three have been seen, although in some winters they are absent completely. You could count yourself unlucky not to see a Kingfisher from here, and Water Rails are often present in this area.

A sizeable gull roost is present on Town Lake from late autumn through to spring, and contains thousands of Black-headed and Common Gulls, hundreds of Lesser Black-backed Gulls and smaller numbers of Herring Gulls. Yellow-legged Gulls are regular, particularly during the autumn, and there are occasional records of Mediterranean, Iceland and Glaucous Gulls.

The footpath leading from Thrapston (Town Walk) passes through some excellent mature trees, shrubs and scrub, which prove attractive to many passage migrants including several species of warbler and sometimes Nightingale. This is often the best place to seek out the first arriving migrants in spring. Parties of Yellow, Pied and White Wagtails feed on emergent insects along the water's edge during April and May. Hobbies can be seen hawking insects over the reserve during the summer, and are sometimes present in small flocks, including 19 in May 2005. Red Kites are often seen and Ospreys and Marsh Harriers turn up every two to three years. Hen Harrier has occurred in the winter.

J.W.

Greenshank

In both spring and autumn, migrating waders such as Grey Plover, Dunlin, Ruff, Black-tailed and Bar-tailed Godwits, Greenshank, Common Sandpiper and Turnstone find plenty of feeding opportunities along with Common Snipe, Curlew and Redshank, all of which breed nearby. Pectoral Sandpiper and Grey Phalarope are the rarest waders to have appeared. Town Lake has a habit of attracting terns and Little Gulls after easterly winds, with sometimes large numbers of both Arctic and Black Terns appearing. Occasionally Little and Sandwich Terns also arrive, as well as the widespread Common Tern.

Titchmarsh Reserve holds the highest number of nesting birds, including significant inland breeding species such as Oystercatcher, Ringed Plover and Common Tern. Grasshopper, Sedge and Reed Warblers also nest, along with Blackcap, Garden Warbler and two or three species of woodpecker.

In all, 213 species have been recorded at this site, including American Wigeon, Blue-winged Teal, Night Heron, Great White Egret, Purple Heron, Red-footed Falcon, Whiskered Tern and two White-winged Black Terns.

Timing
There is always something of interest to see, and this site is worthy of a visit at any time of year. For some reason, the area remains remarkably under-watched.

Access
To reach the Titchmarsh Nature Reserve, leave Thrapston north-east on the A605 and after 2 miles (3.2 km) turn left into Thorpe Waterville. Follow the road into Aldwincle and take the first left (Lowick Lane). The entrance to the reserve is on the left after 300 m (TL 007 813) where there is a small car park and information boards. The Nene Way footpath also runs alongside the reserve. Alternatively, park in the lay-by off the A605 500 m north-east of Thrapston (TL008796) and take the footpath down the side of the field to the disused railway line (Town Walk) which gives views of Town Lake.

Calendar
Resident: Mute Swan, Greylag and Canada Geese, Gadwall, Tufted Duck, Little and Great Crested Grebes, Cormorant, Grey Heron, Red Kite, Kingfisher, Green and Great Spotted Woodpeckers, Lesser Spotted Woodpecker (rare), Skylark, Treecreeper, Tree Sparrow (rare), Reed Bunting.

October–March: Eurasian Wigeon, Common Teal, Shoveler, Pochard, Goldeneye, Smew (scarce), Goosander, Bittern (scarce), Water Rail, gull roost including occasional Mediterranean, Iceland and Glaucous Gulls, Fieldfare, Redwing, Goldcrest, Siskin, Lesser Redpoll.

April–September: Shelduck, Garganey (scarce), Marsh Harrier (scarce), Osprey (scarce), Hobby, Oystercatcher, Little Ringed and Ringed Plovers, Dunlin, Ruff, Black-tailed Godwit (scarce), Bar-tailed Godwit (scarce), Curlew (scarce), Redshank, Greenshank, Common Sandpiper, Little Gull, Yellow-legged Gull (August onwards), Sandwich Tern (scarce), Common Tern, Arctic Tern, Little Tern (scarce), Black Tern, Yellow Wagtail, White Wagtail (mainly April), Nightingale (scarce), Northern Wheatear, Grasshopper, Sedge and Reed Warblers, Blackcap, Garden Warbler.

34B. STANWICK LAKES COUNTRY PARK

OS Landranger 141
OS Explorer 224

Habitat

An international aggregates company finished quarrying sand and gravel in 2004 and undertook a well-planned and executed restoration programme to return some of the meadows stripped of their gravel foundations back to wet grassland and flood meadows. Ditches have been cut, islands created and screening hedgerows planted to try to minimise disturbance from visitors. Alders and other wet woodland tree species have been introduced, along with oak, ash and cherry in the drier sections to maximise the diversity of bird species visiting the site. A large number of lakes, mainly shallow but some deep, of various sizes has developed as they were in turn worked out and allowed to fill up. This has left a rich mosaic of pits, some with permanent islands and others with islets that reappear each year as water levels fall during the hotter drier months. A former silt bed has both willow carr and a large *Phragmites* reed area, managed to prevent willow encroachment.

East Northamptonshire Council purchased 800 acres (240 ha) of the gravel pits and a disused railway line which bisects the whole site and handed it over to the Rockingham Forest Trust to create and manage a regional park. This was opened to the public in January 2006 and further development is planned running through to 2009. It remains to be seen what impact this will have on the birdlife of the area.

Species

The number of wintering wildfowl has increased dramatically in the last few years. Peak counts in the 2001 and 2002 winters included 100 Mute Swans, 380 Greylag Geese, 1,530 Eurasian Wigeons, 280 Common Teal, 140 Gadwall, 100 Shovelers, 210 Tufted Ducks, 80 Pochards and 24 Goosanders. Small numbers of Pintails and Goldeneyes visit every winter, along with a few Smew. Up to 50 Cormorants are regular, feeding on the river and the many lakes. A few Bewick's and Whooper Swans sometimes occur and rarer geese such as White-fronted, Pink-footed and Brent have appeared on occasions.

Wintering waders find the damp meadows to their liking, with recent peaks of 4,500 European Golden Plovers, 1,730 Northern Lapwings and 60 Dunlins. The largest lake between the old railway line and the river is the best for all these species and several rare ducks have appeared on here, including American Wigeon, Green-winged Teal and Ferruginous Duck, as well as the more regular Scaup, Common Scoter and Red-breasted

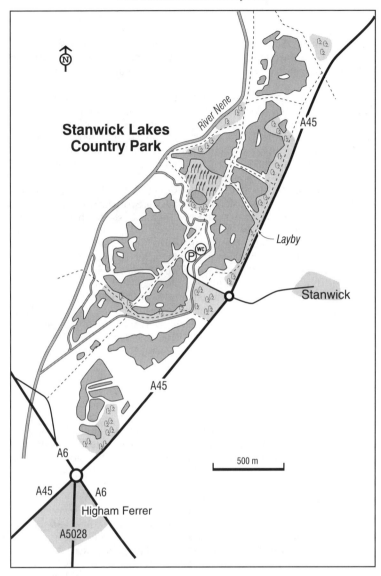

Merganser. The three rarer grebes, Red-necked, Black-necked and Slavonian, have all been recorded on the lake, which is also the location of the night-ly winter gull roost. The usual species in that roost are as expected, being predominantly Black-headed and Common, with smaller numbers of Lesser Black-backed, Herring and Great Black-backed Gulls. As at most of the sites along the Nene valley, Mediterranean, Caspian, Iceland and Glaucous Gulls have occurred several times, and Yellow-legged Gulls are fairly frequent.

This lake, along with the one south of the old railway line adjacent to the layby on the A605, are the most attractive to passage waders. Ruff, Greenshank and Green and Common Sandpipers are regular, especially in autumn when they may be present for weeks on end. Scarcer species which occur more or less annually include Grey Plover, Sanderling, Little Stint, Curlew Sandpiper, both godwits, Whimbrel and Turnstone. There have been eight Temminck's Stints and four Pectoral Sandpipers in the last 14 years, while rarer still have been sightings of Avocet, Kentish Plover, Baird's and Buff-breasted Sandpipers and one of the few Northamptonshire records of Stone-curlew.

Passage terns can be found in both spring and autumn, with Little and Sandwich scarce but regular and Black and Arctic Terns more frequent. A few Little Gulls often accompany migrating terns. Also at migration times, observers are on the lookout for Whinchat and Northern Wheatear, both of which are regular but not common. There is also the chance of locating a Common Redstart, while early spring and late autumn sometimes see records of Rock Pipit or, more rarely, Water Pipit.

A few pairs of Black-headed Gull and Common Tern breed annually, pre-ferring the more vegetated islands, and one or two pairs of Ringed Plover and Redshank nest, along with the occasional Oystercatcher. During the spring most of the common warblers can be found, and in the thicker patch-es of willow scrub a Cetti's Warbler may give itself away with its explosive song, although it will probably remain hidden. Reed and Sedge Warblers are common and even Savi's and Marsh Warblers have been recorded. Water Rails probably breed in the *Phragmites* reedbeds and Spotted Crakes have been seen a few times. The same reedbed hosted a party of Bearded Tits throughout a recent winter as well as a nightly roost of thousands of Starlings, and the first ever Marsh Harrier to overwinter in Northamptonshire regularly roosted here. The latter species is recorded annually in May and/or August and September, usually involving juveniles or immatures dispersing form nest areas further east. Other regular raptors are Osprey, Red Kite, Peregrine Falcon and Merlin, while Hobbies are present daily throughout the summer and are often seen hawking dragonflies over the pits. Rarer rap-tors seen have included Honey Buzzard, Hen Harrier and Goshawk.

Between 1988 – when recording at this site began – and 2006, a total of 204 species had been recorded in a relatively short period, emphasising the potential of the area. As well as the scarcities already mentioned, notable species have included Great White Egret, Purple Heron, Spoonbill, two Caspian Terns, Hoopoe, Richard's Pipit and Firecrest.

Timing

This area underwent a massive transformation during 2005, when it changed from being visited by a handful of birders and walkers to a site pre-dicted to attract 250,000 visitors a year in just the first phase of development. Purpose-built facilities and paved footpaths mean that visitors will swarm over the site. It is hoped that careful management will result in the most sensitive areas receiving degrees of protection from disturbance. Probably the best time to visit will be early morning, avoiding weekends and school holidays if possible.

Access

Stanwick Lakes Country Park is 1.6 miles (2.5 km) east of Irthlingborough. The entrance to the park is from the roundabout (SP971713) on the A45 1.1 miles (1.8 km) north-east of the A6/A45 junction. The large car park has toi-lets, picnic areas, an information centre with rangers in attendance, an assault course, an adventure trail, a state-of-the-art play area for children, cycle and walking tracks. Coarse fishing is allowed on lakes in the south-west corner only and does not affect the birdlife. Non-motorised watersports and boating will be allowed on some lakes in the future and others have been set aside for nature conservation. Parking charges are £1 from October to March, when the car park is open from 7 am to 5 pm, and £2 from April to September (7 am to 9 pm); alternatively, a £20 annual parking permit is available. A hide under construction in March 2006 overlooks one of the best areas.

Alternative free access is available from the loop road next to the A6 roadbridge crossing the River Nene between Higham Ferrers and Irthlingborough (SP957701), or from the small layby next to the A45 250 m north of the Stanwick roundabout (SP973717).

Calendar

Resident: Mute Swan, Greylag and Canada Geese, Gadwall, Tufted Duck, Little and Great Crested Grebes, Cormorant, Grey Heron, Sparrowhawk, Kestrel, Water Rail, Kingfisher, Cetti's Warbler (scarce), Willow Tit, Yellowhammer, Reed Bunting.

October–March: Eurasian Wigeon, Common Teal, Pintail, Shoveler, Pochard, Goldeneye, Smew, Goosander, Peregrine Falcon, European Golden Plover, Northern Lapwing, Dunlin, Common Snipe, Green Sandpiper, Mediterranean Gull, Caspian Gull (scarce), Iceland Gull (scarce), Glaucous Gull (scarce), Long-eared Owl (scarce), Short-eared Owl, European Stonechat, Bearded Tit (rare), Lesser Redpoll.

April–September: Shelduck, Garganey, Little Egret, Marsh Harrier (passage, mainly May and August), Osprey (scarce), Hobby, Oystercatcher, Little Ringed, Ringed and Grey Plovers, Sanderling, Little Stint (August and September), Temminck's Stint (scarce May), Curlew Sandpiper (August and September), Dunlin, Ruff, both godwits, Whimbrel, Curlew, Spotted Redshank, Redshank, Greenshank, Green, Wood and Common Sandpipers, Turnstone, Little Gull, Black-headed Gull (colony), Yellow-legged Gull, Sandwich Tern (scarce), Common and Arctic Terns, Little Tern (scarce), Black Tern, Cuckoo, Turtle Dove, Whinchat, Northern Wheatear, Sedge and Reed Warblers, Lesser and Common Whitethroats.

34C. DITCHFORD GRAVEL PITS

OS Landrangers 152 and 153
OS Explorer 224

Habitat

This site occupies a riverside location on an east-west flyway and is visible for miles to migrating birds; during its heyday in the 1980s, it regularly attracted major national rarities, and has added more species to the Northamptonshire bird list than any other site in the county.

The largest pit, immediately to the west of Higham Ferrers, was designated as a Site of Special Scientific Interest on account of its important selection of breeding birds and the number of passage waders using the locality as a regular stop-over. This status, however, did not stop a new road being built across one side of the pit in 1985 and its subsequent upgrading to dual carriageway ten years later. The associated diversion of the river along a new course seemed to affect the water levels in the pit, which no longer rose and fell as quickly, an important factor in maintaining muddy edges and feeding areas for waders. Since that time the banks have become increasingly vegetated with willows and patches of reedmace, and many of the narrow

Water Pipit

islands left after mineral extraction have become covered in willows. From a human viewpoint, the pits do not look as good as they previously did, and the area now receives far less coverage than it used to, but nevertheless it is still attractive to birds, and occasional rarities continue to put in an appearance.

More pits have since been excavated, and the newest stretch to the west of Ditchford Lane extends almost to the eastern outskirts of Wellingborough. Two hides are located on an area leased by the Northamptonshire Wildlife Trust.

Species

Ditchford varies between the fifth and eighth best county wildfowl site, with the December 2001 count of 1,900 birds being the highest total in recent years. Eurasian Wigeon predominates, with up to 640 birds, followed by Tufted Duck (320), Gadwall (175), Common Teal (100), Pochard (40), Goosander (25) and Shoveler (20), as well as Mallard and a few Goldeneye. Something rarer often appears during the course of a year; Red-crested Pochard, Scaup, Common Scoter and Smew are relatively frequent, and rarer species such as American Wigeon, Green-winged Teal, Blue-winged Teal, Ring-necked Duck, Ferruginous Duck, Common Eider, Long-tailed Duck and Velvet Scoter have appeared over the years. Ducks tend to move around the complex of pits depending upon conditions such as wind strength and direction and the amount of disturbance, but in general the largest lake immediately west of Higham Ferrers holds the best variety and totals.

Gulls often gather in the late afternoon but their choice of pit seems to vary. Large numbers of Herring and Great Black-backed Gulls are sometimes present and these have been accompanied by Iceland and Glaucous Gulls on several occasions. Yellow-legged Gulls are fairly regular, particularly during the autumn when they often associate with Lesser Black-backed Gulls. Mediterranean Gulls have also occurred among the commoner Black-headed and Common Gulls. Most birds fly off just before dusk to roost elsewhere, probably at Grafham Water across the county boundary in Cambridgeshire.

Ditchford is the best site in Northamptonshire for Water Pipit, with up to three wintering annually. The birds tend to favour the area alongside the river but, as is often the case with this flighty species, they can be difficult to observe well as they usually fly long distances once flushed. European Stonechats also like this area in the winter and a pair even stayed to breed nearby on one occasion. Water Rails can usually be found around the more vegetated pits, being most easily observed during spells of hard weather when they are forced to feed out in the open if their favoured areas are frozen. Bearded Tits have found the mass of waterside vegetation to their lik-

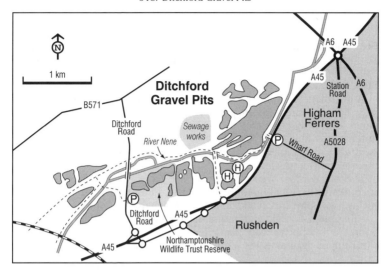

ing but are not annual in occurrence. When not calling they can be very inconspicuous, feeding quietly in the vegetation.

As would be expected with such a variety of habitats, many raptors have been encountered. Sparrowhawk, Common Buzzard and Kestrel are resident and breed nearby, where they are joined in the summer months by Hobbies. Peregrine Falcons have taken to using the huge electricity pylons at the western end of the complex outside the breeding season to roost and keep a look out for potential prey. Osprey, Marsh Harrier, Red Kite and Merlin are seen every couple of years and Goshawk and Hen Harrier have been recorded. Long-eared Owls are sometimes seen in the winter and through into spring and may well breed in the area.

In spring the bushes are alive with Sedge and Willow Warblers, and Reed Warblers are not uncommon. Cetti's Warblers have been in residence at Ditchford since the late 1980s and most county records come from this site; six birds were present in early 2006. Several pairs of Willow Tits find the damp marshy thickets to their satisfaction. There is a small heronry, with up to ten pairs of Grey Heron nesting annually. Purple Herons have been recorded five times on neighbouring pits, in addition to which Spoonbills, Great White and Little Egrets and several Bitterns have been noted over the years, the latter mainly occurring during the winter months. Shelduck, Gadwall, Shoveler, Pochard and Tufted Duck have all bred recently, and Eurasian Wigeon, Common Teal and Garganey have summered.

Common Terns no longer breed but are ever present during the summer, and when inland movements of migrating terns take place some large flocks of this species may be present. At such times, Arctic and Black Terns also arrive with regularity, and the much scarcer Little and Sandwich Terns are also possible. The pits have a good range of breeding waders, with Little Ringed Plover, Ringed Plover, Northern Lapwing and Redshank all nesting when conditions and water levels are suitable. Oystercatchers will hopefully soon follow suit, as birds are occurring with more frequency in the spring and summer months.

Passage waders are mostly found at the western end of the complex. They are more numerous in autumn, with small groups of Little Ringed and Ringed Plovers, Dunlin, Ruff, Greenshank and Common and Green

Sandpipers being the most regular and scarcer species such as Little Stint, Curlew Sandpiper, Black-tailed and Bar-tailed Godwit and Wood Sandpipers being not infrequent. In all, 34 species of waders have been found at Ditchford, including Avocet, Kentish Plover, Temminck's Stint, Pectoral Sandpiper, Purple Sandpiper, Broad-billed Sandpiper, Marsh Sandpiper, Lesser Yellowlegs and Grey Phalarope.

A selection of seabirds has appeared, usually following autumn gales, with Fulmar, Leach's Storm-petrel and Pomarine, Arctic and Long-tailed Skuas all having been recorded. Diligent searching of the site during the autumn has led to the discovery of vagrants normally associated with coastal localities, including Hoopoe, Wryneck, two Yellow-browed Warblers and several Firecrests.

The total number of species recorded at Ditchford currently stands at 238, second only in Northamptonshire to Pitsford Reservoir. The list of rarities is highly impressive and, in addition to those already mentioned, includes such exciting birds as Night Heron, Sabine's Gull, Ring-billed Gull, Caspian Tern, Sooty Tern, White-winged Black Tern, Alpine Swift, European Bee-eater, Red-rumped Swallow, Savi's Warbler and Penduline Tit.

Timing

A visit is worthwhile at any time of day or any time of year. There is so much good habitat here to explore and anything can turn up.

Access

To view the older pits, the best access point is reached by heading south into Higham Ferrers on the A5028 Station Road from the A45/A6 round-about just north of the town. After 1 mile (1.6 km) turn right on to Wharf Road and follow this road to the end, where there is a small car park (SP953687); from here, cross the footbridge over the dual carriageway to the pits beyond. Access is virtually unlimited, although one private lake is fenced off. A hide overlooks this lake, and another gives views over the lake adjacent to the dual carriageway, where a scrape has been constructed.

The newer pits, and the Northamptonshire Wildlife Trust reserve, are accessed by leaving the A45 just west of Rushden and heading north on Ditchford Road towards Irthlingborough. After 500 m there is a small car park on the right (SP931678). Alternatively, continue along Ditchford Road for a further 500 m, cross the river bridge and a gravel track which can be walked down leads off to the left (SP930684).

Calendar

Resident: Mute Swan, Greylag Goose, Canada Goose, Gadwall, Tufted Duck, Little Grebe, Great Crested Grebe, Grey Heron, Sparrowhawk, Common Buzzard, Kestrel, Northern Lapwing, Kingfisher, Cetti's Warbler, Willow Tit, Reed Bunting.

October–March: Eurasian Wigeon, Common Teal, Shoveler, Red-crested Pochard (scarce), Pochard, Scaup (scarce), Common Scoter (scarce), Goldeneye, Smew, Goosander, Cormorant, Peregrine Falcon, Water Rail, Common Snipe, Green Sandpiper, Mediterranean Gull (scarce), Caspian Gull (scarce), Iceland Gull (rare), Glaucous Gull (rare), Long-eared Owl (rare), Water Pipit (scarce), Grey Wagtail, European Stonechat, Lesser Redpoll.

April–September: Shelduck, Garganey (scarce), Marsh Harrier (scarce), Osprey (scarce), Hobby, Oystercatcher, Little Ringed Plover, Ringed Plover,

Dunlin, Ruff, Black-tailed Godwit (scarce), Bar-tailed Godwit (scarce), Redshank, Greenshank, Green Sandpiper, Common Sandpiper, Yellow-legged Gull (July onwards), Sandwich Tern (scarce), Common Tern, Arctic Tern, Little Tern (scarce), Black Tern, Cuckoo, Sedge Warbler, Reed Warbler, Common Whitethroat, Willow Warbler.

34D. EARLS BARTON GRAVEL PITS AND SUMMER LEYS NATURE RESERVE

OS Landranger 152
OS Explorer 224

Habitat

Following cessation of mineral extraction in 1989, this large gravel pit was thoughtfully landscaped and developed into what has become an excellent reserve. It forms part of a chain of both restored and active gravel pits, in the Wollaston-Earls Barton section of the Nene valley, which extend for 3.5 miles (5.6 km). Officially opened in 1994, Summer Leys Nature Reserve, which is managed by Northamptonshire County Council, has already attracted a large number of bird species and has become very popular with local bird-watchers. The main lake is bounded by gently sloping banks which shelve down into the open water, and a series of gravel-topped islands attract breeding terns, waders and wildfowl. The water levels of a purpose-built scrape adjacent to the car park can be controlled to produce ideal conditions for passage and breeding waders. Thousands of mixed deciduous trees have been planted on the reserve and there are hawthorn hedgerows and ash trees around the perimeter. Three well-placed hides and a screen overlook the best parts of the reserve, including the scrape, and a feeding station has been established next to one of the hides.

To the east of the reserve are two large pits known as Pete Wyles' Lake and Mary's Lake, while to the west lie older gravel workings. To the north-west of the reserve, grazed meadows lead down to the River Nene and to the south beyond the road is mixed arable farmland.

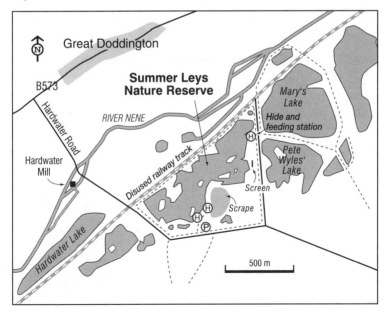

249

Species
This site is now ranked the third best for wintering wildfowl in Northamptonshire, with nearly 4,000 individuals often present. The predominant species (average highest counts in brackets) are Eurasian Wigeon (875), Tufted Duck (425), Pochard (280), Common Teal (275), Shoveler (40) and Goldeneye (40), while Gadwall have peaked at 280, making the site one of national importance for this species. Up to eight Smew are now regular during the winter months. White-fronted and Brent Goose are almost annual, and often join up with the large numbers of resident Greylag and Canada Geese. Ferruginous Duck, Common Eider and Long-tailed Duck have all occurred, as well as Great Northern Diver and Red-necked and Slavonian Grebe.

The hawthorn hedgerows support feeding flocks of Blackbirds, Fieldfares and Redwings, and wintering parties of Meadow Pipits frequent short grass areas around the newer workings. Common Snipe find the shallow water areas and wet grassland to their liking, and odd Green Sandpipers occur throughout the winter months, often feeding on the newly worked pits. Water Rails are present at this time of year but are easier to hear than see, their eerie calls being a feature of still winter evenings.

On a spring day the reserve is alive with birds. Black-headed Gulls and Common Terns have their largest colonies in Northamptonshire at this site, and these compete for space with Little Ringed and Ringed Plovers, Northern Lapwings and Redshanks. The ever-present Cormorants, which breed nearby, are often to be observed resting on the gravel islands with outstretched wings. Singing Sedge and Reed Warblers vie for territories among the reedbeds and rough scrub around the pits, with attendant Cuckoos watching for likely nests in which to lay their eggs. Shelduck and Shoveler sometimes breed and Gadwall and Tufted Duck usually do so, while one or two Eurasian Wigeons stay throughout the summer and Teal linger late into May. Grey Herons and Oystercatchers nest on neighbouring pits and large numbers of Tree Sparrows breed on the reserve.

The ability to lower the water levels, revealing areas of exposed mud, means that this is a good site for observing spring wader passage. Species such as Grey Plover, Knot, Sanderling, Dunlin, Ruff, Black-tailed and Bar-tailed Godwit, Whimbrel, Greenshank and Turnstone are all regular in spring, and even Little Stint and Curlew Sandpiper sometimes appear at this time of year. Avocets are almost annual spring visitors, usually in April, while Temminck's Stint is another scarce but not infrequent visitor, with the middle of May being the peak time to find this species.

This is one of the best sites in the county to chance upon either a Sandwich or Little Tern, both of which are just about annual in occurrence. Parties of Arctic Terns often pass through in April, while Black Terns and Little Gulls often arrive together in with May during periods of east or south-east winds. One or two Garganey appear throughout the spring, a period which often sees records of both Common Scoter and Black-necked Grebe. Whinchat and Northern Wheatear are regular spring passage migrants, as are White Wagtails. Hobbies are seen almost daily throughout the summer, often hawking for insects over the pools. Passage Marsh Harriers and Ospreys are becoming more frequent, with the months of May and August being the peak times to catch up with these exciting raptors.

Little Egrets have been seen regularly in late summer in recent years, in line with the species' recent increase in numbers in southern Britain, and two overwintered 2005-06. One or two Red-crested Pochards usually appear

Smew

in the autumn. The waders present in spring can again be seen in autumn, with Little Stint, Curlew Sandpiper and Black-tailed Godwit being more likely at this time of year. European Golden Plover numbers often build up to around 2,000 as they feed in nearby fields and visit the reserve to bathe and roost.

216 species have been recorded at the site, the fourth highest total in the county. The list of rarities is impressive, especially as all have occurred since 1989, and is headed by a Bridled Tern in 1993, a truly exceptional inland record. Rare waders have included Black-winged Stilt, two Collared Pratincoles, two Kentish Plovers, American Golden Plover, White-rumped Sandpiper, no fewer than six Pectoral Sandpipers, Buff-breasted Sandpiper, Marsh Sandpiper, Red-necked Phalarope and Grey Phalarope, while other exciting species to have been recorded include Green-winged Teal, Blue-winged Teal, Great White Egret, Red-footed Falcon, Caspian Tern, White-winged Black Tern, Little Auk, Hoopoe and Great Reed Warbler.

Timing
This site can be rewarding at any time of the day or year but, as with many inland sites, early morning during spring or autumn probably offers the best chance of locating some of the scarcer species.

Access
Summer Leys Nature Reserve is 5 miles (8 km) east of Northampton and 2.5 miles (4 km) south-west of Wellingborough. Travelling from Northampton, leave the A45 at the Great Doddington exit (B573) and head towards Great Doddington. After 500 m turn right on to Hardwater Road, cross the River Nene at Hardwater Mill and the car park and reserve are clearly signposted on the left after a further 500 m (SP885634). Two hides, both with disabled access, are within 50 m of the car park, and a screen and a third hide are located on the east side of the reserve. A well-marked footpath surrounds the area and gives views over all parts of the reserve. There are guided walks at intervals throughout the year.

The two pits to the east (Pete Wyles' Lake and Mary's Lake) are always worth a look and can be viewed from the gateways along the single-track road, which is first left after turning left out of the car park. The pit further to the west and the newer ones to the east can also be explored.

Calendar

Resident: Mute Swan, Greylag and Canada Geese, Gadwall, Tufted Duck, Red-legged and Grey Partridges, Little and Great Crested Grebes, Cormorant, Grey Heron, Sparrowhawk, Kestrel, Northern Lapwing, Black-headed Gull, Green Woodpecker, Tree Sparrow.

October–March: Bewick's Swan (scarce), White-fronted Goose (rare), Brent Goose (rare), Eurasian Wigeon, Common Teal, Pintail, Shoveler, Pochard, Goldeneye, Smew, Water Rail, European Golden Plover, Common Snipe, Green Sandpiper, Meadow Pipit, Fieldfare, Redwing.

April–September: Shelduck, Garganey (scarce), Red-crested Pochard (scarce, August and September), Black-necked Grebe (scarce), Little Egret, Marsh Harrier (scarce), Osprey (scarce), Hobby, Oystercatcher, Little Ringed and Ringed Plovers, Grey Plover, Knot, Sanderling, Little Stint (mainly August and September), Temminck's Stint (rare May), Curlew Sandpiper (scarce, August and September), Dunlin, Ruff, both godwits, Whimbrel, Curlew, Spotted Redshank, Redshank, Greenshank, Green, Wood and Common Sandpipers, Turnstone, Mediterranean and Little Gulls, Sandwich Tern (scarce), Common and Arctics Tern, Little Tern (scarce), Black Tern, Cuckoo, Yellow Wagtail, White Wagtail (April), Whinchat, Northern Wheatear, Grasshopper, Sedge and Reed Warblers.

34E. CLIFFORD HILL GRAVEL PITS

OS Landranger 152
OS Explorers 207 and 223

Habitat

This extensive area comprises one large and five small flooded gravel pits alongside the southern bank of the River Nene on the south-east edge of Northampton. The largest lake, which has been enclosed by a giant clay and earth bank, is designed as a flood catchment area to receive water when the River Nene is swollen after periods of heavy rainfall. Automatic sluices allow the basin to fill up and lower the level of the river, thereby protecting areas downstream from the threat of flooding. Originally it was thought that the basin would only fill once every seven years or so, but flooding is at present an annual event which can occur at any time of year following periods of heavy rainfall. A large spit of land and a narrower point extend into the lake, and waders, gulls and terns often find these spots to their liking. A small *Phragmites* reedbed has become established on the western side, and there is also a small gravel island at the south-west corner of the basin with willows established around the edge. When not covered in floodwater the area is grazed by sheep and geese. This has consistently been the best of the lakes, but is at times used by coarse fishermen who often camp out overnight around the edge.

The small lakes to the east are not open to the public. The deepest of these lakes is a trout fishery which can be easily scanned from the rim of the largest lake, while another can be viewed from a public footpath which runs along the southern edge. This footpath is the track of a former railway line, and is used for access purposes by farm vehicles. The latter lake is surrounded by willows, many of which overhang the water, and there is a small *Phragmites* reedbed in the south-east corner.

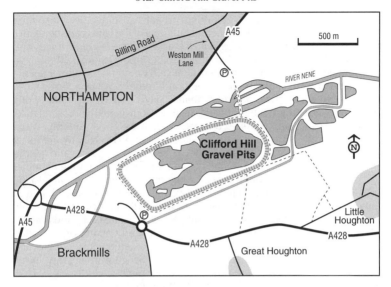

Species

Almost 200 species have been recorded at this rather open site. The locality is the 20th most important wintering site in Britain for European Golden Plover, with up to 5,000 birds present from October through to April; during particularly harsh weather, this species will depart the area, returning with the onset of milder conditions. Several thousand Northern Lapwings are usually present along with up to 30 Dunlins and one or two Green Sandpipers. Clifford Hill averages the fourth best site in Northamptonshire for wildfowl, with regularly over 3,000 and sometimes over 4,000 individuals present (October 2005); these totals often comprise over 2,000 Mallards, as large numbers are released for shooting on the more easterly pits. Some recent peak counts from the 2004-05 winter included 880 Eurasian Wigeons, 170 Tufted Ducks, 120 Pochards, 120 Shovelers, 80 Gadwall, 35 Common Teal and 30 Goosanders, with smaller numbers of Goldeneyes. Eurasian Wigeons find the grassy banks around the main lake to their liking and are accompanied by large numbers of Greylag and Canada Geese, of which up to 400 and 580 respectively were recorded in 2005. These feral flocks sometimes attract singles or small parties of wild geese, and White-fronted, Pink-footed, Tundra Bean and Brent Geese have all occurred regularly. Mute Swan numbers often total 150–200, even during the summer months, Bewick's Swans sometimes pay a visit in November and a Whooper Swan recently wintered. Of the rarer waterbirds, Scaup, Smew and Common Scoter are almost annual, and there have been records of Long-tailed Duck and Red-necked Grebe. The adjacent trout lake is very deep; consequently, even during the most prolonged frosts, there is an ice-free area which acts as a magnet for the remaining wildfowl.

The point area acts as a gathering site for Cormorants and gulls in the late afternoon prior to going to roost. The gulls consist mainly of Black-headed, with smaller numbers of Common, Lesser Black-backed and Herring Gulls. As with most well-watched gull haunts, there have been occasional records of the scarcer species; Glaucous and Iceland Gulls have occurred once or twice, Kittiwakes and Mediterranean Gulls have been seen on several occasions and Yellow-legged and Caspian Gulls are noted on a regular basis.

In March, Sand Martins and Northern Wheatears sometimes make their first county appearance at this site, and numbers of the latter can sometimes reach double-figures. White and Yellow Wagtails like the grassy edges and Ring Ouzels have been recorded on a number of occasions. Little Ringed and Ringed Plovers, Dunlin, Ruff, Redshank and Common Sandpiper are the most regular waders and a good selection of other passage species move through but seldom stay for more than a day or so. Of the rarer spring migrants, Sanderling, Whimbrel and Bar-tailed Godwit are the most reliable, with less regular appearances by species such as Wood Sandpiper and Turnstone, while during the autumn Little Stint and Greenshank are likely. Late summer often sees the appearance of several Little Egrets, and later in the autumn Rock Pipit is a possibility. Common Terns, which breed at other sites in the Nene valley, are present throughout the summer, coming to the pits to fish and bringing their fledged young later in the year. Little and Sandwich Terns are almost annual on passage, with Black Terns and Little Gulls being more reliable given a hint of east or south-east winds during May and July to September. Mute Swan, Greylag and Canada Geese, Tufted Duck, Great Crested Grebe, Coot and Moorhens breed on adjacent pits, and Shelduck are often seen in summer. Reed and Sedge Warblers nest in the reedbeds and sedges, and other breeding birds include Little Owl, Kingfisher, Skylark, Meadow Pipit and Reed Bunting.

Such a well-watched site with a good range of habitats is sure to produce a number of scarce birds over time, and recent years have seen records of Leach's Storm-petrel, Great White Egret, Spoonbill, Marsh Harrier, Osprey, Sabine's Gull, Hoopoe, Shore Lark, Water Pipit, Twite and Snow Bunting.

Timing
The best times to visit are either early morning or just before dusk as the main lake area is popular with joggers and particularly dog walkers, who let their animals run free and seldom keep to the footpaths. During wet and windy weather there is less disturbance and any time of day can be good. In the winter months, Tuesday and Fridays are perhaps best avoided as shooting often takes places over the adjacent private lakes causing disturbance to wildfowl in particular.

Access
Leave the centre of Northampton eastwards on Billing Road and turn right after 2 miles (3.2 km) on to Weston Mill Lane, signposted to Weston Favell Mill. Cross the dual carriageway bridge and there is a car park on the right (SP791608). Leave nothing of value in vehicles as break-ins are frequent here. Walk south down the lane towards the boat club, cross the lock gate and then the footbridge over the river, and the main lake is immediately in front. A footpath encircles the flood storage reservoir. Alternatively, at the A45 (Nene Valley Way)/A43 (Lumbertubs Way) interchange, go north on the A43 for 200 m before turning left along Bewick Road then left on to Weston Mill Lane after half a mile (0.8 km). Access can also be gained from the A428 Bedford Road, which passes the southern edge of the main lake. Half a mile (0.8 km) east of the A428/A45 interchange turn off the roundabout towards the Lakeside public house and a small car park is at SP783596.

Calendar
Resident: Mute Swan, Greylag and Canada Geese, Gadwall, Tufted Duck, Red-legged Partridge, Little and Great Crested Grebes, Cormorant, Northern Lapwing, Little Owl, Kingfisher, Skylark, Meadow Pipit, Reed Bunting.

Northern Wheatear

October–March: Eurasian Wigeon, Common Teal, Shoveler, Red-crested Pochard (scarce), Pochard, Scaup (scarce), Goldeneye, Smew (scarce), Goosander (December onwards), European Golden Plover, Dunlin, Common Snipe, Green Sandpiper, Caspian Gull (scarce), Rock Pipit (scarce, October and November), Grey Wagtail, European Stonechat, Linnet.

April–September: Shelduck, Little Egret, Hobby, Little Ringed and Ringed Plovers, Sanderling, Little Stint (August and September), Dunlin, Ruff, Bar-tailed Godwit (mainly May), Whimbrel, Redshank, Greenshank, Wood and Common Sandpipers, Turnstone, Little and Yellow-legged Gulls, Common Tern, Arctic Tern (mainly April and May), Little Tern (scarce), Black Tern, Yellow Wagtail, White Wagtail (mainly April), Whinchat, Northern Wheatear, Ring Ouzel (scarce), Sedge and Reed Warblers.

35. PITSFORD RESERVOIR OS Landrangers 141 and 152
OS Explorer 223

Habitat

This 800 acre (324 ha) reservoir, constructed in 1955, is owned by Anglian Water and is subjected to intensive recreational use for sailing, cycling, walking and both seasonal trout and coarse fishing. A footpath around the perimeter is a full 13 miles (21 km) in length. The whole reservoir was designated as a Site of Special Scientific Interest in 1970, principally due to the large numbers of wildfowl using the site.

The larger south side of the reservoir, with the exception of the sailing club grounds, is all open to the public, and is surrounded by a hard-packed path/cycle track, but the area north of the causeway is a reserve of the Northamptonshire Wildlife Trust, with access limited to permit holders only. The fishing lodge is also in this section and is situated adjacent to the causeway.

Apart from the dam, the reservoir has natural clay banks, which in turn have a number of mixed woodland plantations of varying ages. Most of the mature plantations, including a copse of oak, are found on the reserve itself. The grassy banks are sometimes grazed by sheep on the reserve side, where there are many willows and hawthorns between the water's edge and the plantations. The surrounding fields are a mixture of arable and pasture, together with a network of hedgerows, and can be seen from within the reserve.

Species

Pitsford Reservoir has attracted 240 species in its 50-year history, more than any other site in Northamptonshire, and is the premier birdwatching site in the county. During the winter months, large numbers of wildfowl are attracted to the reservoir, with average totals of over 5,500 birds and a peak of 9,950 in November 1994. Eurasian Wigeon is the most numerous of the dabbling ducks, with over 1,200 birds regularly present, and there can be up to 800 Mallard and 750 Common Teal present. Gadwall average 420, making the site of national importance for this species and ranked eleventh in Britain. Pitsford is also of national importance for four other species of waterbird (average highest counts given in brackets): Shoveler (157), Tufted Duck (1,690, particularly in the early part of the winter), Great Crested Grebe (250) and Coot (2,250). Fewer Pochard are now present than in the past, with 420 the usual peak, but 630 were present in September 2003. Over 100 Goldeneye are recorded in the coldest months, and up to 50 Goosanders spend the winter at Pitsford. Before the national cull of Ruddy Ducks began here in 2006, numbers regularly built up throughout the winter to over 200.

Of the scarcer species, Scaup, Common Scoter, Red-breasted Merganser and Smew are annual and Red-crested Pochard can turn up at any time of year. The much rarer American Wigeon and Ring-necked Duck have both occurred once, and Common Eider, Velvet Scoter and Long-tailed Duck visit every few years. Red-necked and Slavonian Grebe are just about annual, and at least one diver species is usually found each year, with Great Northern being the most likely. Small parties of Bewick's Swans usually pass through in November and large flocks of Canada Geese, which can be found grazing on the open fields adjacent to the south-east bank, often attract scarcer species such as Brent, White-fronted and Pink-footed Geese.

A large gull roost assembles near the dam between August and March. The total is regularly around 20,000 birds, with the majority being Black-headed and Common Gulls, along with smaller numbers of Herring, Lesser Black-backed and Great Black-backed Gulls. Inevitably, with a roost of this size, the scarcer species are picked out annually. Mediterranean and Yellow-legged Gulls may be found from early autumn onwards, with double-figure counts of the latter being fairly frequent during August, while Caspian Gulls

Eurasian Wigeon

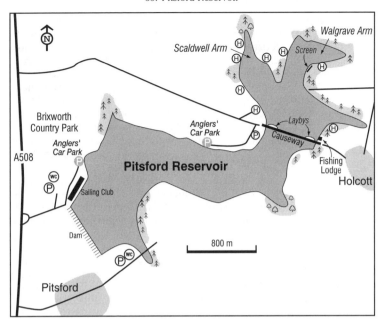

tend to occur later in the autumn and through the winter. Iceland and Glaucous are rarer and are usually found from Christmas onwards.

Yellowhammers can usually be located in the fields adjacent to the dam, and are often found by sheep-feeding troughs. Tree Sparrows are thinly distributed but regularly visit the winter feeding station in the Scaldwell arm, where they are joined by Reed Buntings, Yellowhammers, Greenfinches, occasionally Bramblings and rarely Corn Buntings. Small flocks of Linnets, Goldfinches and Meadow Pipits roam around the banks and attract the attention of the regular Peregrine Falcons, the occasional Merlin and the resident Sparrowhawks.

Spring brings Yellow and White Wagtails to the causeway and the short grass of the dam, along with a few Northern Wheatears. Singing warblers appear in the plantations and thickets, with eight species staying to breed, mostly on the reserve. On cool or overcast days in May, hundreds or even thousands of hirundines and Common Swifts may be hunting for insects low over the water, producing a spectacular sight. A few Common Terns are present throughout the summer, with several pairs breeding on the rafts provided in the Scaldwell arm, while the numbers of visiting Arctic and Black Terns vary enormously from year to year, with counts into three figures in some springs. Much scarcer are Sandwich and Little Terns, although one or two individuals of each are annual. Several species of waterbird breed, including Mute Swan, Tufted Duck and Little and Great Crested Grebes; in addition, a few Gadwall and Shovelers usually nest successfully. Cormorants and a few pairs of Grey Herons breed in the tall willows in the Walgrave arm of the reservoir.

During late summer and early autumn water levels can fall dramatically, exposing acres of mud on the shallower reserve side of the reservoir. However, Anglian Water now has a facility to pump in water from the nearby River Nene, meaning that the regular autumn draw-off of water may not occur with such regularity. At times of low water levels, the eight hides can afford close views of some of the 25 species of wader which are regular: Ringed and European Golden Plovers, Northern Lapwing, Dunlin, Ruff, Common Snipe, Redshank, Greenshank and Green and Common Sandpipers are the most numerous waders, with a scattering of Knot, Little Stint, Curlew Sandpiper, Jack Snipe, Black and Bar-tailed Godwits, Spotted Redshank, Wood Sandpiper and Turnstone. In all, 40 species of wader have been recorded, including such rarities as Black-winged Pratincole, American Golden Plover, Sociable Lapwing, Buff-breasted Sandpiper, Long-billed Dowitcher, Lesser Yellowlegs and Wilson's Phalarope.

Pintail are present throughout the autumn and Black-necked Grebes often arrive in August, a month which is good for seeing wandering Marsh Harriers or Ospreys. Hobbies regularly hunt dragonflies over the water, particularly in the evenings. A walk from the causeway into the Scaldwell Arm can produce migrant warblers, Whinchats or occasionally Common Redstarts on the hedges which are visible from the perimeter fences. Later in the autumn, October is the best time to find Rock Pipits, which particularly favour the stonework of the dam.

A search through autumn parties of Black Terns and Little Gulls, which usually arrive during periods of easterly winds, could be rewarded with a White-winged Black Tern, a south-eastern vagrant that has appeared on no fewer than eight occasions. By contrast, westerly gales in September and October have produced sightings of seabirds, with several records of Manx Shearwater, Leach's Storm-petrel, Shag and Arctic Skua and occasional Fulmar, European Storm-petrel, Gannet, Little Auk and Pomarine and Great Skuas. In addition, other rarities recorded at Pitsford over the years have included Ferruginous Duck, Night Heron, Great White Egret, Caspian Tern and Citrine Wagtail.

Timing

Something of interest can usually be found at any time of year, but the spring and autumn passage periods can be particularly rewarding. Winter sees the largest numbers of waterfowl and some areas of water remain free of ice even in the coldest conditions, when hundreds of birds can become concentrated on small ice-free patches, affording exceptional viewing. Gull watchers tend to assemble near the sailing club at the south-west corner of the reservoir an hour or more before dusk but have to wait until the windsurfers and yachtsmen have finished at weekends before the gulls will settle.

When sailing commences on a Sunday morning, the birds in the deeper water areas near the dam and the sailing club tend to move towards the causeway, which offers excellent views over a large part of the water area.

Access

Pitsford Reservoir is just north of Pitsford village, 6 miles (9.6 km) north of Northampton. Access to the dam end is off the A508; there are car parks and toilets at either end of the dam (SP761686 and SP753693), and also an information centre, café and cycle hire at the north end adjacent to Brixworth Country Park. To reach the causeway, leave the A43 Northampton to Kettering road 1.6 miles (2.5 km) north-east of Moulton on to the minor road signed to Holcot, pass through the village and continue for half a mile (0.8 km). The causeway gives access to the reserve side to the north and open access to the south side. A permit is required for the reserve (no dogs allowed), and is available daily or annually from the fishing lodge by the causeway or from the Northamptonshire Wildlife Trust. Eight hides are always open on the reserve.

Calendar

Resident: Mute Swan, Canada Goose, Gadwall, Tufted and Ruddy Ducks, Little and Great Crested Grebes, Cormorant, Grey Heron, Sparrowhawk, Common Buzzard, Tawny Owl, Green and Great Spotted Woodpeckers, Goldcrest, Marsh and Willow Tits, Tree Sparrow, Yellowhammer, Reed Bunting.

October–March: Bewick's Swan (scarce, mainly November), Brent Goose (scarce), Eurasian Wigeon, Common Teal, Pintail, Shoveler, Red-crested Pochard, Pochard, Scaup (scarce), Common Scoter (scarce, mainly November), Goldeneye, Smew, Goosander, Red-necked Grebe (scarce), Slavonian Grebe (scarce), Little Egret (scarce), Merlin (rare), Peregrine Falcon, European Golden Plover, Northern Lapwing, Jack and Common Snipe, Mediterranean and Yellow-legged Gulls, Caspian Gull (scarce), Iceland Gull (rare), Glaucous Gull (rare), Rock Pipit (scarce, mainly October and March), Grey Wagtail, European Stonechat, Fieldfare, Redwing, Brambling.

April–June: Common Scoter, Black-necked Grebe (scarce), Marsh Harrier, Osprey, Hobby, Ringed Plover, Dunlin, Redshank, Common Sandpiper, Little Gull, Sandwich Tern (scarce), Common and Arctic Terns, Little Tern (scarce), Black Tern, Cuckoo, Yellow Wagtail, White Wagtail (April), Whinchat, Northern Wheatear.

July–September: Garganey, Red-crested Pochard, Black-necked Grebe, Marsh Harrier, Osprey, Hobby, Ringed Plover, Little Stint (scarce), Curlew Sandpiper (scarce), Dunlin, Ruff, Common Snipe, Black-tailed Godwit, Redshank, Greenshank, Green and Common Sandpipers, Turnstone (scarce), Mediterranean Gull (scarce), Yellow-legged Gull, Sandwich Tern (scarce), Common and Black Terns, Yellow Wagtail, Whinchat, Northern Wheatear.

36. SALCEY FOREST

OS Landranger 152
OS Explorer 207

Habitat

Situated alongside the M1 motorway, Salcey is a rectangular-shaped ancient royal hunting forest of 1,250 acres (500 ha) owned and managed by the Forestry Commission. A private farmed area in the centre called Salcey Lawn once used to provide hay and pasture for deer, the quarry of the royal hunt. The forest is famous for its ancient oaks and although these remain in much reduced numbers, there are still some fine stands of these magnificent trees covering 250 acres (100 ha), some of which form part of a 34 acre (13.5 ha) reserve shared by the Northamptonshire Wildlife Trust and the neighbouring Berkshire, Buckinghamshire and Oxfordshire Wildlife Trust. The active forestry industry has felled a large amount of old trees and replanted mainly with the more economic fast-growing softwoods, although with an increasing awareness of the conservation importance of the woodland some oaks have again been planted in recent years. Other trees in the reserve are mainly native ash and field maple with introduced sycamores, sweet chestnut and turkey oaks, while willows and sallows grow mainly along the ride edges.

Once a mecca for entomologists, large areas of the forest were at one time sprayed with the chemical 2.4.5-T, which had a dramatic effect on insect populations; thankfully some rare species still exist today. There are several small ponds used by birds throughout the day for drinking and bathing.

Of the large network of rides some are wide and grassy and managed to provide a diverse ground flora, while others are narrow and overhung by shrubs and trees. Three well-marked trails of various lengths lead through the different areas of the forest and its habitats. A tree-top walkway was opened at the end of 2005 and allows gentle ascent with stairs to the highest platform which gives splendid views over the top of the woodland canopy. The forest stands on heavy boulder-clay soils, and the paths which have not been reinforced with stone chippings can become very muddy during wet weather and in the winter months.

Species

During the winter months, the common resident tits join together with Goldcrests, Treecreepers and the odd Nuthatch to form large foraging flocks moving through the woods searching for food. By spring, the flocks disperse but territorial males can be located by song and calls, with the Treecreepers and Nuthatches being very vocal from late March. Small flocks of Siskins and Lesser Redpolls may also be evidence during the winter months.

Up to 52 species breed in the forest, including all three species of woodpecker. The best times to see Great Spotted and Lesser Spotted Woodpeckers are when the broadleaf trees are bare during the winter and early spring, when the males of each species are drumming. Green Woodpeckers are more often heard than seen, giving away their presence with their loud, laughing calls; they do, however, spend long periods on the ground foraging for ants and other invertebrates. Tawny Owls are widespread and broadcast their presence at dusk, while Long-eared Owl, which has bred, is much rarer. The calls and song of the adult birds are quiet compared to those of Tawny Owls, but the squeaky notes of the fledged young are more obvious in the late spring. Other resident species include Sparrowhawk, Kestrel and Common Buzzard, the latter having recently spread into the area.

In spring and summer the site is well known for Nightingales, although this species has become scarce in recent summers; they prefer the coppiced areas and plantations with a shrub layer. Grasshopper Warblers are fairly common in the younger plantations, and their reeling song is at its strongest during the night. While listening to the calls of Tawny Owls and the reeling of Grasshopper Warblers, the grunts and squeaks of roding Woodcocks may be obvious as dusk approaches, although this is another species which has declined somewhat of late.

Common Redstarts and Wood Warblers are both unusual visitors to the older woodland areas, with the latter species usually announcing its arrival with its shivering song performed from the newly-opened leaf canopy. Spotted Flycatchers are the latest of the summer visitors to arrive, and in some years the occasional Pied Flycatcher is located. The dawn chorus includes the far-carrying song of the Mistle Thrush mixed in with the songs of all the usual summer migrants typical of broadleaved woodland such as Blackcap, Garden Warbler, Common Chiffchaff and Willow Warbler. Lesser and Common Whitethroats prefer the more scrubby areas around the clear-fells and the woodland rides where Cuckoos repeat their name in song. These woodland edges are good spots to see Bullfinches in the spring, when they often feed on the buds of blackthorn and sallows.

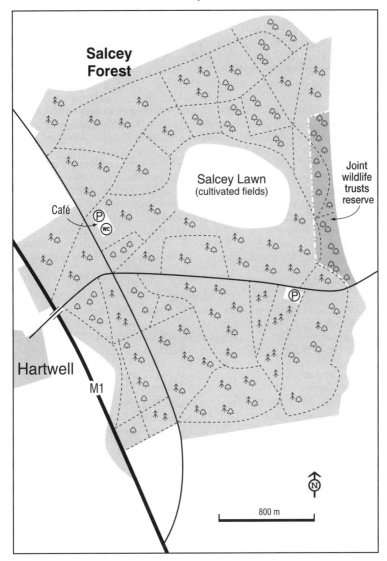

Timing

Spring is the best season to visit and the dawn chorus is particularly impressive, especially when Nightingales are in full song from late April to early June. Late evening is also a good time to listen for this species, when roding Woodcocks should also be evidence. Birdsong diminishes throughout the summer and the increasingly dense foliage makes it harder to actually see the birds, although early autumn can be the best period to see families of Spotted Flycatchers darting out from the bare branches catching insects.

The site is very popular with families and dog walkers, with Sunday afternoon being the peak period of human activity and hence the worst time to look for birds. However, there are plenty of footpaths off the marked trails which can still be of interest even at the busiest of times.

Access

Salcey Forest is 6.25 miles (10 km) south of Northampton on the county boundary with Buckinghamshire. Leave Northampton southwards on the A508 and cross the A45/A5076 roundabout; 0.6 miles (1 km) south of this roundabout turn left on to High Street towards Wootton and pass through the village to Quinton. Continue south through Quinton on the minor road towards Hanslope and after 2 miles (3.2 km) there is a large car park on the left just within the forest (SP795516) with information boards, toilets, a café (open daily), picnic tables and children's playground. Various colour-coded trails start from here and are well signposted, while Tree Top Way is accessed by following the Elephant Walk trail.

By turning left out of the main car park and then left again at the cross-roads on to the minor road towards Horton and Stoke Goldington, a further car park is found on the right after 1 mile (1.6 kilornetres) at SP811508. From here the Green Woodpecker trail starts; this walk takes approximately 2.5 hours and wellington boots are recommended. This car park also gives access to the reserve section of the forest on the northern side of the road. A main track passes down the western edge of the reserve but access is restricted to wildlife trust members to prevent trampling of rare plants growing here.

Calendar

Resident: Red-legged Partridge, Sparrowhawk, Common Buzzard, Kestrel, Woodcock, Stock Dove, Little, Tawny and Long-eared Owls, all three woodpeckers, Mistle Thrush, Goldcrest, Marsh and Willow Tits, Nuthatch, Treecreeper, Jay, Tree Sparrow, Bullfinch, Yellowhammer, Reed Bunting.

October–March: Fieldfare, Redwing, Siskin, Lesser Redpoll.

April–September: Turtle Dove (rare), Cuckoo, Nightingale, Common Redstart (scarce), Grasshopper Warbler, Blackcap, Garden Warbler, Lesser and Common Whitethroats, Wood Warbler (rare), Common Chiffchaff, Willow Warbler, Spotted Flycatcher, Pied Flycatcher (rare).

37. STANFORD RESERVOIR

OS Landranger 140
OS Explorer 223

Habitat

This picturesque reservoir, located in the valley of the River Avon and straddling the Leicestershire and Northamptonshire boundary, is owned by Severn Trent Water and covers 180 acres (72 ha). The majority of the water, including the large Blower's Lodge Bay in the south-east corner, is in Northamptonshire. This bay, and the surrounding bank extending to the disused railway line, has been a 13.6 acre (6 ha) reserve of the Northamptonshire Wildlife Trust since 1968. There are two hides overlooking the bay, which in dry summers provides large areas of exposed shoreline attractive to waders. In these periods, good wader habitat can also be found at the eastern end of the reservoir by the feeder stream.

The northern (Leicestershire) bank is flanked by a narrow belt of trees which grow close to the water's edge, and there are some substantial growths

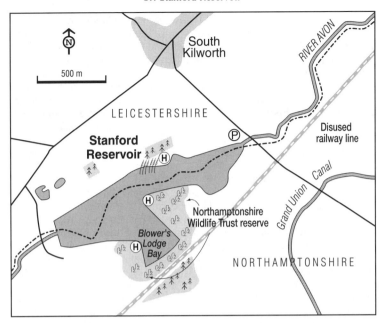

of reed along this shore. A new hide is being built by the Leicestershire and Rutland Ornithological Society in this area in early 2006. The southern bank is more open, with adjoining arable fields, but there is plenty of hawthorn scrub on the reserve.

The reservoir is relatively undisturbed; no water sports are permitted, and only a small amount of coarse fishing takes place between mid-June and mid-March.

Species

Due perhaps to its rather out of the way location, Stanford Reservoir is a very underwatched site and as such offers observers a good opportunity to find their own birds.

Winter birdwatching concentrates mainly on waterbirds, with the added attraction of a substantial gull roost. Numbers of the commoner wildfowl can be impressive, and peak counts within the last 15 years have included 2,000 Eurasian Wigeons, 267 Gadwall, 1,600 Common Teal, 548 Shovelers, 269 Pochards, 420 Tufted Ducks and 274 Ruddy Ducks. It is, however, the humble Coot for which Stanford Reservoir is most important, and exceptional counts have included 2,115 in October 1989 and 1,950 in October 2001. Goosanders are found in good numbers during the winter months, often in groups of over 40. Small flocks of Goldeneye are also regular and Red-crested Pochard is not infrequent. Scarcer species such as Long-tailed Duck, Red-throated and Great Northern Divers and Red-necked and Slavonian Grebes have all been recorded on more than one occasion, and these vagrants are usually found on the deep water near the dam. Flocks of Pink-footed and White-fronted Geese are occasionally seen, usually just passing overhead, and there have been several records of Brent Goose. Bewick's and Whooper Swans are scarce visitors.

The reservoir has a large and easily-observed gull roost, but it is not watched often. However, when coverage of the roost has been attempted, there have been regular records of Yellow-legged and Mediterranean Gulls and occasional Iceland and Glaucous Gulls. The roost's potential was further demonstrated in November 2002 with the finding of a Franklin's Gull, which became a first for both Northamptonshire and Leicestershire in a matter of minutes!

Long-eared Owls have occasionally been seen in the winter months roosting in the scrub on the reserve, but are difficult to locate in dense hawthorn bushes. In recent years Bitterns have become more frequent, usually being glimpsed in the reedbed on the Leicestershire bank. The beech trees on the minor road between Stanford on Avon and South Kilworth, close to the access track to the dam, regularly host a wintering flock of Bramblings, while there have been a few recent records of the elusive Hawfinch around the reservoir.

A ringing group has been active since 1974, and during the spring has trapped such unlikely species as Hoopoe, Marsh Warbler and Red-backed Shrike. Other spring rarities to have been found have included Alpine Swift, Great Reed Warbler, Golden Oriole and Lesser Grey Shrike, an impressive list for a reservoir which lies about as far from the coast as anywhere in Britain.

Spring and autumn tern passage is always notable, and Black Terns in particular often visit in good numbers. Little and Sandwich Terns are fairly regular, and the reservoir has attracted Caspian, Whiskered and two White-winged Black Terns. Small groups of Little Gulls and Kittiwakes are also occasionally noted. Black-necked Grebes often appear during the spring and Marsh Harriers are becoming more frequent, particularly in May and August.

The breeding season can be a little quiet, although a few declining species such as Turtle Dove and Grasshopper Warbler still retain small populations. Good numbers of Reed Warblers nest in the *Phragmites* patches, and Lesser Whitethroats are common during the summer months. A few pairs of Common Terns make use of the specially provided rafts. Hobbies regularly breed nearby and can sometimes be seen during the summer and on passage hunting over the water.

Autumn wader passage is very much dependent on the water levels. In most years very little exposed mud is present, and in these times waders are restricted to the odd Common Sandpiper or Little Ringed Plover on the dam. However, when the water level does drop, Stanford can be an excellent site: species such as Ringed Plover, Dunlin, Ruff, Greenshank and Green Sandpiper are the most frequent, with Little Stint, Curlew Sandpiper, Black-tailed and Bar-tailed Godwits, Spotted Redshank, Wood Sandpiper and Turnstone all likely to put in an appearance. A fine selection of rare waders recorded over the years includes Avocet, Temminck's Stint, Purple Sandpiper, Lesser Yellowlegs and Wilson's, Red-necked and Grey Phalaropes. Low water levels have also attracted Great White Egret and Spotted Crake in recent times. Strong winds and heavy showers in the autumn have produced a good number of storm-driven seabirds, with Leach's Storm-petrel, Gannet, Arctic Skua, Great Skua and Little Auk all being on the Stanford list. After periods of easterly winds in the late autumn, there is the likelihood of a Rock Pipit appearing on the dam.

Timing

This site is worth visiting at any time of year, although the winter and passage periods are perhaps the best. Viewing conditions are more favourable in the morning from the eastern end. To observe the gull roost, arrive at least an hour before dark and watch from a vantage point on the southern shore near the dam.

Access

The eastern end of the reservoir can be viewed from the small car park by the minor road 0.6 miles (1 km) south-east of South Kilworth at SP612812. To reach the western end, take the track south from the minor road between Stanford on Avon and South Kilworth at SP593807 and park in the small car park on the south side of the dam. Access to the reservoir grounds and hides is officially restricted to members of either the Northamptonshire Wildlife Trust or Leicestershire and Rutland Ornithological Society, but birdwatchers who ask at the house below the dam are usually granted permission to view from the dam at least.

Calendar

Resident: Mute Swan, Canada Goose, Little and Great Crested Grebes, Sparrowhawk, Common Buzzard, Kestrel, Kingfisher, Yellowhammer, Reed Bunting.

October–March: Greylag Goose, Eurasian Wigeon, Gadwall, Common Teal, Pintail, Shoveler, Red-crested Pochard (scarce), Pochard, Tufted Duck, Goldeneye, Goosander, Ruddy Duck, Cormorant, Bittern (scarce), Peregrine Falcon (scarce), gull roost including regular Mediterranean and Yellow-legged Gull, Long-eared Owl (rare), Rock Pipit (scarce), Grey Wagtail, Fieldfare, Redwing, Brambling, Siskin.

April–September: Black-necked Grebe, Marsh Harrier, Hobby, passage waders depending on water levels, Little Gull, Kittiwake, Common, Arctic and Black Terns, Turtle Dove, Cuckoo, Yellow Wagtail, Common Redstart (scarce), Northern Wheatear, Grasshopper, Sedge and Reed Warblers, Garden Warbler, Lesser and Common Whitethroats.

38. The Idle Valley
39. King's Mill Reservoir
40. Lound Gravel Pits
41. Sherwood Forest
42. Trent Valley Gravel Pits
42A. Girton, Besthorpe and Collingham Pits
42B. Hoveringham Gravel Pits
42C. Netherfield Lagoons
42D. Holme Pierrepont
42E. Colwick Country Park
42F. Attenborough Nature Reserve

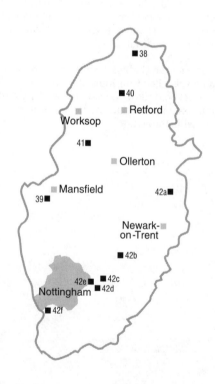

38. THE IDLE VALLEY

OS Landrangers 111 and 112
OS Explorers 279 and 280

Habitat

In the far north of Nottinghamshire the River Idle forms the county boundary with Lincolnshire in the Isle of Axholme. The area, which is less than 3 m above sea level, once regularly flooded and contained extensive marshes, but has long since been drained and brought under intensive arable cultivation. Nowadays the area very rarely floods, although most winters there are usually wet areas at Idle Stop and north of the river at Newington. There are also several small borrow pits which are particularly attractive to dragonflies. Drainage has left the area crossed with wide dykes which, in the case of the larger ones, contain growths of reeds. The main crops on this rich peaty soil are cereals, sugar beet and peas, while areas of set-aside provide winter feeding for flocks of finches and buntings.

Hedgerows and trees are in rather short supply in this area. A small conifer plantation near Carr Farm and the relatively new Nottinghamshire Wildlife Trust reserve of Misson Carr (formerly an old bombing range) stand as isolated pockets of woodland in the wide open landscape.

Species

A feature of winter birdwatching in this area is the flock of wild swans, which usually arrives in late October and often stays into early March. Traditionally the most numerous were Bewick's Swans, with a peak count of 174 in 1972 and up to 99 present as recently as 1998; however, subsequent counts have been much smaller. In contrast, Whooper Swans now visit in larger numbers than ever before, with 67 in January 2005 being the largest flock to date. The swans move about considerably during the course of the winter, and they may also visit Lound Gravel Pits to the south on occasions. Flooded fields along the river, particularly those at Idle Stop, attract good numbers of wintering Shelducks, Eurasian Wigeons, Gadwall, Common Teal, Pintails and Shovelers; if suitable floodwaters persist, many of these birds are likely to remain into the spring, and under these conditions Garganey is fairly regular.

Winter brings large flocks of passerines, especially finches and buntings, which feed in the set-aside areas. Three-figure flocks of Tree Sparrows, Linnets, Yellowhammers and Reed Buntings are not uncommon and a large wintering population of Corn Buntings still exists, with the highest recent

J.W.

Dotterels

count being 200 in March 2004. The wide open fields also hold large flocks of European Golden Plovers, Northern Lapwings and Skylarks. All this avian fodder attracts the attentions of up to three Hen Harriers and one or two Merlins and Peregrine Falcons, along with small numbers of Short-eared Owls to go with the resident Sparrowhawks, Common Buzzards, Kestrels and Barn Owls.

By early spring marshy areas attract good numbers of Common Snipe. Similarly, flooded fields may hold small flocks of Curlews and Redshanks, small numbers of both staying to breed. During April, groups of northern European Golden Plovers often pass through, but it is for another wader that the area is best known: Gringley Carr is a regular stop-off point for small groups of Dotterels, which arrive in late April or early May. In some years flocks may stay for extended periods, with numbers rising and falling as further birds arrive and depart; the largest number recorded is 38 in 1980. Dotterels tend to favour pea-fields, the locations of which change annually. Any areas of floodwater are worth checking during spring and autumn passage periods for other waders; species such as Ringed Plover, Dunlin, Ruff, Greenshank and Green Sandpiper are regular, and there have been recent records of Grey Plover, Little Stint, Black-tailed Godwit, Whimbrel and even Avocet and Temminck's Stint.

The dykes and drainage channels are important areas for dragonflies and damselflies during the summer and these, along with the large flocks of Common Swifts and hirundines which feed over the cereal fields, prove attractive to Hobbies, which are regular from May to early September. Other raptors may well be in evidence; Marsh Harriers are not infrequent, particularly in late summer and early autumn, while Montagu's Harriers have been seen in at least five years since 1994 and have often remained for several weeks.

The summer months are usually enlivened by the sound of a singing Quail or two, and the area is a traditional site for this elusive gamebird. Good numbers may be present in influx years; a remarkable 48 singing males were counted in July 1998! Areas of reeds adjacent to dykes and the borrow pits hold breeding Grasshopper, Sedge and Reed Warblers while Water Rails, which occur on passage, may also breed. The areas of scrub have nesting Lesser and Common Whitethroats and Turtle Dove, with the reserve at Misson Carr being a good site for the latter species. An intriguing record from this area in June 2004 was of a Cetti's Warbler carrying food.

The Idle Valley has produced several rarities over the years, the most notable being Britain's only ever inland Blyth's Pipit in December 2002 and January 2003. Three different American Golden Plovers have been found among the autumn European Golden Plover flocks, and a Red-footed Falcon graced the area in June 2002. Other scarcities have included American Wigeon, Common Crane, Kentish Plover, Grey Phalarope, Richard's Pipit, Golden Oriole and Lapland Bunting.

Timing

Winter is the best period to see large numbers of birds, with the added bonus of wild swans and raptors. Dotterel may arrive any time between mid-April and mid-May, but are most frequently seen in early May.

Access

The whole area between Misterton, Gringley on the Hill and Misson can only be watched from a series of minor unclassified roads and a public footpath which runs along part of the northern bank of the River Idle. Many of

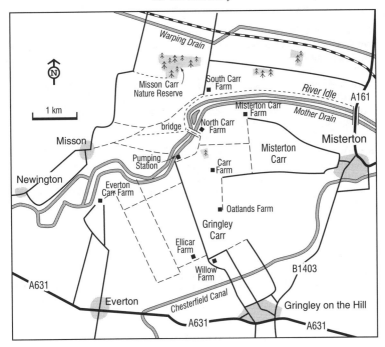

these unclassified roads are privately maintained and as such are only open to the public at the discretion of the local farmers; responsible birdwatchers should encounter no problems, as long as all local signs are obeyed and vehicles are parked sensibly.

Gringley Carr is reached by turning north-east off the A631 on the western edge of Gringley on the Hill on to West Wells Lane at SK731906. After 100 m turn left on to Wood Lane and follow the road for 2.8 miles (4.5 km) to the pumping station (SK713949). Vehicles should not be taken beyond this point and, in the last few years, access on foot along the track towards North Carr Farm, which leads to the bridge across the River Idle (SK717957), has also become more problematical. If in doubt, stay on the roads and only enter other areas if given express permission.

Misterton Carr is approached by turning west off the B1403 in Misterton village on to Carr Lane at SK762948 (signed to Cornley). After 100 m the road forks into two and either of these two roads give views over the area.

The northern side of the valley can be viewed from a minor road which runs west from the A161 1.6 miles (2.6 km) north of Misterton. At the T-junction 2.8 miles (4.5 km) along this minor road, turn left to the Idle bank (SK721967). From here, a public footpath heads off both east and west, with the westward route leading via Idle Stop to an area of scrub.

During times of flood, the fields south of Newington are often the most retentive of water. These can be viewed either from the A614 immediately north-east of Bawtry or from Slaynes Lane, which is the minor road that runs north-east from Newington to Misson.

The Nottinghamshire Wildlife Trust reserve of Misson Carr is 1.8 miles (3 km) north-east of Misson and is accessed via Station Road which leads north out of the village. The entrance to the reserve is at SK711971.

Calendar
Resident: Grey Partridge, Sparrowhawk, Common Buzzard, Kestrel, Water Rail, Northern Lapwing, Barn Owl, Tree Sparrow, Linnet, Yellowhammer, Reed and Corn Buntings.

October–March: Bewick's and Whooper Swans, Shelduck, Eurasian Wigeon, Gadwall, Common Teal, Pintail, Shoveler, Hen Harrier, Merlin, Peregrine Falcon, European Golden Plover, Common Snipe, Redshank, Long-eared Owl (scarce), Short-eared Owl, European Stonechat, Fieldfare, Redwing.

April–September: Garganey (scarce), Quail, Marsh Harrier, Montagu's Harrier (scarce), Osprey (scarce), Hobby, Dotterel (scarce, April and May), Ringed Plover, Dunlin, Ruff, Curlew, Redshank, Greenshank, Green Sandpiper, Turtle Dove, Cuckoo, Yellow Wagtail, Whinchat (passage), Northern Wheatear (passage), Grasshopper, Sedge and Reed Warblers, Lesser and Common Whitethroats.

39. KING'S MILL RESERVOIR

OS Landranger 120
OS Explorer 270

Habitat
King's Mill is a medium-sized reservoir covering approximately 70 acres (28 ha), maintained naturally by the River Maun. Most of the edge of the reservoir is vegetated with trees and scrub, predominantly willow but also ash, birch, poplar, oak and sycamore. Patches of *Phragmites* and reedmace can also be found in several areas. In close proximity to the reservoir are a number of paddocks and areas of arable land, although these have been significantly reduced recently with the construction of a bypass. A tern raft has been built and has proved to be successful.

Species
During the winter months, the main focus centres on wildfowl and gulls. The sailing club by the main car park is an ideal spot from which to scan the open water for wildfowl, which should include Eurasian Wigeon, Shoveler, Pochard and Goldeneye. Common Teal favour the shallow water in the south-west corner, an area which also attracts Water Rail and Common Snipe in the winter months. Species such as Pintail, Scaup and Goosander are scarce, but fairly regular, visitors, while vagrant waterbirds have included Brent Goose, Ferruginous Duck, Common Eider, Velvet Scoter, Great Northern Diver and Slavonian Grebe.

The King's Mill roost is the most reliable one in Nottinghamshire for Mediterranean Gull, and records are regular between November and March. Yellow-legged, Iceland and Glaucous Gulls are less frequent, but not unusual, and there have been an increasing number of sightings of Caspian Gull.

Winter can be the best time to see some of the more interesting resident species. Willow Tits favour the south-eastern car park and the scrub to the rear of the viewing platform, while the area around the viaduct on the east side of the reservoir is the best spot for Grey Heron, Kingfisher and Grey Wagtail. Of particular note was a Dipper that stayed in the latter area during December 2004.

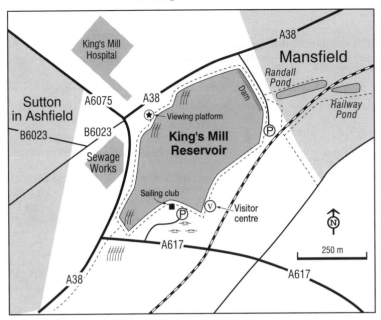

Spring sees the arrival of good numbers of warblers, with the reedbed in the south-western corner holding Sedge and Reed Warblers and the area around the south-eastern car park being good for Blackcap, Lesser and Common Whitethroats, Common Chiffchaff and Willow Warbler. Searching the hedgerows and paddocks during the spring and autumn may reveal Whinchat or Northern Wheatear, both of which are regular, or perhaps a Common Redstart or Pied Flycatcher, of which there have been several records of each. A Nightingale which took up temporary residence near the viewing platform in 2004 was noteworthy, as was a Wood Warbler in the paddocks in 2001. Arctic and Black Terns move through in the spring in suitable weather conditions, and a single pair of Common Terns nests on the raft on the reservoir. Spring and summer have also produced several records of Common Scoter, Black-necked Grebe and Osprey in recent years, while Rock Pipits have occasionally been found on the dam wall in early spring or late autumn.

Common Sandpipers are regular on migration, but the appearance of most other waders is dictated by water levels; if suitable conditions exist, the south-western corner is usually the best spot. As well as the more regular species, there have been records of Temminck's Stint, Pectoral Sandpiper and Grey Phalarope.

King's Mill Reservoir is well-known locally for its significant visible migration, particularly between September and November. Large numbers of hirundines, Meadow Pipits, thrushes, finches and other migrants are regularly recorded; in total, over 200,000 birds have been logged during these watches since 1990.

For such a small area, the total site list of 216 is particularly impressive. Highlights among the rarities have included Lesser Scaup, Shag, Rough-legged Buzzard, Corncrake, Arctic and Great Skuas, Sabine's Gull, Whiskered Tern, Wryneck and Lapland Bunting.

Timing
The reservoir is probably of most interest in the winter months, when wild-fowl numbers at their greatest and there is the chance of a scarcity in the gull roost. There are several good areas to view from, meaning that bright sunlight can easily be compensated for. The gull roost is best watched from the viewing platform on the north shore. Visible migration is greatest on clear days with a light south-westerly breeze.

Access
King's Mill Reservoir is on the south-western outskirts of Mansfield. From junction 28 of the M1 take the A38 eastwards towards Mansfield and after 4.5 miles (7.2 km) turn right onto the A617 towards Newark on Trent. A newly-constructed car park is signed on the left after 200 m (SK515593). An additional car park is accessed off the A38 at the north-eastern corner of the reservoir (SK509596). A footpath runs round the whole reservoir, giving ample viewing opportunities; in addition, a viewing platform is located on the north shore (SK514597).

Calendar
Resident: Grey Partridge, Sparrowhawk, Kestrel, Northern Lapwing, Kingfisher, Grey Wagtail, Willow Tit, Reed Bunting.

October–March: Eurasian Wigeon, Common Teal, Pintail, Shoveler, Pochard, Scaup (scarce), Goldeneye, Goosander, Water Rail, Common Snipe, Mediterranean Gull, Yellow-legged Gull (scarce), Caspian Gull (rare), Iceland Gull (rare), Glaucous Gull (rare), Rock Pipit (scarce, mainly October and November), Fieldfare, Redwing.

April–September: Common Scoter (scarce), Black-necked Grebe (scarce), Osprey (scarce), Common Sandpiper, Common Tern, Arctic Tern (scarce, passage), Black Tern (scarce, passage), Common Redstart (scarce), Whinchat, Northern Wheatear, Grasshopper, Sedge and Reed Warblers, Blackcap, Lesser and Common Whitethroats, Common Chiffchaff, Willow Warbler, Pied Flycatcher (scarce).

40. LOUND GRAVEL PITS

OS Landrangers 111, 112 and 120
OS Explorers 271 and 279

Habitat
Lound Gravel Pits is the overall term for a huge site in north-east Nottinghamshire which stretches from the outskirts of Retford in the south to near Mattersey in the north and is centred on the village of Lound. It is essentially a gravel and aggregate extraction complex, but the site has a much greater variety of habitats than most such areas and its extensive size means that it has developed into one of the foremost birdwatching locali-ties in Nottinghamshire.

All of the pits at present lie on the western side of the River Idle, but as the site is a working area the local geography is constantly changing, and good spots for birding one year may become featureless reclaimed land the

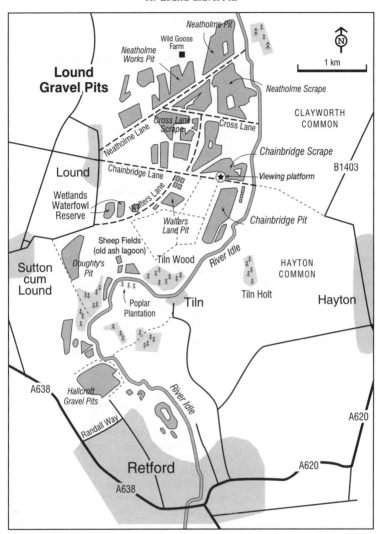

next. The pits offer a variety of shallow and deeper water areas, with muddy margins and grass of varying heights growing around the edges and on any islands. The variable water levels and the extent of recent excavations have rapid effects on the numbers of wildfowl and breeding gulls and terns which use the site. Apart from the older pits, which have been filled and returned to agricultural usage, others have been left for fishing, water-skiing and windsurfing, while in the centre of the complex is a captive wildfowl reserve. One of the best pits, known as Chainbridge Scrape, along with a small area of willow carr by the side of the River Idle, has been purchased by the Nottinghamshire Wildlife Trust as a nature reserve.

The wide access tracks which run through the complex are bordered with large old hedgerows left over from times prior to the excavations. These hedgerows consist mainly of hawthorn but there are also a number of old oaks and a wide variety of other tree species including ash, elm, willow,

273

alder and elder. There is a healthy understorey of bramble and in more open areas willow herb, gorse and broom dominate, with areas of long rough grassland, thistles and docks being found on colonised spoil heaps.

By the side of Chainbridge Lane, where it leaves Lound village, are grazed horse paddocks which offer a further area of interest. Additional habitats include a riverside poplar plantation near Tiln, a number of willow plantations and extensive areas of grazing fields around Sutton cum Lound village. The River Idle itself winds around the eastern edge of the complex and although fairly narrow, it offers running fresh water and is an important dragonfly habitat. To the east are Clayworth Common and Hayton Common, which are essentially areas of arable fields attractive to wintering swans and raptors.

To the south of the main complex is the relatively new site of Hallcroft Gravel Pits, which has produced several interesting birds in recent years. The main pit here is relatively steep-sided, with several large vegetated islands.

Species

Wildfowl are the principal winter attraction, with the dominant species being Eurasian Wigeon, Common Teal, Pochard and Tufted Duck. Gadwall have increased substantially in recent years and their numbers have peaked at over 200 on occasions. Goosander and Goldeneye are regular during the winter, as are Shoveler and Pintail, although numbers of the latter two are usually at their highest in the autumn. One or two Smew are seen most winters. Shelducks and Red-crested Pochards are now more or less resident and both have bred in the past. Of the scarcer species, Scaup are not infrequent, and there have been records of American Wigeon, Green-winged Teal and Ring-necked and Ferruginous Ducks, as well as Red-necked and Slavonian Grebes.

Clayworth Common is a fairly regular site for small numbers of wintering Bewick's and Whooper Swans, which join up with larger herds of Mute Swans; these birds often move between here and Gingley Carr further north in the Idle valley. Groups of White-fronted or Pink-footed Geese may occasionally associate with the swans, although skeins of the latter species are more often seen overflying the area in October and January. The arable land to the east of the Idle also attracts raptors, with one or two Hen Harriers and Merlins being seen most winters and occasional Peregrine Falcons being noted. Short-eared Owls are usually present between November and March in small numbers, although their appearances can be erratic and their numbers variable. Water Rails are evident during the winter and possibly remain to breed in some years.

The winter gull roost varies with the state of filling of some of the larger pits, but is still a sizeable roost nonetheless; for instance, peak counts in January 2004 were 6,300 Black-headed, 1,176 Great Black-backed, 925 Common and 855 Herring. Inevitably, there have been regular records of Mediterranean and Yellow-legged Gull and occasional Glaucous and Iceland Gulls.

Waders are a special feature of this locality and it attracts significant totals of some normally coastal species, although it must be stressed that numbers are greatly affected by water levels and the state of development of various pits throughout the year. Most species occur during the migration periods of April to June and late July to October, but there are regular winter records of Jack and Common Snipe and Green Sandpiper, along with the occasional Dunlin and Ruff. Oystercatchers, Little Ringed and Ringed Plovers, Northern Lapwings and Redshanks all breed in small numbers, with the latter reaching peak totals in March and April of maybe up to 30 birds.

Long-eared Owl

Northern populations of Ringed Plovers pass through in late April and May, and this is the best period for spring records of Grey Plover, Sanderling, Dunlin, Ruff, both godwits, Whimbrel, Spotted Redshank, Greenshank, Wood Sandpiper and Turnstone. Autumn numbers are larger and birds often stay for longer periods of time so the chances of seeing them are greater. Dunlin may peak at over 100 birds, and more regular species at this season include Little Stint, Curlew Sandpiper and Black-tailed Godwit. Curlew may occur at any time and have been known to breed, but usually peak in autumn. A good selection of scarcer species has been recorded, including Avocet, Temminck's Stint, Pectoral, Purple and Buff-breasted Sandpipers and Red-necked and Grey Phalaropes.

Spring is a good period to find transient flocks of Common Scoters, although this species may occur at virtually any time of year; an exceptional party of 115 was noted in October 1990. Garganey is also regular in spring and has on occasion bred. Marsh Harriers have become frequent passage migrants in spring and especially autumn, with the favoured month being August; these birds are often juveniles which are presumably dispersing from breeding sites not too far away in Lincolnshire. Ospreys are more or less annual and Hobbies have also increased, with the large numbers of dragonflies around the pits during the summer and autumn providing ideal hunting for this dashing falcon.

Given suitable weather conditions, the spring migration period brings arrivals of parties of terns. Both Arctic and Black Terns are regular, sometimes in large numbers, while Sandwich and Little Terns have both been recorded. Often accompanying passage terns are groups of Little Gulls, and small flocks of Kittiwakes may appear between March and June. The migration periods usually produce a few records of species such as Common Redstart, Whinchat and Northern Wheatear, with less frequent Black Redstart and Ring Ouzel. Westward-moving flocks of Skylarks and Meadow Pipits may be in evidence during the late autumn, and Rock Pipits are occasional in March and October.

All three woodpeckers occur, with Green being the commonest, and many other species breed in the area. Breeding waterbirds include Mute Swan, Greylag Goose, Gadwall, Tufted Duck and Little and Great Crested Grebes, along with irregular nesting by Pochards. Up to 15 pairs of Common Terns breed, as do large numbers of Black-headed Gulls; this colony has attracted a few pairs of Lesser Black-backed Gulls in the past, and even a pair of Little Gulls attempted to breed one year. A wide variety of passerines include Grasshopper, Sedge, Reed and Garden Warblers, Lesser and Common Whitethroats and Willow Tit, while Nightingale has bred in the past in plantations near Tiln. Turtle Doves nest and there are large numbers of Skylarks and Meadow Pipits with attendant Cuckoos during the spring.

Lound lies on a known migration route, and with such a wide variety of habitats it is no surprise that it has a long list of bird species. Since 1979, the site has produced no fewer than seven firsts for Nottinghamshire; in chronological order, these were Bluethroat (1979), Killdeer (1981), Ring-billed Gull (1990), Lesser Scaup (1990), Long-billed Dowitcher (1996), Baird's Sandpiper (1998) and Blue-winged Teal (2000). Other rarities have included Spoonbill, Rough-legged Buzzard, Red-footed Falcon, Common Crane, American Golden Plover, Great Skua, Caspian, Whiskered and White-winged Black Terns, Razorbill, Shore Lark, Richard's Pipit, Golden Oriole, Red-backed Shrike, Arctic Redpoll and Lapland and Snow Buntings.

Timing

With its wide variety of habitats, this locality will repay a visit at any time of year. Spring and autumn are favoured for the variety of passage waders recorded, but the winter is productive for wildfowl and a good range of breeding birds are present in summer.

Access

The main area of the Lound complex is approximately 2 miles (3.2 km) north of Retford. Leave Retford north-west on the A638 towards Blyth and after 1 mile (1.6 km) turn right on to a minor road to Sutton cum Lound. In Sutton cum Lound turn right onto another minor road signed to Lound. Once in Lound village, access to much of the complex is reached by turning right on to Chainbridge Lane at SK692850. This gravel track, which is very bumpy, continues for 1.2 miles (2 km) to the River Idle and passes a variety of habitats. Care should be taken on this track as it is used by large lorries, and if parking make sure that no access routes are blocked. The Nottinghamshire Wildlife Trust reserve, which is open at all times, is on the left and has a raised viewing platform which is an excellent vantage point for scanning the area. The pits nearest to the Idle to the south of Chainbridge Lane are worthy of a look, and should only be viewed from a footpath which runs along the western bank of the river. North of Chainbridge Lane and to the east of the river is Clayworth Common, which can be viewed from the raised bank on the east side of the Idle. By following the raised bank northwards it is possible to reach the Neatholme Lane area of pits. Neatholme Lane can also be accessed from Lound village 100 m north of Chainbridge Lane (SK692862), although it is not possible to drive along this track from the village as it is blocked by a gate after 200 m. Approximately halfway along Chainbridge Lane at SK702858 a track leads off south (Walters Lane), which gives views over several more pits and eventually rejoins the minor road between Lound and Sutton cum Lound at the Wetlands Waterfowl Reserve.

Hallcroft Gravel Pits are reached by turning east off the A638 on the northern outskirts of Retford on to Randall Way (signed to Household Waste and Recycling Centre) and then turning left at the end of the road. Park at the dead end (SK693829) and the largest pit is viewable from here. A footpath runs along the southern and eastern banks of this pit.

Calendar

Resident: Mute Swan, Greylag and Canada Geese, Shelduck, Gadwall, Shoveler, Red-crested Pochard, Pochard, Tufted Duck, Little and Great Crested Grebes, Cormorant, Sparrowhawk, Kestrel, Northern Lapwing, Redshank, Black-headed Gull, Barn and Long-eared Owls, Kingfisher, all three woodpeckers, Skylark, Meadow Pipit, Willow Tit, Tree Sparrow.

October–March: Bewick's Swan, Whooper Swan, Pink-footed Goose, White-fronted Goose (scarce), Eurasian Wigeon, Common Teal, Pintail, Scaup (scarce), Goldeneye, Smew (scarce), Goosander, Hen Harrier, Merlin, Peregrine Falcon, Water Rail, European Golden Plover, Jack and Common Snipe, Green Sandpiper, Short-eared Owl, Rock Pipit (scarce, October and March), Grey Wagtail, European Stonechat, Fieldfare, Redwing, Brambling, Siskin, Lesser Redpoll.

April–September: Pintail (August onwards), Garganey, Common Scoter (scarce), Marsh Harrier, Osprey (scarce), Hobby, Oystercatcher, Little Ringed, Ringed and Grey Plovers, Sanderling, Little Stint (scarce, August onwards), Curlew Sandpiper (scarce, August onwards), Dunlin, Ruff, both godwits, Whimbrel, Curlew, Spotted Redshank, Greenshank, Green, Wood and Common Sandpipers, Turnstone, Little Gull, Common, Arctic and Black Terns, Cuckoo, Yellow Wagtail, Common Restart (scarce), Whinchat, Northern Wheatear, Grasshopper, Sedge and Reed Warblers, Blackcap, Garden Warbler, Lesser and Common Whitethroats.

41. SHERWOOD FOREST

OS Landranger 120
OS Explorer 270

Habitat

The area of central Nottinghamshire between Worksop and Nottingham, which has long been associated with the myths and legends of Robin Hood and the Sheriff of Nottingham, has changed a great deal since the time when the Royal Forest of Sherwood stretched in an unbroken belt of ancient woodland for 20 miles (32 km) north to south and 8 miles (12.8 km) east to west. The area of ancient forest has been reduced to small fragments, but successive generations of landed gentry have created estates with areas of parkland, ornamental lakes and younger woodlands, which have all added to the diversity of the landscape and make this an exceptional area for birdwatching. The present landscape is a wonderfully varied mix of old deciduous woodland, parkland, lakes, heathland, shelter-belts and younger coniferous plantations, interspersed with arable farmland.

This section deals with a number of different birdwatching sites within Sherwood Forest, including the following three major areas: Clipstone Forest (Sherwood Pines Forest Park), the Birklands (Sherwood Country Park and Budby South Forest) and the Dukeries (Clumber Park and the estates of Thoresby and Welbeck). Some of the estates and woodlands are well known

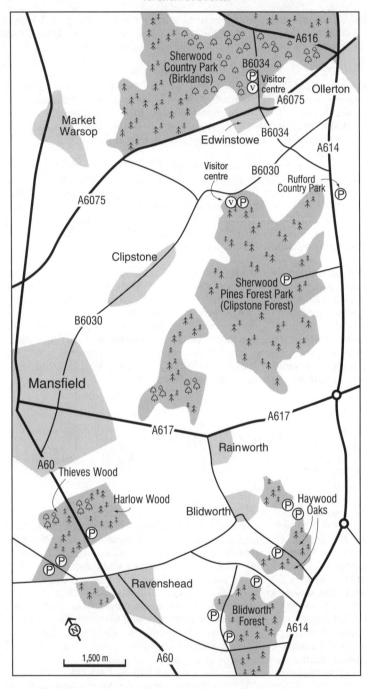

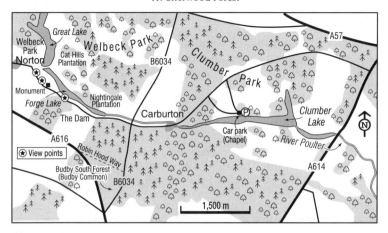

for their scarce breeding and wintering birds and the area as a whole is a very popular tourist attraction.

Sherwood Pines Forest Park (Clipstone Forest) is the largest area of woodland open to the public in the East Midlands, covering some 2,965 acres (1,200 ha), and is managed by the Forestry Commission. The main habitats are areas of coniferous woodland, which are at varying ages and states of felling and replanting, and open sandy heathland. Wide open rides and tracks dissect the woodland blocks, including colour-signed trails of 1 mile (1.6 km) and 2.5 miles (4 km). A forest conservation plan has been designed to benefit the wildlife of the site; sandy heathland is being maintained for European Nightjars, Woodlarks and Tree Pipits among other species, and the coniferous woodland is being managed in an attempt to increase its potential value to wildlife. Nearby, there are other Forestry Commission woodlands open to the public, including Thieves Wood, Harlow Wood, Blidworth Wood and Haywoods Oaks, the latter named after the collection of ancient oaks which have now been made more visible by conifer harvesting.

Of the remnants of the ancient forest, characterised by its stunted gnarled old oaks, one of the best known is Sherwood Country Park, which is often referred to as the Birklands. This 450 acre (182 ha) tract of woodland, which contains the famous Major Oak, is managed by Nottinghamshire County Council with advice from English Nature. It has been designated as an SSSI and, in 2002, was granted National Nature Reserve status. Many of the other woodlands in the region are managed by the Forestry Commission, and recent developments within these areas has seen a marked shift to more wildlife-orientated schemes, increasing their value to birds and birdwatchers alike.

The area known as the Dukeries contains the three well-known estates of Clumber Park, Thoresby Park and Welbeck. The 3,800 acres (1,538 ha) of Clumber Park are owned and managed by the National Trust, and the park boasts the longest continuous avenue of lime trees anywhere in Europe. Among its wealth of other woodlands are large blocks of old oak, sweet chestnut, horse chestnut and beech, interspersed mainly along the park boundaries with younger plantations of conifers. There are also ornamental trees and an understorey of rhododendron around the chapel area, where a block of yews is of importance to the Hawfinch population. Farmland and some open heathland make up most of the rest of the area, along with a large man-made lake set in the valley of the River Poulter, which runs through the centre of the park. The wide roadside verges are mainly short grass which spread into a mixed cover of longer rough grasses, bracken and birch scrub around the heathland clearings. Thoresby Park is mainly private with restricted access, and viewing is from a minor road which crosses the northern side of the park. The Welbeck estate is also private and contains much the same mix of woodland and farmland; it has an impressive series of ornamental lakes, some of which can be overlooked from the minor road which runs from Carburton to Cuckney. Nearby, Cuckney Flash provides a habitat for passage waders.

Species

The coniferous woodlands, especially Sherwood Pines Forest Park (Clipstone Forest), hold a typical cross-section of associated species, with good numbers of Goldcrests, Coal Tits, Treecreepers and Great Spotted and Green Woodpeckers. As with all coniferous woodlands, winter sees feeding flocks of small passerines rove over large areas of woodland, being absent from extensive blocks for long periods when such spots can seem totally birdless. Depending on the fruiting of the birch trees and the pines there will be variable sized flocks of Lesser Redpolls and Siskins, with a few of both species staying into late spring and breeding occasionally. Common Crossbills occur annually but their numbers vary from year to year. Irruptions very often occur in June, and the number of birds staying to winter will then depend upon the local pine and larch cone crops. The heathland to the north at Budby (known locally as Budby Common) is also a good area for Lesser Redpolls, Siskins and Common Crossbills. The common was formerly a traditional wintering site for Great Grey Shrike; although they are now infrequent, one arrived nearby in Clumber Park in January 2004 and it is to be hoped the species will again become regular. Hen Harriers are seen occasionally over the heathland areas in winter, and Merlin and Peregrine Falcon are annual.

The areas of old deciduous forest found in the Dukeries and Sherwood Country Park (the Birklands) support a rich variety of woodland birds. During the winter months Clumber Park is a particularly good locality, with feeding flocks usually apparent in the woodland blocks around the main car park area, the chapel and the oak woodland near the main road. As the birds are regularly fed by visitors, they can become very tame and give superb views at very close quarters. Species such as Nuthatch, Great Spotted Woodpecker, Marsh Tit and even the normally timid Jay will take food very close to people and make the use of binoculars almost redundant. Large flocks of up to 400 Chaffinches occur and there may be variable numbers of Bramblings associating with them. One of the major attractions at Clumber Park in winter, however, is the gathering of Hawfinches in the trees behind the chapel, where yews and two hornbeams provide food for these heavy-billed finches. Up to ten birds were present in 2005, although they are best seen in the early mornings before disturbance from large numbers of tourists forces the birds to quieter areas. Nearby, the car park at Rufford Country Park is another good spot to look for Hawfinches; at least ten were here in early 2006. The area near the chapel in Clumber Park is one of the better places to see the elusive Lesser Spotted Woodpecker, especially in the late winter and early spring when they indulge in drumming and territorial displays. Firecrest, another scarce wintering species, has occurred in the rhododendron scrub around this particular spot, as well as in other areas of Sherwood Forest, and is worth looking and listening for.

A wide variety of wildfowl occurs on the lake in Clumber Park, ranging from the ubiquitous Mallard to flocks of Gadwall, Common Teal, Tufted

Honey Buzzard

Ducks, Pochards and Ruddy Ducks. A small resident population of Egyptian Geese has recently become established, and the area is now the county stronghold for Mandarin Ducks, with a peak of 23 in November 2004. Eurasian Wigeon and Goosander are regular, the latter often in reasonable sized flocks, while Goldeneye appear irregularly. There are occasional records of scarcer species, which since 2001 have included Scaup, Common Scoter, Smew, Red-breasted Merganser, Great Northern Diver and Black-necked Grebe. In addition, the lake at nearby Welbeck has seen recent records of Whooper Swan and Brent Goose. Skeins of Pink-footed Geese pass over between October and January; those in the autumn are usually travelling south-east, while flocks in December and January head north-west. A Caspian Gull regularly winters in the area, usually dividing its time between the lakes at Clumber Park and Welbeck.

Early February sees the arrival of the first returning Woodlarks to the heathland areas, and by the end of the month most birds are back on territory. This is a species which has shown a tremendous increase over the last 15 years, and by 2005 there were perhaps as many as 70 pairs in Sherwood Forest. By mid-April, Tree Pipits will be parachuting over the clearings and heaths, with Budby Common being one of the most favoured spots. European Nightjars return in mid-May and breed in good numbers in the forest and on the heaths. Appropriate habitat management should ensure the continued presence of this special bird within Clipstone Forest, where they inhabit the clear-fells as well as the natural heathland sites. Full census work in the whole Sherwood district in recent years has shown a peak population of 70 churring males, although the total in 2005 was nearer 40 pairs. During the evenings from June to August, young owls may be heard calling from the edges of the conifer plantations. Tawny Owls are the most common, but a few pairs of Long-eared Owls are present and the squeaky-gate call of the young is a characteristic heathland sound on warm evenings. Roding Woodcocks traverse the skyline giving their distinctive grunts and squeaks.

The woodland bird population is swelled in the spring by Blackcaps, Garden Warblers, Common Chiffchaffs, Willow Warblers and Spotted Flycatchers, and on the heaths Common Whitethroats and Yellowhammers are numerous. Wood Warblers may occasionally take up a territory in suitable habitat, but this is a species which has shown a marked decline in recent years. Common Redstarts breed in some areas, and although there are still reasonable numbers in the Birklands, they too have shown a recent decrease. The former population of Whinchats has now unfortunately disappeared altogether, although by way of compensation a pair of European Stonechats bred in a restocked conifer plantation in Clumber Park in 2003 and 2004. Hawfinches breed in the vicinity but are very elusive; the best way of locating them is to listen for their distinctive 'tic' calls as they fly over the tree-tops. Nuthatch and Marsh Tit also breed locally.

The Welbeck area is best known in the summer for Honey Buzzards. This was one of the first publicised breeding sites of this species in Britain, as the birds could be watched from a public road without disturbance. Honey Buzzards have been present in summer here for over 40 years, although of late they have proved to be rather unpredictable in their appearances. In better years they generally arrive in late May and are present through to late August, but often become more difficult to see towards the end of their stay. They are best looked for from the minor road which runs along the southern edge of the estate (see Access), as they soar and display over the woodlands to the north. It should be noted that the birds can often be very difficult to see as they spend a great deal of time just sitting around in trees; on some days they are not seen at all or just for a few minutes. Warm sunny days with broken cloud and light to moderate winds during the early part of their stay are usually the best; this is when the birds will be most active and can sometimes be seen in their wing-clapping display flight. Honey Buzzards are not the only large raptors in the area, however, as many pairs of Common Buzzards nest in the same locality and, as they spend much more time on the wing, they are more likely to be seen than the Honey Buzzards, so caution is needed with identification. Goshawk is another species which has increased here, although they are at their most visible earlier in the year: they can be seen on most days in February and early March if weather conditions are suitable. Ospreys are frequent visitors in spring and autumn and have summered on occasions, while Marsh Harriers occur some years on passage. Midsummer watches will often produce sightings of Hobby, while Red Kite records are increasing and Sparrowhawks and Kestrels are abundant, giving a possible day list of nine species of raptor. Raven has also become more regular in the last five years and pairs are often seen flying across the area. Conversely, the large heronry, which contained 54 nests as recently as 1993, has for some reason been abandoned since the late 1990s. Inevitably, with so many observers regularly overlooking the Welbeck estate, a few scarce passage migrants have been seen; Little Gull, Kittiwake and Sandwich Tern have all been noted in recent years over the lake, and a White Stork passed over in May 2002. The small flash on the edge of the nearby village of Cuckney is worth a look, particularly in the autumn, as it sometimes attracts small numbers of waders, including a Pectoral Sandpiper in September 2003.

Rarities in the region over the years have included, at Clumber Park, a Ring-necked Duck on the lake in 1990, three Red-rumped Swallows in the autumn of 1994 and another in May 1996, and an obliging male Golden Oriole in May 2005. In addition, a Red-backed Shrike was at Blidworth in 1987, an Arctic Redpoll frequented Budby Common in 1995 and seven Parrot Crossbills were in the Dukeries in 1990.

Timing

This area is worth visiting at any time of year due to the varied selection of species present. Winter is perhaps best for woodland birds, which can become very tame at certain sites; this is the period when Hawfinches are at their easiest to see, particularly early in the morning before too much disturbance occurs. Woodlarks are normally back on territories by mid-February, while Lesser Spotted Woodpeckers are best looked for when they are at their most vocal in March and April. European Nightjars return in mid-May and warm still evenings are the ideal conditions for this species.

Raptor-watching may involve a long vigil so an early start is recommended on a day with broken cumulus cloud, sunshine and moderate winds. Early spring is the peak time for watching displaying Goshawks, while Honey Buzzards arrive in late May and are best seen in June and early July; they may, however, show through to late August. Ospreys and Hobbies are most likely from May to August.

Access

Clumber Park, which is open all year, is 4.5 miles (7.2 km) south-east of Worksop and 6.5 miles (10.4 km) south-west of Retford. From the A1/A57/A614 roundabout 3.1 miles (5 km) east of Worksop, take the A614 south for half a mile (0.8 km) and turn west into the park through a stone archway (SK645772). The road runs through the avenue of limes for 4 miles (6.4 km) to two ornamental gatehouses at Carburton (SK608726). There are numerous parking places off the side of this road. To reach the chapel and lake, turn south off the road after 2 miles (3.2 km) to the car park (SK622742), where there are toilets, a café and bicycle hire facilities. An access fee of £4.30 is charged for cars and motorcycles.

To reach Welbeck from Clumber Park, continue on the road which runs through the park and go straight over the crossroads at Carburton by the Old School Tea Rooms. Alternatively, if approaching from Worksop turn west off the B6034 at the crossroads 3 miles (4.8 km) south-east of the town. There are two suitable spots for parking along this road: (1) after 1.2 miles (2 km) there is an obvious parking area on the north side of the road at SK590721, and (2) a little further west there is limited parking by the Bentinck monument at SK583720. From either of these two points, look north across the lake and over the woods for raptors. Viewing is slightly restricted by the monument, so alternatively walk 200 m west along the road and view from the wide verge. Do not enter the fields or private woodlands here. Cuckney Flash is 2 miles (3.2 km) to the west and can be watched from the road next to the church at SK566714.

Sherwood Pines Forest Park (Clipstone Forest) lies 13 miles (20.8 km) north of Nottingham and 3 miles (4.8 km) north-east of Mansfield. The main car park, which has a visitor centre, toilets and catering facilities, is reached by turning west off the A614 on to the B6030 1 mile (1.6 km) south of Ollerton; the car park is well signed on the left after 2 miles (3.2 km) at SK612646. There is an entry charge of £2 per vehicle and colour-signed trails lead from this car park. Another car park can be found by turning west off the A614 3.5 miles (5.6 km) south of Ollerton (SK620616). Rufford Country Park is nearby, and the well-signed car park is on the east side of the A614 2.5 miles (4 km) south of Ollerton.

For Sherwood Country Park (Birklands), take the A6075 west out of Ollerton and turn north on to the B6034 at Edwinstowe. The visitor centre (with toilet facilities) is on the left after half a mile (0.8 km) at SK626677. The car park is open from 8 am to 5 pm and a fee of £2.50 is charged.

Budby South Forest (Budby Common) is reached by leaving Budby north-west on the A616 and joining the B6034 at the two small roundabouts just outside the village. The main area of heath is on the left after half a mile (0.8 km) at SK612714. This is a military training area and visitors must keep to designated footpaths.

Haywoods Oaks and Blidworth Wood are 6.25 miles (10 km) south-east of Mansfield and are accessed from minor roads off the A614 south-east of Blidworth village. From the A614/A617 roundabout 6 miles (9.6 km) east of Mansfield, head south on the A614 and cross another roundabout. Take the first minor road on the right after 1 mile (1.6 km) to reach the Baulker Lane car park for Haywoods Oaks, which is situated on the left after 0.8 miles (1.2 km) at SK611558. A second car park for Haywood Oaks is found by returning to the A614, heading south and taking the next minor road on the right for 0.6 miles (1 km) to the Oaks Lane car park on the right at SK605549. Blidworth Wood has three car parks: (1) the Blidworth Bottoms car park is reached by turning west off the A614 on the next minor road south of Oaks Lane and the car park is on the left at SK595543; (2) return to the A614, head south and take the next minor road west to access the Longdale Lane car park, which is on the right after half a mile (0.8 km) at SK591524; (3) turn right out of the Longdale Lane car park, turn right again after half a mile (0.8 km) and the Rigg Lane car park is on the right after another half a mile (0.8 km) at SK584534.

Harlow Wood and Thieves Wood both lie just south of Mansfield. For Harlow Wood, park in the small car park at the Portland College on the east side of the A60 1.5 miles (2.4 km) south of Mansfield at SK552568; from here, footpaths lead through the woodland. To access Thieves Wood, turn west off the A60 on to the B6020 0.8 miles (1.3 km) south of Portland College, and then turn right again after half a mile (0.8 km) on to the B6139. There are car parks on the right and left at SK542558 and SK537559, from where waymarked trails lead through this popular recreational area.

Calendar

Resident: Egyptian Goose, Mandarin Duck, Gadwall, Ruddy Duck, Grey Heron, Goshawk, Sparrowhawk, Common Buzzard, Kestrel, Woodcock, Stock Dove, Tawny and Long-eared Owls, all three woodpeckers, Marsh and Willow Tits, Nuthatch, Treecreeper, Jay, Raven, Hawfinch, Yellowhammer.

October–March: Pink-footed Goose, Eurasian Wigeon, Common Teal, Tufted Duck, Goldeneye, Goosander, Hen Harrier (scarce), Merlin (scarce), Peregrine Falcon, Caspian Gull, Firecrest (rare), Great Grey Shrike (scarce), Brambling, Siskin, Lesser Redpoll, Common Crossbill (irregular).

April–September: Honey Buzzard, Marsh Harrier (scarce, passage), Osprey, Hobby, European Nightjar, Woodlark, Tree Pipit, Common Redstart, Garden Warbler, Common Whitethroat, Wood Warbler (rare), Common Chiffchaff, Willow Warbler, Spotted Flycatcher, Common Crossbill (irregular).

42. TRENT VALLEY GRAVEL PITS

OS Landrangers 121 and 129
OS Explorers 260 and 271

The River Trent flows roughly south to north through Nottinghamshire before reaching Lincolnshire and ultimately draining in to the Humber estuary. As in Derbyshire, there are extensive areas of aggregate extraction along its course, and the sites detailed here are listed from north to south.

42A. GIRTON, BESTHORPE AND COLLINGHAM PITS

OS Landranger 121
OS Explorer 271

Habitat

Sand and gravel extraction in the vicinity of Girton and Besthorpe, north of Newark on Trent, has created a series of pits to the east of the River Trent; several of these are now disused and flooded, with areas of scrub having grown up around their periphery. Tarmac are currently quarrying areas further to the north. One of the large pits at Girton is used for water sports, with a sailing club in existence, while the other large pit, next to the A1133, currently has no use and is very deep. There are several smaller pits, which have an extensive growth of sallow and willow scrub around their edges, along with some small areas of *Phragmites*. Some of the larger pits at Besthorpe were used as settlement lagoons for flyash, which was pumped there from the power stations further along the Trent valley, although most no longer exist.

Nottinghamshire Wildlife Trust (NWT) has a reserve at Besthorpe, centred on Mons Pool with its Grey Heron and Cormorant colonies. There is an SSSI grassland grazed by Hebridean sheep, with a scrubby reedbed, areas of open ground and a disused settling lagoon by the river. The old flyash lagoons are no longer present, having been restored to arable land. To the south of the reserve is an active Lafarge quarry, with pits at various stages of excavation. This area, which will become part of the NWT's reserve when quarrying ceases, has become known as Collingham Pits by local birdwatchers and has recently provided the best wader habitat in the vicinity. Large old hawthorn hedges flank some of the area.

At Girton, a small stream known as The Fleet widens into a broad shallow sheet of water, backed by old gnarled willows. It has sedges round the edge and often muddy margins, which can prove attractive to waders and wagtails.

The River Trent here is tidal and relatively wide, with high grass banks grazed in places by cattle and sheep but with longer rough grass dominating in other stretches. The surrounding area is composed of old grazing marshes in areas of flat land, called holmes, to the south of Girton and Besthorpe pits and to the west across the River Trent. Some remnants of the old mature hawthorn hegderows which were used to divide up the grazing pastures remain. In very wet winters, the River Trent may flood some of these fields, making them particularly attractive to wildfowl, as was the case in 2000.

The two sites have been brought to life in words and drawings in *Shorelines: Birds at the Water's Edge*, a collection of paintings and drawings by local artist Michael Warren, published in 1984 and now out of print.

Species

The area is of interest throughout the year but is best known for the high numbers of wintering wildfowl which make the site of particular importance within Nottinghamshire. During the winter months, however, there is considerable movement of birds between different sites in the Trent Valley in response to disturbance, feeding conditions and weather. During severe freezing weather, when areas of water may be ice-bound, the birds will move to the open water of the Trent to feed, but this happens less often now winters are generally milder. Nationally important numbers of Tufted Ducks occur, with smaller numbers of Pochards and up to 60 Goldeneyes. The wintering flock of Goosanders, which used to number up to 90 birds, has all but

285

disappeared; in most recent winters only a few birds have been present at Girton, either on the river or pits. Smew are less than annual and their presence depends on whether there has been an influx into the county. A large flock of Eurasian Wigeons moves between the pits and feeding areas on grazing meadows, especially when the fields are flooded, and small numbers of Gadwall also winter. Common Teal favour the marshy areas at Besthorpe and Trent Pit, Girton, where their population has peaked at 400 birds in February. A large flock of Canada Geese may reach 500 birds in midwinter, and Greylag Geese are also on the increase with a few pairs breeding at Besthorpe. Occasionally one or two Egyptian Geese occur. Skeins of Pink-footed Geese usually just fly over the area on their migration route between north-west England and the Wash, although small numbers sometimes linger for a few days on the wetter arable fields and the North Pit at Girton. Smithy Marsh, an area of open flat farmland between Besthorpe and Girton, usually has a herd of Mute Swans that sometimes attracts a few Bewick's and Whooper Swans. There is always the chance of rarer waterbirds, and vagrants have included Tundra Bean and Brent Geese, Common Scoter, Red-throated and Great Northern Divers and Red-necked and Slavonian Grebes.

As with most inland wetland sites, the number of Cormorants has increased dramatically of late, from peaks of about 45 in the early 1990s to an average peak of 367 in recent years. This species now nests in trees on the large island at Mons Pool, Besthorpe.

Pits with muddy edges and sedge beds prove attractive to Common Snipe, and in winter they usually hold one or more Jack Snipe but, as everywhere, a considerable amount of good fortune is needed to bump into one of these superbly camouflaged waders. The surrounding fields attract flocks of up to 800 Northern Lapwings and 300 European Golden Plovers. Redshanks feed along the Trent and are usually found at Collingham Pits and North Pit, Girton. A few Dunlin are often to be found at Collingham. There is a gull roost at Girton comprising mainly Black-headed and Common Gulls, and in the past there have been records of Glaucous and Mediterranean Gulls.

Flocks of Chaffinches, Greenfinches, Goldfinches and Linnets feed on the rough ground around the pits, while the fields and hedgerows hold Tree Sparrows, Yellowhammers and Reed Buntings. Areas of rough grassland often attract one or two wintering European Stonechats. Merlins are seen infrequently and occasional Short-eared Owls may pass through or perhaps remain for the winter in good years. Sparrowhawks and Kestrels are a common sight, and records of Common Buzzard and Peregrine Falcon are increasing.

By March, the main island at Mons Pool is a cacophony of sound and alive with the breeding activity of Grey Herons, Cormorants and Rooks. The colony of Cormorants is in the dead guano-covered ash trees and numbers around 100 nests. The heronry of about 40 nests is more hidden, with birds nesting in the tops of tall hawthorns. Other interesting breeding species include a few pairs of Shelduck, two or three pairs of Oystercatchers and Redshanks and a few Little Ringed and Ringed Plovers and Northern Lapwings. One or two pairs of Curlews cling on in the grass fields of the holmes. Good numbers of Great Crested and Little Grebes breed at Girton, and Kingfishers are seen frequently.

Nine species of warblers breed in the area. Lesser Whitethroats occur in the mature hedgerows along with Bullfinches and Linnets, and Garden Warblers can be found in areas of scrub, especially around the old reedbed at Besthorpe, which also has Turtle Dove, Cuckoo, Willow Tit and Reed

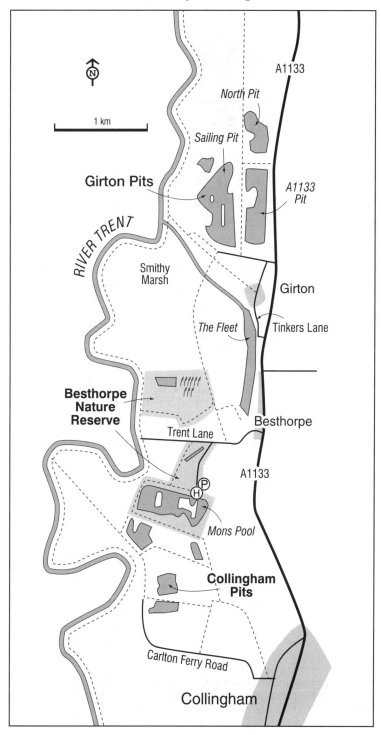

Short-eared Owl

Bunting. Rough grassland at Girton may contain reeling Grasshopper Warblers, and Reed Warblers nest in the small areas of *Phragmites*. The reedmace beds at Besthorpe played host to Nottinghamshire's first Savi's Warbler in May 1990. Sand Martins nest in the banks of the Trent at Girton and in a specially created bank at Besthorpe Nature Reserve.

Common, Arctic and Black Terns all pass through in most years, with the last days of April and the first week of May being the most productive periods. Inclement weather often brings the highest numbers of passage terns, and in such conditions large flocks of hirundines and Common Swifts may be found feeding over the water areas. The sheep fields at Girton are favoured by Yellow Wagtails, while small numbers of Northern Wheatears appear in the spring and occasional Ring Ouzels have been found. Hobby has increased as a breeding species in Nottinghamshire and birds can be seen hunting over the pits, especially in autumn when hirundine numbers build up.

The variety and number of migrant waders in both spring and autumn is highly dependent upon the availability of suitable muddy areas and shallow margins. Species such as Green and Common Sandpipers can be relied upon, with numbers of the former sometimes reaching double-figures, but the appearance of rarer waders is rather more unpredictable. In the last few years Collingham Pits has been the best area for waders, with small numbers of Dunlin, Ruff and Greenshank in autumn; scarcer species such as Knot, Little and Temminck's Stints, Curlew Sandpiper, Black-tailed Godwit, Spotted Redshank and Wood Sandpiper have all occurred there.

The autumn sees Shovelers peak at 40 or so birds in August and September at Besthorpe, and sometimes the odd Garganey may also be present. Later in the autumn, flocks of Stock Doves can exceed 100 birds, and passage Skylarks and Meadow Pipits have numbered 250 and 100 per day respectively in October. Westward-moving flocks of Redwings and Fieldfares stop off to feed on the hawthorn berry crop, sometimes staying for several weeks in productive autumns.

Being situated in the Trent Valley on a major flyway, this site receives its fair share of vagrants, although the area is relatively underwatched and there is great potential for finding more good birds. Perhaps the most notable record is of a well-watched Great Snipe found in nettle beds along the bank of the Trent in August 1989, while other exciting birds have included Green-winged Teal, Leach's Storm-petrel, Gannet, Avocet, American Golden Plover, Buff-breasted Sandpiper, Arctic and Great Skuas, Caspian and White-winged Black Terns and Richard's Pipit.

Timing

This is a good place to visit at any time of year. Wildfowl numbers are highest in midwinter, the range of habitats provides a good selection of breeding species and during both passage periods the site attracts migrants, notably waders. At weekends, early morning visits are best at Girton, where sailing may disturb waterfowl later in the day.

Access

The area is situated 5 miles (8 km) north of Newark on Trent, off the A1133 Newark on Trent to Gainsborough road.

Collingham Pits (Besthorpe New Workings): Approaching Collingham village on the A1133 from the south, turn left on to The Green and then right on to Low Street; if approaching from the north, turn right on to Low Street on the northern edge of the village. On Low Street take the turn signposted to the River Trent opposite the church (SK 829620) – this road is called Carlton Ferry Road on some maps. The new workings are visible from by a gate on the right. Further along park by a footpath sign on the right, from where by crossing the stile the pits can be viewed. Another pit is visible on the right a little further along, and a track to the west of this pit leads to the rear of Mons Pool. There are several footpaths through this area so an Ordnance Survey map is recommended. Do not trespass on working areas of the quarry.

Besthorpe Nature Reserve: Besthorpe village is 1.5 miles (2.4 km) north of Collingham on the A1133. Turn west off the A1133 on to Waddington Lane, a minor road at the south end of Besthorpe village, signed River Trent. This becomes Trent Lane, which soon narrows to a track beyond some obvious pylons. For the scrubby reedbed take the first track on the right (SK821645) and the reedbed is on the left as the track opens out onto farmland. A footpath runs through scrub and along the edge of the reedbed and then onto the open area of the reserve next to the Trent. For Mons Pool continue along Trent Lane and turn left into the track with the reserve sign. There is a car park at the end of the entrance track (SK817640). For the part of the reserve next to the Trent continue along Trent Lane until it bends right. It is possible to park at Mons Pool and walk back along the entrance track to access the two other two areas.

The Fleet: From the north side of Besthorpe, continue north on the A1133 for 800 m then turn left on to Tinkers Lane, signed to Girton village (SK826656). This minor road runs alongside the northern part of The Fleet and a public footpath runs south along the eastern side.

Girton: For the main Girton pits, turn left off the A1133 on to a minor road signed to Girton 1 mile (1.6 km) north of Besthorpe (SK828665), and at the left bend after 100 m go straight on. The large pit next to the A1133 is visible through the hedge and the main sailing pit comes into view on the right after 600 m. There is limited parking on the side of the pit and a public footpath runs north alongside the western bank of the pit and around a smaller pit, Trent Pit, and onto the disused works area next to the Trent. A track runs north between the A1133 Pit and the Sailing Pit, and by following this north there is another pit on the right, North Pit. This latter pit can also be accessed by turning west off the A1133 on to the track at SK 827675.

Calendar

Resident: Gadwall, Tufted Duck, Great Crested and Little Grebes, Cormorant, Grey Heron, Northern Lapwing, Redshank, Stock Dove, Barn Owl, Kingfisher, Green Woodpecker, Meadow Pipit, Willow Tit, Tree Sparrow, Linnet, Bullfinch, Yellowhammer, Reed Bunting.

October–March: Pink-footed Goose (scarce), Shelduck, Eurasian Wigeon, Common Teal, Shoveler, Pochard, Goldeneye, Smew (rare), Goosander (scarce), Common Buzzard, Merlin (rare), Peregrine Falcon, Water Rail, European Golden Plover, Dunlin, Jack and Common Snipe, Green Sandpiper, gull roost, Short-eared Owl (rare), Grey Wagtail, European Stonechat, Fieldfare, Redwing, Siskin, Lesser Redpoll.

April–September: Shelduck, Little Egret (scarce), Hobby, Oystercatcher, Little Ringed Plover, Ringed Plover, Dunlin, Ruff, Curlew, Spotted Redshank (rare), Greenshank (scarce), Green Sandpiper, Common Sandpiper, Common, Arctic and Black Terns, Turtle Dove, Cuckoo, Sand Martin, Yellow Wagtail, Whinchat, Northern Wheatear, Grasshopper, Sedge, Reed and Garden Warblers, Lesser and Common Whitethroats.

42B. HOVERINGHAM GRAVEL PITS

OS Landranger 129
OS Explorer 271

Habitat

Much of the land between Hoveringham and Bleasby has been subject to extensive gravel and sand extraction by Tarmac Ltd for many years, but current plans are for work to finish in the area in the near future. The pits created by these extractions have proved to be of ornithological interest over the years but, in contrast to some other such complexes, many of the pits have now been filled and returned to agricultural use. However, a number remain and, because of their size and location, make Hoveringham one of the premier birdwatching sites in Nottinghamshire. The Trent valley is a major overland migration route for birds and the lakes at Hoveringham are often a magnet for such migratory species.

One of the largest pits in the complex, known locally as the Sailing Pit, is used by Nottinghamshire County Sailing Club for sailing and windsurfing from March to December. There is a very small pool to the west of the main lake, used for training by the sailing club, and another slightly larger lake to the north-east which is undisturbed by water sports. These lakes are bordered on one side by the River Trent and on the other two sides by farmland with, on the west side, a meadow which has SSSI status.

The main lake has rather steeply sloping grassed sides, but the other pools are surrounded with more mature vegetation and have some shallow edges. The river has many bushes along its bank nearest the lake, and on the other side there is a steep wooded escarpment,

In addition, there are several other pits in the area, but only one is accessible to the public. This lake, the largest of the complex, is known locally as the Railway Pit and lies to the north of Hoveringham village. The lake, about

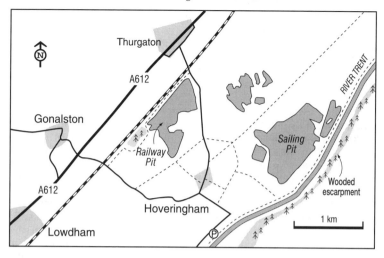

a mile (1.6 km) in length, has the railway line running alongside but is otherwise surrounded by farmland and has a small mixed deciduous wood next to it.

Species

The winter months bring wildfowl and gulls to the complex and a variety of species to the surrounding farmland and small woodlands. Typical wintering species include Mute Swan, Mallard, Eurasian Wigeon, Gadwall, Common Teal, Shoveler, Pochard, Tufted Duck, Goldeneye, Goosander, Little and Great Crested Grebes and Cormorant. Small numbers of Smew have been regular in recent years. Records of the rarer grebes and the occasional diver occur in most winters.

The gull roost on the main lakes is probably the largest in Nottinghamshire, and is regularly watched; on some occasions more than 15,000 gulls are to be seen. Records of Mediterranean, Yellow-legged, Iceland and Glaucous Gulls are annual, and Caspian Gulls are now being identified more frequently, so the roost is always worth close scrutiny during the winter months.

The surrounding fields often have flocks of Northern Lapwings and European Golden Plovers during the winter, and groups of Redwing and Fieldfare may be encountered in the early winter period. Wild geese and swans often pass through but seldom linger in the area. Small passerines are represented by such species as Linnet, Reed Bunting, Yellowhammer, Long-tailed Tit and Meadow Pipit, all of which are common, while Rock and Water Pipits are occasional and one or two European Stonechats, Green Sandpipers and Grey Wagtails usually winter around the lakes. Green and Great Spotted Woodpeckers are frequently heard and seen in the areas of woodland and raptor sightings include regular Kestrel, Sparrowhawk and Common Buzzard, with the occasional Peregrine Falcon or Merlin wintering in the area.

The first summer migrants, Sand Martin, Common Chiffchaff and a few Northern Wheatears, arrive during late March when local breeding birds such as Shelduck, Oystercatcher and Redshank first appear on the surrounding fields. The banks of the lakes and the River Trent unfortunately offer little suitable wader habitat so only small numbers of Common and

Green Sandpipers are regular in spring, with occasional visits from Sanderling, Greenshank and Turnstone. The recently re-flooded Railway Pit no longer provides much wader habitat, so Ringed and Little Ringed Plovers are going to find breeding much more difficult. The two large lakes attract passage parties of Arctic and Black Terns in suitable weather conditions, and occasional Kittiwakes appear during the early spring.

The main lakes also attract feeding flocks of hirundines during the spring and summer when insects are emerging and on the wing, and summer migrants such as Yellow Wagtail, Sedge Warbler, Common Whitethroat and Willow Warbler all join resident Meadow Pipits and Reed Buntings in breeding around the lakes. The small woodland across the River Trent has breeding Tawny Owl and most of the common woodland species, and in addition has a small heronry. Hobby is also an occasional visitor during the late spring and summer months.

The autumn return migration period often brings in good numbers of Black Terns, and these are joined now and again by Arctic Terns and Little Gulls. The more regular waders such as Common and Green Sandpipers are sometimes complemented by rarer species including Grey Plover, Little Stint, Ruff, Bar-tailed and Black-tailed Godwits, Wood Sandpiper and the occasional Curlew Sandpiper. Little Egrets are seen with some regularity from late July onwards. Passage Northern Wheatears and Whinchats are regular, the latter often favouring areas of tall weedy stems and small bushes.

Owing to its strategic location in the Trent Valley, the site has produced a creditable list of scarce and rare birds for an inland county. Waterbirds have included Red-throated, Black-throated and Great Northern Diver, the three rarer grebes and wildfowl such as Tundra Bean Goose, American Wigeon, Ring-necked Duck, Common Eider and Long-tailed Duck. Seabirds, always a prize inland find, have included Fulmar, Leach's Storm-petrel and Gannet. Scarce waders have been represented by American Golden Plover, Temminck's Stint, Pectoral and Buff-breasted Sandpipers and Red-necked Phalarope. More expected finds include nearly annual Bitterns, Marsh Harriers and Ospreys. The best of the scarce passerines in recent years have been Black Redstart, Twite and Snow Bunting. Nearby, Bleasby Pits shot to fame in March 1996 when it hosted the first Redhead for the Western Palearctic.

Timing

Hoveringham pits have something of interest to birdwatchers at all times of year and because they are large stretches of water on a migration route, unusual birds can drop in at any time. However, the best periods are probably November to March when there is little disturbance from water sports on the Sailing Lake, and during the spring and autumn migration periods. Late afternoon and evening during the winter months is the time to watch the gull roost.

Access

Hoveringham Gravel Pits are situated about 8 miles (13 km) north-east of Nottingham. From Lowdham village, travel north-east on the A612 for about a mile (1.6 km) and turn right on to a minor road signposted to Hoveringham. In the village turn right at the T-junction near the church, continue to a sharp right-hand bend and a few hundred m further on park in the large car park on the left at SK702462. Walk back along the road to the bend and go through the gate on to the public footpath along the River Trent, with the river to the right. Continue along the footpath through the

SSSI meadow for a few hundred m, go through another gate and the Sailing Pit is on the left. The best views are obtained a little further on, when the footpath is closer to the lake. There is also another smaller pool at the far end of the Sailing Pit. It is not possible to walk all the way around the lake, since much of the land is private.

To reach the Railway Pit, park near the railway crossing just south-east of Thurgaton village (SK697484) and follow the public footpath to the south-west, adjacent to the railway line. Please note that parking here is severely limited. An alternative is to park on Gonalston Lane, between Gonalston and Hoveringham, and use the public footpath from there (SK686469). Visitors should remain on public rights of way at all times.

Calendar

Resident: Mute Swan, Red-legged and Grey Partridges, Little and Great Crested Grebes, Grey Heron, Sparrowhawk, Common Buzzard, Kestrel, Northern Lapwing, Little and Tawny Owls, Kingfisher, Green and Great Spotted Woodpeckers, Skylark, Meadow Pipit, Marsh and Long-tailed Tits, Linnet, Yellowhammer, Reed Bunting.

October–March: Eurasian Wigeon, Gadwall, Common Teal, Pintail (scarce), Shoveler, Pochard, Tufted Duck, Common Scoter (scarce), Goldeneye, Smew (scarce), Red-breasted Merganser (scarce), Goosander, divers (rare), Red-necked Grebe (rare), Slavonian Grebe (scarce), Black-necked Grebe (scarce), Merlin (scarce), Peregrine Falcon, European Golden Plover, Jack Snipe (scarce), Common Snipe, Green Sandpiper, gulls (including annual Mediterranean, Yellow-legged, Caspian, Iceland and Glaucous), Rock Pipit (scarce), Grey Wagtail, European Stonechat, Fieldfare, Redwing, Brambling (scarce), Goldfinch, Siskin, Lesser Redpoll, Bullfinch.

April–September: Shelduck, Garganey, Little Egret, Hobby, Oystercatcher, Little Ringed and Ringed Plovers, Sanderling, Dunlin, Ruff, Black-tailed Godwit (scarce), Bar-tailed Godwit (scarce), Whimbrel, Curlew, Redshank, Greenshank, Wood Sandpiper (scarce), Common Sandpiper, Turnstone, Little Gull, Kittiwake (scarce), Sandwich Tern (rare), Common and Arctic Terns, Little Tern (rare), Black Tern, Turtle Dove, Cuckoo, Common Swift, Sand Martin, Swallow, House Martin, Yellow and White Wagtails, Whinchat, Northern Wheatear, Grasshopper Warbler.

42C. NETHERFIELD LAGOONS

OS Landranger 129
OS Explorer 260

Habitat

The disused gravel pits at Netherfield have been used to some extent as a dump for coal slurry and the two remaining gravel ponds are frequently used by anglers. The two slurry pits are separated by a raised causeway, which is elevated some 50 feet (15 m) above the pits, giving a commanding view of the area. The largest tank is virtually full but retains some water, with muddy edges attractive to waders and roosting gulls and terns. The smaller tank is mainly deep water, and harbours good numbers of wildfowl, with smaller birds feeding and breeding around the tank edges. The area has recently been acquired by the Gedling Conservation Trust and will be managed by them as a nature reserve with free public access.

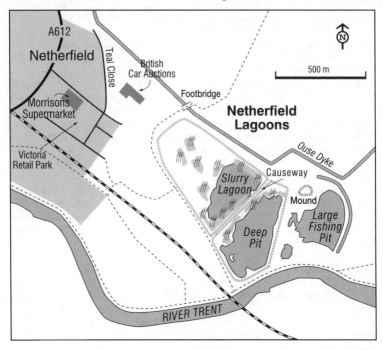

Species

Because of the largely temporary nature of the main slurry lagoon sites, much of the avian interest is restricted to passage and wintering birds. A railway embankment, which forms the western boundary of the site, holds Turtle Dove and Lesser Whitethroat during the summer and occasionally Long-eared Owl in the winter. Grasshopper Warblers sing from the scrubby banks of the gravel ponds, and these areas are frequent stopping-off points for small numbers of Whinchat and a regular wintering site for European Stonechat. Northern Wheatears can often be found during passage periods on the bank tops and fence posts by the first slurry lagoon. Cormorants roost on the electricity pylons and parties of wild swans sometimes feed on the extensive sewage farm fields to the east.

During the spring, pools created on the slurry attract most of the common species of wader, with Little Ringed Plovers being common from April to September. Regular species in autumn include Ruff, Dunlin, Greenshank, Redshank and Green and Common Sandpipers. In the late autumn up to 4,000 European Golden Plover and 1,000 Northern Lapwings use the pools as a roost site, along with several hundred Eurasian Wigeons, smaller numbers of Common Teal, Shovelers and Pintails and the occasional Garganey. Gulls also use the pools to roost and loaf, and during late summer both Yellow-legged and Mediterranean are often located. The weedy banks and fields attract good numbers of Skylarks and Meadow Pipits, with Yellow Wagtails being common in the summer. The reedbed areas, which are now more extensive than previously, hold good numbers of Reed and Sedge Warblers during the summer and Water Rails during the winter.

A good selection of rare birds has been located at this site, the most famous being a Little Swift in May 2001 which attracted many thousands of observers during its four-day stay. Regular checking of the migrant waders has produced records of Avocet, Stone Curlew, Dotterel, Pectoral, Purple and Buff-breasted Sandpipers, Lesser Yellowlegs and Grey Phalarope, an impressive list for an inland site. Other scarcities that have been found over the years have included American Wigeon, Gannet, Bittern, Spoonbill, Common Crane, White-winged Black Tern, Richard's Pipit, Marsh and Great Reed Warblers.

Timing

April to June is the best time for passage waders, with terns and gulls also moving through the area. In autumn, birds begin to arrive from late July onwards, with passage peaking in September and October. Winter produces good numbers of birds, especially gulls, when the pools freeze over in harsh conditions. Dawn and dusk are the best times to visit, but passage birds can drop in throughout the day.

Access

There is unrestricted access at all times, although the slurry lagoons are, in theory at least, private. Netherfield railway station is a 15 minute walk away and buses arrive from Nottingham city centre on a regular basis. Vehicle access is directly off the A612; park in the large retail park (look for Morrisons) at SK627407 and then walk 300 m to Teal Close. Walk to the end of Teal Close and cross the Ouse Dyke by the footbridge, follow the footpath to the east and recross the Ouse Dyke at the next footbridge, on to the site.

Calendar

November–March: Eurasian Wigeon, Gadwall, Common Teal, Pochard, Tufted Duck, Goldeneye, Goosander, Great Crested and Little Grebes, Peregrine Falcon, European Golden Plover, Jack Snipe, gull roost, Long-eared and Short-eared Owls.

April–June: rarer grebes, Hobby, passage waders, gulls, terns, hirundines, Yellow Wagtail, Whinchat, Northern Wheatear, Grasshopper Warbler, passage migrants.

July–October: wildfowl, Peregrine Falcon, Little Ringed and Ringed Plovers, Dunlin, Redshank, Greenshank, Green and Common Sandpipers, gulls (including Mediterranean and Yellow-legged), terns, passage migrants.

42D. HOLME PIERREPONT

OS Landranger 129
OS Explorer 260

Habitat

This large site comprises disused gravel workings, a water sports centre, meadows, grassland and scrub, with some small sections of woodland. Many of the best areas are private, although there is some access to view parts of these.

The site is dominated by two water areas, the 2,000 m national rowing course and the 140 acre (56 ha) A52 Pit. The rowing course has attracted a good number of county rarities over the years, and the A52 Pit has also produced a creditable number of rarities since its formation in the early 1980s; unfortunately, it is located on private land and even local birdwatchers are finding it increasingly difficult to gain access. To the east of the A52 Pit is Blotts Pit, which often proves attractive to waders, gulls and terns. Moving further east towards the end of the rowing course are the old 'finger ponds', an area largely neglected by birdwatchers. There is also the 27 acre (11 ha) Skylarks Nature Reserve, owned by the Nottinghamshire Wildlife Trust, which is mainly composed of small ponds and an extensive willow holt.

The only woodland of note is around Holme Pierrepont Hall and its surrounding gardens. The main grassland areas are around the A52 Pit and at the eastern end of the rowing course.

Species

Winter wildfowl flocks are usually made up of all the regular species including Eurasian Wigeon, Gadwall, Common Teal, Pochard, Tufted Duck, Goldeneye and Ruddy Duck, with the rowing course and A52 Pit being favoured spots. Small numbers of Smew are often located in the winter months, the rarer grebes occur occasionally and seaducks such as Scaup may arrive in severe weather. There is a reasonable gull roost on the A52 Pit, which sometimes produces records of Mediterranean, Yellow-legged, Caspian, Iceland and Glaucous Gull. Small numbers of Jack Snipe winter, but as everywhere are difficult to locate.

All three species of woodpecker occur, although Lesser Spotted is now infrequent. Other resident breeding species include Gadwall, Sparrowhawk, Kingfisher and Willow Tit, and these are joined in summer by good numbers of warblers, among which are Lesser Whitethroat and Grasshopper, Sedge and Reed Warblers.

During favourable conditions in the spring and autumn, good numbers of migrant birds pass through the site, especially terns and Little Gulls. Early spring is a worthwhile time to look for Water Pipits, which have occurred several times in recent years, often in late March. Rock Pipits may also be found at this time of year, as well as in the late autumn. During April, groups of migrant Yellow Wagtails may contain a few White Wagtails. One or two Garganey are seen most years, mainly in the spring, and small flocks of Common Scoters sometimes pause on their overland migration in April. Hobbies are seen regularly on passage and through the summer months, and Little Egrets are becoming regular visitors, particularly from July onwards.

Migrant waders favour the A52 Pit and Blotts Pit, although their appearance is unpredictable due to the constantly changing water levels of the lakes. Passage species include the usual mix of Little Ringed and Ringed Plovers, Dunlin, Ruff, Redshank, Greenshank and Green and Common Sandpipers, with occasional records of other species such as Grey Plover, Sanderling, Little Stint, Curlew Sandpiper, both godwits, Spotted Redshank and Wood Sandpiper. The best of the rarer waders have been American Golden Plover, Lesser Yellowlegs and Pectoral and Spotted Sandpipers, while Avocet, Temminck's Stint, Purple Sandpiper and Grey Phalarope have all been seen in recent years. In addition, records of American Wigeon, Green-winged Teal, Great White Egret, Spotted Crake, White-winged Black Tern, Richard's Pipit and Golden Oriole all show the wide variety of scarce species which may be located on an obvious migration route, even at inland localities.

Timing

For passage birds, as with most sites in Nottinghamshire, spring is the best period of the year (from April to early June). Apart from the private A52 Pit, most areas are open to the public and therefore suffer from disturbance, particularly the rowing course. Early morning visits are therefore recommended,

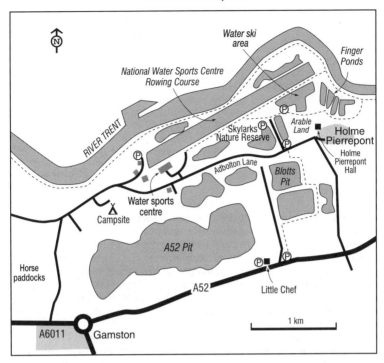

with most visible passage taking place during the first few hours of daylight. During high summer, birds are more elusive and the public more numerous. Avoid national water sports events at all costs!

Access

There is open access to the rowing course, the finger ponds and the bank of the River Trent, as well as to Skylarks Nature Reserve. Viewing of the A52 Pit is difficult as the whole lake is on private farmland. The south-western corner can be watched from the A52 just east of the Gamston roundabout (SK610377), although parking here is difficult. The whole pit can be seen by parking in a lay-by on the A52, 150 m east of the Little Chef restaurant (SK622380); a concrete track, the southern part of which is a public foot-path, runs northwards from here, but the views over the pit are rather distant and a telescope is essential. From this spot a public footpath leading off north-east gives access to Blotts Pit, which can also be approached from the northern end of this public footpath along Adbolton Lane, 200 m east of the watersports centre (SK623390).

There is public transport available from Nottingham city centre to the water sports area and the whole site can be walked around in three to four hours. Car parking is easy, although some parks charge a fee and, as usual, beware of car thieves in quiet car parks.

Calendar

Resident: Gadwall, Tufted and Ruddy Ducks, Little and Great Crested Grebes, Sparrowhawk, Kingfisher, Green and Great Spotted Woodpeckers, Lesser Spotted Woodpecker (scarce), Skylark, Willow Tit, Nuthatch, Reed Bunting.

October–March: Eurasian Wigeon, Common Teal, Pochard, Goldeneye, Smew, rare grebes, Jack Snipe, gull roost, Water Pipit (scarce), Rock Pipit (scarce), Fieldfare, Redwing.

April–September: Garganey (scarce), Common Scoter, Hobby, Little Ringed and Ringed Plovers, Dunlin, Ruff, Greenshank, Green and Common Sandpipers, passage waders, Little Gull, Common, Arctic and Black Terns, Yellow and White Wagtails, Whinchat, Northern Wheatear, Grasshopper, Sedge and Reed Warblers, Lesser Whitethroat.

42E. COLWICK COUNTRY PARK

OS Landranger 129
OS Explorer 260

Habitat

Officially opened in 1978, Colwick Country Park is located on the eastern outskirts of Nottingham and covers 250 acres (101 ha). It is based on former gravel workings which have been landscaped and planted with a variety of trees and shrubs. Lying within the city boundary, the park forms a recreational facility for the city of Nottingham. Prior to the extraction of gravel the area was a natural rough island, flanked by the Trent Cut, a man-made navigation canal, and the River Trent itself. The site has a history going back to the Domesday Book, with several notable archaeological finds having been made in the area.

The park proper is dominated by two lakes, of 62 acres (25 ha) and 24 acres (10 ha) respectively. The southern boundary is the River Trent, which separates the park from Holme Pierrepont. To the north lies the Colwick Woods escarpment, a well wooded glacial ridge with extensive public access.

Within the park are a number of different habitats which prove attractive to birds. The nature reserve is dominated by sycamore with the occasional oak and birch trees, in addition to which there is a small narrow lake and overgrown marsh area. Scattered throughout the park are numerous small and relatively new plantations, with food trees such as alder, beech and hazel. There are several quiet woodland rides and some areas of damp grassland, although these are heavily used by the public.

The West Lake, the smaller of the two lakes, is used for coarse fishing and windsurfing with consequent disturbance all year round. The larger Colwick Lake is a trout fishery with a running season from mid-March to the end of November. Trout boats are often active on the lake, especially at weekends.

Whinchat

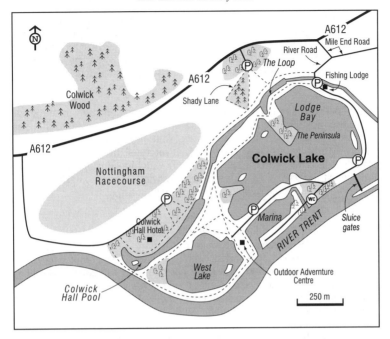

Species

The park list stands at around 220 species. Because of its location in the Trent Valley migration corridor, passage movements of many species are often a feature of a visit with thrushes, pipits and larks moving through in considerable numbers at times.

The large expanse of water draws a good mix of wildfowl including Pochard, Tufted Duck, Gadwall and Eurasian Wigeon. Winter counts of Goldeneye can exceed 100 birds, while Smew are becoming increasingly regular. All three species of diver and the rarer grebes have been recorded. The site came to national prominence in March 1994, when a drake Bufflehead was present for just over a week, attracting 4,500 observers during its stay. This in turn led to the finding of several other rare birds including Long-tailed Duck and Lapland Bunting, showing the potential for discovery of unusual birds at the site. Blackcap and Common Chiffchaff regularly winter and are often found with roving tit flocks; there have also been several recent winter records of Firecrest (including up to four together in 2002-03) and, rarer still, a Yellow-browed Warbler wintered in 2003-04.

Parties of terns pass through in the spring and autumn, with Black and Arctic Terns and Little Gulls often present after a period of easterly winds. Kittiwakes are occasionally recorded in early spring, and Mediterranean Gulls are annual, with some individuals remaining for several days.

In excess of 60 species breed within the park annually, with Great Spotted Woodpecker and Kingfisher both being common. Eight species of warbler are present in summer including Reed and Sedge Warblers. From April to September Hobbies appear regularly, taking advantage of the large hirundine and Common Swift flocks feeding over the insect rich area. Both Sparrowhawk and Kestrel breed and are a common sight in the park.

As well as Bufflehead and Yellow-browed Warbler, rare birds recorded in recent years have included Night Heron, Purple Heron, White Stork,

Red-footed Falcon, Caspian Tern, White-winged Black Tern and Shore Lark. Periods of gales during the autumn have produced a number of seabirds, including Manx Shearwater, Fulmar, Grey Phalarope and Great, Arctic and Long-tailed Skuas. In addition to the ornithological value of the site, 27 species of butterfly and 17 species of Odonata have occurred.

Timing

Owing to disturbance, mainly by dog walkers and anglers, early morning visits are the most productive. Weather conditions are also most important as Colwick is situated within a geographical funnel, which means it is almost always windy to varying degrees. Birdwatchers' favourite conditions, easterly winds with drizzle, provide good watching during April to May and August to October. Light north-westerly winds with clear skies usually guarantee some visible migration, especially in autumn.

Access

The park is open at all times but visitors are asked to exercise care when on the footpaths. The area has three major parking areas which are free, in addition to which there is ample parking within the park for an entrance fee of £1. Sheltered car parks are best avoided as car crime does occur; the safest car parks are next to the fishing lodge and outside Colwick Hall. Buses for Colwick leave Nottingham city centre frequently and Netherfield railway station is about 15 minutes walk away. Vehicular access to the park is off the A612, which passes Nottingham Racecourse; follow the signs for water user entrance only, and turn off Mile End Road on to River Road at SK611400. Disabled birdwatchers can view both lakes from their vehicles at several points.

Calendar

Resident: wildfowl, Little Grebe, Great Crested Grebe, Sparrowhawk, Kestrel, Great Spotted Woodpecker, Kingfisher, tits, woodland species.

October–March: Red-crested Pochard, Goldeneye, Smew (scarce), scarce grebes (rare), Mediterranean Gull (scarce), Water Rail, Siskin.

April–September: Hobby, Little Gull (scarce), Common Tern, Arctic Tern (scarce), Black Tern (scarce), Sedge Warbler, Reed Warbler, Blackcap, Garden Warbler, Lesser Whitethroat, Common Whitethroat, Common Chiffchaff, Willow Warbler.

42F. ATTENBOROUGH NATURE RESERVE

OS Landranger 129
OS Explorer 260

Habitat

Attenborough Nature Reserve is situated 4.3 miles (7 km) south-west of Nottingham city centre and covers approximately 240 acres (97 ha). In 1982 the reserve was designated a Site of Special Scientific Interest due to the importance of its wintering wildfowl population. It is owned by Cemex (Ready Mixed Concretes) and jointly managed with the Nottinghamshire Wildlife Trust. As a result of decades of gravel extraction and careful restoration, the area has a wealth of bird interest throughout the year. There are two hides and two viewing screens, and the Attenborough Nature Centre has enhanced the visitor experience by providing a venue for refreshments and opportunities for education.

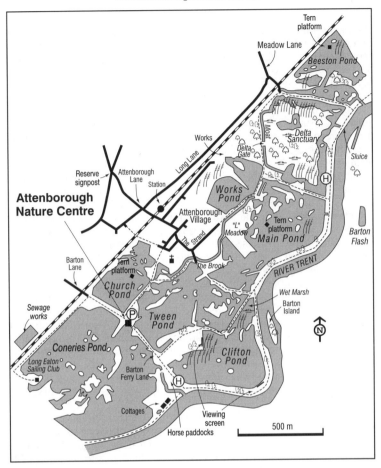

The reserve comprises a diverse range of habitats along an important migration route. Mature willow and alder fen habitat dominates the Delta Sanctuary. The drier areas are providing opportunities for broad-leaved species including ash and sycamore to colonise, with a shrub layer of hawthorn and small patches of blackthorn. The area is fringed by common reed, with a substantial area at the Delta Front. Valuable areas of reedbed have also developed at the Wet Marsh and Clifton Pit following a creation scheme by Nottinghamshire Wildlife Trust. Away from here, the reserve comprises a mosaic of flooded pits of varied depths with vegetated islands, exposed spits and meadow with accompanying scrub. To the south of the River Trent the patchwork of fields and mature hedgerows with mixed woodland on the valley sides provide habitat for a further range of species.

The River Trent, which runs south-west to north-east, acts as a migratory corridor and therefore must be considered an important factor in attracting birds to the area. During periods of extremely cold weather, when the pits become frozen, the open water of the Trent greatly increases its value to wildfowl.

Species

During the winter months the main attraction for visitors is the presence of Bitterns, and Attenborough is one of the most reliable places in Britain to see this species. In addition, the views obtained are often exceptional. Over the last decade up to three birds have been present between November and March; they are regularly seen from the hide overlooking the Delta Front and from the screens that look out on to the Wet Marsh.

Typical wintering wildfowl include Gadwall, Common Teal, Pochard, Tufted and Ruddy Ducks and Little and Great Crested Grebes, while a feature of recent winters has been the presence of around 40 Goosanders. Small numbers of Eurasian Wigeons and Goldeneyes occur and Shelduck is an uncommon visitor. Pintail is a scarce passage and winter visitor, while Scaup, Smew and Red-breasted Merganser are rare winter vagrants that can turn up during periods of hard weather; there have also been records of sea-ducks such as Common Eider and Velvet Scoter. Black-necked Grebes sometimes arrive at this time of year, but this species is generally a rare spring passage migrant. The other grebes and divers are genuine vagrants. Wild swans are rare visitors to the reserve and do not normally linger. Of the geese, Pink-footed is an irregular winter visitor, while White-fronted and Brent are true vagrants.

The islands in Coneries Pond provide an ideal roost site for Cormorants, with maximum counts exceeding 200 birds during the winter. This species is ever-present and although breeding has yet to be confirmed, one was seen sitting on a nest in 2004. The winter period also features an influx of Water Rails, which can be quite confiding as they forage among the marginal vegetation of the ponds. During late afternoon large numbers of Black-headed Gulls, together with smaller groups of Common, Herring, Great Black-backed and Lesser Black-backed Gulls, gather before flying off to roost. It is always worth scanning through the assembled birds for Mediterranean Gull.

The alders around the Delta attract small flocks of Siskin and Lesser Redpoll and the roving tit flocks are always worth checking for additional species; Firecrests have been noted on several occasions, and Common Chiffchaffs winter regularly. This is also an excellent area to see Willow Tit. Although the Delta Sanctuary is not open to visitors, the Delta Woodland Path runs along one boundary of it and from here it is possible to see all three woodpeckers; Lesser Spotted is regularly seen among the standing deadwood by the Delta Sanctuary gate in late winter and early spring. The sewage farm off Barton Lane attracts large numbers of Pied Wagtails, and Grey Wagtail has become more numerous in recent years.

Spring normally brings a reasonable passage of waders, the more regular being Ringed and Little Ringed Plover, Dunlin, Ruff, Curlew, Greenshank, Redshank and Green and Common Sandpipers. Irregular species include the two godwits and Whimbrel, with rarer visits by Grey Plover, Knot, Wood Sandpiper and Turnstone. The key sites for these species are the islands and shallow areas on Clifton Pit and Tween Pond and the Works Pond Delta, while the river flash north-east of Barton village is an ephemeral water body that is worth checking during the spring.

April and May offer the best chance of seeing a passage Marsh Harrier or Osprey – the latter is annual, although invariably birds do not linger. Arctic and Black Terns are recorded most years in spring but the timing and number of birds involved are governed by the prevailing weather conditions. Main Pond is generally the best place to look, as they tend to mix with the breeding Common Terns. Little Gull and Garganey occur most years during

Great Grey Shrike

April and May and Sandwich Tern is an irregular visitor. This time of the year can also produce rarer visitors including Kittiwake and Black-necked Grebe, while true spring vagrants have included Purple Heron, Bluethroat, Savi's Warbler, Marsh Warbler and Golden Oriole.

Nottinghamshire Wildlife Trust manages the site in order to maintain a variety of habitats that consequently provide nesting opportunities for a wide range of species during the summer. The paths around the Delta Sanctuary are the best places to view Blackcap, Garden Warbler and Common Chiffchaff, while the scrub and grassland mosaic between the River Trent and the pits will produce Grasshopper and Sedge Warblers, Lesser and Common Whitethroats and Willow Warbler. Reed Warbler is also a fairly common breeding species, largely concentrated in the areas of reed around the Delta Sanctuary, Wet Marsh and Clifton Pit. South of the River Trent is a heronry that generally holds around 40 pairs of birds; this is best viewed from the riverbank adjacent to Clifton Pit. Kingfisher is a regular breeding species that can be seen in the vicinity of all the water bodies within the reserve, but the posts in front of the hide on Barton Lane and the banks of the River Trent are the best sites for this species. Common Terns are conspicuous during the summer as they nest on purpose-built platforms on Main Pond, Church Pond and Beeston Pond. Water Rails probably breed most years but, given their elusive nature, proving it is not always possible. A recent addition to the reserve's breeding birds is Egyptian Goose, and a small population is now well established.

Autumn migration begins in July with the first returning Dunlin, Greenshank and Green and Common Sandpipers. More waders occur in autumn than in spring and birds tend to linger for longer periods due, in part, to the greater availability of suitable habitat. Favourable weather conditions can produce Ruff, Black-tailed Godwit and Redshank along with rarer species such as Spotted Redshank and Wood Sandpiper. Garganey occurs regularly during August and September, often in association with returning Common Teal – check around the reedbeds on Clifton Pit and the Delta Front from the hide, or from The Bund. The autumn is also a good time to see Hobbies as they are attracted by the large number of Common Swifts and hirundines that feed over the pits. Little Egrets are usually found during the late summer and autumn, and are often seen flying in to roost with Cormorants on Coneries Pond in the evening. Adult Yellow-legged Gulls also feature regularly in late summer, tending to favour the Works Pit.

Attenborough is a long established and well-watched site, and as such has an impressive list of rare and scarce birds to its credit. It is probably best known for Britain's first ever inland Sora, in December 2004, but equally as notable are three records of Little Crake, in 1975, 1976 and 1983. Other national rarities have included Squacco Heron, two Great White Egrets, Black-winged Stilt, Caspian Tern, Red-rumped Swallow and Penduline Tit. Rare wildfowl have been represented by Green-winged Teal and Ring-necked and Ferruginous Ducks, while the wader list includes Avocet, Kentish Plover, Temminck's Stint, Pectoral and Purple Sandpipers and Grey Phalarope. Even a few seabirds have been found after strong gales, and there have been records of Fulmar, Manx Shearwater, Leach's Storm-petrel, Gannet and Arctic Skua. Other notable species recorded at this excellent site over the years have included Spoonbill, Spotted Crake, Wryneck, Shore Lark, Bearded Tit, and Red-backed and Great Grey Shrikes.

Timing

Attenborough Nature Reserve is worth visiting throughout the year although spring and autumn can be particularly rewarding periods. During the winter, the best time to see Bitterns is generally dawn and, especially, dusk, when the birds often fly to roost in favoured areas of reeds.

Access

Attenborough Nature Reserve is situated off the A6005 between Beeston and Long Eaton, 5 miles (8 km) south-west of Nottingham. From junction 25 of the M1 take the A52 eastwards signposted to Nottingham; after 1.5 miles (2.4 km) turn right at the roundabout on to the B6003 signed to Long Eaton and Toton. A further 1.25 miles (2 km) on turn left at the traffic lights on to the A6005. After half a mile (0.8 km) turn right at the traffic lights and proceed through Chilwell Retail Park. Continue straight on at the roundabout on to Barton Lane, over the railway crossing and onwards to the designated parking area (SK516339). All areas are easily accessible from here. The Attenborough Nature Centre provides refreshments and toilets and is open from 10 am to 4 pm Monday to Friday and 9 am to 5 pm at weekends. Entry to the reserve is free though a £1 parking donation is requested. Keys for the hide overlooking the Delta are available from the Nature Centre.

Calendar

Resident: Egyptian Goose, Gadwall, Tufted Duck, Little and Great Crested Grebes, Cormorant, Grey Heron, Sparrowhawk, Water Rail, Little and Tawny Owls, Kingfisher, all three woodpeckers, Willow Tit, Tree Sparrow, Linnet, Bullfinch, Reed Bunting.

October–March: Bewick's Swan (rare), Whooper Swan (rare), Pink-footed Goose (scarce), Shelduck, Eurasian Wigeon, Common Teal, Pintail, Shoveler, Red-crested Pochard, Pochard, Scaup (scarce), Goldeneye, Smew, Red-breasted Merganser (rare), Goosander, Ruddy Duck, Bittern, Northern Lapwing, Common Snipe, Mediterranean Gull (scarce), Long-eared and Short-eared Owls, Grey Wagtail, European Stonechat, Fieldfare, Redwing, Siskin, Lesser Redpoll.

April–September: Garganey, Common Scoter (irregular), Black-necked Grebe (scarce), Little Egret (July onwards), Marsh Harrier (scarce), Osprey (scarce), Hobby, Little Ringed and Ringed Plovers, Dunlin, Ruff, Black-tailed Godwit, Whimbrel, Curlew, Spotted Redshank (scarce), Redshank, Greenshank, Green Sandpiper, Wood Sandpiper (scarce), Common Sandpiper, Little Gull (passage), Yellow-legged Gull (July onwards), Common Tern, Arctic Tern (April and May), Black Tern, Cuckoo, Yellow Wagtail, White Wagtail (April), Whinchat (passage), Northern Wheatear (passage), Grasshopper Warbler, Sedge Warbler, Reed Warbler, Blackcap, Garden Warbler, Lesser and Common Whitethroats, Common Chiffchaff, Willow Warbler.

USEFUL ADDRESSES AND PUBLICATIONS

DERBYSHIRE

Joint County Recorders
Roy Frost, 66 St Lawrence Road,
North Wingfield, Chesterfield,
Derbyshire S42 5LL.
Telephone: 01246 850037.
Email: frostra66@lepidoptera.force9.co.uk

Richard James, 10 Eastbrae Road,
Littleover, Derby DE23 1WA.
Telephone: 01332 771787.
Email: rmrjames@yahoo.co.uk

Rodney Key, 3 Farningham Close,
Spondon, Derby DE21 7DZ.
Telephone: 01332 678571.
Email: r.key3@ntlworld.com

Carsington Bird Club
Maria Hopwood, Lydgate House,
West End, Brassington,
Derbyshire DE4 4HL.
Telephone: 01629 540556.
Website: www.carsingtonbirdclub.co.uk

Derbyshire Ornithological Society
Barrie Staley, 20 Lancelot Drive, Stretton,
Burton upon Trent, Staffordshire DE13 0GJ.
Telephone: 01283 567325.
Email: barrie@staley3176.fsnet.co.uk
Website: www.derbyshireos.org.uk

Derbyshire Wildlife Trust
East Mill, Bridge Foot, Belper,
Derbyshire DE56 1XH.
Telephone: 01773 881188.
Email: enquiries@derbyshirewt.co.uk
Website: www.derbyshirewildlifetrust.org.uk

Ogston Bird Club
Malcolm Hill, 2 Sycamore Avenue,
Glapwell, Chesterfield, Derbyshire S44
5LH. Telephone: 01623 812159.
Email: aamahaamah@yahoo.co.uk
Website: www.ogstonbirdclub.co.uk

Pleasley Pit Nature Study Group
Geoff Walker, 28 Poplar Drive, Glapwell,
Chesterfield, Derbyshire S44 5LB.
Telephone: 01623 811378.
Email (Loz Brooks):
loz.brooks1@btinternet.com

LEICESTERSHIRE AND RUTLAND

County Recorder
Rob Fray, 5 New Park Road, Aylestone,
Leicester LE2 8AW.
Telephone: 0116 2238491.
Email: r.fray2@ntlworld.com

Leicestershire and Rutland Ornithological Society
Ken Goodrich, 6 Riversdale Close,
Birstall, Leicester LE4 4EH.
Telephone: 0116 2674813.
Email: kjgood1532@aol.com
Website: www.lros.org.uk

Leicestershire and Rutland Wildlife Trust
Brocks Hill Environment Centre,
Washbrook Lane, Oadby,
Leicestershire LE2 5JJ.
Telephone: 0116 2720444.
Email: info@lrwt.org.uk
Website: www.lrwt.org.uk

Loughborough Naturalists' Club
Leslie Hall, 47 Victoria Road, Woodhouse
Eaves, Leicestershire LE12 8RF.
Telephone: 01509 890200.
Email: leslie@hall4774.wanadoo.co.uk
Website: www.loughboroughnats.org.uk

Rutland Natural History Society
Linda Worrall, 6 Redland Close,
Barrowden, Rutland LE15 8ES.
Telephone: 01572 747302.
Website: www.rnhs.org.uk

Rutland Water Nature Reserve
Anglian Water Birdwatching Centre,
Egleton, Oakham, Rutland.
Telephone: 01572 770651.
Email: jfisher-robins@lrwt.org.uk
Website: www.rutlandwater.org.uk

LINCOLNSHIRE

County Recorder
Steve Keightley, Redclyffe, Swineshead Road, Frampton Fen, Boston, Lincolnshire PE20 1SG.
Telephone: 01205 290233.
Email: steve.keightley@btinternet.com

Frampton Marsh and Freiston Shores RSPB Reserve
Parker House, 61a Horseshoe Lane, Kirton, Boston, Lincolnshire PE20 1LW.
Telephone: 01205 724678.

Gibraltar Point National Nature Reserve
Gibraltar Road, Skegness, Lincolnshire PE24 4SU.
Telephone: 01754 762677.
Email: gibpoint@lincstrust.co.uk

Lincolnshire Bird Club
Mike Harrison, Baumber Park, Baumber, Horncastle, Lincolnshire LN9 5NE.
Email: michael@michaelharrison1.wanadoo.co.uk
Website: www.lincsbirdclub.co.uk

Lincolnshire Wildlife Trust
Banovallum House, Manor House Street, Horncastle, Lincolnshire LN9 5HF.
Telephone: 01507 526667.
Email: info@lincstrust.co.uk
Website: www.lincstrust.org.uk

NORTHAMPTONSHIRE

County Recorder
Gary Pullan, 21 Banbury Lane, Byfield, Northamptonshire NN11 2UX.
Telephone: 01327 262671.
Email: gary.pullan@nationwide.co.uk

Northamptonshire Bird Club
John Showers, 103 Desborough Road, Rothwell, Northamptonshire NN14 6JQ.
Telephone: 01536 710831.
Email: ShowersJohn@aol.com
Website: www.connect2northamptonshire.com
(and then follow the links)

Northamptonshire Wildlife Trust
Lings House, Billing Lings, Northampton NN3 8BE.
Telephone: 01604 405285.
Email: northamptonshire@wildlifebcnp.org
Website: www.wildlifebcnp.org

NOTTINGHAMSHIRE

County Recorder
Andy Hall, 10 Staverton Road, Bilborough, Nottingham NG 8 4ET.
Telephone: 0115 9169673.
Email: andy.h11@ntlworld.com

Attenborough Nature Reserve
Barton Lane, Attenborough, Nottingham NG9 6DY.
Telephone: 0115 9721777.
Email: enquiries@attenboroughnaturecentre.co.uk
Website: www.attenboroughnaturecentre.co.uk

Nottinghamshire Birdwatchers
Howard Broughton, 5 Park Road, Plumtree, Nottingham NG12 5LX.
Telephone: 0115 9374474.
Email: forestrub@aol.com
Website: www.nottmbirds.org.uk

Nottinghamshire Wildlife Trust
The Old Ragged School, Brook Street, Nottingham NG1 1EA.
Telephone: 0115 9588242.
Email: nottswt@cix.co.uk
Website: www.wildlifetrust.org.uk/nottinghamshire

Lound Bird Club
Gary Hobson, 23 Milne Road, Bircotes, Doncaster, South Yorkshire DN11 8AL.
Telephone: 07712 244469.
Email: loundbirdclub@tiscali.co.uk
Website: www.piczo.com/loundbirdclub

REGIONAL

English Nature (East Midlands Region, Eastern Area Team)
The Maltings, Wharf Road, Grantham,
Lincolnshire NG31 6BH.
Telephone: 01476 584800.
Email:
eastmidlands@english-nature.org.uk

English Nature (East Midlands Region, Peak District and Derbyshire Team)
'Endcliff', Deepdale Business Park,
Ashford Road, Bakewell,
Derbyshire DE45 1GT.
Telephone: 01629 816640.
Email: peak.derbys@english-nature.org.uk

National Forest
Enterprise Glade, Bath Lane, Moira,
Leicestershire DE12 6BD.
Telephone: 01283 551211.
Email: enquiries@nationalforest.org
Website: www.nationalforest.org

Royal Society for the Protection of Birds (Central England Regional Office)
46 The Green, Banbury,
Oxfordshire OX16 9AB.
Telephone: 01295 253330.

NATIONAL

British Birds Rarities Committee
Colin Bradshaw, 9 Tynemouth Place,
Tynemouth, Tyne and Wear NE30 4BJ
Telephone: 0191 257 2389.
Email: secretary@bbrc.org.uk
Website: www.bbrc.org.uk

British Trust for Ornithology
The Nunnery, Thetford,
Norfolk IP24 2PU.
Telephone: 01842 750050.
Email: info@bto.org
Website: www.bto.org

English Nature
Northminster House,
Peterborough PE1 1UA.
Telephone: 01733 455000.
Email: enquiries@english-nature.org.uk
Website: www.english-nature.org.uk

Environment Agency
Millbank Tower, 25th floor,
21/24 Millbank,
London SW1P 4XL.
Telephone: 08708 506506.
Website: www.environment-agency.gov.uk

Forestry Commission
Silvan House, 231 Corstorphine Road,
Edinburgh EH12 7AT.
Tel: 0131 3340303.
Email: enquiries@forestry.gsi.gov.uk
Website: www.forestry.gov.uk

Friends of the Earth
26-28 Underwood Street,
London N1 7JQ. Tel: 020 7490 1555.
Website: www.foe.co.uk

Greenpeace
Canonbury Villas,
London N1 2PN.
Telephone: 020 7865 8100.
Email: info@uk.greenpeace.org
Website: www.greenpeace.org.uk

National Trust
PO Box 39,
Warrington WA5 7WD.
Telephone: 0870 4584000.
Email: enquiries@thenationaltrust.org.uk
Website: www.nationaltrust.org.uk

Ordnance Survey
Romsey Road,
Southampton SO16 4GU.
Telephone: 08456 050505.
Email:
customerservices@ordnancesurvey.co.uk
Website: www.ordnancesurvey.co.uk

Royal Society for the Protection of Birds
The Lodge, Sandy,
Bedfordshire SG19 2DL.
Telephone: 01767 680551.
Website: www.rspb.org.uk

Woodland Trust
Autumn Park, Dysart Road, Grantham,
Lincolnshire NG31 6LL.
Telephone: 01476 581111.
Email:
conservation@woodland-trust.org.uk
Website: www.woodland-trust.org.uk

INDEX OF PLACE NAMES
BY SITE NUMBER

Index of place names by site number

INDEX OF SPECIES BY SITE NUMBER